University of Pennsylvania Studies
in Germanic Languages and Literatures

Edited by
ANDRÉ VON GRONICKA and OTTO SPRINGER

With the cooperation of ADOLPH C. GORR,
ADOLF D. KLARMANN, EGBERT KRISPYN,
ALBERT L. LLOYD, HEINZ MOENKEMEYER,
GEORGE C. SCHOOLFIELD, ALFRED SENN

Inquiry
and Testament

Robert Walser

Inquiry
and Testament

A Study of the Novels and Short Prose of Robert Walser

by George C. Avery

University of Pennsylvania Press · Philadelphia · 1968

For D. C. N.

Preface

The aim of this study is to introduce the Swiss writer Robert Walser to the general reader and to the student of German literature. Virtually unknown in this country, Walser has now begun to engage the interest of critics and scholars in German-speaking countries. Until after his death in 1956 Walser was known, if at all, as the author of engagingly written short prose pieces who disappeared from the German literary scene in the twenties. What was not generally known was that mental illness had disrupted Walser's literary career; his death in 1956 recalled to the literary public a nearly forgotten author.

The publication of Walser's collected works, which started in 1966, has already shown that Walser was more prolific than had been recognized and that the largely unknown work from the last decade of his career adds significantly to the scope and the quality of his work as a whole. Thus the need for a reassessment of Walser had become clear even before the completion of the present edition. The emphasis on Walser's three published novels in this study is meant to contribute to a reassessment that will assure Walser the place in our literary consciousness that he deserves.

Up until now Walser's novels have been neglected and it is accurate to say that even at the time of Walser's greatest success as a writer in the decade before the end of World War I the reputation which depended on readers of divergent literary tastes and standards gained little from the novels. Yet a study of the novels is essential to understanding the rest of Walser's work. Hopefully the five chapters devoted to the novels will also indicate to the general reader the degree to which the literary problems posed in German novels of the first two decades of the century made a sensitive and prophetic contribution to the creation of the contemporary novel.

A principal premise of this study is the modernity of Walser's work, or more specifically, of the features his novels share with the European novel as it developed in the first third of the century. It is, however, valid to question this premise since Walser himself never professed any interest in avowedly modern literary schools, never wished himself regarded as an adherent of a particular literary movement, and—except for the early work of Thomas Mann—is not known to have either praised or admired the work of his contemporaries. The few Swiss critics who have written about Walser and whose work was inspired by more than patriotic interest have not raised this question. Instead they have been more interested in defining the limits of Walser's artistry against the implicit presumption that the cost of political freedom is an ethically conformistic society reacting to practical realities. Yet the most manifest expression of Walser's modernity, his symbolic concentration on the consciousness of single protagonists, underlies his work from his early verse dramolets, through the novels, the short prose, and the dialogs and so-called essays in the final phase of his career. The refraction of Walser's response to man's role in modern society through this particular optic inheres in the cohesiveness of the central images in his work. It objectifies and transforms into paradigmatic art Walser's preoccupation in his writing with a transparently autobiographical first-person persona. It examines and gives literary shape to a range of human experience in a way that identifies Walser's Swiss heritage—a more positive and more profound testament to his homeland than civic shibboleths can measure—as part of an essential European tradition: a pervasive knowledge of the need to accept change as the precondition for human understanding and growth. Walser gives this poetic vision a modern esthetic formulation as an interaction between absolute subjectivity and its metaphoric function. Together these establish the possibility of revitalization in the awareness of man's variegated appearance and not in the subservience to institutions or the defense of systems.

Walser's modern perspective is evident too in an anti-esthetic creative ethos that appears throughout his writing in various guises but is always informed by compassion and artistic skill. Walser's relevance to the modern temperament resides in the dichotomy this opposition implies. Using a fragmentarily portrayed creative personality as a symbol of the dynamic continuum of life, Walser's career demonstrates a testament—in art—of ambivalence toward the function and the efficacy of verbal art that he shares with contemporaries as different as Franz Kafka, Thomas Mann, and Bertolt Brecht. What distinguishes Walser from these contemporaries is his apparent disregard for the tradtions of the genres he wrote in. While there is no evidence for grouping Walser with conscious experimenters in German letters after 1900, and the practice of his craft suggests a persuasion of the equivalence of genres with regard to their esthetic utility and their metaphoric statement, his novels anticipate the refinement in his short prose of extensive statement in a restricted form by emphasizing the primacy of a personalized, anti-traditional literary language.

The central figures in Walser's novels are referred to in the study as heroes because Walser portays them in the only way that modern literature can still lay claim to the term: for figures who resolutely resist the pretense of being any more or anything different than what they are. They do not, however, share with their present-day literary descendants a moral neutralism or an amorality the intention of which is to signify a higher morality in the absence of generally accepted ethical norms in society as a whole. The heroes' subjectivity is the affective core of the novels but Walser's subjectivity cannot be read as moral insensitivity— either in the novels or in the rest of his work. Walser's failure to expressly justify his heroes gives them an enigmatic dimension that provokes the mind. Because they communicate a response to the wonder in human life, they simultaneously speak to the heart. Walser's late "essays" achieve a synthesis of the implicit opposition between the creator and the critic in his earlier work and thereby enlarge a literary structure for experiencing human perception, consciousness, and cognition.

The division of this study reflects the emphasis on the novels. Following an introductory chapter, separate chapters on each of the three novels' heroes provide interpretative summaries and characterizations of these works. These form a background for detailed discussion of recurrent motifs and themes(Chapter Five) and distinctive elements of style(Chapter Six). The intentional reexamination of previously presented works from a more synoptic perspective is intended to provide the reader without German a more extensive analysis of one significant part of Walser's writing. Chapter Seven gives an overview of Walser's remaining prose production by discussing characteristic shorter prose works. Here the emphasis is on the development of the thematic and stylistic elements found in the novels. The final chapter seeks to establish a basis for a historical view of Walser's writing by comparing his work with a number of representative contemporary works.

All of the translations used in the text are my own. Whether or not some of the intentional rough spots in the translations give an adequate approximation of the sense of Walser's prose, readers with a knowledge of German will judge. The German originals of the indented extracts are printed at the bottom of the page to permit readers who know German to discover for themselves the importance of sentence rhythm in Walser's prose.

Of the many whose assistance facilitated my work on the book, I should like first of all to acknowledge most gratefully the help and encouragement of Professor Adolf D. Klarmann, at whose suggestion I first began to read Walser. The ready generosity of Dr. Jochen Greven, the editor of Walser's works, in making available Walser material before its publication in *Das Gesamtwerk* enabled me to support the presentation in Chapter Seven with more texts than would otherwise have been possible at present. I want also to express my appreciation to Dr. E. Fröhlich, President of the Carl Seelig Foundation in Zurich, for kindly agreeing to make available the photographs in the text. The Frontispiece and Plates 1, 2, 4, 5, 7 and 8 were previously published in Robert Mächler, *Das Leben Robert Walsers. Eine dokumentarische Biographie* (1966), and are reproduced here with the kind permission of the Helmut Kossodo Verlag. Yale University Library gave me permission to copy the correspondence between Walser and the Kurt Wolff Verlag in the Kurt Wolff archive in the German Literature Collection. I am also grateful to Professor André von Gronicka, co-editor of the University of Pennsylvania Studies in Germanic Languages and Literatures for his thoughtful suggestions. My deepest debt of gratitude is to my wife for the constancy of her faith in my ability to write this book.

George C. Avery

Swarthmore, Pennsylvania

June, 1968

Contents

List of Illustrations

(Following Page 140)

Bibliographical Note

The varied sources of the texts used for this study due to the lack of a complete edition of Walser's prose works at the present, make necessary a prefatory note on the book publications of his writings. During his active literary career Walser published the following volumes:

> *Fritz Kochers Aufsätze* (Leipzig: Insel, 1904).
> *Geschwister Tanner* (Berlin: Cassirer, 1907).
> *Der Gehülfe* (Berlin: Cassirer, 1908).
> *Jakob von Gunten* (Berlin: Cassirer, 1909).
> *Gedichte* (Berlin: Cassirer, 1909).
> *Aufsätze* (Leipzig: Kurt Wolff, 1913).
> *Geschichten* (Leipzig: Kurt Wolff, 1914).
> *Kleine Dichtungen* (Leipzig: Kurt Wolff, 1914).
> *Prosastücke* (Zurich: Rascher, 1917).
> *Kleine Prosa* (Bern: Francke, 1917).
> *Der Spaziergang* (Frauenfeld/Leipzig: Huber, 1917).
> *Poetenleben* (Frauenfeld/Leipzig: Huber, 1918).
> *Komödie* (Berlin: Cassirer, 1919).
> *Seeland* (Zurich: Rascher, 1919).
> *Die Rose* (Berlin: Rowohlt, 1925).

All of these titles have long since been out of print; if available, they are sold as collector's items. Even the reprintings of Walser's novels (*Geschwister Tanner* [Zurich: Rascher, 1933]; *Der Gehülfe* [St. Gallen: Schweizer Bücherfreunde, 1936]; *Jakob von Gunten* [Zurich: Steinberg, 1950]) are difficult to find.

In 1953 a projected ten-volume edition of Walser's prose works, entitled *Dichtungen in Prosa*, began to appear under the editorship of Carl Seelig. At the time of Seelig's accidental death in 1962, the five volumes listed below had appeared, the first two published by Holle Verlag (Geneva), the others by Verlag Helmut Kossodo (Geneva):

Vol. I (1953): *Aufsätze | Kleine Dichtungen.*
[This volume contains all of the prose pieces originally published under the first title and more than half of those originally included in *Kleine Dichtungen.*]

Vol. II (1954): *Unveröffentlichte Prosadichtungen.*
[This volume contains only a small portion of the prose writings not previously collected in book form.]

Vol. III (1955): *Der Gehülfe.*

Vol. IV (1959): *Fritz Kochers Aufsätze | Die Rose |*
     Kleine Dichtungen.
[In addition to the first two titles, this volume contains the thirty-one pieces from *Kleine Dichtungen* not included in Vol. I.]

Vol. V (1961): *Komödie | Geschichten | Der Spaziergang.*

Late in 1962 Dr. Jochen Greven, the author of the first dissertation on Walser in German, accepted the editorship of the interrupted collected edition. Greven's edition, the first two volumes of which appeared in 1966, will consist of twelve volumes in all and will include—in addition to the complete prose works—a selection of Walser's poetry and letters.

Greven's decision to reorganize and expand the edition that is now appearing in Verlag Helmut Kossodo (Geneva/Hamburg) under the title *Das Gesamtwerk* was based in part on Seelig's indifferent editorship. Equally important was Greven's discovery of a large number of prose pieces by Walser in defunct, hard-to-find magazines or newspapers. Greven's edition also includes works in manuscript not published in Seelig's edition. The present editor is rearranging the work that appeared in Seelig's edition so as to publish more nearly contemporaneous texts in the same volume of *Das Gesamtwerk*. As a result, only volume II of the uncompleted *Dichtungen in Prosa, Der Gehülfe,* will be taken over unchanged into *Das Gesamtwerk*.

Key to abbreviations

Works by Walser:

GW IV = *Das Gesamtwerk.* Herausgegeben von Jochen Greven, Band IV (1967): *Geschwister Tanner; Jakob von Gunten.*

GW VI = ——, Band VI (1966): *Phantasieren: Prosa aus der Berliner und Bieler Zeit.*

GW VII = ——, Band VII (1966): *Festzug: Prosa aus der Bieler und Berner Zeit.*

Dichtungen in Prosa. Herausgegeben von Carl Seelig [1953–1961].

AKD = Vol. I (*Aufsätze / Kleine Dichtungen*).

UP = Vol. II (*Unveröffentlichte Prosadichtungen*).

G = Vol. III (*Der Gehülfe*).

FKR = Vol. IV (*Fritz Kochers Aufsätze / Die Rose / Kleine Dichtungen*).

KGS = Vol. V (*Komödie / Geschichten / Der Spaziergang*).

T = *Geschwister Tanner* (in *GW*, IV).

JvG = *Jakob von Gunten* (in *GW*, IV).

PS = *Prosastücke.*

KP = *Kleine Prosa.*

P = *Poetenleben.*

S = *Seeland.*

UG = *Unbekannte Gedichte,* ed. Carl Seelig (St. Gallen: Tschudy, 1958).

GKW = *Grosse kleine Welt. Eine Auswahl,* ed. Carl Seelig (Zurich/ Leipzig: Eugene Rentsch Verlag, 1937).

Other works and studies:

Albérès = R. M. Albérès, *Geschichte des modernen Romans.* Aus dem Französischen übersetzt und bearbeitet von Karl August Horst (Düsseldorf/Cologne: Eugen Diedrich, 1964).

Allemann = Beda Allemann, *Ironie und Dichtung* (Pfullingen: Neske, 1956).

Bänziger = Hans Bänziger, "Robert Walser," in *Heimat und Fremde. Ein Kapitel "Tragische Literaturgeschichte" in der Schweiz: Jakob Schaffner, Robert Walser, Albin Zollinger* (Bern: Francke, 1958), pp. 63–106.

Beach = Joseph Warren Beach, *The Twentieth Century Novel: Studies in Techniques* (New York/London: Century, 1932).

Benjamin = Walter Benjamin, "Robert Walser," in *Schriften.* hrsg. von Theodor W. Adorno und Gretel Adorno unter Mitwirkung von Friedrich Podszus (Frankfurt am Main: Suhrkamp, 1955), II, 148–151.

Benn = Joachim Benn, "Robert Walser," *Die Rheinlande*, 24. Bd. (1914), 131–134.

Brod = Max Brod, *Streitbares Leben. Autobiographie* (Munich: Kindler, 1960).

Emrich = Wilhelm Emrich, *Protest und Verheißung. Studien zur klassischen und modernen Dichtung* (Frankfurt am Main/Bonn: Athenäum, 1960).

Friedman = Melvin Friedman, *Stream of Consciousness: A Study in Literary Method* (New Haven: Yale University Press, 1955).

Greven = K. J. W. Greven, *Existenz ,Welt und reines Sein im Werk Robert Walsers. Versuch zur Bestimmung von Grundstrukturen* (Cologne: W. Kleikamp, 1960 [photomechanic reproduction of dissertation typescript]).

Janouch = Gustav Janouch, *Gespräche mit Kafka. Erinnerungen und Aufzeichnungen* (Frankfurt am Main: Fischer Bücherei, 1961).

PA James Joyce, *Portrait of the Artist as a Young Man* (London: Jonathan Cape, 1960).

Briefe = Franz Kafka, *Briefe 1902–1924*, hrsg. von Max Brod (New York: Schocken, 1958).

Erzlgg = ————, *Erzählungen*, in *Gesammelte Werke*, hrsg. von Max Brod (Frankfurt am Main: S. Fischer, 1946).

Tgbch = ————, *Tagebücher. 1910–1923*, in *Gesammelte Werke*, hrsg. von Max Brod (Frankfurt am Main: S. Fischer, 1951).

Kayser = Wolfgang Kayser, "Die Anfänge des modernen Romans im achtzehnten Jahrhundert und seine heutige Krise," *DVLG*, 28 (1954), 4. Hft., 417–446.

Mächler = Robert Mächler, *Das Leben Robert Walsers. Eine dokumentarische Biographie* (Geneva/Hamburg: Verlag Helmut Kossodo, 1966).

Middleton = J. C. Middleton, "The Picture of Nobody. Some Remarks on Robert Walser, with a Note on Walser and Kafka," *RLV*, XXIV (1958), 5, 404–428.

MOE = Robert Musil, *Der Mann ohne Eigenschaften* (Hamburg: Rowohlt, 1952).

YT = ———, *Young Törless*, tr. Eithne Wilkins and Ernst Kaiser (New York: Pantheon Books, 1955).

MLB = Rainer Maria Rilke, *The Notebooks of Malte Laurids Brigge*, tr. M. D. Herter Norton (New York: W. W. Norton, 1949).

Wdgg = Carl Seelig, *Wanderungen mit Robert Walser* (St. Gallen, Tschudy, n.d. [1957]).

Thalmann = Marianne Thalmann, *Das Märchen und die Moderne. Zum Begriff der Surrealität im Märchen der Romantik.* Urban Bücher, Nr. 53 (Stuttgart: Kohlhammer, 1961).

The sources of works by Walser that have not yet appeared in book form are given in the text. Further references are cited in the notes.

Inquiry
and Testament

1

INTRODUCTION

Robert Walser (1878–1956) will in all likelihood emerge as German Switzerland's most significant author in the first half of the twentieth century. As such he will take his place as the successor to the remarkable nineteenth century triumvirate of Jeremias Gotthelf, Gottfried Keller, and Conrad Ferdinand Meyer. The fact that until very recently Robert Walser has been a neglected figure even in German-speaking countries and practically unknown abroad has several causes. In his own lifetime Walser resolutely held to the position of an outsider, both literarily and socially. Until now only a part of Walser's work has been accessible. He himself probably destroyed four novels he had written and only a fraction of his work appeared in book form during his lifetime. This applies particularly to the final phase of Walser's career, when, in the face of almost complete critical disregard, he was not only very productive but was able to improve the literary quality of his work. Another element contributing to the lack of knowledge about this author is the widespread incapacity of the German critical intelligence to deal with the short prose form which makes up the bulk of Walser's writing. Despite the achievement and the advocacy of short prose forms by Lichtenberg, Nietzsche, and Karl Kraus, it is difficult to dislodge the onus of "minor" implicitly attached to a literary *oeuvre* either modest in size or lacking an encounter with the times in extended novelistic form. Still another factor has been the often contradictory character of the literary success Walser did enjoy. His literary fortunes depended to a large degree on the interest and promotion of widely varied literary groups. The literary journals that originally published Walser's prose pieces constitute a melange of variously oriented literary programs and ideals. As a literary novice at the turn of the century, Walser contributed to the consciously exclusive, esthetically oriented *Die Insel.* In the first period of his magazine publications in Berlin, in the years 1907–1909, Walser's work appeared in avowedly modern journals such as *Die Neue Rundschau, Die Schaubühne,* and *Kunst und Künstler.* From 1911 on he published in *Die Rheinlande,* a traditional, middle-of-the-road journal whose ideological base was the cultivation of a specifically regional heritage, accompanied by a stylized, neo-romantic preference for atmospheric color. Concurrently however, Walser was also publishing in the most catholic and least dogmatic of the journals of literary Expressionism, *Die Weißen Blätter,* Critical interest in Walser's work was similarly varied, extending from writers as different as Kafka and Musil, through Hesse, Morgenstern, and Oskar Loerke to an organ of conservative literature, *Romantik.* In both instances the explanation lies in the difficulty of immediately locating the nexus of work and artist.

At the same time the quality of Walser's works and the nature of his artistry made it unlikely that he would appeal to a wide audience. His work contains contradictory, often paradoxical ideas, while both the form and the content resist categorization under traditional literary norms. Finally, the heretofore confused status of Walser's literary canon and the fact that the bulk of his work was either never collected for publication in book form or consists of *inedits* has impeded critical discussion of Walser as a writer. It is accurate to say that during the period of Walser's greatest reputation, the second decade of this century, he was read and admired by a limited, nearly exclusively literary audience. Frequently only isolated elements within his work were praised. By the time of his death in 1956 he had become a marginal figure in literature, another name among the scores of writers who had contributed to the unparalleled fecundity of German literature in the first three decades of the century, but whose works were either out of print, temporarily or permanently lost with the demise of literary magazines, or the victims of a deteriorating cultural and political climate.

Robert Walser was born April 15, 1878 in the Swiss city of Biel (Bienne) in the Canton of Bern, the seventh of eight children of Adolf and Elise Walser. Walser's ancestors had settled in eastern Switzerland at the end of the seventeenth century. His great-grandfather, Johann Jakob Walser (1770–1849) was a cultivated, well-to-do physician in the town of Teufen (Canton Appenzell), where the Walsers had become franchized citizens. One of Johann Walser's twelve children was Johann Ulrich Walser (1798–1866), himself the father of thirteen children, who left the Protestant clergy to follow a successful career as a Radical pamphleteer and editor in Canton Basel.[1] Robert's father, Adolf Walser

(1833–1914), was trained as a bookbinder. In 1864 he opened a notions and toy store in Biel. The city was growing rapidly thanks to the burgeoning watch industry, yet the father was never able to provide his family with more than a modest living. In 1868 he married Elise Marti, a smith's daughter from the nearby Emmental region. In contrast to the jovial, modest, and harmonious character ascribed by Robert to his father,[2] the mother is described as an imperious figure, irritable and highly sensitive. She died in 1894 of a coronary thrombosis following a period of mental illness. Her husband outlived her by twenty years, generally rooming alone and in poor circumstances. After giving up his unsuccessful business he occasionally sold soap, oils, and wine. Although Adolf Walser descended from families with many children, none of his eight children had any progeny.

One of his five brothers died before Robert was born. One older brother, Ernst, was a secondary school teacher. A talented pianist and an amateur poet, he fell victim to schizophrenia after a restless and unsatisfying teaching career and died in a mental institution in 1916. Hermann Walser, another brother, was Lecturer in Geography at the University of Bern until his death in 1919. Only two of Robert's siblings survived him: another older brother, the accountant Oskar, who died in 1959, and Fanny, the youngest of the children, who now lives in Bern. Walser was closest to his older sister Lisa and his brother Karl. Lisa taught school at a village in the Bernese countryside before working as a governess in Leghorn, Italy for several years. After her return to Switzerland she taught languages at Bellelay in the Swiss Jura for thirty years. Through the years she was the mainstay in the modest family relations Walser knew. She died in 1944 without Robert having heeded her wish for a final visit. Karl Walser (1877–1943) made a name for himself as a stage designer for Max Reinhardt in Berlin in the early years of the century and as a book illustrator. He illustrated the original edition of Thomas Mann's *Disorder and Early Sorrow* as well as works by Cervantes, Kleist, E. T. A. Hoffmann, Hugo von Hofmannsthal, and Hermann Hesse. Although less well known as a painter, Karl did exhibit with the Berlin Secessionists and Robert spoke and thought of his brother primarily as a painter.[3]

Autobiographical episodes in Walser's first two novels, *Geschwister Tanner* and *Der Gehülfe* provide some fragmentary information about Walser's childhood. The prose piece "Fanny" (*AKD*, originally published in 1912 in *Die Schaubühne*) tells how Robert was often charged with entertaining his younger sister and her playmates with stories or with original plays.[4] Family finances forced Walser to conclude his formal education in 1892, when he left the German section of the *Progymna-*

sium, probably just before his fourteenth birthday. On the evidence of his writing and the correspondence so far available, Walser's education from then on consisted of extensive reading—almost exclusively in *belles lettres*—through the rest of his life. He had probably learned French as a child in his bilingual native city and was studying English in his late teens (cf. "Luise" *KP*). After leaving school he worked in Biel for three years as an apprentice bank clerk. During this period, the lifelong interest in the theater that had begun with the plays written for home consumption took the form of amateur roles in the productions of a local dramatic club (*Wdgg,* 101). He renewed this activity after his return to his home town from Berlin in 1913.

In the spring of 1895, Walser left home. He first worked as a private secretary in a Basel banking firm for three months. He then accepted his brother's invitation to join him in Stuttgart, where Robert worked in the advertising office of the *Deutsche Verlagsanstalt,* as well as with the publishing firm of Cotta briefly. His theater passion was fed by frequent visits to the Stuttgart Royal Theater. His plans for an acting career ended abruptly after an unsuccessful reading for one of the most famous actors of the period, Josef Kainz.[5] He then decided—"God willing," as he wrote Lisa—to become a poet.

Walser's literary career began with his arrival in Zurich in the fall of 1896, after having journeyed by foot from Stuttgart.[6] In strictly biographical terms this career can be divided into four roughly equal periods of eight years each, in Zurich, Berlin, Biel, and finally, Bern, Switzerland. Walser's first published works from the Zurich period are the poems accepted by the influential feuilleton editor and author Joseph Viktor Widmann for the Sunday supplement to the Bern newspaper *Der Bund* on May 8, 1898. Walser had submitted a notebook with 40 poems to Widmann at the beginning of the same year. These poems attracted the interest of Franz Blei, the renowned man of letters, whose best-known contribution to German literature was the discovery and advancement of promising authors.[7] Through him Walser made contact with the editors of *Die Insel,* a literary magazine most notable today for its support and publication of Rainer Maria Rilke and Hugo von Hofmannsthal. Poems by Walser appeared in 1899, its first year of publication.[8]

In Zurich Walser supported himself through a large number of positions held for short periods of time. He successively worked for an insurance firm, two different banks, a lawyer, a bookdealer, an electrical equipment firm, a sewing-machine factory, an electric company, a copying office for the unemployed, and as a servant in the home of a wealthy Jewish lady. He also took jobs outside of Zurich. He worked for a brewery in Thun in the spring of 1899, spent eight months in Solothurn from the fall of 1899 until spring 1900, and was employed in a rubber factory in Winterthur in the spring of 1903. From the summer until the end of 1903 he worked as a secretary in the home of an engineer in the town of Wädenswil on the lake of Zurich. His stay in Zurich was also interrupted by at least one lengthy visit to his sister Lisa, by military service in Bern during the summer of 1903, and by one known visit to Munich in the autumn of 1901, where he read his verse dramolet *Die Knaben.* Although documentary proof is lacking, it is likely that Walser had already visited Munich in the spring of 1899 to meet with Blei and the founders of *Die Insel.* Among other writers and painters Walser met through his association with the magazine, the best known are the poet-translator Rudolf Alexander Schröder, the Impressionists Max Dauthendey and Eduard von Keyserling, the playwright Frank Wedekind, and the painter-illustrator Alfred Kubin (cf. *Wdgg*, 29, 138, 148). In a partially autobiographical prose piece, Walser says that at nineteen he was reading Heine, Börne, Lenau, "and the noble Friedrich Schiller, whom incidentally I shall never cease to esteem in the highest sense" ("Luise," *KP*, 99).

As frequent as were the job changes in Zurich, the changes of lodgings during the Zurich period were still more frequent—seventeen times in all. He felt that both were prerequisites for the freedom he needed to write. In 1899, after a literateur (Franz Blei?) had advised Walser to write "something from within" instead of a drama he was planning based on the Battle of Sempach (1386), he wrote in quick succession the prose dramolets *Die Knaben, Dichter,* and the two verse dramolets *Aschenbrödel* and *Schneewittchen.* According to Carl Seelig, the dramolets followed an intensive reading of Shakespeare and Büchner (*KGS*, 351). Walser's first prose pieces, published in *Die Insel* and in *Der Bund,* also date from this period. Walser's first book, a collection of prose pieces under the title *Fritz Kochers Aufsätze,* was published by Insel Verlag in 1904, after some of the pieces had appeared in *Der Bund* in 1902 and 1903. The book was not successful and was remaindered in a Berlin department store the year following its appearance.

In the spring of 1905 Walser moved to Berlin. It was his third attempt at a literary career in the metropolis. Two earlier exploratory visits, in December, 1897 and in January, 1902, had not proven encouraging. In a letter to J. V. Widmann dated February, 1902, Walser wrote that he had returned from Germany with the knowledge that he could not earn his living as a writer in a peaceful and honest way, and he asked Widmann to help him find work as a clerk or as a copyist (*Mächler*, 77). Nor did he immediately become part of the city's literary life.

Early in his stay in Berlin he attended a training school for servants; this was followed by some six months as a butler in a count's castle in Upper Silesia. By the beginning of 1906, however, he was back in Berlin. Within a matter of weeks he wrote his first novel, *Geschwister Tanner*. Later, he worked briefly as secretary for the *Berliner Sezession*, the group of young painters, who, after "seceding" from the *Verein Berliner Künstler* early in the nineties, had become the rallying point against artistic authoritarianism, particularly as it was practised by the Imperial Court. The leading members of the group, Max Liebermann, Lovis Corinth, and Max Slevogt painted successfully in the blend of styles that made up German Impressionism.

Having made artistic contacts through his brother Karl, Walser now settled in Berlin as a writer. The years that followed, until his return to Switzerland in 1913, were without a doubt the most successful in his career. Judging by the number of book publications, it has also been regarded as his most productive period. The *inedits* in Walser's literary papers, and the uncollected (or lost) prose publications in newspapers and magazines, however, suggest that the final productive period of Walser's career, his eight years in Bern from 1921 to 1929, will match the Berlin period in quantity as well as in quality. Walser's first Berlin publication was a prose piece in the November, 1905, issue of *Kunst und Künstler*, an art journal published by Cassirer. Walser's reputation as a master of the short prose form derives from the response to the prose pieces originally published in literary journals and then collected in book form. Besides *Kunst und Künstler*, Walser published in such historically important magazines as *Die Schaubühne, Die Neue Rundschau, Die Zukunft, Die Rheinlande, Simplicissimus, Pan,* and, less frequently, in *Saturn, Das Blaubuch,* and *Der Bildermann,* as well as in short-lived, literarily significant journals such as *Morgen, Die Opale,* and *Der lose Vogel.* Some of these prose pieces fill in details about his personal life at the time, such as his balloon trip from Bittersfeld to the Baltic coast with the influential Berlin art dealer Paul Cassirer ("Ballonfahrt," *AKD*). Walser's conversations with Seelig and his correspondence with Resy Breitbach, the younger sister of the Alsatian author Joseph Breitbach, between 1925 and 1932[9] corroborate the impression gained from the prose pieces that Walser was an enthusiastic participant in metropolitan attractions ranging from theater, ballet, and art galleries to cabarets and what Walser himself termed "vulgar dives" (*Wdgg,* 42). The Berlin prose pieces also record an active interest in the works of Schiller, Lenz, Büchner, Kleist, and Brentano as well as less highly regarded authors such as Kotzebue and the actress-playwright Birch-Pfeiffer. Privately-held correspondence also indicates that in Berlin

Walser for a time entertained the notion of taking employment in an exotic land. Walter Rathenau, the Jewish industrialist, writer, and later cabinet minister helped him find a position in the German colony of Samoa but Walser decided to stay in Berlin. The Seelig conversations refer to meetings in Berlin with the painters Max Liebermann and Max Slevogt, with Gerhart Hauptmann, Ellen Key, and Efraim Frisch and his wife Fega. A section of the actress Tilla Durieux's memoirs from this period relates how the Walser brothers ruined a Christmas party by insisting on demonstrating a Swiss style of wrestling on Frank Wedekind and the sculptor Niklaus Friedrich.[10]

Retrospectively Walser indicates that his ambitions at the time were directed more toward the novel than short prose. "At that time I was mad for writing novels," he told Seelig (*Wdgg*, 72). Walser was introduced to the publishers Samuel Fischer and Bruno Cassirer by Karl, who did book illustrations for both of their firms. Walser's first novel, *Geschwister Tanner*—which Walser claims to have written in some three or four weeks, "so to speak without any corrections" (*Wdgg*, 48)—was published by Cassirer early in 1907 in an edition of one thousand copies. Undoubtedly Christian Morgenstern's high praise of the book after reading it in manuscript significantly influenced Cassirer's decision to publish the novel, since Cassirer himself did not like the book and subsequently urged Walser to delete several sections he regarded as boring.[11] Walser submitted his second novel, *Der Gehülfe* (1908), as an entry in a novel competition sponsored by the Scherl Verlag in Berlin but gave it to Cassirer after the editor for the competition returned the manuscript unread on hearing the amount Walser was asking for it (*Wdgg*, 62). The author later said of the novel—which he wrote in six weeks (*Wdgg*, 92)—that it was intended as "an excerpt from everyday Swiss life" (*G*, 315). Walser's last published novel, *Jakob von Gunten* (1909), was probably written in 1908. In a late prose piece Walser says that he wrote three more novels in Berlin, which he found it necessary to destroy ("Ueber eine Art von Duell," *GW*, VII, 360–365). Questioned by Seelig about the truth of this claim, Walser merely said that it was possible and changed the subject (v. *Wdgg*, 72). Why he destroyed the novels, if in fact he did, is unknown. Karl Walser later suggested to Seelig that his brother had not been able to find publishers for the novels (*Mächler*, 113). Walser was certainly always extremely sensitive to criticism; he remarked that he once destroyed a whole novel because of a single criticism made of it (in "Fragment," first published in 1929; also, cf. Walser's reaction to a review of his poems [*Wdgg*, 47 *passim*]). His first publisher in Berlin, Cassirer, constantly suggested authors whom Walser might use as models to improve his own writing, and other acquaintances repeatedly reminded him of his failure to achieve critical success. An unpublished letter to Christian Morgenstern sketches the plot of a novel which does not correspond to any of the three extant novels. Later in his career, Walser wrote two more novels, neither of which was ever published. In a letter written shortly before Walser moved to Bern he offered the Zurich publisher Rascher a novel entitled "Tobold." This novel was probably completed by 1919 and seems to have been based on Walser's Berlin experiences. "Theodor," another novel based on the years in Berlin, was probably begun shortly after Walser moved to Bern in January, 1921, and appears to have been completed by the end of November. The circumstances surrounding the disappearance of the manuscript are not clear. Rascher Verlag turned it down, claiming a post-war shortage of paper. Walser read selections from the work in Zurich in March, 1922 (*Wdgg*, 144) and two sections of the novel appeared in a literary magazine in 1923, previous to its anticipated publication by Grethlein Verlag (Zurich) in 1924.[12] Grethlein ultimately rejected the manuscript, reportedly because of the retainer Walser asked. In an unpublished letter from 1928, Walser said that the manuscript was in Berlin at the Rowohlt Verlag for four years. In a conversation with Seelig in 1953, Walser asserted that he didn't know its whereabouts (*Wdgg*, 144).

Cassirer's final book by Walser in this period was the publication of poems in 1909 under the title *Gedichte*. Although the poems as well as the first two novels appeared in second editions, the first editions were small. The original lithographs by Karl Walser accompanying the poems were certainly a speculative factor in the production of the book. In order to fill in the picture of Walser's reputation during this period it is necessary to bear in mind that while Walser's prose pieces appeared in liberal journals presenting avowedly modern authors in German literature, they often appeared in the back pages of a particular issue, sometimes as "glosses" or as "sketches." As Greven points out, the location of the pieces suggested "second rate" (*Greven*, 8). Walser's difficulty in establishing himself may be seen in Cassirer's decision to withdraw the financial support he had been giving Walser, following the publication of the poems. From 1910 on the number of magazine acceptances also decreased. The reasons for Walser's return to Switzerland in 1913 are largely due to what Walser regarded as the failure of his literary ambitions. The personal crisis immediately preceding his departure from Berlin, which Walser referred to in conversations with Seelig, seems to have been directly related to this experience of failure (cf. *Mächler*, 124–126). During his last two years in Berlin, part of Walser's support had come from a well-to-do unidentified benefactress, in whose home he had a room, but her support ended with her death in 1913. Also, Walser's increased drinking at the end of the Berlin period, combined with his inability (or unwillingness) to conform to rules of decorum seem to have made him *persona non grata* in the artistic circles to which he had had access. His failure to achieve even *succès d'estime* with his novels,[13] however, seems to have been the most important element in the artistic crisis of his final years in Berlin. "The more earnestly I longed to put firm ground under my feet, the more clearly I saw that I was tottering."[14] A prose piece, an interpretive gloss entitled "Meine Bemühungen," sheds some light on Walser's decision to abandon the novel. This piece is one of the many prose commentaries on his own writing during the final period of his literary career. It retains the ironic voice found in most of them, but is distinguished by its forthrightness. Walser says he gave up writing novels

> . . . because the diffuseness of epic continuity had, so to speak, begun to irritate me. My hand developed into a kind of conscientious objectress. To appease her, I gladly demanded less extensive attestations of her proficiency, and, lo and behold, by showing such considerateness, I gradually won her back. Subduing my ambition, I directed myself to be satisfied with very modest little successes.*

To Seelig, Walser said that the only proper thing left for him to do after what he termed "the Berlin debacle" (*Wdgg*, 94) was to retreat to Switzerland. He returned to his home town, Biel, where he lived until the end of 1920 as a "ridiculed and unsuccessful author" (*Wdgg*, 101). For most of his eight years in Biel, Walser occupied a small room under the roof in a hotel run by a temperance society. His life was a solitary one despite the renewal of some earlier acquaintances and despite the cordiality and interest shown Walser by Emil Schibli, a teacher and writer from a nearby town. The already tenuous relation to his family was further affected by the death of his father in 1914 and of his brother Hermann in 1919. He seems to have made a positive relation between his extreme independence as a writer and the enforced material simplicity of his life. When writing he wore home-made slippers; in the winter he wore an army overcoat and left his room unheated. A physical counterbalance to the practise of his craft in these circum-

---

* . . . weil mich weitläufige epische Zusammenhänge sozusagen zu irritieren begonnen hatten. Meine Hand entwickelte sich zu einer Art Dienstverweigerin. Um sie zu begütigen, mutete ich ihr gern nur noch geringere Tüchtigkeitsbeweisablegungen zu, und siehe, mit derartiger Rücksichtnahme gewann ich sie mir allmählich wieder. Meine Ambition bändigend, erteilte ich mir die Weisung, mich mit bescheidensten Erfolgelein zu begnügen (*GKW*, 196–197).

stances were the frequent walks and hiking tours through the Lake of Biel region and into the Jura. He regularly visited Lisa in Bellelay. There he made the acquaintance of Frieda Mermet, a service employee at the sanatorium and friend of Lisa's, to whom Walser subsequently made what appears to have been too casual a proposal of marriage for Mrs. Mermet to have accepted. They did remain friends, however, and Mrs. Mermet became Walser's most frequent correspondent. (Lisa appears to have destroyed her brother's letters to her.) The only other known interruptions in this life were a visit in 1914 to Berlin and Leipzig in connection with the publication of *Kleine Dichtungen*, periods of border patrol duty with a National Guard battalion during the First World War, and a journey on foot to Zurich in 1920. There he was to read from his works to the *Hottinger Lesezirkel* but the reading was actually given by an alternate, with Walser sitting unrecognized in the audience, after it had been decided (according to one account) that Walser read poorly.[15]

Although Walser did write the lost novel "Tobold" and an undetermined number of verse stories or verse dramolets in Biel, the production of the Biel years was devoted primarily to the cultivation of small prose forms. After his return to Switzerland in 1913, the number of magazine publications increased and Walser again published in magazines very diverse in literary taste and audience. His prose works appeared most frequently in *Die Rheinlande*, edited by Wilhelm Schäfer. He also published regularly in *März* while Hermann Hesse and Theodor Heuss were editing it; in *Die Neue Rundschau;* in the least polemical of the three most important journals of literary Expressionism, René Schickele's *Die Weißen Blätter;* in Efraim Frisch's *Der Neue Merkur;* and in the representative Swiss literary journal *Wissen und Leben.* Single works appeared in *Wieland, Jugend, Der Bildermann.* At irregular intervals Walser also published his prose in newspapers such as the *Vossische Zeitung* and the *Frankfurter Zeitung,* as well as in Swiss newspapers, principally in the *Neue Zürcher Zeitung.* Walser's difficulties in placing his prose pieces are ironically recited in "Das letzte Prosastück" (*Die Rheinlande* (1919); now: GW VII, 70–76). Conversely, Eduard Korrodi, then feuilleton editor of the *Neue Zürcher Zeitung,* said the appearance of a piece of Walser prose would occasion angry letters from readers threatening to cancel their subscriptions "if the nonsense didn't stop" (Schibli, *op. cit.*). Max Brod, who held the same post on the *Prager Tagblatt* in the twenties, reports reluctance on the part of the managing editor to continue to accept work by Walser until after the competing *Prager Presse* started publishing him at frequent intervals (*Brod,* 390f.)

While still in Berlin, Walser's work was accepted for publication by the Kurt Wolff Verlag in Leipzig, the publishing house most intimately associated with the generation that started to publish around 1910. *Aufsätze* (1913), the first of three collections of prose pieces to appear there, came out shortly before Walser's return to Switzerland. It contained work written during the Berlin years. *Geschichten* (1914) was a collection of work dating from the early Berlin years as well as early prose originally published in *Die Insel* in 1900 and 1901. *Kleine Dichtungen* (1914), Walser's final volume with Kurt Wolff,[16] contained material taken predominantly from *Die Rheinlande* and *März*, much of it based on Walser's new encounter with his homeland. Upon the initiative of Wilhelm Schäfer, *Kleine Dichtungen* was awarded a prize of the "Women's League for Awards to Rhenish Poets" and appeared both in a small subscription edition for the League and a larger trade edition. The final book publication in Germany during the Biel period was the collection of the four dramolets written in 1899, which Cassirer published in 1919 under the title *Komödie*. Four more collections of new prose were published in Switzerland during Walser's years in Biel: *Prosastücke* (Rascher, 1917); *Kleine Prosa* (Francke, 1917); *Poetenleben* (Huber, 1918); and *Seeland* (Rascher, 1919). A separate edition of *Der Spaziergang*, the longest and best of the prose pieces in *Seeland*, had already appeared in Huber Verlag in 1917. Before he included it in *Seeland* Walser made stylistic revisions. Contrary to Walser's reputed practice in the Berlin years of refusing to correct or rewrite his work (see the quotation above on his writing *Geschwister Tanner;* the retrospective prose piece "Geschwister Tanner" [*FKR*, 243]; and his remarks to Carl Seelig about the composition of *Der Gehülfe* [*Wdgg*, 47, 55, 62]), a comparison of three of the longer prose works in *Seeland* with the versions previously published in magazines show that Walser did undertake extensive revisions. In one of the more important of the later prose works, *Die Ruine* (*UP*)[17] Walser refers to the emphasis he put on style during these years: "I was always a sort of an esthete who practically tore out bushels of hair for a turn of phrase, and who was quite unhappy when his lines didn't flow along flowingly enough."

The considerations that underlay Walser's move to the Swiss capital of Bern in 1920 were again artistic, and, in part, financial. His savings, consisting principally of the prize money awarded for *Kleine Dichtungen,* were deposited in Germany, and were lost in the inflation. At the beginning of his stay in Bern Walser worked for six months at a job his sister Fanny had found him in the Cantonal Archives before being discharged because of an altercation with a superior. He apparently believed that a change of locale would prove beneficial in his search for new motifs and a different style after having exhausted the motifs he could draw from the region around Biel. Walser's remarks to Seelig on the move indicate the decisive character he himself imputed to this change (cf. *Wdgg*, 21).

While in Bern Walser changed rooms almost as frequently as he had during his Zurich years. Otherwise his life was outwardly little different from what it had been in Biel. He stated to Seelig that his social contacts were restricted almost entirely to waitresses. He also mentions as acquaintances the daughter of a Jewish publisher and the painter and sculptor Hermann Hubacher. The need for human communication seems to have been partially satisfied in his correspondence during this period. In addition to his letters to Resy Breitbach and Frau Mermet, he corresponded with Max Rychner, the editor of *Neue Schweizer Rundschau/Wissen und Leben,* and with Otto Pick, the feuilleton editor of the *Prager Presse.*

Notwithstanding the loneliness of his personal life and what appears to have been an income hardly above subsistence level, Walser was extremely productive in Bern. Indeed, rather than the laziness that has been imputed to him, he seems to have been obsessed by his work, producing more than one third of his entire *oeuvre* in these years. He continued to publish work in *Die Neue Rundschau* and in *Der Neue Merkur,* and, as a cordial and mutually respectful correspondence with Max Rychner developed, his work began to appear more regularly in *Neue Schweizer Rundschau/Wissen und Leben.* In the early twenties Walser also succeeded in finding new outlets for his writing in *Das Tagebuch,* in the second half of the decade in Willy Haas' *Die Literarische Welt* (1925ff.), in *Die Weltbühne,* in the anthroposophist organ *Individualität,* and, with one known publication in each, in *Bimini* and in *Orplid.*

Although he is known to have negotiated with publishers on six separate titles, Walser's single book during the final phase of his career was the collection of prose pieces entitled *Die Rose.* The extremity of style in this book has been read as an indication of incipient mental illness in Walser, yet in an unpublished letter to Resy Breitbach, Walser makes clear that the style is conscious and that he intended the book for sophisticated readers. *Die Rose* was published in 1925 by Rowohlt, the firm established in 1919 after the business association between Ernst Rowohlt and Kurt Wolff took an abrupt end.[18] Many of the prose pieces in *Die Rose* appeared shortly before book publication in the Rowohlt-sponsored literary magazine *Vers und Prosa.* In a privately owned letter Walser says that Ernst Rowohlt paid him less for the book than Berlin newspapers would for eight prose pieces. Walser's publications in literary magazines, however, only made up a fraction of his total published work in these years. The largest part of his published work appeared in the literary sections of newspapers.

Of the three newspapers Walser himself referred to in the conversations with Seelig as his principal outlets—all of them associated with the German-Jewish intelligentsia—the *Berliner Tagblatt* was the most selective and paid the best fees. (The newspaper once suggested that Walser stop writing altogether for a time. A hiatus of nearly a year ensued until Walser's work began to reappear.) In the *Prager Tagblatt* Walser found an outlet for some of his prose and the poems he had started to write again in the twenties. Walser's main source of publication during the second half of the decade was the *Prager Presse*, a government-subsidized German-language newspaper whose literary columns gave concrete and persuasive evidence of Czechoslovakia's claim to represent a cultural bridge between East and West. The newspaper paid low retainers, but from 1925 on Otto Pick, its literary editor, accepted everything Walser submitted, both prose and poetry. Close to two hundred works by Walser (some seventy of which were poems) first appeared in the *Prager Presse*. Nearly one hundred of the prose works were not included in the second volume of Seelig's edition, *Unveröffentlichte Prosadichtungen*. The absence of this material from the corpus of Walser's work has made it impossible to estimate fairly the final phase of his career. The appearance of Walser's work in the *Prager Presse* as late as 1937, four or five years after he had stopped writing completely, also complicates the accurate dating of this work. Walser seems often to have sent Pick a number of manuscripts under a single cover, which then appeared at Pick's discretion.

Despite whatever private misgiving Walser may have had about the consequences of this shift in the place of publication of the larger part of his work in the twenties, his claim to have been content with the designation "newspaper writer" ("Meine Bemühungen," *GKW*, 197) does illustrate his independence and separation from conventional literary life. As one of the large number of aliterary self-definitions he used to designate his writing career, his statement also indicates his knowledge that the formally essayistic analyses of human situations that dominate his final period are less than ever dependent on the traditions and conventions of narrative development (cf. *Wdgg*, 14). Coming after the publication of *Die Rose*, the exploratory and experimental character of the narrative technique in this late prose, together with the refinement of earlier themes, makes it a significant part of his entire *oeuvre*. A distinguishing characteristic of his work in the twenties is the development of a tendency already apparent in the second half of the Biel period, a renewed interest in literary personages as the subjects for his prose and poems.[19]

At the end of the twenties Walser again began to drink heavily (*Wdgg*, 72). The nervous exhaustion that went with it may have resulted from his unsuccessful efforts to gain critical acknowledgement of his work and the compulsion he felt to continue to write. Again Walser claims to have experienced difficulty in finding new motifs: "During the final months in Bern my head was as if nailed shut. I simply couldn't find any motifs" (*Wdgg*, 34). Walser tells Seelig of the nightmares and hallucinations he experienced at this time (*Wdgg*, 21) and of the attempts he made to take his own life. In January, 1929 he acceded to Lisa's urging to commit himself to a sanatorium. He entered the Waldau Sanatorium on the outskirts of Bern, where he was diagnosed as schizoid.[20]

During his first years at the Sanatorium (through 1931 or 1932), Walser wrote some one hundred poems as well as some new prose pieces. (A selection of the poems appeared after Walser's death in *Unbekannte Gedichte*.) After that, however, Walser disregarded the encouragement of physicians to continue his writing (*Wdgg*, 59) and turned down their offer of a separate room where he could write. He defended this decision by asserting that the age of litterateurs was past (*Bänziger*, 70) and that he had no right to thus set himself apart from his fellow patients. In his conversations with Seelig he was frequently critical of the literary and personal independence that distinguishes his work. He professed for himself a conformistic moral code that viewed the culturally apostate artist as an injurious influence (*Wdgg*, 16, 42, 72, 106). Other, less personally colored remarks, on the other hand, express Walser's belief in an art whose vision is directed at "the whole of mankind" (*Wdgg*, 104), created by artists whose relationship to society is based on the tension of uncompromised independence (*Wdgg*, 79, 117). In 1933, after having rejected the physicians' suggestion that he try to take up residence again outside the institution, Walser was moved to a mental hospital-sanatorium in Herisau in eastern Switzerland, where, had he ever become destitute, he would have had legal claim to welfare facilities. From 1936 on, Walser was visited regularly by Seelig and the two of them took extensive walking tours in the surrounding countryside. The conversations Seelig transcribed took place mainly on these walks. His commentary on their meetings indicates that Walser was not oppressed by the routine of daily chores expected of him at Herisau. Nor was Walser notably friendly in his relations with other patients. And his attitude toward the physicians was one of distinct reserve. Yet in 1937 Walser still could speak hopefully of "the great breakthrough" that might come if he were to live two or three years on the outside in freedom (*Wdgg,* 13f.). Although Seelig records meetings when Walser was excessively irritable and uncommunicative, the dominant impression Walser gives in the conversations is that of an intellectually curious, informed, and articulate commentator on contemporary social and political events, whose literary judgments were incisive and enthusiastic, and whose memory for events, people, and his own earlier reading was astonishing.[21]

The twenty-seven years of self-imposed isolation and silence at Waldau and Herisau ended with Walser's death on Christmas day, 1956, some four months before his seventy-ninth birthday. Walser was crossing a snow-covered field during a solitary hike to the top of the Rosenberg outside of Herisau when he was overcome by a fatal heart attack. On June 16, 1962 the town of Herisau dedicated a square with a sculpture commemorating Walser and his brother Karl.

The Novels

Walser's claim to our attention derives from the thematic, stylistic, and structural elements in his work that identify him as a participant in and contributor to the creation of modern literature on the continent. His three extant novels exemplify the early abandonment of what Joseph Warren Beach has termed "the well-made novel" in an attempt to refine and expand the province and the sensibility of contemporary prose. In his own reaction to the confrontation with traditional literature, Walser instinctively utilized two of the principal responses with which his generation sought to satisfy the urge for new modes of literary expression: an author-imposed limitation on the literary devices to be used in the execution of his craft, and the circumscribed form dictated by a restricted narrative point of view.[22]

An attempt to approach Walser by "locating" him within movements or by comparison to contemporaries is an undertaking of only limited promise and one that will be most instructive after the interpretation of the novels themselves (see Chapter Eight). Even then, Walser's production will appear to confirm the adage about the discrepancy in German literature between the frequency of gifted writers and the absence of a cohesive literary tradition comparable to that found in England and France. Despite the breadth of his reading of writers from the eighteenth century through to his own time, Walser never associated himself with a particular literary tradition, and it is difficult to identify a pervasive literary influence on Walser's work. Nor did he regard himself as an innovator, or wish himself viewed as an adherent of a modern school. It is therefore useful to begin from an assumption of Walser as a literary "Einzelgänger."

Even a cursory view of Walser's writing reveals divergencies of style and attitude on the author's part from one period of his career to the next, thus limiting the usefulness of any single characterization of Walser's work according to traditional literary criteria. Walser's first known work, the dramolets from the Zurich period, has at its core a fairy-tale hermeticity which shuns contact with the world beyond their author's private sensibility; the novels and prose of the Berlin period present a radical attempt to delineate and participate in this world; the prose works of the Biel period, the dominating body of which are descriptions of nature by a solitary walker, represent an increasingly abstracted encounter with a solipsistic nature which is depicted as harmonious and which lacks the social engagement of the Berlin period; and the prose written in Bern exhibits still another *volte-face*—as a culmination of Walser's stylistic and thematic probings and inquiries, it embodies a final testament in Walser's documentation of a symbolic existence at the beginning of a new cultural and literary era.

Before proceeding to an interpretation of the central figures in the novels, a selection of the critical response to Walser's short prose will illustrate the divergency of the assertions about Walser's "place" in contemporary German letters. An awareness of the opposing positions in criticism that claim Walser for their own may serve as a point of orientation for a largely unknown writer and prepare for the thematic ambivalences found in the novels.

In a recently published revision of his history of twentieth century German literature, the conservative critic Wilhelm Duwe revives a view of Walser that has its antecedents in some of the well-intentioned, but superficial contemporary reviews at the time of the appearance of the volumes of prose pieces.[23] Duwe sees Walser essentially as a bourgeois romantic, an Impressionist in style, skillful in the use of his palette, but with hardly more than water colors at his disposal.[24]

Duwe discusses Walser in terms that confuse a fair judgment. His remarks on the novels are superficial; he dispatches *Jakob von Gunten,* the novel which, more than any other, is of interest to the literary historian, with the misleading adjective "cheerful."

Duwe's discussion centers around Walser's shorter prose. The substance of his remarks is to take issue with what he sees as the attempt of the contemporary poet and critic Walter Höllerer to claim Walser for the literature of the absurd. In an afterword to his selection from

Walser's shorter works (*Prosa*, ed. W. Höllerer) Höllerer tried to identify the variety of level in Walser's prose by ascribing to him the complexity and simultaneity of perceptions found in Expressionists like Georg Heym, Alfred Lichtenstein, and Jakob von Hoddis, in combination with the sense of experience of a Hugo von Hofmannsthal. He spoke of the language as one veering "between the heretofore conventional simile and an emblematic (*zeichenhafte*) speech that moves away from simile" (*Prosa*, 205). Noting that the content of many prose pieces in large measure resides in the rhythm and the gestic movement (*Gestik*) of Walser's sentences, he quotes Walser's "Unter einer Linde" as a piece whose stylistic elements combine to present a self-portrait of the author. Duwe objects specifically to Höllerer's remarks on the style of this piece but does not support his objections. Instead he interprets the following quote from Fritz Kocher's essay "Vocation" ("Der Beruf"):

> To be able to lead an upstanding life in this world one has to have a vocation. One can't just work. Work has got to have its specific character and a goal to which it ought to lead. So as to achieve this, one chooses a vocation. This happens upon leaving school and by virtue of this event one is a grown person, that is to say, one now faces a different school: life.*

Duwe attributes to this presumed counter-portrait of the author a greater degree of modernity than in the piece cited by Höllerer, defending what he identifies as Romantic author-intrusion here as opposed to its use by a novelist like Uwe Johnson, where the result is not a novel, but "a description." Duwe recognizes a tone of melancholy in Walser, but claims "that it is completely free of present-day complexes." He cites the Fritz Kocher essay as proof of the impossibility of identifying Walser with a sacrifice of the self, "for despite its transcendental quality, [Walser's] prose remains gratifyingly clear and simple in its substance" (*op. cit.*).

Dismissing the gratuitousness of some of his remarks and the illogicality of denying the complexity of author irony in the late prose piece quoted by Höllerer in favor of a simpler, much earlier instance of narrator-directed self-irony, it must be said that Duwe's selective receptivity prettifies Walser but talks itself past him, just as his praise for the sim-

* Um in der Welt ein rechtschaffenes Leben führen zu können, muß man einen Beruf haben. Man kann nicht nur so in den Tag hinein arbeiten. Die Arbeit muß ihren bestimmten Charakter und einen Zweck haben, zu dem sie führen soll. Um das zu erreichen, wählt man einen Beruf. Dies geschieht, wenn man aus der Schule tritt, und mit diesem Ereignisse ist man ein erwachsener Mensch, das heißt, nun hat man eine andere Schule vor sich: das Leben (*FKR*, 31).

plicity of Walser's prose strongly suggests a rather limited knowledge of some of the prose Walser wrote in Biel, not to mention the bravura style of pieces in *Die Rose.*

Regarding the quoted text, Duwe overlooks first and foremost the skillful expression of author irony towards Fritz Kocher's sentiment. Admittedly the language is clear and simple, but two elements prevent us from taking the sentiments expressed at face value: the boldness of presenting what pretends to be a most uncomplicated social credo as a literary creation, and, allied to this, the author's double remove from Fritz Kocher through the fiction of an editor who has gained permission to publish Fritz Kocher's essays only on condition that he not "correct" them. This adds dimension to the naïveté and limited perspective of first-person narrative. Then too, by employing a language made up of nearly equal measures of sentiment and self-indulgence, Walser characterizes Fritz Kocher as a little pedant. The tone of the writing throws the assuredness and assertiveness of Kocher's axiomatic statements into doubt. The tune of Fritz Kocher's hopes that life will provide him the security of a vocation sounds like an unpractised melody being whistled in the dark.

The appraisal of Walser's writing by Carl Seelig, the original editor of the collected edition, must in sum be viewed as standing closer to Duwe than to Höllerer,[25] despite the fact that Seelig's critical capacity undoubtedly responded to the complexity of Walser's creations. His claim to have seen in him "the most peculiar personality" among contemporary Swiss authors when he made Walser's acquaintance in 1936 (*Wdgg,* 9) and the admirably representative selection of Walser's work—including important *inedits*—that he made in *Große Kleine Welt* in 1937 attests to this.

Seelig's remarks on Walser emphasize the human values which lie at the root of the works: the freedom of creative existence; the acceptance of poverty, misfortune, or subordination as the natural and equally glorious counterparts of life's exalted moments; and the celebration of man and nature, especially in their neglected, customary aspects. Seelig's attitude is one of admiration and respect, whereas critical insight and a confrontation with the artistic elements at work in Walser would be more illuminating. Essentially an anthologist, Seelig's principal injustice to Walser's work comes from his separation of elements within the work from their literary context, thereby sacrificing the force of complexities and tensions that often lie beneath the surface of the work, but which run deep enough to give internal shape in theme, language, and structure to a large part of Walser's work. Without the contrasts of tone, the equipoise of light and dark, or intellect and unreflected existence, and the alternation between light-hearted sensual enjoyment and momentarily unveiled forebodings of death or destruction, Walser's work is unfairly divested of its representational aspect as a reaction to the contemporary world.

In discussing the novels, we shall make reference to other essays on Walser, the larger number of which are contemporary reviews of Walser's books. It is, however, necessary to refer presently to two further essays, both of which emphasize the shorter prose, and both of which are important contributions to Walser criticism.

Walter Benjamin's essay on Walser, originally published in 1929, was even then an "Ehrenrettung" of Walser's reputation. The insights and the suggestiveness of this short study remind us that Benjamin himself is the author of "Einbahnstraße" (1929), a classic modern example of short prose. With his typical critical brilliance, Benjamin pierced the happiness and euphoria surrounding the solitary protagonists of Walser's short prose to identify their existence, their "so exacerbating, so completely inhuman, imperturbable superficiality" (*Benjamin*, 151) as a recovery after madness or as an existence after the end of a fairy tale. These formulations follow Benjamin's bold attack on Walser's apparent linguistic "formlessness," on the irrelevance and frequent near absence of "plot" in his short prose, and the contradictory emotional factors at hand in the prose. By focusing on this euphoric state, Benjamin thereby broke ground for the perception of a binary existence in Walser's protagonists, even though he admitted that, in Walser, we never learn about the process of this recovery from madness. As Greven has said, "these remarks of Benjamin's are only hints, but they indicate paths to follow toward an understanding of Walser, paths on which the all too obvious nature of certain foreground phenomena in his work are not to be naïvely taken for the whole truth about Walser, but rather as a simple spoor of hidden, complicated structures" (*Greven*, 13).

An article nearly thirty years later by the English translator, poet, and scholar J. C. Middleton presented the first persuasive attempt to view Walser "whole."[26] As such Middleton's essay unqualifiedly stands as a landmark in Walser criticism and scholarship. His general characterization of Walser describes him as a "pre-eminently non-ideational intelligence," a typically Swiss countercurrent to "the socratic imagination which nowadays electrifies critics." Central to Walser's writing "is an independence from influences, movements and vogues . . ." In "Walser's sense of the absoluteness of the elements" and his "indelible vision of an absolute purity in creation," Middleton finds the source of Walser's "moral vision" and many of his "stylistic peculiarities." Middleton's essay parallels Benjamin's study where he defends Walser, "the rejected, daring, capricious Ariel of modern German prose," against the disinterest of critics and characterizes his gaiety as "a conquest of the vacuum, a conquest which could not have been made were not the healing of doubt the sign that doubt has been understood" (*op. cit.*, 425f.). He goes beyond Benjamin, however, in his excellent analysis of the style of the short prose. After warning that in reading Walser "one must discard prejudices against mannerism," he illustrates instances of Walser's "delight in rhythmical patterns," the "synergies of sound and sense" Walser achieves through shift of perspective, caricature, and parody, and the "form of arabesque discourse" which "can explore dimensions of verbal comedy which are inaccessible to any prose of a representational nature."

These critics concentrate their remarks and analyses on Walser's shorter prose works in the belief that they can thus best introduce a neglected author to a larger audience. However, the emphasis on the novels in this present study seems justified by the central position they occupy in the total *oeuvre*. Although Walser's three published novels were completed before mid-career, they shed light on the work coming before the novels and are a critical transitional stage to his later concentration on short prose forms. The novels trace Walser's spiritual and artistic development through the first half of his career and contain as well the stylistic and formal elements he employs in his later career. This study devotes itself to the relation in the novels between content, form, and style and to an investigation of themes from the novels as they recur in representative shorter prose works, written in Biel and Bern. The aim of the study is to thereby facilitate reading Walser from the perspective of the crises, experiments, and new modes of twentieth century prose fiction.

Before turning to the novels it may be useful to review predominant characteristics in German prose fiction that helped form the literary environment in which Walser began to write. We do not intend thereby to provide even a tentative basis of comparison for Walser's novels. In what follows we want rather to direct our attention to the emergence of lyricism as a characteristic mode in a normatively "epic" form and to refer schematically to the historical development of this lyricism into the objectified inwardness which enabled writers to derive from it social and anthropological commentary.

If, then, we look back to the German novel in the final decades of the nineteenth century, we realize how notoriously meager was its claim to any more than a provincial audience. Yet the one novel that more than any other was determinative for the German novel's course in the nineteenth century, Goethe's *Wilhelm Meister,* breathed a cosmopolitanism which had its social base in a reaction to the centrifugal forces of the French Revolution and its philosophic foundation in German Idealism. The balance Goethe's novel maintains between exterior and interior reality was possible because of the coincidence for Goethe of the universal and the particular, between reality and its idea. In Germany's post-Napoleonic political and social stagnation, the imitations of this balance became more and more tenuous in the face of economic and political forces that were undermining the vision of the integrality both of the individual and his society. The precariousness of the faith in this integrality is evident in Adalbert Stifter's novels *Der Nachsommer* and *Witiko,* where a rarefied esthetic-pedagogic realm, and a historical myth replace the missing social nexus. In Walser's homeland, Gottfried Keller's masterpiece, *Green Henry* (1854–55; 1879–80) can only demonstrate the integration of the hero with his society through an erasure of the hero's death in the original version and a consciously didactic rewrite of the conclusion. Underlying Keller's final novel, *Martin Salander* (1886), is the realization that even Switzerland had reached the end of a period of relative serenity and calm, during which it had been spared the disruptive effects of a bourgeoisie asserting itself under the political banner of nationalism. The factors contributing to Switzerland's social stability had been its long-established nationalism, its recently secured political integrity, and the early acquisition of ruling power by the middle class, obviating political dissension aimed at replacing an older ruling class. Whereas the tendency of nineteenth-century German prose fiction to localize its subject matter regionally posed a serious hindrance to the creation of realistic prose fiction, it encouraged the development and refinement of the novella in German literature. In its representative practitioners from Heinrich von Kleist and the Romantics through to the young Gerhart Hauptmann, the novella at its best combined its subjectively oriented narrative technique, lyric scenicism, and dramatic immediacy with rich symbolic allusiveness. Yet the formal limitations of the novella made it increasingly difficult to esthetically objectify the confrontation of the individual with a complex, rapidly changing exterior reality. The sensitive, ironic intimation of latent, unsolved social, political, and psychological problems in the novels set in Brandenburg that Theodor Fontane wrote in the last two decades of the century are an isolated phenomenon in the German novel of the late nineteenth century. Following the road Fontane nearly single-handedly marked out, Thomas Mann's *Buddenbrooks* reestablished the missing connection with the European tradition of the novel. The locale of Mann's first novel in a port city whose populace and traditions look out to the rest of Europe as much to their own hinterland is symptomatic for Mann's subsequent attempts in his work to transcend a narrowly German perspective both esthetically and thematically. Thomas Buddenbrook's catastrophic encounter in the novel with Schopenhauerian philosophy also furnishes a historical demarcation line for the termination of the *Bildungsroman* as Goethe created it. Thomas' doubt parallels Nietzsche's frontal attack on the German concept of *Bildung*. Mann's own further variants of the *Bildungsroman, The Magic Mountain* and *The Confessions of Felix Krull, Confidence Man* are highly stylized parodies of the *genre.*

The response of novelists to the passing of belief in a causally ordered world, to what Hermann Broch has called the "decay of values," was the creation between 1900 and 1930[27] of a form only nominally related to the traditional novel. This new novel revived the argument about the novel's illegitimacy of form. In declaring itself free of the commitment to external public "reality" no less than from the obligation to depict this reality, the novel followed the lead of Dostoevski, in viewing man more as a metaphysical organism than as a social and psychological being. Shifting the emphasis from plot and sacrificing the author's omniscience, the novel writer undertook the esthetic risk of assuming the perspective of fellow man (*Albérès*, 137) to deal with creatures who are "enormous, shadowy and intractable, and three-quarters hidden like an iceberg" (Forster, *Aspects of the Novel*, p. 85).

In the words of a recent critic, "the development of the novel since the later James and Proust shows an increasing inwardness of vision, the progressive limitation of definite plot and subject matter, and the intensification of the focus of narration" (*Friedman*, 23). As the novel became more intent on the incalculable and the unpredictable in an attempt to recreate a riddle or tell an undefinable story, the author acknowledged his incomplete knowledge of himself in the openness of his form, in the "torsi" or incompleted novels (Kafka, Musil), and in the amorphousness of his characters. The technical lapses in certain instances of the modern novel and the disregard for the conventions of narrative method are part of an effort to enrich the province of the novel by the inclusion in it of realms of experience that the "well-made novel" carefully extirpated. Critics, and, not least of all, novelists themselves, have noted the "crisis of the novel" that resulted from the author's recall of allegiance to the organizing intellect as prime principle. Virginia Woolf's novels have been charged with tediousness and triviality (*Kayser*, 442); Joyce with the hubris of creating a new language (*Emrich*, 186), and Mann, Broch, and Musil with essayism. Wilhelm Emrich's somewhat paradoxical observation that a significant number of representative modern novels are not really novels at all (*Emrich*, 176) is justified in view of the qualitative "otherness" of the modern novel and the great diversity in technique and style among agreed-upon masterpieces. The definition of the modern novel is a task for critics; what is certain is that the novel has become a veritable "cosmopolis of destiny's possibilities" (*Albérès*, 420).

The multiplicity of reference in this cosmopolis suggests to the critic of the modern novel the overlay of distinct but phylogenetically related evidences of human existence at an archeological site rather than a comprehensive city plan. In the profusion of techniques the novelist employs in his attempt to come to terms with the complexity, diversity, and eccentric tendencies of an expanded reality, "destiny's possibilities" necessarily assume a quantitatively larger mass in the novel. The description, documentation, and analysis of these possibilities accelerates what Beach has called the "tendency to deformalization" among the moderns (*Beach*, 334), whether in the subtle descriptions and analyses of emotional states in Proust or in the successive analyses of untenable intellectual redoubts in Robert Musil. The loss of a commonly accepted definition of reality not only results in the emergence of the paradoxical tendency to make relativity an absolute (thematically and formally), but is very likely the source of the post-Freudian "tendency to present that one abstraction which includes within itself all the others—the human consciousness. Such writers as Proust, Joyce, and Virginia Woolf used person and event merely as a necessary scaffolding to present the abstraction of consciousness itself" (*Friedman*, 7f.). One of the most frequently remarked consequences is the isolation of the hero. Thematically his isolation stems either from the sterility of his own interior life, his role as critic of the society he confronts, or as a seeker of a world in which man's potential can be achieved. The other major consequence is the development of an author's irony whose function can perhaps most simply be described as the self-critical attempt to puncture the apparent reality of literature. As the German novelist perhaps most consistently conscious of his own use of irony, Thomas Mann has provided his own commentary to the author intrusions, the commentaries and the scientific knowledge found in his novels from *The Magic Mountain* on.[28] These place Mann in the context of novelists whose (often unexpressed) aim it is to write the novel as art in contrast to adding to the art of the novel. When Mann in his address on *Joseph and His Brothers* protests that author explanation belongs to the game of art, that it "is not actually the speech of the author but of the work itself" (Mann, *Neue Studien*, p. 160) he sets himself off, it is true, from the desire in modern writers to "achieve absolute directness of expression" (*Emrich*, 119) which reaches its culmination in Expressionism and Dadaism, but he shares with other modern authors the integrality of the form (a persuasion with Mann, a hope for other novelists) whether as art or as expression.

Critics of the modern novel have been justifiably reluctant to ascribe to it an organizing intellectual or even emotional idea beyond the awareness of the ineffability of human existence. They have, however, distinguished the preponderance of a highly individualized language in the modern novel—whatever its particular "voice"—as opposed to the stylized literary language of the conventional novel. Beach describes this phenomenon as an increase in lyricism at the expense of dramatic effect and demonstrates how the novels of Virginia Woolf and James Joyce rely heavily on devices heretofore restricted to poetry. In his study of the stream-of-consciousness novel, Friedman emphasizes this lyricism still more. He proceeds beyond the recognition of poetic devices in the novel to discuss the compositional analogy with music (*Friedman,* Chapter Five). Seeking an explanation for the frequent use of musical borrowings for characterization, he suggests that perhaps "the only analogy with the unfolding states of consciousness is musical structure or pattern" (*Friedman,* 126). But it is necessary to mention the writer's relation to his basic tool of language, too. If we can speak of the musicalization of form in the modern novel in its attempt to reproduce the simultaneity of contrasting states of being or thereby provide a contrapuntal continuity to the discontinuity of external reality, it must be noted that such musicalization was possible only after a critical encounter with the efficacy of language.

The classical expression in German literature of the twentieth century writer's doubt in the viability of traditional literary language is contained in Hugo von Hofmannsthal's "A Letter of Lord Chandos" (1900). Hofmannsthal's Chandos is depicted as a Renaissance writer whose creative sustenance lies in tradition. His letter to his mentor, Francis Bacon, describes a creative paralysis resulting from the loss of "the ability to think or speak about anything coherently."[29] His anguish and despair are heightened by his certainty that he will never find the "language" to particularize intellectually the near mystic, yet unquestionably creative visions he has experienced and now describes. "Abstract words" he writes, "dissolved in my mouth like rotted mushrooms." Since for Chandos these visions could not be epiphanies, or articles of faith for a new creative mode as they are for us, he abdicates his literary career.

Although there is no document in Walser's writing paralleling the programmatic nature of "The Letter of Lord Chandos," the possibilities latent in the medium of language and its proximity to silence were always his crucial concern. His probing of the limits of verbal expression attest to his participation in the linguistic revolution characterizing German literature after the turn of the century. Two quotations, separated in time by nearly the length of his career, attest to this concern. The first, a selection from an "essay" by Fritz Kocher entitled "Free Topic" ("Freithema"), is an exercise in characterization undertaken in a typically modern absence of an organizing idea, where both author and narrator wish to emphasize a preoccupation with language.

> I am too lazy to think something up. And what might that be anyway? I like writing about anything. It's not the looking for a specific topic that excites me, but picking out fine, lovely words. Out of one idea I can form ten, even a hundred ideas, but no basic idea. What can I say? I write because I find it nice to fill out the lines with delicate letters in this way. *What* I write is a matter of complete indifference to me.*

The second quotation is from the late prose piece "My Efforts" ("Meine Bemühungen"), first published in *Große Kleine Welt*. The piece belongs to a group of essay-apologues from the twenties that show Walser's reaction to his awareness that the scorned and secretly courted "imago" of fame had eluded him. The selection is distinguished by its pairing of two apparently contradictory attitudes toward language, spontaneity and experimentation.

> The occasions on which I just wrote along spontaneously may have perhaps seemed a bit funny to the serious; but in fact I was experimenting in the linguistic field in the hope that there is present in language an unknown vivacity, which it is a pleasure to awaken.†

The spontaneity Walser refers to is indeed a characteristic element of a large part of his writing. It can be traced throughout his work as the symbolic element in his confessed need to depict his inner life (cf. "Aus meiner Jugend," *UP*, 254ff.), since both spontaneity and chance are stylistic reflections of an unanswerable reality of the self. The relation

---

* Ich bin zu faul, etwas zu ersinnen. Und was könnte das auch sein? Ich schreibe über alles gleich gern. Mich reizt nicht das Suchen eines bestimmten Stoffes, sondern das Aussuchen feiner, schöner Worte. Ich kann aus einer Idee zehn, ja hundert Ideen bilden, aber mir fällt keine Grundidee ein. Was weiß ich, ich schreibe, weil ich es hübsch finde, so die Zeilen mit zierlichen Buchstaben auszufüllen. Das "Was" ist mir vollständig gleichgültig (*FKR*, 27).

† Wenn ich gelegentlich spontan drauflos schriftstellerte, so sah das vielleicht für Ernsthafte ein wenig komisch aus; doch ich experimentierte auf sprachlichem Gebiet in der Hoffnung, in der Sprache sei irgendwelche unbekannte Lebendigkeit vorhanden, die es eine Freude sei zu wecken (*GKW*, 198).

of this need to the quest for joy that is posited as the result of the experimentation points to a source of the richness and uniqueness of the personal idiom Walser created. The uncertainties and the night figures are nearly always banished in his work but their shadows reside within the limits of the risk the spontaneity assumes. With reference to the novels, this verbal spontaneity parallels the incidence of chance in structure and plot.[30]

In Walser's own work, the novels represent a victory over the implicit attraction of silence as it is suggested in the encapsulated, fairy-tale like world of the early dramolets (cf. discussion of Simon Tanner and Chapter Seven). In other words, whatever the spontaneity and chance tell us about the form of Walser's work adds to our understanding of its structure when we identify silence as the opposing risk. Historically his three novels contribute to the attempt of the modern German novel to transcend the thematic and stylistic limitations of its nineteenth-century forebear. Thus his novels both figuratively and actually take their starting point at the threshold between the German inwardness whose literary antecedents lie in Romanticism and the prospect of a contemporary novel of more ambitious symbolism after it has forsaken the premise that the novelist's province is exterior reality.

Analogous attempts to broaden the context of subjectivism or even to repudiate it can be found in the careers of Rilke and Hugo von Hofmannsthal. Rilke's lyric journal-novel *The Notebooks of Malte Laurids Brigge* (1910) is a late, perhaps final monument to German inwardness. More chastened and much less sensually indulgent than Rilke's earlier prose poem, *The Lay of the Love and Death of Cornet Christoph Rilke* (1904), Rilke nevertheless still disavows his hero's solipsism. Yet "The Notebooks" are the necessary prelude to Rilke's beginning to write the *Duino Elegies,* just as Hofmannsthal's Lord Chandos letter sets off the "pre-existence" of his early works and marks the beginning of the road that leads via the opera libretti[31] to the social comedy *The Difficult Man (Der Schwierige* [1919]).

The most apparent evidence of subjectivism in Walser's novels is the almost unbroken concentration on a central figure and the stark reduction of exterior action. The following plot resumés indicate this.

In *Geschwister Tanner,* the hero, Simon Tanner, appears in a lakeside city, where he is variously, if irregularly, employed. For a few months he and his artist brother Kaspar share a luxurious room in the home of Klara Agappaia, the wife of an archaeologist. The Agappaia home is sold, Kaspar drops out of sight after an affair with Klara, and Simon, unwilling to stick to any work, pays an extended visit to his sister Hedwig in the village where she teaches school. During these three months he is unemployed. On his return to the city he drifts aimlessly in the backwaters of the city's life, usually unemployed and without means. His solitary life is once interrupted by a chance meeting with Klara, now apparently divorced. Beyond that he associates briefly with a homosexual male nurse, he dreams and daydreams much, takes lonely walks, exhibits an extreme volubility, and remains unaffected by the admonitions of another, older brother to alter his way of life. The novel ends without any clear resolution nearly two years after its beginning, as Simon visits what was formerly the Agappaia home on the edge of the forest "around Christmas time."

The external action is reduced both in scope and in time in the second novel, *Der Gehülfe*. Joseph Marti, twenty-four years old and obviously kin to Simon Tanner, works for some six months as secretary for an unsuccessful, prodigal inventor named Karl Tobler and his family in a villa overlooking a Swiss lake. Episodes from the hero's recent past, trips to the nearby city, descriptions of nature, and introspective mediations by Marti about his role in the Tobler menage fill out the book. His employer's precarious financial position worsens steadily, while Marti's hope of finding a spiritual home is disappointed. Marti leaves together with his predecessor in the job as bankruptcy becomes imminent and the family is preparing to leave Villa Abendstern and the extravagant life they led there.

Jakob von Gunten, finally, is the journal which the scion of an industrialist and councillor writes after running away from home and enrolling in a dilapidated boarding school for training servants. Subordinate just as are the two previous heroes, Jakob is to learn patience and obedience at the Institute Benjamenta. Undated journal entries treat of random subjects: Jakob's ambivalent relation to the school, his characterizations of his fellow pupils, his relations to the brother and sister who conduct the school, the repetition over and over again of the single lesson which constitutes the curriculum of the school, forays into the teeming metropolis, and meetings with a successful but blasé artist brother. Still other entries describe dreams, fantasies, and presentiments of the approaching disintegration of the school. After the self-prophesied death of Lisa Benjamenta, the school's only teacher, Jakob decides during the death watch he keeps together with her brother to agree to the principal's offer to go out into the world with him. They are to leave Europe and journey to the east.

The foregoing plot summaries do not indicate the tension created in the novels by the interplay between reflection and feeling, between the reception of the exterior world and nature, and the investigations of self, since they do not indicate the pervasiveness of the personalities of the three heroes, the prime source of the novels' "subjectivity." The significance of the spare plots is further diminished by the rarity with which resumés, interpolation, conventional exposition, and analysis are used to portray character or develop a theme. In varying degrees these traditional devices are replaced in the novels by a lyric juxtaposition of episodes closer to the structure and statement of poetry than to conventional prose fiction. In this way the subjectivity serves to expand the form and illuminate the spiritual temper of the new century. The progressive attenuation in the novels of an author-narrator—a characteristic self-imposed technical limitation—imposes a new obligation on the reader to deal with a variety of levels of human logic.

In each of the three novels, lyrical compositional elements such as repetitions and variations, formal contrast or juxtaposition, the use of the precognitive and subrational not only to forecast character and plot but to portray critical interior states, and the presentation—both in theme and style—of existence as a spiritual continuum[32] contribute to the esthetic effect and the meaning of the novels. The novels stemming from this creative process require a reader response similar to the response necessary for comprehending two otherwise dissimilar novels that were contemporary with Walser's, Robert Musil's *Young Törless* (1906) and Rilke's *The Notebooks of Malte Laurids Brigge* (1910). In them the reader must synthesize the slow accretion of states of mind, the thoughts and dreams of a hero who seeks to illuminate visually apprehended objects with a surcharge of perception, and what is veiled behind confessional monologs.

Typical of all three novels is a youthful hero, the "seeker of his true self" (*Middleton,* 410), who disappears at the "open" end of the novel with no explanation of what has happened or what will happen to him. In Greven's words, a "structurally isolated I" faces "the total opposite" of an inaccessible world (*Greven,* 27). All three arrive devoid of the usual credentials with which an author seeks to legitimatize his central characters. They are seen in an external locale that is filled in by frequently assiduous description but the geographic location of which is not specified. They hesitatingly knock at the door of life and are granted or are refused access. At the end, they move on to a spiritual "address unknown." It is the form and the atmosphere of each of the novels that creates a correlative of the heroes' essence as human beings. Judged by the traditions of the novel of development, the portrayals of the heroes are incomplete. By omitting any explicit synthesis of the dimensions in their portraiture, Walser depicts his heroes as remaining open to the possibilities of their fate. They are unaware of a curious inviolateness they bring with them that adds to the mystery of their personalities. They do not develop their gifts, and they leave unanswered the question implicitly posed in the modern novel: is man his actions or his secrets and his dreams?[33]

The three heroes recreate Walser's own confrontation with external reality.[34] The novels describe a line moving from a symbolistic introspectiveness in *Geschwister Tanner* to a more objective awareness of the threat urban society presents to man's nature in *Jakob von Gunten.* In *Geschwister Tanner,* the plot and themes reflect the enthusiasm of the new century for the "reform of life," while the abstraction of subjectivism, the distrust of rhetoric, and the struggle to articulate the ineffable in terms of the single life in *Jakob von Gunten* could be called a chastened Expressionism.

All three heroes hunger for the experience of life, but are estranged from life through their isolation from society. In Simon's case the very vociferousness of the search for the self, his rebellion against the spiritual subordination of office work and the wistful, melancholic tenor of the novel achieve this estrangement. In Joseph Marti's case the uncertainty of the outcome in this confrontation with life is added to his reservation towards the life the Toblers symbolize. In *Jakob von Gunten,* a highly developed irony acts as a regulator and shield in the hero's contact with the world outside the Institute Benjamenta. All three heroes reject society, but offer themselves in service to its individual members, thereby reestablishing a basis for the vitality of the inner life in a post-bourgeois era. Implicit in all three is the struggle to achieve grace by an affirmation of the plurality of life. This is the interior locale of the novels (cf. *Greven,* 97).

The heroes' affirmation of the plurality of life is, at the same time, a condition of their failure to achieve external realization of the self, since this means an accommodation to an objectified and therefore limited concept of life. Any such realization is an inward one; its nature dictates certain formal and stylistic elements used to depict it. With all three heroes, their "voice," their dreams, their fantasies and visions unremittingly emphasize the insufficiency, the metaphysical irrelevancy, and their own intuitive distrust of systematic or intellectual dicta (cf. *Greven,* 97f.). Although this suggests the creation in the novels of an autistic imaginative realm, what in fact links earlier critics of the novels is their uniform attempt to articulate the novels' symbolic breadth.[35]

Notes

1. See Hans Bänziger, "Pfarrer Johann Ulrich Walser aus Grub," *Neue Zürcher Zeitung,* August 8, 1955.

2. Especially in "Bild des Vaters" (S), written shortly after the father's death. Cf. "Brief eines Vaters an den Sohn" (AKD).

3. The mythological frescoes in the Council Chambers in Bern's Old City Hall were done by Karl Walser as was the fresco on wood, "Hirtenvolk" in the Reinhardt Museum in Winterthur.

4. A short play in Bernese dialect, "Der Teich," in the possession of Frau Fanny Hegi-Walser, probably belongs to *juvenilia* that followed these familial entertainments. As far as is known, it is the only exception to Walser's claim never to have written in Swiss dialect, which he regarded as "an unseemly accommodation to the masses" (*Wdgg*, 27).

5. See "Wenzel" (KGS), originally in *Die Schaubühne* (1901).

6. According to Franz Blei, some of Walser's published poems were written as early as 1894–95 ("Prolog über Walser," *Die literarische Welt*, I [1925], Nr. 1, 4). Blei may well have had a substantial source for his comparison of the emergence of Walser's literary talent with that of Hofmannsthal in the "Loris" period. Walser's anonymously printed untitled poem in Blei's literary magazine *Der lose Vogel* (1912–13) is dated 1894.

7. Franz Blei's very active literary career in the first decade of the century, especially his prominent role in the founding of new literary journals, is described in: Paul Raabe, "Franz Kafka und Franz Blei, samt einer wiederentdeckten Buchbesprechung Kafkas," *Kafka-Symposium* (Berlin: Verlag Klaus Wagenbach, 1965), pp. 7–20.

8. Documentary and historical material relating to the literary magazine may be found in "Die Zeitschrift 'Die Insel' und die Anfänge des Insel-Verlages 1899–1905," *Die Insel: Eine Ausstellung zur Geschichte des Verlages unter Anton und Katharina Kippenberg* (Marbach: Deutsches Literaturarchiv im Schiller-Nationalmusem, 1965), pp. 11–52. Walser in 1907 unsuccessfully offered his poems to Kippenberg for publication in the Insel Verlag (*loc. cit.*).

9. Selections reprinted in *Du*, Schweizerische Monatsschrift, February 1960.

10. Tilla Durieux, *Eine Tür steht offen. Erinnerungen* (Berlin, 1954).

11. All of the extant deletions in the original manuscript are appended to volume IV of *Das Gesamtwerk*. According to Greven, Walser himself made three (more likely four) deletions of longer passages in the course of composition. Further deletions (these done with pencil instead of ink) Greven identifies as Walser's concessions to Cassirer's wish to shorten the novel. These were done as the manuscript was being prepared for publication. Altered, incomplete pagination and crossed-out passages indicate that three further deletions have been lost: a story entitled "Gräfin Kirke" and one whose original title, "Ein Jüngling," was changed to "Mein Leben" before being dropped altogether, both of which originally stood at the present location in the text of Simon's dream of Paris, and, finally, the central part of an imaginary "letter" Simon writes, which may have represented a preliminary sketch for Walser's second novel, *Der Gehülfe*. Where necessary, the deletions are referred to below.

12. *Wissen und Leben—Neue Schweizer Rundschau*, XVII, 25 (1924), 269–288.

13. In a letter to Resy Breitbach dated January 15, 1926, in which Walser recalls the Berlin art dealer and publisher Paul Cassirer, he quotes Cassirer as having said of *Geschwister Tanner* "This book was a colossal success and at the same time a colossal failure" (*Du*, Schweizerische Monatsschrift, February 1960).

14. From an uncollected prose piece "Heimkehr im Schnee," originally quoted in: *Vom Glück des Unglücks und der Armut,* ed. Carl Seelig, Sammlung Klosterberg (Basel: Schwabe, 1944), p. 17; now in: *Mächler,* 124–125.

15. Emil Schibli, "Die Vorlesung. Kleiner Beitrag zu einer Biographie Robert Walsers," *Der kleine Bund,* February 15, 1957.

16. Twenty-two letters and post cards to the Rowohlt Verlag and the Kurt Wolff Verlag dating from 1912 to 1919 are now deposited in the Kurt Wolff Archive in the German Literature Collection at Yale University Library. In 1918 Walser tried to interest Wolff in a collection of prose works he planned to title "Kammermusik." A brief reminiscence of Walser is found in: Kurt Wolff, "Vom Verlegen im Allgemeinen und von der Frage: Wie kommen Autoren und Verleger zusammen," *Sprache im technischen Zeitalter,* 1964, 894ff.

17. Originally published in: *Neue Schweizer Rundschau—Wissen und Leben,* XIX, 3 (March 1926), 252–259.

18. Kurt Pinthus describes the founding of Rowohlt's first publishing firm and Wolff's relation to it in a foreword to: *Rowohlt Almanach 1908–1962,* herausgegeben von Mara Hintermeier und Fritz J. Raddatz (Reinbek and Hamburg: Rowohlt, 1962), pp. 9–40.

19. Some of the authors referred to or written about in these two periods are Goethe, Schiller, Jean Paul, Wilhelm Hauff, Gottfried Keller, Kleist, Brentano, Lenau, Byron, Dickens, Balzac, Verlaine, Baudelaire, Rimbaud, Tolstoi, Dostoevsky, Ibsen, Adalbert, Stifter, Hermann Hesse, Georg Trakl, Lesage, Alfred de Vigny, Stendhal, Voltaire, and Flaubert.

20. The discovery by psychologists and psychiatrists of clinical evidence of emotional disturbances and mental illness in contemporary literature and the analysis of the same literature by critics as meaningful poetic statements is caution enough to resist the equation of the medical diagnosis of the soul with its creative manifestations. Both Bänziger and Greven list features in Walser's writing, such as verbosity, flight of ideas, and the contrast between an objective situation and the emotional reaction to it, that may be regarded as indicative of schizoid tendencies (*Bänziger,* 103–104, 157; *Greven,* 208). That Walser was personally and literarily conscious of these "symptoms" seems to be clear from the intentional emphasis they receive in his literary work when compared with his correspondence and the objectivity he brings to the portrayal of psychologically "revealing" episodes (cf. "Brief an die Geduldige," *UP,* 78; "Schwäche und Stärke," *FKR,* 221).

21. The most frequently praised author in *Wanderungen mit Robert Walser* is Gottfried Keller. Walser also expresses admiration for Goethe (*Wdgg,* 28, 35), Lessing (*Wdgg,* 15) and Wieland (*Wdgg,* 18) among the classical authors, praises Wedekind as nobler and more human than Strindberg (*Wdgg,* 110), admits jealously of the kind of fame Theodor Storm and Wilhelm Raabe achieved (*Wdgg,* 18), allows for the "astonishing" quality of Thomas Mann's early work but is put off by the length and pedantry of the Joseph tetralogy (*Wdgg,* 15, 103), and denies a more famous miniaturist than himself, Peter Altenberg, the title of poet (*Wdgg,* 22). Whereas he speaks disparagingly of both Hesse (*Wdgg,* 16, 42) and Rilke (*Wdgg,* 11), he reveals a taste for lesser known authors such as Nestroy (*Wdgg,* 57), Börne (*Wdgg,* 20), and Keyserling (*Wdgg,* 104).

22. Clemens Heselhaus investigates this phenomenon as it applies to lyric poetry in the section of his *Deutsche Lyrik der Moderne* (Düsseldorf: Bagel, 1961), entitled "Lyrische Zyklen," where he discusses the poetry of Mombert and Otto zur Linde.

23. Two further histories of modern German literature have included greatly expanded treatments of Walser in recent revisions: Albert Soergel and Curt Hohoff, *Dichtung und Dichter der Zeit. Vom Naturalismus bis zur Gegenwart*, revised edition (Düsseldorf: Bagel, 1961), I, 815–828 and the addition of Bernhard Rang's "Exkurs über Robert Walser" to the fourth edition of *Deutsche Literatur im 20. Jahrhundert* (Heidelberg: Rothe, 1961), I, 99–110.

24. Wilhelm Duwe, *Deutsche Dichtung des 20. Jahrhunderts* (Zurich: Orell Füssli, 1962), I, 174, 176; II, 15–20, 45, 60. In a more recent publication that claims to trace the development of modern style, Duwe claims for Walser the role of predecessor for German Expressionism without substantiating this assertion. See *Ausdrucksformen deutscher Dichtung vom Naturalismus bis zur Gegenwart: Eine Stilgeschichte der Moderne* (Berlin: Erich Schmidt Verlag, 1965), pp. 83–85.

25. Seelig never undertook a comprehensive critical study of Walser. He wrote about Walser principally in the appreciative essays that introduce his new edition of the *Gedichte* (Sammlung Klosterberg [Basel: Schwabe, 1944], in *Unbekannte Gedichte* (St. Gallen: Tschudy, 1958), in the sampler of prose selected from the novels and the shorter works entitled *Vom Glück des Unglücks und der Armut* (Sammlung Klosterberg [Basel: Schwabe, 1944]), and in the article "in memoriam Robert Walser" (*Jahresring 57–58*). Two newspaper essays that appeared shortly after Walser's death ("Am Grab Robert Walsers," *National-Zeitung* [Basel], January 6, 1957; "Robert Walser als Dichter der Armut," *Volksrecht* [Zurich], January 3, 1957) and the essay "Robert Walsers Lebensbild" in *Die Welt von Robert Walser*, a keepsake edition distributed at Christmas, 1961 by the book printers Gebrüder Fritz, AG (Zurich) are predominantly biographical in character.

26. J. C. Middleton, "The Picture of Nobody." The same author did the first translations of Walser's work into English: Robert Walser, *The Walk and Other Stories,* trans. Christopher Middleton (London: John Calder, 1957).

27. 1900 is not intended as a terminological *ante pro quem*. In German literature it is convenient to regard the reaction to German Naturalism as the inception of forces that inspire modernist movements, notwithstanding Professor Emrich's essay showing Arno Holz, the founder of so-called "consistent Naturalism," anticipating the linguistic theories of German Expressionism (cf. *Emrich*, 155ff.). The pre-symbolist poetry of C. F. Meyer, Stefan George's poems, Hugo von Hofmannsthal's early work, and Frank Wedekind's plays are German parallels to the forerunners of a revolution in literature anticipated in French Symbolism and its English variants (in the Pre-Raphaelites, George Moore, and Henry James). In whatever form this reaction to Naturalism took place, artists clearly did not concern themselves with the dogmatic compartmentalization of the reaction which literary historians through the thirties imposed on the period under such names as *Neuromantik, Impressionismus, Neuklassizismus,* or *Das heimliche Deutschland*.

28. Cf. Thomas Mann, *Die Entstehung des Doktor Faustus* (Berlin and Frankfurt a.

M., 1949), and "Joseph und seine Brüder, ein Vortrag," in *Neue Studien* (Berlin and Frankfurt a. M., 1948).

29. Hugo von Hofmannsthal, *Gesammelte Werke in Einzelausgaben,* ed. Herbert Steiner (Frankfurt a. M.: S. Fischer, 1951), vol. 5 (*Prosa II*), 12.

30. Walter Benjamin recorded a similar intuition when he spoke of Walser's "farmer-like modesty about speech" (*Benjamin,* 149). Hardly does Walser have pen in hand, Benjamin writes, when a desperado mood breaks out: "He feels all is lost, a flood of words is loosed, in which the object of each sentence is to make you forget the one before" (*loc. cit.*). Unfortunately the force of Benjamin's insight is dissapated by his illustration. He cites the first line of Walser's parody of the famous monolog by Schiller's Wilhelm Tell before he shoots the tyrant Gessler: "He has got to come along this sunken road, I think" (*AKD,* 46).

31. Cf. Hilde D. Cohn, "Hofmannsthal's Libretti," *German Quarterly,* XXXV (1962), 149–164.

32. Middleton speaks of the sense of "rhythm as existence" which gives *Geschwister Tanner* its "peculiar energy." Actually Middleton's perception can be applied beyond *Geschwister Tanner,* since the phenomenon of rhythm or, more appropriately, movement and repose, has both stylistic and thematic ramifications that extend to the rest of the *oeuvre.*

33. "While Zola, Duhamel and Maurois put the question of where they stand in the state of human existence, Musil, Kafka and Joyce—but no less Cocteau, Hofmannsthal, Thomas Mann and Breton—struggled with those other questions inevitably posed by the relationship between humanity and chance, between human wisdom and man's impotence, between the known and the unknown" (*Albérès,* 241).

34. Walser's remarks to Seelig about his novels are colored by the consequences of his decision to stop writing. He charged his novels with excessive subjectivity and said that they disregarded the rules of art (*Wdgg,* 14, cf. 42).

35. See Felix Poppenberg's review of *Geschwister Tanner;* Franz Kafka's intimation of Simon's personality after having read only *Jakob von Gunten* (*Briefe,* 75–76); Joachim Benn's recapitulative critical essay on Walser's work through 1914 in *Die Rheinlande,* XXIV (1914), 131–134; and the letter and "aphorism" Christian Morgenstern wrote Bruno Cassirer after reading *Geschwister Tanner* in his capacity as publisher's reader (*Ein Leben in Briefen,* ed. Margarete Morgenstern [Insel, 1952], 242–243).

2

SIMON TANNER

Simon Tanner, a young man in his early twenties, is the first of Walser's three self-seekers. He moves through the three segments of the plot (the first stay in the city, dominated by the relationship to Klara Agappaia; the sojourn in the country with his sister Hedwig; and his aimless life after his return to the city) with so strong an appearance of resiliency and insouciance that he might be mistaken for a light-hearted drifter, an eternally blissful "Sonntagskind." Such a view would overlook the fact that Simon's joy is a precariously held island threatened by a tide of unhappiness often hinted at as the rootlessness of a marginal existence, but rigorously disregarded. The Simon we see as a carefree human being represents the freedom implicit in his still-unrealized possibilities of life. Seen against the background of the search for relation to and integration in the world he faces—a search that parallels his search for identity through the book—his failure to utilize his talents becomes as insistent a threat of psychological extinction as that experienced by the artist-journal writer in Rilke's *The Notebooks of Malte Laurids Brigge*.

If we seek to understand Simon as a human being and as a literary creation symptomatic for a particular historical perception of reality, we are confronted with contradictions and inconsistencies.[1] He is brash, daring, and unperturbedly outspoken in the many, frequently lengthy "speeches" in which he presents himself to the exterior world and which are his principal medium for seeking a relation to it.[2] As public utterances they establish an initial ambivalence in Simon's personality in the "childish" contradiction between their opinionated, forceful expression and Simon's aversion to the display of emotion, which he holds to be a weakness (cf. *T*, 38, 130–133). The tone and the substance of these speeches varies with what occasions them, but they all exhibit a pathos of rhetoric, a high degree of self-awareness, and an unmistakable irony reflecting the uncertainty of Simon's situation.

The book begins abruptly with such a speech, the volubility of which takes the reader by surprise. Yet the image Simon creates of himself, with the successful intention of persuading a book dealer to employ him on the spot, is misleading. In a turnabout after eight days, during which a "quiet, shy" Simon had worked "so very reliably" (*T*, 17), he quits the job, scolds his employer in a long pronouncement on the meanness of the employment, and appends a gratuitous threat "to sell his freedom for good" by going into the army rather than continue to deny his talents their full development behind the bookdealer's "old, scroungy, narrow" desk.

The opening scene typifies Simon's resistance to the institutionalization of his life. His ambition to utilize his talents is correspondingly directed more at relationships with individuals than toward his own advancement. Simon's most meaningful encounters in the book are with women, but his relationship to them is ambiguous and there is no easy identification of them with his ambitions. When he once fancies himself married, his imagined behavior toward his wife is alternately maudlin or sadistic (*T*, 126f.). During his brief employment as a servant in the home of a rich lady, he senses the failure of his service to effect a human contact, and insult is substituted for reverence (*T*, 204–205). More often, his wish is to revere and idealize women, as is the case with Klara Agappaia. The book never treats of Simon's sexual impulses; they are dormant or are consumed in the idealized gift of himself to Klara.

Behind Simon's personal ambition is a desire to function as a part of a larger whole. His opportunity to do so in the first segment of the novel is the various employment he takes. He departs from each position as precipitously as he did from the bookdealer's. A short time later, when he is seeking work at an employment office, he defends the frequency of his job changes by insisting that a marginal existence such as his demands the courage needed to discover where he can serve his fellowman (*T*, 19–20). This same speech ends with an initial, exaggerated instance of Simon's desire to equate employment with service and divorce it from livelihood in his ironic refusal to take a job with a vacation.

> I won't have anything to do with vacations. I absolutely hate vacations. Just don't get me a position with a vacation. That doesn't attract me in the least; as a matter of fact, I would die if I were to get a vacation. I want to do battle with life, I don't care if I collapse,

> I don't want to experience either freedom or comfort, I hate freedom
> if it's just tossed at me, the way you throw a bone to a dog.*

The above quotation concludes a speech in which a tone of humility provides a counterweight to the more obvious irony. We come closer to Simon, however, if we recognize behind the irony a criticism of a bourgeois ethos which makes it impossible—other than through the indirection of this irony—to plead for a morality no longer existent.

The social criticism of the mercantile world representing the society Simon seeks to enter becomes more explicit in Simon's speech to the director of a large bank (*T*, 42–44). He denounces bank employment as too costly in terms of its damage to the human spirit. Simon assures the director of his willingness to do any work that demands all his abilities, but he brusquely rejects the director's offer of a letter of recommendation. As a fictional hero, Simon enters the novel unburdened by, and not identifiable with a conventional view of social reality. In the context of society, he starts morally from scratch so as to better justify an absolute claim on reality.

> A testimonial? No, don't write one out for me. . . . From now
> on I'll make up my testimonials myself. All I will do from now on if
> anybody asks me for references is give them my own name. . . . I
> don't want a future, I want to have a present. That seems more valu-
> able to me. You only have a future when you don't have any present
> and if you do have a present you forget to even think about a future.†

Simon's conversation in Chapter Four with Klaus, his scholar brother, gives the first overt indication of a discrepancy between Simon's outer and inner person and cautions against too complete a reliance on the appearance Simon creates. The conversation is one of those held during the nocturnal lakeside scenes when the single meeting of all the Tanners occurs. This chapter represents a first climax; all of the characters have

---

* Ich will mit Ferien nichts zu tun haben. Ich hasse die Ferien geradezu. Verschaffen Sie mir nur nicht einen Posten mit Ferien. Das hat nicht den geringsten Reiz für mich, ja ich würde sterben, wenn ich Ferien bekäme. Ich will mit dem Leben kämpfen, bis ich meinetwegen umsinke, will weder Freiheit noch Bequemlichkeit kosten, ich hasse die Freiheit, wenn ich sie so hingeworfen bekomme, wie man einem Hund einen Knochen hinwirft (*T*, 20).

† Ein Zeugnis? Nein, stellen Sie mir keines aus. . . . Ich selbst stelle mir von jetzt an meine Zeugnisse aus. Ich will mich von nun an nur noch auf mich selbst berufen, wenn jemand nach meinen Zeugnissen fragt. . . . Ich will keine Zukunft, ich will eine Gegenwart haben. Das erscheint mir wertvoller. Eine Zukunft hat man nur, wenn man keine Gegenwart hat, und hat man eine Gegenwart, so vergißt man, an eine Zukunft überhaupt nur zu denken (*T*, 44).

been introduced, most of the themes have been touched on, and, consistent with the compositionally lyric nature of this work, these themes are repeated in much greater proximity to one another during this single meeting of the Tanner siblings. The conversations in this chapter and the next, during the "glorious evening" climaxed by the speech in which Simon makes the spiritual gift of himself to Klara Agappaia (*T*, 83–86), terminate the first segment of the novel. The speech adds a new perspective to his person since the fate of lovelessness he foresees is spoken of with a passionate certainty that precludes irony.

The conversation with Klaus attempts to answer his older brother's concern about the goallessness of Simon's life. Simon's concept of the role he may be destined to fill considers the possibility a unilateral accommodation to life in which the world does not participate. This gives Simon's irony a more humane cast. It reveals much of Simon's previous and subsequent aggressiveness as more than the provocation it clearly intends to be; Simon is indeed "the *eiron* of Greek comedy . . . the ironic outsider" (*Middleton*, 410), but his irony also comprehends a special plea for communication and contact. Simon's words are the first articulation in the novels of the *primus agens* for all three heroes, the incontrovertible reality of individual existence.

> I'm not in the habit of showing that I feel respect for many things. That's the sort of thing I keep to myself, for I tell myself, what use is it to put on an earnest air if one is destined by fate, I mean maybe chosen, to play the fool. There are lots and lots of fates and it's before these that I want first and foremost to curb my pride. There's no choice in the matter.*

The subsequent change of locale from city to country brings with it a change in Simon's character. Until he returns to the city from the country at the beginning of Chapter Eleven, he is, by comparison, strangely mute and incommunicative. The speeches subside; he takes comfort from the thought "of being a forgotten person" (*T*, 115); the world of the first phase of the novel silently recedes. Kaspar devotes himself to his painting, Klara Agappaia's husband leaves on an expedition in search of a lost Greek city, and Klara herself unaccountably vanishes from the scene of the novel after the transitional sixth chapter.

* Es ist nicht meine Gewohnheit, zu zeigen, daß ich Ehrfurcht vor vielen Dingen besitze. So etwas pflege ich für mich zu behalten, denn ich denke, was nützt es, eine ernste Miene aufzusetzen, wenn man vom Schicksal dazu bestimmt, ich meine vielleicht dazu erwählt ist, den Narren zu spielen. Es gibt viele, viele Schicksale, und vor ihnen will ich in allererster Linie meinen Nacken beugen. Es bleibt nichts anderes zu tun übrig (*T*, 71).

Simon lives secluded and withdrawn until he sets out to visit his sister. There is no external reason to explain why the verbal and emotional energies of the first part subside; there is only the decisiveness of this elliptical transition at the beginning of Chapter Seven: "Winter came" (*T*, 115). The new rhythm that asserts itself thereafter is marked by a reestablished intimacy between Simon and his sister Hedwig based on their mutual respect and their shared childhood, by the fantasies sparked in Simon by the placidity of rural life, and the expository essay "Country Life" which he writes to earn money. Life proceeds in this new rhythm with a "presentness" and immediacy that leaves no room for retrospection or commentary on what transpired through Chapter Five.

From the time of Simon's return to the city until the end of the book still another tonality predominates. The final phase of the novel is a modulation of the first phase, dealing with the phenomenon of an urban society increasingly subject to the dictates of a modern economy. Simon's figure as an unabsorbed individual is in no way diminished in this setting, but Simon is missing the foil of society. His confrontations are now with individuals and with himself; his vociferousness of statement is unimpaired, but it is uttered in markedly greater isolation. Simon wouldn't now be able to muster the *sang-froid* and indulgent self-importance such as are found in the restaurant scene, where he reflects gratefully that he can enjoy modest pleasures "more impetuously and more sensually" than others do greater ones (*T*, 65). He can still be vain, opportunistic, and relentless in his imagination, but it is now his tolerance, sensitivity, and respect for the denizens of the world between the urban anonymity of respectability and the anonymity of the uprooted and the rootless where he himself dwells that stand out in sharpened relief.

In contrast to the first phase of the book, the portrayal of Simon is gradually shifted to the interior person, preparatory to the open end of the final chapter. Simon's long defense of unhappiness in Chapter Fourteen is a step toward this. The impassioned tone of this speech is comparable to and implicitly adds to the significance of Simon's remarkable declaration of enduring love to Klara on the lake shore—a gift of love given on the premise that it not be requited. Simon delivers this speech after overhearing two men discuss the decline into madness of a young man who is revealed as a heretofore unmentioned Tanner sibling.

As with the speech to Klara, Simon's words here attest to the balance struck between strong emotion and reflection. To Klara he had projected a vision of human relations based on his acceptance of a fate of lovelessness. Now Simon carries his tactic of definition in a new direction, radically postulating the origin of the soul and describing a metaphysics for it that is free of the categories of formalized or intellectual religion. Underlying Simon's inquiry and statement is the antithesis between the implicit belief that the affirmation of life's plurality is grace and the absence or remoteness of God (cf. the snow-child fairy tale below and *Greven,* 99). In Simon's own thinking the antithesis is bridged here by a spiritualization of the body in terms impossible in German literature before the advent of Modernism. The sensualist orientation of Simon's idealism in itself reveals a shift in the cognitive role of perception. Of equal historical significance is the linguistic form of the will to encounter a new age with an appropriate moral commitment. Whereas the fragileness of post-Goethean idealism can be seen in the increasing reliance in literature on the themes of renunciation and resignation to shore it up, here an individual moral impulse is articulated in a verbally flamboyant, "public" statement. Simon has "forgotten" his brother because of the completeness of his struggle for moral and personal identity. "You see," he says, "I never get around to thinking about him, for I am a person who has to fight with his hands and feet to be able to stand up in the world. I won't give in until it's impossible to think of getting up off the floor again" (*T*, 239). Consistent with the derivation of Simon's knowledge from the alogical level of dream, misfortune is perceived as an inevitable, transcendental force, unrelated to Idealism (or poetry [*T*, 242f.]) but based rather in a vitalistic concept of nature that replaces idealized nature with reverence for the manifestations of life. The completeness of identification Simon seeks with all things underlies the unsparing breadth of a view of reality in which suffering and misfortune, as integral parts of reality, are given the same consciousness of experience as their more courted opposites.

> Misfortune is formative. . . . Misfortune is the friend in our lives who is all the more honest for being rather morose. It would be quite impudent and dishonorable of us to overlook that. We never comprehend misfortune in the first moment, that's why we hate it at the moment of its coming. . . . Yes; fate, misfortune is beautiful. It is good, for it also includes happiness, its opposite. . . . It awakens new life when it destroys old life it didn't like. It's an incitement to live better. All beauty—if we still hope to experience beauty—we owe to it. . . . Most people don't have the courage to greet misfortune as something in which you can bathe the soul, like limbs in water. . . . Misfortune has to be added to this abundance of splendor and happiness—if one is really ready to regard the naked, taut, mobile, warm member that came with our life on earth as such an

abundance. It keeps us from frothing over, it gifts us with soul. It develops our ears to hear the sound made when the soul and the body, blended into one, having crossed over into one another, respire together. It makes something corporeal-soulful of our bodies, and the soul settles down in our very middle, so that we can, if we like, feel our entire body as a soul. . . . It lets us love, for where would there be love without some unhappiness? Dreams are more beautiful than reality, for when we dream, we suddenly understand the sensuality and the rapturous goodness of misfortune.*

In the unbroken rhythm of physical isolation and transient human encounters characteristic of the final phase of the novel, Simon's temporary association with the homosexual male nurse (*T*, 253–268) actualizes the sharpening anomaly between his insistence on absolutes and provisional and ephemeral existence. This emerges both in his conduct with the nurse during their association and in his lengthy and unusually fair self-appraisal at the beginning of their acquaintanceship (*T*, 254–258). Implicit throughout the speech to the nurse is Simon's determination to give meaning to his existence by insisting on man's responsibility to fulfill his own fate, thus placing him near to the development towards a *homo dei* which Emrich sees climaxing, in Hans Castorp in *The Magic Mountain* the development of Thomas Mann's heroes (*Emrich*, 174). But the primacy of experience that Simon posits ("I am always afraid that a single experience of life might escape me. To this end I am as ambitious as ten Napoleons" [*T*, 258].) sees a unique-

---

* Das Unglück bildet . . . Das Unglück ist der etwas mürrische, aber desto ehrlichere Freund unseres Lebens. Es wäre ziemlich frech und ehrlos von uns, das zu übersehen. Im ersten Augenblick verstehen wir das Unglück nie, deshalb hassen wir es im Moment seines Kommens. . . . Ja, das Schicksal, das Unglück ist schön. Es ist gut; denn es enthält auch das Glück, sein Gegenteil . . . Es weckt neues Leben, wenn es altes erschlagen hat, das ihm nicht gefallen hat. Es reizt zum Besser-Leben. Alle Schönheit, wenn wir noch hoffen, Schönes zu erleben, verdanken wir ihm . . . Den meisten mangelt der Mut, das Unglück zu begrüßen als etwas, worin man die Seele baden kann, wie Glieder im Wasser . . . Zu dieser Fülle von Pracht und Glück, wenn man wirklich geneigt ist, das nackte, straffe, bewegliche, warme, mit auf das Erdenleben bekommene Glied als eine solche Fülle zu betrachten, muss eine Art Gegengewicht treten: das Unglück! Es kann uns hindern überzuschäumen, es schenkt uns die Seele. Es bildet unsere Ohren dafür aus, den schönen Klang zu vernehmen, der tönt, wenn Seele und Körper, ineinandervermischt, ineinanderübergetreten, zusammen atmen. Es macht aus unserem Körper etwas Köperlich–Seelenvolles und die Seele bringt es zu einem festen Dasein mitten in uns, daß wir, wenn wir wollen, unseren ganzen Körper als eine Seele empfinden . . . Es macht uns erst lieben, denn wo liebte man, mit nicht auch ein wenig Unglück? In den Träumen ist es noch schöner als in der Wirklichkeit, denn wenn wir träumen, verstehen wir auf einmal die Wollust und entzückende Güte des Unglücks (*T*, 240–242).

ness in experience that determines its quality of individual inevitability. The measured, almost defensive tone of his remarks to the nurse bespeaks Simon's readiness to accept poverty as the price for freedom and the opportunity to remain a human being. Seeking an undefined absolute and as yet unwilling to acknowledge any norm or law as binding, he is ready to pay any price in personal terms for a fiat for his unlimited, but arbitrary commitment.

> ". . . why don't they let me try to wrest from life its excitment in my own way, everyone tries that, everyone; they just don't all do it in the same way. . . . You see, I don't want any wreaths on my grave, that's the whole difference. I don't care what my end will be. They keep telling me, the others do, that I am going to have to atone for my high spirits. Good enough, then I'll atone and then I'll know what it means to atone."*

Before their relationship collapses under the single-mindedness of the nurse's interest, Simon exhibits a disquieting tolerance toward the nurse's advances, even restraining his own instinctive repugnance by telling himself: "One has to get to know everything, and you only get acquainted with everything if you contact it without flinching" (*T*, 266). This instance of Simon's "absolute 'lack of prejudice'" (*Greven*, 54) is one of many affronts to accepted social mores, which, since they are motivated in Simon by momentary, wholly subjective impulses, only cumulatively achieve the force of criticism.

The remainder of Simon's portraiture and his increasingly real exile within the homeland he refuses to leave can be easily summarized. Unemployed and without the ambiguous solace of his siblings, he copies addresses to stave off starvation and inveigles his landlady into lending him money. Even the coincidental meeting with Klara, to whom he is lead through a subconscious divination, is unable to brake the momentum of his descent. Immediately after his return to the city he had accepted an offer to care for a sickly child in a wealthy home in the belief that his individualism was less valuable than the chance to serve others. The life he had "frittered away" because it had seemed "quite without value" would, he said, merge into other's needs and he would live for their "purposes, interests and intentions" (*T*, 187). By contrast,

* . . . sie mögen mich auf meine Weise dem Leben seinen Reiz abzureißen versuchen lassen, das versuchen alle, alle, nur nicht alle auf die gleiche Art . . . Sehen Sie, ich will keine Kränze auf mein Grab bekommen, das ist der ganze Unterschied. Mein Ende ist mir gleichgültig. Sie sagen mir immer, jene andern, ich werde meinen Übermut noch büßen müssen. Nun wohl, dann büße ich und erfahre dann doch, was büßen heißt (*T*, 257f.).

the absence of a grantee after his descent into an emotional and social "lower depths" seems to mock the donor. In the final scene of the novel Simon wanders back to the site of what used to be the Agappaias' *Waldhaus*, where the club manageress who befriends him listens to the last and longest of Simon's speeches. As a climactic résumé placed where the conventional novel resolves plot, Simon's final public statement merits our attention. This unparagraphed twelve-page outpouring begins with a chronicle of the Tanner parents and their children, after which Simon relates his own school life, his unsuccessful bank apprenticeship, his hypersensitivity, and his subsequent removal to another town. Throughout the book Simon had foresworn the promise of a "smooth future" (*T*, 258) in his search for a vital present. Now he adduces recollection and memory not as nostalgia but as the definition of a past from which he seeks release, knowing that youth is often "more difficult and more pensive than the life of many an old man" (*T*, 328). His estimate of his present situation is in two parts. On the one hand he stresses the human irrelevancy of his encounters with the mercantile world when he denies a failure due to having followed the wrong road: "I would have been just as far along as I am now, in any profession" (*T*, 329). Then he employs a critical image of himself as beggar and dreamer vainly awaiting admission at the door of life. We shall refer to this image in the following section. We should note here that the reappearance of a dream at the conclusion of an individual segment of emotional discourse, such as found in the following quotation, establishes an interrelation between inner and outer reality as well as a connecting road of unimpeded access between them.

> As for myself, up until now I've remained the most incompetent of men. . . . I still stand before the door of life, knocking, to be sure not too impetuously, and I just listen intently, whether someone might come to push back the bolt for me. A bolt of this sort is a little heavy, and if someone has the feeling that it's a beggar standing outside and knocking, he doesn't like to come. I am nothing but a listener and a waiter, but as such absolutely perfected, for I have learned how to dream while I wait . . .*

---

* . . . Was mich betrifft, so bin ich bis jetzt der untüchtigste aller Menschen geblieben . . . Ich stehe noch immer vor der Türe des Lebens, klopfe, allerdings mit wenig Ungestüm, und horche nur gespannt, ob jemand komme, der mir den Riegel zurückschieben möchte. So ein Riegel ist etwas schwer, und es kommt nicht gern jemand, wenn er die Empfindung hat, daß es ein Bettler ist, der draußen steht und anklopft. Ich bin nichts als ein Horchender und Wartender, als solcher allerdings vollendet, denn ich habe es gelernt, zu träumen, während ich warte . . . (*T*, 329).

In the climax and conclusion of the speech Simon acknowledges an indebtedness to the world which he promises to satisfy; he expresses a love for human beings coming from his realization of his dependence on them. He renews and strengthens his offer of service to people, "to be used by them" (*T*, 330). In this climactic situation Simon makes his first admission to others of what is at least a guilt of omission. He also repudiates the longings that previously occasioned indifference and scorn of mankind; these have been dissolved in the knowledge that the repayment of his debt will call on all his energies and faculties.

Simon's final speech poses a problem of interpretation. The reader may be puzzled by Simon's sudden abdication of a sense of absolute individual responsibility. Recognizing the figure he cuts in the world, or being, as he says, "aware of my virtues and my weaknesses" (*T*, 329) seems insufficient to enable Simon to sidestep the burden of his own person and its inwardness. The discrepancy of Simon's apparent surrender, the abandonment of principle in one whose existence was given shape—if not meaning—by principle, and the abrupt termination of the novel with no apparent esthetic logic raise questions which neither the plot nor the author answer. Even if we allow for the critical juncture of this "speech," note the absence of nearly all vestiges of mimicry, pose, self-intoxication, and irony, and acknowledge its sincerity and judiciousness, we still question the claim of this new promise for greater credibility than the earlier resolves to undertake a "useful" life (*T*, 101, 105, 248, 299). Is it the truncation of the narrative one short paragraph after the end of the "speech" that accounts for the undeniable sense of skimpiness of statement? Or is it the contrast between the final scene and the richness and suggestiveness of the rest of the novel, which an early critic sensed when he characterized the novel as a *Weltgedicht* (*Benn*, 133)? More than our concentration on Simon's public life has been able to indicate, *Geschwister Tanner* succeeds in giving substance to a complex, richly modulated existence at whose isolated center stands Simon. This richness is in part due to the depiction of this existence as one revolving about his vital concern that he maintain an equilibrium between his inner and outer life and that the primacy of this existence, if not absolutely based on the inner life, at least not be abrogated by rationally derived dicta. For another part it is due to the insight and human wisdom of his reflections on his encounters (*i.a. T*, 36f., 183f., 256, 271), on the death of the poet Sebastian, and on religion (*T*, 263–265), even where the human contact is not permanent and reflections do not advance the plot (cf. *Greven*, 53–54).

The symbolic expansion given his presentiment of this existence in his self-appointed role as fool makes the conclusion of the novel seem an esthetic and logical *lapsus memoriae*. Two passages, one a rare intrusion by the author as omniscient observer to comment on Simon, immediately before the final scene, the other Simon's definition of his debt from the final "speech," shed further light on the ending of the novel. In the first passage Simon is seen exercising in his unheated room, his courage bolstered by the knowledge that he had after all been able to live into the winter whose advent he so feared. The author says of his spiritual and physical exertions that "at the time he resembled a person who has lost money and who sets all his willpower on gaining it back, but who does nothing more to regain it than merely to set his will to it and does nothing beyond that" (*T*, 309). Simon thus enters the final scene under the shadow of the author's doubt about the effectiveness of an act of will divorced from the context of human relations. What is noteworthy about the world, as Simon defines it in his subsequent promise to accommodate himself to it, is that it is not the world of social and commercial enterprises, at whose extremity Simon had ventured to live, but a "maternal earth" closer to the isolated center Simon occupies, a world he can only articulate as an opposite.

> ". . . [the world] stands facing me like an angered, offended mother; wondrous visage that infatuates me: the countenance of maternal earth demanding expiation! I am going to pay off what I've neglected, what I've transgressed, and what I've lost in playing and dreaming."[3]

The second section of this chapter attempts to relate interior action in the hero to what has been summarized above. The purpose of the contrast of the two will be to indicate the possibility of reading Simon's final speech as an unintentional but nonetheless real admission of defeat in a spirit whose sensitivity and difficultly bridled pride permitted only a promise of an accommodation whose fulfillment lies in an unknown future, but which is more appropriately read as the questions concerning the nature of existence to which his society provides no answers. Simon's failure to achieve personal form outweighs the protestations of sanguineness in his monolog, his reversion to the interior realm symbolized by the image of the earth (in contrast to "the world") gives a meaning of poetic statement to a conclusion which is not a conclusion as much as a structural *fermata*.

Before proceeding to characteristic interior episodes we shall deal with the commentaries on Simon's character by his brother Klaus and

---

* ". . . [die Welt] steht mir gegenüber wie eine erzürnte, beleidigte Mutter: wundervolles Antlitz, in das ich vernarrt bin: das Antlitz der Sühne fordernden, mütterlichen Erde! Ich zahle ab, was ich vernachlässigt, verspielt, verträumt und verbrochen habe" (*T*, 332).

by the novel's principal female figures as a further perspective on Simon from the expository level of the novel. These will, it is hoped, provide a balance to the confinement of our discussion so far to Simon's own actions and utterances.

Klaus' analysis of Simon occurs during his brief reappearance in the novel's second autumn. In contrast to the uniformly sympathetic commentary on Simon by the women in the book, Klaus' well-meaning pedantry and his antipodal bourgeois role to Simon fault his brother's "immaturity." He complains that Simon has "something too wild" about him which "in the twinkling of an eye" can be a tenderness, "which for its part demands much too much tenderness of people, to be able to abide" (*T*, 305). Klaus also imputes to his brother an imbalance of values, saying that he senses offence "from entirely self-evident things that emerge from life and the world" (*ibid.*) while he is insensitive to things that should hurt him. Neither Klaus' recitation of Simon's capabilities nor the charge that Simon's longings are unworthy of a "citizen, a human being and above all a man" (*T*, 305) elicit a response from Simon. Although the curt termination of the scene leaves it without commentary, its juxtaposition to the two remaining scenes of the final chapter effectively achieves implicit commentary.

Hedwig is the only other Tanner to comment on Simon. She speaks of him in a long monolog at the end of his stay in the country (*T*, 176–180). Characteristically frank in its insights, the monolog shares with the comments of other women in the novel the quality of idealizing and somewhat abstract interpolation. The fate of lovelessness in one who claims to love all of life's manifestations elicits a reaction in Hedwig compounded of superiority towards the selflessness that she feels would allow Simon to commit "much that is indecent" if it were asked of him and the knowledge that behind the unprepossessing impression of love he makes on people the same selflessness is capable of an act of heroism. Behind Simon's lack of concern for his prospects, Hedwig finds a person who can elicit unconstrained self-expression in his opposite number. Hedwig too asks him to try to change, since "for most people you will be an uninteresting phenomenon, for you'll seem dull to girls, insignificant to women, and to men untrustworthy and lethargic" (*T*, 177), but her long list of contradictions between outward appearances and inner resources is not her last word. As the alternating emotions of scorn, gratitude, and the resolutely unemotional leave-taking at the end of Chapter Ten make clear (*T*, 180–181), her discursive analysis of her brother leaves unarticulated the significance of her brother's presence for Hedwig, namely the fullness of human response and communication they shared.

Whereas the figure of Hedwig achieves esthetic integrality through the creation of an area of emotional resonance between her words and her being, the rich lady who temporarily employs Simon is too sketchily traced to warrant reading her thoughts on Simon as anything but a projection of the author on the hero. She too intuits a contrast in Simon between a special gift of accommodation and "a slight addition of shamelessness and defiance" (*T*, 196). Like Klaus, with whom she shares bourgeois ideals, her personal association with Simon is based on a wish to reform his character. She is no more successful than Klaus, despite the sensitivity she brings to the undertaking. "He has soul, this young man" she thinks, "and for that reason one has to approach him soulfully, with an awareness of the soul, in order to accomplish anything with him" (*T*, 197).

Simon's attitude toward this woman (*T*, 204f.) might be described as gingerly submissiveness; it complements the uncritical idealization that characterizes his relation to Klara. The two attitudes coalesce in Walser's later writing, principally in the prose of the twenties, into adoration of a beloved who retains this position only if she remains separated from her "troubador." This development is not yet discernible in the relation between Simon and Klara. Her few remarks on Simon are spoken in emotion (following the revelation of her love for Kaspar and at the time of Simon's gift of himself to her) and are restricted to the enigma of Simon's personality. "One can't describe you" she says. "Your heart is what is beautiful about you. I understand that one doesn't understand you. You understand everything" (*T*, 58).

The club manageress who listens to Simon's final speech is a more significant figure than the briefness of her appearance and the artistic incongruity of her role as spokesman for the author would indicate. She establishes her credentials for this role by immediately recognizing Simon as "an exceptionally lonely young man" who desires "to come into contact with human beings" (*T*, 311). She reveals herself as the Egeria of Walser's first novel through her capacity for divining the composition of Simon's personality. The curiosity and fascination she feels in Simon's presence are a mirror image of the persuasion in Simon that the insignificant and the unobtrusive partake of an uncharted profundity and ineffable complexity. In speaking to him she realizes that one easily misjudges Simon and fails to sense his inner resources "because one has been dealing with a completely composed person who simply disdained assuming an attitude and who wouldn't want to appear better and more dangerous than he is . . ." (*T*, 319).

The manageress succeeds in touching Simon as no other figure in the novel has done because she speaks assuredly of a utopian human

society still bound to the "maternal earth" which Simon finally acknowledges as his mistress. She spells out her hopes for the "brothers and
sisters," for the "human beings on this lonely, forlorn planet" (*T*, 312)
in views that coincide with Simon's own liberal Christianity. As reluctant
as Simon is to evade the present, she hesitates to shift her gaze to
a future she characterizes as "this bold arch across a dark water . . . this
forest full of trees . . . this child with radiant eyes" (*T*, 315), believing,
as does Simon, that "the present is the future" (*T*, 315). That she herself
is not deluded by Simon's assuaging promise of a different future for
himself is manifest in the final paragraph of the book. There, as Simon's
"poor, happy captive" she leads him not into the world but into the
adjoining forest, thus returning Simon to the realm of nature.

Interior Search

The search undertaken by Simon in his public life ends abortively
with his untenable equation of the world into which he, as a non-com-
mitted participant seeks entrance, to the sub-cognitive world of nature,
drawn together in the image of the "maternal earth." This situation,
accurately conveyed by Simon's depiction of himself as a beggar at
the door of life, a "listener and a waiting man," consummates as he
says, "I have learned to dream while I wait" (*T*, 329). An interior search
paralleling the outer one takes shape in the monologs during Simon's
extended periods of solitary life, in his experience of nature, and in
the statements found in Simon's two pieces of writing (the essay "Land-
leben" and the reminiscences of his youth); this fragmented search culminates in Simon's dream of Paris and his final fantasy before he visits
the *Waldhaus*. A separate treatment of the exterior and the interior
person suggests itself in seeking to define the emotional integer that
contrasts with the failure of Simon's public life. Such a treatment, too,
is dictated by the style and form of the novel. In a novel of which
Walser himself said he had disdained esthetic conventions "in order
to simply make music" (*Wdgg*, 14), the cadences that unify a superficially discursive work have their source in the tension between these
two modes of experience.

Simon's search for clarification and identity proceeds at two levels,
corresponding to the two esthetic levels of discourse in the novel. The
esthetic rationale for these two levels of Simon's life parallels the symbolic irreconcilability of the two. As a public figure Simon is astonish-
ingly voluble, yet in explaining his decision not to answer a letter from
Klaus he touches on a crucial impediment to the transferral of the interior search into conscious, specifically intellectual modes of expression.

"I don't know how to depict my situation," he says, "it is not even worth describing. I have no reason to complain, just as little as to leap for joy, but every reason for being silent" (*T*, 18).

Using a more abstract approach than that utilized by the novel, a bridge can be made between Simon's public and private life by seeking to find his ideals, since ideals may signify a public designation for a segment of personal commitment. The characterizations of Simon by other figures in the book all implicitly pose the question of the nature of such ideals. As Simon admitted to Klaus (*T*, 71) and as the manageress correctly intuits (*T*, 319), he does not bare his ideals. He expressly rejects the suggestion of the two men before whom he defended unhappiness that he is motivated by ideals: "I am in the habit of making rules for myself and in general am hardly inclined to be swept off my feet by fantasies and ideals, since I regard that as extremely unwise and presumtuous" (*T*, 242f.).

Simon's single consciously creative act in the novel, the essay "Land-leben" (*T*, 146–153), is written during the restorative interlude in the country. It aims to do no more than describe and document the presumptuousness of ideals in their disengagement from the conduct of life. Paralleling this reform ethos is the intentional transparency of a creative effort that presumes to be no more than description and documentation based on a reflective appraisal of the visible present. As such Simon's essay develops the form used in *Fritz Kochers Aufsätze* and parallels the short prose Walser wrote during his Berlin period. As a personal document the moral probity and balanced linguistic vigor of the essay contrast to the "wild talk" (*T*, 258) and the aggressiveness of some of Simon's "speeches." The thematic antithesis inherent in the essay contrasts city and country. Simon describes his own situation when he writes of the dignity one can maintain in rural poverty against the degradation and ostracism it means in the city: ". . . for there everything is judged by what people say and do, while here grief grieves on silently and pain subsides naturally in pain" (*T*, 148). His most incisive insight is based on his knowledge of the loss of contact between rich and poor in modern urban life. He perceives a human dilemma so acute that he pleads for a relationship even at the price of sustaining it through cruelty and self-advantage rather than have the propertied ignore the poor.

> Better to torment them, to force them into bondage, to let them feel hardship and blows, then a relationship ensues at least; rage, an agitation of the heart, and that's a kind of communication too. But to keep oneself holed up behind gold garden gates, in

elegant homes, and to be afraid of sensing the warm breath of human beings, not to dare to live lavishly any more for fear the embittered oppressed might notice it, to oppress and yet not have the courage to show that one is an oppressor, to fear even the people one oppresses, neither to feel comfortable with one's wealth nor to afford others comfort, to use ugly weapons which don't presume any real defiance or manly courage, to have money, just money, and not any splendor along with it. This is the present image of the cities and it seems to me an unbeautiful image, one in need of improvement.*⁴

Simon's disavowal of ideals follows from his obstinate insistence that "it is a question of this world" (*T*, 255). In this sense his brother Klaus is correct when he says that Simon asks too much of the world (*T*, 305), for what Klaus sees as Simon's omissions, his lethargy, fatuousness, and the insouciance of his public life, are a disquieted renunciation of a world that shares neither his hierarchy of values nor the tolerance he brings to their definition. The vitality of Simon's encounter with the world cannot be mistaken either for estheticism or *fin-de-siècle* lassitude since his actions reveal his endeavor to guide his life according to intuitive convictions and aspirations. When, in the context of his final speech, he says "I should like to take definitive form as late as possible" (*T*, 330) his freedom of spiritual movement not only expresses his concern that many of his contemporaries have incontrovertibly abdicated their claim to a unified life while still professing ideals, and thereby falsifying them, but he becomes the medium for what should have been their own continuing awareness and inquiry.

An earlier instance of interior definition are Simon's reminiscences of his youth, written after the disappearance of the figures who had so compellingly enlivened the first segment of the novel (*T*, 115–124). The creativity of the essay "Landleben" lies in its attempt to fuse the present with Simon's imagination. The reminiscences, on the other hand,

---

* Besser, man peinige sie, zwinge sie zu fronen, lasse sie Druck und Schläge fühlen, so entsteht doch ein Zusammenhang, eine Wut, ein Herzklopfen und das ist auch eine Art Verbindung. Aber sich in eleganten Häusern, hinter goldenen Gartengittern verkrochen zu halten und sich zu fürchten, den Hauch warmer Menschen zu spüren, keinen Aufwand mehr treiben zu dürfen, aus Furcht, er könnte von den erbitterten Gedrückten wahrgenommen werden, drücken und doch den Mut nicht besitzen, zu zeigen, daß man ein Unterdrücker ist, seine Unterdrückten noch zu fürchten, sich in seinem Reichtum weder wohl zu fühlen, noch andere wohl sein zu lassen, unschöne Waffen zu gebrauchen, die keinen echten Trotz und Mannesmut voraussetzen, Geld zu haben, nur Geld, und doch damit keine Pracht. Das ist gegenwärtig das Bild der Städte, und es scheint mir ein unschönes, der Verbesserung bedürftiges Bild zu sein (*T*, 149f.).

successfully form an essay in self-knowledge undertaken at the realized risk of re-experiencing the grief and the traumatizing brutality (*T*, 119–120) as well as the love that constituted the original experiences. The author is careful to dissociate what Simon writes from even the suggestion of literary creativity by having him say that he started to write "unintentionally without thinking" (*T*, 115), simply to document "what I still know from those days" (*T*, 119). That Simon's reminiscences are intended to fill no other function than to help him define an emotional locale from which he can do battle with life is unmistakable when Simon immediately destroys what he has written: "Then he tore up what he had written, without ill-humor and without deliberating much, simply because it had no further value for him" (*T*, 124).

The area of paradox between Simon's public appearance—with the disdain and denial of fantasy appropriate to this figure (*i.a. T*, 242f.)—and the dreamer and daydreamer is enlarged in monologs and fantasies. Many of these are highly discursive and lack formal integration. The principal monologs are those dealing with resolutions to lead a more socially purposeful life (*T*, 99–102; 248–249) and Simon's fear of the approaching winter (*T*, 281–283). A fantasy about the possibility of a settled life in the country (*T*, 125–129) points to Simon's awareness of the lack of resolution at the end of the first section of the novel. A crude, tasteless fantasy concerning Hedwig (*T*, 139–143) is a literarily honest indication of Simon's willingness to approach his sister in her new role as a mature woman, while it in itself is a tangle of unbridled associative fancy (cf. also *T*, 215f.; 248).

Both in his defense of unhappiness and in his remarks to the club manageress, Simon refers to dreams as the vehicles of insight. The most determinative dream in the novel, Simon's dream of Paris (*T*, 218–227), providing a conjunction of the creativity of imagination and the self-restriction demanded by the exterior world, successfully integrates into the structure of the book a revelation of Simon's inner life and an anticipation of plot. The narrative isolation of this dream within the novel is accentuated by the complete absence of any commentary on the dream by the author. No further indication is given that Simon ponders the dream he himself characterizes as "melancholy" (*T*, 228) after awakening, despite the remark introducing the dream: "He had a strange dream that occupied him for a long time afterwards" (*T*, 218). The remainder of the novel makes clear that Simon in fact does occupy himself with the dream, but at a cognitive level beneath, albeit parallel to that of the narrative of his public life.

The first of the dream's three sections is a street scene that heightens and synthesizes other street scenes in the novel (*i.a. T*, 183–184; 197f.;

245–246) and anticipates passages in the two later novels where the transient heroes encounter humanity. The description of Parisian streets captures an atmosphere at once graceful and elegantly light to the point of almost tangible mobility, yet invested with the illogical, piercing beauty of a nocturnal paradise. This scene contrasts to the street scenes in the last six chapters of the book, where they are dominated by the meanness and hopelessness of an existence that drives men to degrading acts (*T*, 300f.). It focuses and heightens the "glorious evening" on the lakeshore and the dissolution of that evening into motion, thereby transforming this dream street into a royal road for humanity. The figures in the dream belong to Simon's world, just as many of the elements in it can be recognized as a pot-pourri from the events of Simon's waking life, but he stares at them with the awe of a stranger and non-participant. In contrast to the demonic energy of the street scenes in *Jakob von Gunten* the precision of detail in this synesthaesia of sound, color, music, and motion is Simon's projection of a *theatrum mundi* beyond the reality of life.

The second section of the dream adds to its irreality. Simon finds himself on a dark staircase. He enters a room where Klara had been sleeping on a divan. She awakens and they are sumptuously served by a Negro "while a soft, muffled music rustled down from the ceiling of the room, like the gurgling of a rare ingenious fountain, which now sounded far away and then next to his ear" (*T*, 222). Klara identifies herself as a sorceress and, taking her wand, successively opens three doors to show Simon visions of his siblings. Klaus is hard at work, but anxious about Simon. Hedwig's corpse lies under a white linen, a victim of the sorrow she had expatiated on to Simon (*T*, 171 *passim*). Her death is presented in terms stressing the separateness of all the Tanners: "She leaves without having answered the question the world asked her: 'why don't you come?'" (*T*, 223). The third of these magic chambers or dreams within a dream, shows Kaspar at work painting. This vision is the most important of the three, permitting Klara to appear both as an idealized selfless lover and as an advocate of art, and suffering only from its disproportionate length in the dream.

A "wondrous, incomprehensible music" (*T*, 226) begins the final section of the dream. The apparitions have dissolved; now Klara opens a window to show Simon a summer snowfall that will eventually cover the houses and imprison the inhabitants of the city for an entire month. During this time Klara will sleep. Then spring will return, trees will blossom overnight, the heavens will descend into the Paris streets and even the poor will have money. "Then you'll see," Klara prophesies, "how people will embrace right out on the streets after the long confinement and weep for joy at seeing one another again" (*T*, 227). Shortly thereafter Klara falls asleep and Simon awakens.

The climax of the dream, the chiliastic re-birth of humanity following the purity of the snowfall and the fruition of spring,[5] uses metaphors drawn from nature to express Simon's utopian hopes more expansively than he expresses them in his final "speech." But Simon is neither the agent of his own vision nor even its prophet. It is clear from the two street scenes in the dream—the first "real" within the dream, the second a promise in the future of the dream—as well as from the pertinency of the release "after the long confinement," that the direction and the details of the dream stem from Simon. The prophet of Simon's ideals is a Klara whose past he distorts in the dream to make of her a sorceress and near vestal virgin. The remoteness of the synthesis in the dream of art and self-restriction is apparent in the setting of this vision in a future within the dream and in the suspension of time at the scene of the vision ("There aren't any definite seasons of the year here," Klara says in explaining the summer snow [*T*, 226]). Two factors account for the transferral to Klara of Simon's own latent ideals: the stringency with which the author separates Simon's imaginative life from art and Simon's inability to articulate or even dream of a relation between nature and society. Thus Klara has to "explain" the disordered chronology in terms of gracious behavior, cautioning Simon not to show his surprise at the summer snowfall (*T*, 226).

The thematically most integrated fantasy and the one most revelatory of the symbolism of Simon's inner life occurs after Klaus' visit in the final chapter (*T*, 306–308). Besides circumscribing Simon's isolation it indicates, in contrast to Simon's passivity in the Paris dream, the extent and area in which the author sanctions creativity in Simon. The passage begins as a presentation of Simon's thoughts during the first snowfall. He is exulting in the transformation the snow works on the city scene, while he is ridiculing his recurrent fears that he would not live to see the winter. Relying solely on the associative force of the metaphoric purity of snow, a transition is made to Simon's inner life using as a threshold between his thoughts about the winter scene and the following tale no more than the remark that the scene seemed like a fairy tale to him (*T*, 306).

> Once upon a time there was a man. He was completely black. He wanted to wash himself, but he had no soap and water. When he saw that now it was snowing, he went out to the street and washed himself with snow water and this made his face as white as snow. Now he could show it off and he did. But he started to cough and now he was always coughing; the poor man had to cough for a whole

year, until the next winter. Then he ran up the mountain until
he began to sweat, but he still had the cough. The coughing just
wouldn't stop any more. Then a little child came up to him, it
was a beggar child. In its hand it had a snowflake. The flake looked
like a delicate little flower. "Eat the snowflake," the child said. And
now the big man ate the snowflake and the cough was gone. Then
the sun went down and all was dark. The beggar child was sitting
in the snow and yet it wasn't cold. It had gotten a beating at home;
why, it didn't really know. You see, it was a little child and didn't
know anything yet. Its little feet weren't cold either and yet they
were naked. A tear gleamed in the child's eye, but it wasn't yet
clever enough to know it was weeping. Perhaps the child froze in
in the night, but it felt nothing at all, it was too small to feel anything. God saw the child, but it didn't move Him. He was too great
to feel anything.*

Taken together with the dream of Paris this brief scene helps reduce
the "querying and astonishment" (*T*, 318) the manageress feels before
Simon. Permitting us to see Simon without the public mask of rhetoric
he assumes in his long speeches, it suggests why, in the Paris dream,
the prophecy is attributed to Klara. The dream thus enables us to understand more clearly the implications of the final scene of the book, where
a compositional termination of the narrative sequence is lacking and
the intimation of a new direction in Simon's life is so presented as
to be ambiguous both by the logic of human nature and that of literature.

The syntactical parataxis in the narrative style, the nearly exclusive
concentration on the "action," the diminutives and the archaizing vocabulary, all identify the story of the snow-child as a fairy tale. The

---

* Es war einmal ein Mann, der war ganz schwarz, da wollte er sich waschen, aber
er hatte kein Seifenwasser. Als er nun sah, daß es schneite, ging er auf die Straße
und wusch sich mit Schneewasser und davon wurde sein Gesicht weiß wie Schnee.
Da konnte er prahlen damit, und das tat er. Aber er bekam den Husten, und nun
hustete er immer, ein ganzes Jahr lang mußte der arme Mann husten, bis zum
nächsten Winter. Da lief er den Berg hinauf, bis er schwitzte, und noch immer
hustete er. Das Husten wollte gar nicht mehr aufhören. Da kam ein kleines Kind
zu ihm, es war ein Bettelkind, das hatte einen Schneeflocken in der Hand, der
Flocken sah aus wie eine kleine zarte Blume. "Iß den Schneeflocken" sprach das
Kind. Und nun aß der große Mann den Schneeflocken, und weg war der Husten.
Da gang die Sonne unter, und alles war dunkel. Das Bettelkind saß im Schnee
und fror doch nicht. Es hatte zu Hause Schläge bekommen, warum, das wußte es
selber nicht. Es war eben ein klein Kind und wußte noch nichts. Seine Füßchen
froren ihm auch nicht, und doch waren sie nackt. In des Kindes Auge glänzte eine
Träne, aber es war noch nicht gescheit genug, um zu wissen, daß es weinte.
Vielleicht erfror das Kind in der Nacht, aber es spürte gar nichts, es war zu
klein, um etwas zu spüren. Gott sah das Kind, aber es rührte ihn nicht, er war zu
groß, um etwas zu spüren (*T*, 307f.).

first, fable-like half deals with the man "who was completely black," the second section, following the sharp transition made at the fall of night, with the beggar child. This second section utilizes restricted, parabolic analysis, the submerged rhetoric and implied question of poetry. The dominant structural element in both halves is contrast: black and white, large and small, perspiration and cold, the man's energetic activity and the child's impassiveness, pain and insentience, the timelessness of the flower-snowflake.

Here a child appears as a servant-redeemer. It cures mankind of an inner estrangement from nature through the spiritual gift of the flower-snowflake (cf. Klara's prophecy of the summer snowfall). After the performance of the redemptive mission the child is abandoned to an unpeopled and loveless night. The child's insentience to the beating and the frost establish its genderless purity and validate its sacrificial fate. The tragedy and the resolution of the fairy tale have one and the same source: the child's gift. Too untutored to know the world, it is too small and insignificant to be cared for by the world, while God, Who is remote and intractable, has discharged His responsibility by leaving the child in the hands of man. The parable of the snow child ends less conclusively than this resumé indicates because of the intermingling of contrast with aural associations in the anaphoric use of the verb *spüren* relating both to the child, and, in the last sentence, to God. The near zeugma thereby created intimates a relationship between them expressly denied in the tale.[6]

Superficially only an episodic connection exists between the three scenes of the final chapter (the meeting with Klaus, the fairy-tale scene, and the return to the *Waldhaus*). Actually, the fairy tale links the other two by commenting on them thematically. The fairy tale is, first of all, Simon's answer to Klaus' admonitions to conform to the society around him. It reiterates at a less conscious level their inability to communicate with one another. More importantly the fairy tale depicts Simon's own situation at a more intimate level than his conscious temporizing does, since it irrevocably separates the elements of the equation Simon has made to the manageress between the world and the spontaneous affirmation of life as part of nature.

Very shortly after this scene, taking up the image found in the fairy tale, Simon characterizes himself as a beggar at the door of life. If he is not clever enough to know that his long speech is a lament and an admission of his failure to combine the freedom of nature with the self-restriction of society, the manageress is. She responds to the plea implicit in his speech and allegorically anticipated in the passivity and the willingness to serve that Simon shares with the fairy-tale figure.

Whereas the principal figures in Walser's earliest work, *Komödie*, consciously renounce the world as a threat to their self-sufficient inwardness
(*Greven:* "reine Innerlichkeit," 29 *passim*), Simon's share of the world
is the freedom of isolation, much as the snow-child is left to the care
of the world.

The presence in the first part of the Paris dream of the mysterious
fleet-footed, blue-frocked linkboys called "Teufelsjungen" (*T*, 220) is
an earlier variant within the novel of the snow-child's minority life.
Seeing them Simon wonders: "Where did they live; did they too have
parents, brothers, sisters; did they too go to school; could they grow
up, marry, procreate children, get old and die?" (*op. cit.*). Like the
fairy-tale child they stand outside the course of normal life and are
unaffected by the demands implicit in the symbiosis an idealized Klara
embodies. Like the fairy-tale child they represent an anthropological,
and therefore moral problem because their freedom lacks any integration
with the world which they illuminate with "a magical, white light" (*op.
cit.*). Only in *Jakob von Gunten*, and after, does Walser raise such figures
from the realm of dream and fantasy and provide them with the mixture
of playfulness and earnestness that Thomas Mann associated with mythic
existence and creativity when he discussed his Joseph figure.[7] In Simon
Tanner they are still part of the silent subterranean stream of life within,
where the knowledge of isolation and the experience of sorrow live
on despite its public suppression by the will. The evidences of this
life dictate the depth of Simon's awareness of himself as beggar and
dreamer. The greater esthetic persuasiveness of the interior life and
the failure of the attempt to subsume the interior life to a commitment
to society points to their ultimate opposition in this book. From
Geschwister Tanner on the tension between irreconcilable opposites remains a thematic constant through all of Walser's formal and stylistic
variations.

Taken as a whole *Geschwister Tanner* derives its vitality from the
presentation in a solitary figure of the infinite quality of one human
life. Simon's commitment to his fellow man is encompassed by his vision
of a love whose completeness of sacrifice provides for its own sufficiency.
On the acceptance or rejection of this love rests the answer to whether
his contact with society and the implementation of his nominal acceptance of its demands will prove viable or ineffectual. To the manageress
he says: "I offer any person my knowledge, my strength, my thoughts,
my achievements, and my love, if he can make use of them. If he points
his finger and motions to me, in that event someone else might hobble
up, but I run, you see, . . . bowl over and tread carelessly on all my
memories just to be able to run all the more freely" (*T*, 330). At the

base of his keenness of receptivity are the moral compassion of his
celebration of misfortune, the knowledge of the intricacies of the heart
in the sense of communion he feels with the underprivileged (*T*, 68–69;
272–275), and the vision of humanity in the Paris dream. It would thus
be misleading to regard this sensitivity as solipsistic or as the "complete
sentience" associated with Neo-Romanticism. The restriction of Simon's
creativity within the realm of nature or its sublimation in Klara illustrates
the role this novel played in Walser's attempt to counteract the post-1900
sentiment of esthetic resignation. Early in the novel Klaus accurately
judges Simon's intemperate outbursts less as disaffection with the world,
than "as a certain search in his younger brother's soul for clarification
of his own condition in relation to the world" (*T*, 72). The definition
and the attempted actualization of this relation define the quality and
the point of view of the novel; they never leave Simon's conscious or
unconscious mind and explain what was to remain among all of Walser's
work the unique breadth of canvas of this first novel.[8] The statement
of the novel is the paradigmatic function of this search through its
variations in the denunciation of a mercantile society, the objectivation
of boredom and vacuity outside this society, the courage to sacrifice
his identity in service, and in the fact and the metaphor of his wanderings punctuated by human encounters.

Notes

1. Greven (*Greven*, 225) has noted as essentially one-sided the attempts to characterize Simon or the novel by speaking, on the one hand, of "seeing the world as
   an unabating miracle" (Christian Morgenstern), or as the "unique personalization
   of the given reality" (*Middleton*, 411), as well as views, which in contrast,
   speak of Simon's "sterile individualism" (Jean Moser, *Le roman contemporain
   en Suisse allemande de Carl Spitteler à Jakob Schaffner* [Lausanne, 1934], p.
   73) or of his "disrupted" relation to the world (*Bänziger*, 73).
   The quotation from the poet Christian Morgenstern comes from an "aphorism"
   Morgenstern probably wrote after reading the manuscript of *Geschwister Tanner*.
   He appended it to a letter written to Cassirer on January 22, 1907, when he
   was reporting on what we must assume was the manuscript of a novel Walser
   subsequently destroyed. Despite Morgenstern's tendency to read Walser from
   the vantage point of his own spiritualizing proclivities, his remarks deserve mention as the earliest attempt to describe the quality of Walser's art. Morgenstern
   correctly emphasizes Walser's loquaciousness, the relation between nature and
   freedom, the naïveté, and the aimlessness of his wandering, all critical aspects
   of Walser's work.
   Morgenstern's remarks on the "new novel" begin as follows:

   . . . was Walsers neuen Roman betrifft, so kann ich nur wiederholen, was
   ich schon früher gesagt habe, nur daß es mir jetzt noch viel berechtigter
   erscheint. Ich glaube nicht zu große Worte zu gebrauchen, wenn ich meine,

daß diese neue Arbeit eine der größten Versprechungen bedeutet, ·die je von jungen Dichtern gegeben worden sind. Sie enthält Partien von so reiner und rührender Schönheit, daß kein reifer Leser unbewegt davon bleiben kann und daß keiner den Glauben wird unterdrücken können, daß hier jemand auf dem Wege zum schlechtweg Außerordentlichen begriffen ist (*Ein Leben in Briefen,* ed. Margarete Morgenstern [Insel, 1952], p. 242–243).

2. Friedman speaks of the prevalence of such "rites of identification" in the heroes of stream-of-consciousness novels from Proust through Joyce (*Friedman,* 158).

3. Thomas Mann's nearly contemporaneous *Tonio Kröger* (1903) undertakes an analogous search for identity following from a failure of acceptance. Kröger turns his back on society from the time of his departure from his birthplace until the revelatory visions on the island of Aalsgard. Yet Simon, despite his isolation, never wittingly follows this path. Tonio Kröger explicitly anticipates Simon's belief that every man must follow his own path, no matter how aberrant it may seem, but whereas Tonio takes solace in a career as an artist, the trenchancy of Simon's encounters and his determination to comprehend them comes from his acceptance of the limitless variety of life as personally pertinent. In the more drastic terms of the Nietzschean dichotomy between life and art as found in Walser, the denial to art of even a stop-gap efficacy is indeed more reminiscent of Hofmannsthal's substitution of an adventurer for the artist in the comedies following the "Letter of Lord Chandos" (cf. Martin Stern's Afterword to his edition of Hofmannsthal's *Florindo:* Bibliothek Suhrkamp, Bd. 112 [Frankfurt a. M., 1963]).

4. The praise of the unnoticed and unsung formative aspects of the country upon its people and the timeless, ritualist, and near-religious significance of the land in contrast to the atrophying city ("Who wants to own a house in the city? . . . The houses are filled with the greatest variety of human beings, all of whom pass one another by without knowing one another, without expressing the desire to be able to get to know each other" [*T,* 150]) is thematically related to the work of the poet Georg Trakl. The central presence of a speaker as against Trakl's receding narrator, however, and the absence of the mute, self-enclosed images that create the ghostly beauty in Trakl's earliest poems ("Die schöne Stadt" and "Kleines Konzert") create an incomparably different tone.

5. In his usually impressive dissertation, Greven interprets Walser's extensive use of a snow image as the symbol of a death wish, principally on the basis of the poems and dramolets written before the novels. He assigns this meaning to the snow image in a discussion of the early works as responses to the question of how to live (See *Greven,* 38f.; 41–43; and Notes 45 and 46), while recognizing that the same image—often simultaneously—also stands for purity. By emphasizing the philosophical implications of the early work, both its artistic statement and its stylistic relation to later work are neglected. As a consequence, the snow image is too narrowly defined. As a death symbol the image fits neither Simon's dream of Paris nor the beggar child in the fairy tale who "was sitting in the snow and still wasn't cold" (*T,* 307). Nor does it fit Jakob von Gunten's transformation of the garden behind the Institute Benjamenta when he imagines snow falling on it. After the early work the snow image is just as often the medium for transition—a tangible, transitory mask for transformation that offers

respite and attests to endurance and to the ability to out-last vicissitudes. Even Greven's quotations can as easily be read in their contexts as literary manifestations of Nietzsche's "eternal return" as of the desire for death.

6. The pathos and the disspiriting tone of the fairy tale parallel the bleak fairy tale told by the grandmother in the final scenes of Georg Büchner's *Woyzeck* (according to Seelig, Walser read Büchner intensively early in the Zurich period [*KGS*, 351]). The eight negatives in seven sentences underlining the unbridged separation between man and God that exists despite man's longings is a stylistic device found in Kafka's crystalline, inexorable parables.

7. Und ist nicht vor allem der Held dieses Romanes ein solcher Zelebrant des Lebens: Joseph selbst, der mit einer anmutigen Art von religiöser Hochstapelei den Tammuz-Osiris-Mythos in seiner Person vergegenwärtigt, sich das Leben des Zerrissenen, Begrabenen und Auferstehenden "geschehen läßt" und sein festliches Spiel treibt mit dem, was gemeinhin nur aus Tiefe heimlich das Leben bestimmt und formt: dem Unbewußten? Das Geheimnis des Metaphysikers und des Psychologen, da die Geberin alles Gegebenen die Seele ist,—dies Geheimnis wird leicht, spielhaft, künstlerisch und eulenspiegelhaft in Joseph; es offenbart in ihm seine *infantile* Natur . . . (Thomas Mann, "Freud und die Zukunft," *Adel des Geistes* [Stockholm, 1948], pp. 583–84).

8. The publisher Bruno Cassirer's decision to excise material from the original manuscript because it seemed boring to him was a mistake of judgment, since Simon is only comprehensible if his portrayal includes the counterweights to his insight and emotional and intellectual energies.

    The novelist's personal relation to this novel was, however, greater than to his two other novels. When Walser thought of himself as a novelist, it was generally with *Geschwister Tanner* in mind (cf. " 'Geschwister Tanner' " (*FKR*); "Walser über Walser" (*Prager Presse*, July 27, 1925). The determinative role Simon's figure occupies in Walser's imagination can be seen in a forerunner of the novel hero in "Simon, eine Liebesgeschichte" (*KGS*).

3

JOSEPH MARTI

The Silent Seeker

Each of Walser's novels represents a stylistic experiment to find a form adequate to the personality of the hero and the quality of his ceaseless redefinition of his relation to his world. We witness Simon's alternating reactions of passion and lethargy; we see with what easy access he moves back and forth (cf. *Middleton*, 419) between a historically specific, geographically indeterminate urban mercantile society and the interior life from which he is awakening and seeks release. *Geschwister Tanner* succeeds as a novel by intermeshing the division into chapters of the exterior action with the cross rhythm of Simon's interior life, thereby objectifying and giving dimensions to an unresolved, individualistic vision that rests on an intuitive base.

The sentience of Joseph Marti, the hero of *Der Gehülfe*, is no less acute than Simon's, but a basic difference is apparent from a comparison of the initial appearance of the two in their respective novels. In place of the protective shield of irony, brashness, and overdone servility behind which Simon engages the attention of a prospective employer at the beginning of *Geschwister Tanner*, Marti stands silently in the rain before the door of Villa Abendstern, surprised at having an umbrella in his hand. "In his earlier years, you see, he had never owned an umbrella" (*G*, 5), the narrator says. From this consciously inauspicious initial meeting until his departure six months later in the company of his predecessor, his kinship to both Simon Tanner and Jakob von Gunten as an interrogator of reality is obvious, but he is unmistakably quieter than either of them, more reserved and incomparably more concerned that he not compromise his prospects for accommodation with the world he has entered.

A deemphasis of the hero takes place in *Der Gehülfe*. Joseph Marti shares with Simon the re-examination and embroidering of his experiences in dreams and daydreams. He, too, is an introspective diarist and, even more than Simon, an indefatigably vigilant observer. Marti faces questions of self-identity and self-realization similar to Simon's, but the torrent-like musical accompaniment of the "speeches" is suppressed, Simon's contradictory behavior and complex motivation are reduced and disciplined. Marti's past failures seem to have chastened him. Simon's exploratory speeches are replaced by Marti's laconic queries, by questions that hover more in the mind, in a glance, in an unspoken word.[1] The reason for the muting of Simon's internal volatility and external vociferousness is that the encounter with Villa Abendstern presents the new hero with a tangible object for what in Simon was an undirected voraciousness for experiences. The novel begins with the actualization of Simon's ideal of service when Marti enters the door of life at which Simon was left waiting with unanswered questions. On entering Villa Abendstern, however, Marti passes through a Janus door.

The necessity to meaningfully delineate the world of Villa Abendstern is consistent with the greater realism in the depiction of society in *Der Gehülfe* and the subtlety of its typefying psychological characterizations. The pathos of Simon's questions is now rechanneled into comedy and irony, dictating a distance between the author and his figures that facilitates commentary.[2] Marti patiently holds his unresolved questions in abeyance for what he takes to be the critical encounter with the "world" while the selectively omniscient author painstakingly utilizes a delicately manipulated irony to underline the contrast between Marti's world and that of the Toblers. Because of the more dominant role of exterior reality in *Der Gehülfe* than in Geschwister Tanner, the hero does not monopolize the terrain of the novel with nearly the frequency of either Simon Tanner or Jakob von Gunten, nor is there the facility of movement from exterior to interior. Moreover such movement may be ridiculed or disguised. Marti is protected and estranged by a stillness that is evident in the first expository episodes. Set off from the world of Villa Abendstern, these episodes are sealed entities which do not intrude and which foreshadow the permanence of the separation between the two worlds.

They have their source in, but are distinguishable from the physical world because, whether through selection of details, through their tone, or the reactions they elicit in Marti or the narrator, they are like planets separated from him by varying radii, yet describable only as part of his system.

Most of the novel's spare exposition contributes to an image of diffidence and social rootlessness. Thus the letter Marti writes to his former landlady shortly after his arrival at the Toblers shows him reacting to a past only two days distant as if it were long removed. Marti simulates cordiality in the style of his letter only to then scrutinize this behavior critically (*G*, 17–19). When he encounters a fellow recruit from his recent military service, he pretends pressing errands only later to give himself over to sententious reflections on the relationship of fraternity and democracy in the army (*G*, 19–20). In a previous job as a bookkeeper, Marti forestalled a feeling of distress at the temporary nature of the job by thinking of "the 'temporariness' of the position" as a "consolation" (*G*, 21). The author, too, chooses to emphasize this transitoriness: "In his entire personality he seemed merely a corner of something, a transient appendage . . . " (*G*, 21). At the time he was rooming with an acerbated old maid and boarding with students. Marti's difficulty in conversing with the students is related without sympathy. There is only the irony of the use of a clothing metaphor to show the provisional character of Marti's life: "Yes, his existence was only a provisional jacket, a suit that didn't quite fit" (*G*, 22).

The stillness surrounding Marti is expanded in the direction of an inviolability of personality in one further expository episode. In an earlier job Marti's ignorance of accounting procedures had resulted in a costly error and a reprimand which made him tremble and his vision blur. An hour later, however, while walking in the streets he is nearly overwhelmed with joyousness at the sight of people.

> Joseph hadn't forgotten the ugly thing that had just occurred; abashed, he bore it within, but it had been transformed into something unconcernedly sorrowful, into something composedly disastrous. He was still trembling a bit and thought: "So, I have to be aroused to pure pleasure in God's world by humiliations."*

The comment given is not an explanation, it is an indication of an existence lived under a charm, a person Greven describes in speaking of both Simon and Marti as "not proper partners for people who stand firm at one spot in the world" (*Greven*, 58).

---

* Joseph hatte das eben Vorgefallene, das Wüste, nicht vergessen, er trug es beschämt mit sich, aber es hatte sich in etwas Unbekümmert-Leidvolles, in etwas Ebenmäßig-Verhängnisvolles verwandelt. Er zitterte noch ein wenig und dachte: "Also muß man mich mit Demütigungen zur reinen Freude an der Welt Gottes aufpeitschen" (*G*, 24).

An element of exposition that contributes to the comic tone of the novel is Marti's distrust of his intellectual capacities. Marti is apprehensive that his "muddle-headedness" (*Kopflosigkeit*) compromises his chances to succeed. It is therefore not surprising that Marti's (partly assumed) ingenuousness is intimidated by his employer's bluff insistence that the job will require "a brain." Just as Jakob von Gunten's later, more frequent references to his "stupidity" are not intended as an objective measure of Jakob's intelligence, instances of Marti's intellectual limitations, such as his pride at having acquired a glossary of glib phrases to stave off creditors, his absent-mindedness in the interview with the prospective investor Herr Fischer, or his clumsy mismanagement of telephone conversation with Tobler's attorney, are the comic variation in *Der Gehülfe* of the juxtaposition of interior and exterior world in Simon Tanner, or in more specific terms, the ironic criticism of a more overtly symbolic form of society distorted by commerce.

In *Geschwister Tanner* Simon Tanner's duality is given its most persistent expression in such a juxtaposition. A corresponding thematic duality in what is referred to in *Geschwister Tanner* as "the world"—the mutually exclusive parts of a utopian realm in which Simon would sacrifice his individuality for his fellows and the static society of hollow ideals and commercial careers—preclude Simon's achieving the self-restriction that he professes. The resulting simultaneity of conflicting and paradoxical traits in a single literary figure identifies Simon as a modern fictional hero. By comparison, the channeling and narrowing of energies and character in the portrayal of Joseph Marti and the external placidity of his person that drastically reduces the need for lengthy self-identifying monologs give Marti the appearance of a more conventional novel hero. In fact a duality pervades *Der Gehülfe* which is projected into the work itself as its most consistent structural feature. In Marti himself this duality is identified by the supernumerary in the expository sections and the comic view of Marti as hapless secretary in the Tobler menage. But this comedy does not exhaust the figure of Marti nor describe the mystery of the part of his person that is communicated in his silences and reflections. In the Villa Abendstern itself, a characteristically Swiss combination of family residence and business establishment in one and the same building, the duality of the outside world is more skillfully evinced than in *Geschwister Tanner*. The exterior impressiveness of this structure is always present in Marti's sensibility, and soon he adds a further duality to those existing in the Villa Abendstern itself and his relation to it. Returning from one of his "flights to nature," the secure appearance of Villa Abendstern has a reassuring effect on him until he "corrects" the initial impression as follows:

Now it is true that a house is composed of two parts, of a visible and an invisible one, of exterior joinery and of an interior strength, and the inner structure is perhaps just as important, in fact, sometimes perhaps even more important for carrying and supporting the whole than the outside one.*

Early in the book both parts have been expressly denominated as Marti's province and as the purpose of his presence at Villa Abendstern: "It was Joseph's debt and duty to learn to fathom the two sorts of houses" (*G*, 26), the narrator remarks.

Marti pursues this investigation at two levels. The investigation of the business enterprise proceeds at the level of the understandable distrust of his intellectual gifts documented in the expository episodes; the investigation of the family proceeds at the level of the silent sharer who feels happiest in the performance of physical tasks such as bottling wine from a cask, hanging a clothesline, or putting up storm windows. Although Marti again and again realizes that his "assistance" in Tobler's affairs is not very fruitful, we gradually understand that his prime concern is not the foredoomed mercantile aspect, but its most intimate neighbor, the familial one: "If anything could compose a person, watering the lawn could, for while doing this job one had a distinctively pleasant feeling of appertaining to the Tobler house in a tight-knit way" (*G*, 87).

The impetus for Simon Tanner's rhetorical energies is his struggle to find a focal point, in social terms, from which to conduct his self-investigation. Having such a focal point, Marti is consequently not hindered by Simon's verbal shields, and is thus free to view the world around him more directly. Marti's is a "double vision" (cf. *Middleton*, 414), a constant transmutation of the visual image to the vision of the heart, making this vision the organ recording both Villa Abendstern's Janus-faced existence and Marti's acute awareness of the discrepancy between the image of the world and its reality.

As with Simon, Marti's introspection and quest for self-awareness also take written form, principally in two highly reflective diary notes. He writes the self-styled *Memoiren* to overcome the pique and the "hateful thoughts" following Tobler's suspicion that, left alone, he would flirt with the maid (*G*, 96–98). The gloss "Bad Habit" clarifies his reaction to the visit by the employment agency manager who had arranged for

---

* Nun besteht ja allerdings ein Haus aus zwei Seiten, aus einer sichtbaren und einer unsichtbaren, aus einem äußeren Gefüge und aus einem inneren Halt, und der innere Bau ist vielleicht ebenso wichtig, ja manchmal vielleicht noch wichtiger zum Tragen und Stützen des Ganzen, wie der äußere (*G*, 108).

his employment at the Tobler's (*G,* 197). Both share, with comparable writing by Simon and Jakob von Gunten, an awareness of isolation which is countered by heightened consciousness in the style and inquisitiveness about the writer's relation to the world. More consciously analytical than Simon, Marti in the *Memoiren* admits the false feelings he assumed in his letter to Frau Weiss but recognizes that the letter was "an invention, figured out in a spirit which is startled that simpler and more immediate relationships are completely lacking" (*G,* 97). As with Simon, these writings are destroyed in order to corroborate their informational character. The quality which Marti castigates in "Bad Habit" is his penchant "to immediately ponder every vivid experience I have," or his concern that "the most trivial occurrence animates a peculiar desire in me to speculate" (*G,* 197). The burden of Marti's diary leaf is the paralyzing enormity the seemingly trivial can assume for him, momentarily consuming his experience of exterior reality or, as Marti describes it: " . . . while the live, driving present has become inexplicable to me" (*G,* 197). Yet the supposedly debilitating involvement with "these apparently trifling and worthless things" (*G,* 197) that momentarily obscures his perception of exterior reality rarely obtrudes as such. As another symbol of the distance between the Toblers and Marti it is perceived more in the pregnant silences, in questions posed as a thought, in the critical moments when Marti "flees" to nature or withdraws to the seclusion of his room in the tower. Although the three principal figures of the novel are enmeshed in a single web of "everyday" circumstances, the outbursts and provocations that justify Werner Weber's calling the novel "the uncanny idyll"[3] come from Herr Tobler, or from his wife, but rarely from Marti. The restriction of Marti's passion to the privacy of his infrequent writing is consistent with his self-effacement, his concern for problems of conscience, and his disturbing recognition that he is "neglected by life" (*G,* 149).

But the same diary leaf voices the author's intention that Marti act as perceptive recorder of the interstices of reality which familiarity has allowed to exist unnoticed, unquestioned, and without affection. "I may be somewhat exaggerated, but I am also a precise person," he says. "I feel the slightest loss . . ." (*G,* 197). Marti's analytic sensibility is the prism which transforms his descriptions into commentary. This sensibility inspires his vision in the description of his first return to the city (*G,* 133–138). The long description of Marti's walk through the city is perhaps the best single example in the book of this duality of vision. The walk is first of all an immediately perceived notation of the city scene. Marti, sustaining this primarily pictorial perception, simultaneously elicits the sense of his own feeling of estrangement from what was once so familiar to him. The most uniform stylistic characteristic within the entire passage is the propelling of a thought forward through the apperception of its contrast or by the "correction" of a previously perceived and described image, either by redefinition or by question. The first such redefinition is the dissolution of his "Sunday mood" as he is struck by how poor the urban strollers appear: "To be sure, they were indeed people from the poor working class, no gentlemen and ladies; but something piteous that had nothing to do with the meanness of material poverty permeated this whole, bright walking scene" (*G*, 134).

Marti's gradual apprehension of the significance of the contrast between the Toblers and the city scene before him effects the first articulate, consciously sought-after insight into the Toblers and events at Villa Abendstern.

> The small and narrow always did seem a rather grand and significant world unto itself after a time when one hadn't been looking into anything else, while conversely what is expansive and truly significant initially seems small and mean, because it is far too dispersed, extensive, and gay. But in the Tobler house there prevailed from the very outset a certain little plumpness and fullness . . .*

The style of the above selection and indeed the entire scene is not pure; it reflects the crosscurrents in Marti's own soul that attract him to Villa Abendstern although he recognizes the life he sees in the city as his own spiritual home (*Greven*, 73). Walser's attempt to portray in Marti a symbiosis of "Gedankenlosigkeit" and heightened psychological perceptiveness is illustrated in Marti's ability to distinguish the discrete elements in the organizing image with which he concludes the first part of the walk: "What humility there was in such a dissipated portrait of strollers. What a bitterly poor appearance a human Sunday could make!" (*G*, 138).

The walk also contains a parallel to the irrepressible joyousness that followed the reprimand from his office superior. The joy as it occurs on the walk explains the apparent inconsistency as well as the effect of estrangement caused by Marti's designation of what he sees to be

---

* Das Kleine und Enge sei immer eine ziemlich große und bedeutende Welt für sich, sobald man eine Zeitlang in nichts anderes mehr hineingeschaut habe, während gerade umgekehrt das Weite und wirklich Bedeutende anfangs klein und unansehnlich erscheine, weil es gar zu verbreitet, ausgedehnt und lustig sei. Im Toblerschen Haus herrschte eben von Anfang an eine gewisse kleine Dicke und Fülle . . . (*G*, 134–135).

a dream. "Soon everything that Joseph saw appeared to have become a natural, quiet, accommodating dream, not an especially beautiful one, no, a modest one and for all that so beautiful" (*G*, 136). Simon Tanner knew such a joy only in the street scene in the dream of Paris; Joseph Marti is able to make this a part of his waking world through a more conscious knowledge of his empathy with the poor.

The Sunday walk as a whole reveals more about Marti than his own diffidence or the author's irony up until this point have been able to do. A final example of Marti's complementary perception here suggests that the metaphoric quality of his reticence has its source in his compulsive accuracy. The contrasts, the corrections, and the dualities in the walk are not impressionistic images garnered for the wanderer's own pleasure, but are rather Marti's perception of an existential incommensurability.

> And this girl vis-à-vis, was she a coquette or was she a chaperone, or a well behaved, prim, affected little decorative plant that turns away from the experiences the world holds out to man—like a wonderful bouquet—on two, rich, warm arms? Or could she be a double, or even a triple species at one and the same time? Possible, for that had happened before, too. One just couldn't separate life into compartments and categories that easily.*

Marti's reflections during a short military imprisonment for failure to report for reserve duty provide a situation that parallels the all-encompassing pictorial image in the walk, the single parts of which are treated with little overt interrelation. Toward the end of his two days in prison Marti feels guilty for having taken part in the diversions of his fellow prisoners rather than utilizing the forty-eight hours to find forty-eight answers either to topical problems or "about his life up until then, for example" (*G*, 221). Common to the walk and the reflections in prison is the emergence of a particularizing truth that shies away from generalizing abstraction but is instead adumbrated in single sensibilities.

> These forty-eight charming, estimable, laboriously thought-up thoughts, what good would they do the young man, since it could be predicted that he would forget them the next day? A single

---

* Und dieses Mädchen da vis-à-vis, war sie eine Kokette oder eine Anstandsdame oder ein artiges, zimperliches, den Erfahrungen, die die Welt mit beiden reichen, warmen Armen den Menschen, einem wundervollen Blumenstrauß ähnlich, darbietet, abholdes Zierpflänzchen und -Püppchen? Oder konnte sie zweierlei oder gar dreierlei Gattung auf einmal sein? Möglich, denn das war ja auch schon vorgekommen. Das Leben ließ sich nicht so leicht in Kasten und Ordnungen abteilen (*G*, 137).

directive thought would certainly be much better here, but this one couldn't be thought, this one melted away into perception.*[4]

Thus is formulated in *Der Gehülfe* the essentially Nietzschean promulgation of the experience of life which in each of Walser's novels takes precedence over socially or culturally imposed dicta. For the starkly "reduced" hero of *Der Gehülfe* the experience in the military prison is a relatively straightforward example of the cohesiveness of Marti's inner life, whereas the author's own diffidence towards Marti, his use of Marti's uncertainty regarding his intellectual capacities and inability to contact the Toblers are all devices for exposing Marti's interior integrity.

A Kind of a Home

Marti's modest self-introduction as he enters Villa Abendstern, "I am the new employee" (*G*, 5), brings him into contact with a world in which he hopes his service will vouchsafe him a home. Although this world is presented in nominally realistic terms, the affective core of the book is the creation of an atmosphere of beguiling illusions which ultimately dissolves the reality to fall back on the single certainty of Marti's existence. The assistant himself is the most frequent victim of the illusions created by the heterogeneous home in Villa Abendstern. However, to the extent that is possible to speak of a "development" in Marti at all,[5] its primary characteristic is the "de-poeticizing" that more and more frequently results from the author-imposed obligation "to learn to fathom both sorts of houses" (*G*, 26). The resolution and the dissolution of Marti's relationship to the Toblers, their children, and to the reality and the idea of their home, provide the basis for the gentle collision of these two worlds; using the irony of a comic novel they lead to an ambiguous, open end, typical to all three novels, in which love and rejection take equal shares.[6]

Herr Karl Tobler, the engineer who brings his family to the brink of bankruptcy after having used his inheritance to settle his family in Villa Abendstern and establish himself as a free-lance inventor, is depicted with a terseness that relies on Tobler's own words and actions to provide the commentary on his mind and his motivations. Tobler's

---

* Diese reizenden, achtunggebietenden, mühsam zusammenerdachten achtundvierzig Gedanken, was konnten sie dem jungen Menschen nutzen, da es doch vorauszusehen war, daß er sie morgen vergaß? Ein einzelner richtungangebender Gedanke war da gewiß viel besser; aber dieser Gedanke war nicht zu denken, dieser Gedanke zerfloß in die Empfindungen (*G*, 222).

prodigality at Villa Abendstern stems from his romantic desire to imitate the class he aspires to, the Swiss patriciate whose social prestige rests on mercantile wealth.[7] Unable to find financial backing for his inventions, he continues to conduct his home "comme il faut" in an attempt to give the lie to the townspeople's growing suspicions regarding his solvency. As the need for money becomes more urgent, the harangues of the creditors more pressing, and the disdain and ridicule of the people of Bärensweil more outspoken, Tobler withdraws to the false security of his home, where he is disturbed not to find the veranda light burning when he arrives home late at night, the light seeming to him "each time the brightly glimmering proof of the secure continued existence of his home" (G, 238). The festivities at Villa Abendstern become fewer in number, although "heaven preserve us, you could still find something to drink at the Toblers' " (G, 234). More and more frequently, however, he avoids his house (cf. G, 172). When he is not travelling through Switzerland on his general commutation ticket, impressing chance acquaintances and making small loans from friends and relatives, he is drinking away the evening at the town tavern or spending hours there waiting for his train: "one might almost believe he missed [his train] intentionally. In such cases it was his custom to grumble: 'Now that blasted train has passed me right by again' " (G, 161).

Tobler's vainglorious prodigality supplies the good food, the plentiful wine and "customary" cigars, new coppersmithing work on a tower of the house, high-powered fireworks to celebrate Swiss Independence Day, new landscaping, and the erection of a "fairy grotto" in the gardens. But from the outset his liberality is paternalistic and ultimately tyrannical: "What a way Tobler had about him of laughing and looking at someone superciliously as soon as it came to handing out cigars" (G, 92). Instead of an agreed-upon salary, Marti receives pocket money on Sundays. When the topic of salary comes up Tobler says: "For a person who eats as you do and enjoys the kind of air you breathe up here at my place, you have a long way to go before you can complain. You're living!" (G, 154).

A contradiction in Tobler's character which is utilized through the major part of the novel to achieve ironic commentary is evident in the opening scene (G, 5–12). His manner as seigneurial head of the family at whose table Marti is invited to eat, his conviviality and "folksy" disregard for the niceties of speech, contrast to the leonine pose of hardheaded practicality when, as Marti's employer, he takes him into the office. After long drawn-out preparations for work nothing more tangible results than Tobler's trail of cigar smoke as he leaves for the afternoon on "business."

During the subsequent decline of the Tobler fortunes that register "the fall of the house" (*G*, 269)[8] the master never becomes conscious of the discrepancy between appearances and reality. His own personable exterior—Marti remarks Tobler's gleaming teeth (*G*, 12) and his "sonorous voice" (*G*, 47)—makes him the embodiment of the Villa Abendstern's pleasing facade set on an insecure foundation. "What good is it," Marti thinks, "if a house stands there smart and pleasing, if the people who live in it are not capable of supporting it and bearing it" (*G*, 108).

Despite all evidence to the contrary, Tobler's hopes for the success of his inventions periodically reassert themselves to buoy up his flagging spirits. The context in which the narrator presents such hopes makes them patently illusory. Thus, after Marti has let a prospective investor get away, "just the mere thought" that they could "indeed" reach him by telephone "early tomorrow morning" "revived the hopes" of both Tobler and Marti (*G*, 90). Similarly Tobler arrives in the office "around ten o'clock" one morning, in such high spirits after having caroused the night before, that Marti has no trepidation about relighting his cigar. "The figure of the head of the firm and Marti's superior really exuded an extraordinary joviality. Every single one of his gestures said: 'Well, now I know where the trouble lies. From this moment on a new direction will come about in the progress of my affairs'" (*G*, 152; cf. *G*, 157–158).

The discrepancy is apparent between the rhodomontade, "choice" diction Tobler uses to depict himself in the role of inventor and the "rather romantically colored speech" Tobler addresses to the dour townspeople who attend the inauguration of the fairy grotto (*G*, 184–185). In this speech Tobler celebrates the creative spirit, "manly soul," the "heart that can bear up under storms," and the creator whose aim is to realize his inventions and thereby alter the "existing structure of the world" (*G*, 185). Tobler gambles all but he never invests the effort needed to back up his risk. "Tobler didn't introduce a new order into his house," the author says: "baton and key remained the same in Abendstern. The conductor had too many other things on his mind and the assistant conductor was by nature too modest and too contented" (*G*, 207).

Tobler's violent outbursts are an even more frequent sign of the discomfort he feels in his role as inventor than are his linguistic feints, extending to his relationships with his family and thus reflecting the instability of his home and its way of life. As a partner to the failure of Tobler's projects, Marti has to suffer considerable abuse at his employer's hands. Hearing of the sudden departure of Herr Fischer, the prospective investor, Tobler screams at his "cluck of an employee" and bewails the "misfortune . . . of being betrayed by [his] own wife and a useless assistant" (*G*, 89). This volatile man's irascibility under the misery of his financial crises reaches a climax when he hurls Marti against a door jamb in his fury at Marti's telephone shyness (*G*, 280–281). In a masterfully deft use of dry mockery, it is Tobler who goes to bed, to recover from his nerves. To the children's questions whether their father is ill, their mother answers: "Yes, child, father is ill. Joseph made him angry" (*G*, 281). Another climactic instance of Tobler's apoplectic anger lies in the area where business and family overlap. Tobler had succeeded in wresting four thousand francs from his mother by means of what Tobler described as the "trick" of threatening to take his own life if he didn't get the money (*G*, 238–241). When he tries to "borrow" again and is informed by her lawyer that she irrevocably refuses to give further financial assistance he "behaved like a wild animal, uttered unnatural words of abuse at his mother, in direct address, as if she were present . . ." (*G*, 300).

The intemperate quality of Tobler's relationship to his family casts an oblique, disturbing light on the other side of the house. Tobler is too preoccupied by "the progress of his affairs" to indicate even once either affection or regard for his wife or his children. There is no indication whatsoever that he is aware of the cruel "training" being inflicted on his black-sheep daughter Silvi, although he "disciplines" his son by mercilessly flailing him (*G*, 206). When Marti, "in a flight of cosmopolitan chivalry," notes that Tobler's insulting tone had hurt his wife, he answers: "Go on, hurt! What is there to hurt there?" (*G*, 91). Nor does Tobler express disapproval when Marti and his wife spend time together. Yet one violent, irrational outburst points to a jealousy Tobler has never admitted and cannot articulate. The scene occurs at the end of the evening during which Marti has finally brought himself to complain to Frau Tobler about her treatment of Silvi. Persuaded that she will "report" him, he waits up for Tobler and tells him himself. Tobler pays little mind to what Marti says, he is made suspicious by the bravado in Marti's tone and at first wonders whether Marti is intoxicated. Tobler's revealing behavior from that point on is described as follows:

> Tobler screamed, as loud as he could: "My wife is a goose and you are a goofy bird! These damned books!"
> He took the rental library book and hurled it to the floor. He searched his memory for insulting words, but didn't find them. . . .
> "Robber" was on the tip of his tongue, but this word wasn't at all insulting. As a result of this confusion his rage was beyond all limit. He would have liked to have said "You dog," but then again this

word made a shambles of all reason. Since he saw himself incapable of crushing his opponent in a decent manner, he was silent. Finally he laughed. No, he roared.

"Get moving, and go straight up to your sack."*

It is not easy to gauge Frau Tobler's view of her husband on the basis of what she says. When trying to encourage Marti she says she finds it impossible to take his enraged outbursts seriously, since they strike her "rather as a comedy than a tragedy" and she has to burst out laughing at him (G, 85). Her implied attitude—as she explains to Marti her willingness to assume the onerous mission to her mother-in-law—is more sympathetic but hardly more respectful. She realizes that husbands prefer, when there is a duty that requires acting contrary to their own soul, to shove their wives up front saying: " 'You go. You can do that better than I.' And one is almost forced to take that as a kind of favor and caress" (G, 261). Yet it is in this same speech to Marti, that she explains Tobler's failures as the result of his directness and his "beautiful, full personality" (G, 263).

Marti reacts to the person Tobler, as distinguished from the inventor suffering under the self-assertiveness Tobler feels compelled to exhibit toward his assistant from the beginning. The palliative, if brusk, words of apology that frequently follow Tobler's abuse of the assistant mesh with Marti's own "too modest and too contented" personality. The infrequency with which Marti is willing to defend himself[9] until he is physically maltreated by Tobler is due in part to his temerity, but more to his wish to accommodate himself to the Toblers, or to use the more general term of Marti's prison dream of his role in his homeland, "to enter the rank and file" (G, 226). Only late in the novel does Marti pose the question the reader may long since have asked: "What induced him to remain the employee of this man any longer?" (G, 301). In his answer Marti "reduces" the figure of Tobler to the basic denominator of his existence as a human being. Paralleling the contradictory emotions Marti felt on the street after the shameful reprimand for his accounting

---

* Tobler schrie, so laut er konnte: "Meine Frau ist eine Gans, und Sie sind ein verrückter Kerl! Diese verdammten Bücher!"

Er nahm das Leihbibliothekbuch und schmiß es zu Boden. Er suchte nach beleidigenden Worten in seinem Gedächtnis, fand sie aber nicht . . . "Räuber" schwebte ihm auf der Zunge, aber dieses Wort konnte ja gar nicht beleidigen. Seine Wut kannte infolge seiner Verwirrung keine Grenzen. Er hätte sagen mögen "Hund," aber dieses Wort machte dann wieder alle Vernunft zu schanden. Er schwieg, da er sich außerstande sah, seinen Gegner in anständiger Weise niederzuwerfen. Schließlich lachte er. Nein, er brüllte.

"Machen Sie, daß Sie sofort hinauf in Ihr Nest kommen!" (G, 252–253).

error (cf. above p. 66), is Marti's remembrance of the abuse or the repugnance and dismay he felt at the wantonness of Tobler's recent drinking bout, when "the earnestness of a manly view of the world lay in a glass of wine that had fallen, had shattered and spilled its contents out on the floor" (G, 276). Marti promulgates a view of human relations free of intellectual constructs and based on apperception of individual existence.

> . . . he loved this person from the bottom of his heart. The un-
> tainted complexion of this feeling made one forget the blemishes
> of the other three [pity, scorn, fear]. And because of this one feeling
> the other three had always been there, too, almost from the beginning,
> and all the more vividly. For what someone is fond of, what some-
> one feels bound to is just what preoccupies him; he would argue
> with it, there was much about it that didn't suit him, once in a
> while he even hated it, because he had always felt powerfully
> attracted to it.*

The portrayal of Frau Tobler and of Marti's relation to her stand apart from that of her husband to Marti in the attention given to details whose effect carries over to subsequent scenes. Marti's relationship to Tobler lies almost entirely within the comic range of the novel. This is determined by Tobler's role as the bluff, harassed businessman in whom the familial aspect is reduced almost entirely to the maintenance of Villa Abendstern's appearances. The de-poeticizing of Tobler reveals the human being behind Tobler's role as inventor and the fact that he is the victim of the illusion of compatibility of family and business in a modern age. The assistant's relations to Frau Tobler are psychologi-cally more complex, the narrator himself providing the psychological commentary on Tobler principally through the irony of judicious quota-tion and question; the conflicting emotions Frau Tobler elicits in Marti appear earlier and regularly contribute to the lyric tone of *Der Gehülfe*.

With Frau Tobler, Marti has first to overcome his initial distrust of her and accept the contradictory woman he gets to know through their day-to-day encounters. Thereafter, he has to suppress his perpetual urge to succumb to the temptation to idealize and enhance her image. The

---

* . . . er liebte aus dem Grund seines Herzens diesen Menschen. Die reine Farbe dieser einen Empfindung machte die Flecken der drei anderen vergessen. Und wegen dieser einen Empfindung waren auch die drei andern immer, beinahe von Anfang an, dagewesen, und um so lebhafter. Denn was einer gern hat, an was einer sich gebunden fühlte, das machte ihm eben zu schaffen, mit dem stritt er sich, an dem paßte ihm vieles nicht, das haßte er gelegentlich, weil er sich mächtig von ihm immer angezogen gefühlt hatte (G, 301).

implied contrast of these two images of Frau Tobler is introduced into the composition of the novel as the tension between narrated "data" on the encounters of the two and Marti's implied interpretation of the data, his musings about Frau Tobler, and his projections and idealizations of her. The realism that Walser defended in this novel ("*Der Gehülfe* is an absolutely realistic novel. I needed invent almost nothing. Life took care of that for me" [*Wdgg*, 55].) is persuasive as it applies to Frau Tobler. It is difficult to idealize this proud, classic specimen of Swiss matronhood without disregarding distinctly unsavory personality traits. The realism and psychological acuity developed in her portrayal complement other, clearly unflattering, and at times severely critical features. The triviality of her social pleasures and the pallidness of her indulgences (cf. *G*, 200) are never glossed over. The method and the result are impressive. The original antipathy toward Frau Tobler is never rescinded by either author or hero. By the gradual accretion of situations and moods the narrator builds her character until it assumes its own perspective and justification. In so doing the narrator nearly succeeds in making esthetically credible the shift of emphasis that occurs in the final third of the novel. Marti himself recedes beyond the sharper focus given his portrayal through the narrator's irony while Frau Tobler emerges as a lawgiver larger than life. Without undergoing a "change of character" she bears the brunt of the reduction of circumstances which overtakes the Toblers and accepts, as her husband never does, the certainty that life at Villa Abendstern must become a memory, the sole reality of which will be its corroboration of the illusion Villa Abendstern represented.

From the outset conflicting pressures are evident in the relationship between Marti and Frau Tobler. At their first meeting Marti instinctively thinks: "an ordinary woman," only to amend this immediately to: "and yet not really" (*G*, 9). Marti reacts to her appraising, ironic glance immediately, but at a complicated level. He bows to the " 'Mistress of the house.' This is what he called her in secret. He didn't do it to elevate her to something finer, but to offend her, swiftly and covertly" (*G*, 9). He is repelled by her social imperiousness, by the coldness heard in her sigh of pity as well as in her laughter (*G*, 46), by her stereotyped commiseration, by the arrogance "of this haughty bourgeois Frau Tobler, this woman born and raised in warmth and plenty" (*G*, 39). Both Frau Tobler and Marti start from a defensive position: Marti, as the "new man" in response to the test to prove himself and to protect himself from the smarting wounds Frau Tobler might inflict (cf. *G*, 167); she from the pride and superciliousness she regards as the prerogative of her class, which obviate for her the need to respond to situations which might tax her arrested emotional development. The relationship that develops between them although never free of harassment, makes each reliant on the other. To be sure, Tobler's frequent absences encourage this reliance. They await Tobler's return together and recognize the approaching footsteps as "his" (*G*, 88). The house assumes a different character in Tobler's absence: "The entire house was different when the master wasn't there, and his wife seemed to be quite different too . . ." (*G*, 80). The limits of the social intercourse between them during their hours together is prescribed by their respective positions. As "assistant," Marti instinctively lowers his eyes when their gazes cross (*G*, 127–128). Probably only Marti is aware of a repressed emotional attachment. One side of his temperament never forgets or forgives her bourgeois birth, while the estranged seeker in him reveres and idealizes her for it. Their only intimacy is their desire to touch the other in the moral border area of annoyance or hurt. This emerges in the frequently irrational nature of their arguments.

Marti's combination of naive frankness, bridled infatuation, and declassé cosmopolitanism makes him well-suited for the role of companion to a wife who is not her husband's primary concern. In the course of the mid-morning and mid-afternoon pauses for coffee he begins to count as one of the advantages of his position taking coffee "in the company of a woman who is certainly pretty nice" (*G*, 26). In the conviviality of the coffee hours he gains the detachment to study her laughter: "It is an obstructed laughter, it doesn't come out of her mouth quite naturally. It is as if, earlier, it had always been curbed, just a bit, by an all too exacting upbringing. But it is lovely and womanly, yes, it is even slightly frivolous" (*G*, 29). Although Marti has replaced his predecessor Wirsich in the office because he is more trustworthy, Frau Tobler's repeated references to Wirsich make him aware that, even though he is less dangerous, he has not been able to usurp the position Wirsich enjoyed in the family (cf. Tobler's decisive reason for firing Wirsich; *G*, 48). Marti's jealousy of Wirsich is part of the reason for his admonitions to concern himself more with Tobler and less with his wife: "Instead of thinking about the technical enterprises every hour and every half-hour, I make it my concern to persuade a woman of my character" (*G*, 131).

The "muddle-headedness" that limits, Marti feels, the effectiveness of his "assistance" to Tobler has its counterpart in the paralysis of feeling that so frequently overcomes Marti in his mistress' presence (e.g., *G*, 176). His shock at her unfeeling treatment of Wirsich and his mother during their disastrous visit is all the greater for his suppressed erotic involvement with her. What he does is to flee to the privacy of his tower room. "Here he felt freed," the narrator comments, "from what, he wasn't actually able to say" (*G*, 42).

Marti's most pervasive reaction to Frau Tobler—the interior basis for his subsequent relation to her—occurs in the nocturnal boat ride on the lake early in the book; at the same time is created the figure he must "de-poeticize" to accord it with the reality of her person (*G*, 50–55). The gondola ride is suggested by Frau Tobler, who wants to take advantage of the lovely evening; Marti, as the "proper man for everything" (*G*, 50), fetches the boat and rows. The entire scene is an excellent example of Walser's skill in the modulation of tone. The section will be referred to again in Chapter Six; we cite it here as a constitutive instance of the imaginative insight in Marti which the author carefully hides in order to amplify the levels of contrast in his relation to Frau Tobler. Riding on the lake, Marti's attention is riveted on Frau Tobler's dark figure. At a level of awareness still close to consciousness, but increasingly prey to the movements of the boat on the dark water, Marti recapitulates for himself the effect Frau Tobler's bourgeois upbringing has had on her by describing the stratum on which her unused affective and imaginative capacities live on in a secret half-life. As the level of his own consciousness is lowered he provides a verbal parallel for the transport she is experiencing at the same moment (cf. *G*, 53 and 52). His empathetic probing into her character concludes as follows:

> No, this woman has no sense of color whatever or anything like that; she has no understanding at all of the laws that govern beauty, but that is precisely why she feels what is beautiful. She has never had time to read a book filled with noble thoughts . . . but now the noble thought itself descends upon her and deeper feeling itself—attracted by her lack of knowledge—moistens her consciousness with its wet pinion.*

The climax of the boat ride is an apostrophe to the deep from Marti's subconscious. From the end of the reverie verbal and imagistic parallels anticipate the apostrophe: the sense of movement and support imparted by a star-filled sky, the "filled space" in the images of night, the perception of depth above and below, "the dark fragrant body of summer night stillness," and the anticipation of the boat's transfiguration in the

---

* Nein, diese Frau hat keinerlei Farbensinn oder dergleichen; sie versteht nichts von den Gesetzen der Schönheit, aber gerade deshalb fühlt sie, was schön ist. Sie hat nie Zeit gehabt, ein Buch voller hoher Gedanken zu lesen . . . aber der hohe Gedanke selber besucht sie jetzt, und das tiefere Gefühl selber, angezogen von ihrer Unwissenheit, netzt ihr mit dem nassen Flügel das Bewußtsein (*G*, 53).

apostrophe, in the words: "Her bright eyes shone placidly and beauti-fully along with the gliding of the boat" (*G*, 52). The apostrophe itself reads:

> Rise up, deep. Ascend. Yes, from the water's surface the deep rises in song and creates a new, immense lake of the space between sky and water. It has no shape and no eye exists for what it represents. It sings too, but in sounds that no ear can perceive. It stretches out its long, wet hands but there is no hand that could join with them. It works its way up from both sides of the nocturnal boat, but no knowledge present in any way is aware of it. No eye looks into the eye of the deep. The water disappears, the crystalline abyss opens and now the boat seems to float along peacefully beneath the water, making music.*[10]

To read the final apostrophe, as does Werner Weber,[11] as a foreshad-owing of the demise of Villa Abendstern is to ignore the relation of what precedes it; more significantly, it confuses the realistic basis of the plot with the hero's symbolism. What the passage does presage is the unresolved relation to Frau Tobler and the necessity for recogniz-ing that the source and inspiration of Marti's creative imagination, Frau Tobler's own life in the depths, is an incongruity at Villa Abendstern. If we remind ourselves that the apostrophe is an amplified parallel to his analysis of Frau Tobler's personality, using related metaphors, we see that this single instance of Marti's creative imagination relies on her as an unwitting muse. To concur with Werner Weber's view would, too, necessitate overlooking the positive poetic union of heaven and earth and the use of music as accompaniment to and symbol for the imagination. Certainly the conclusion of the apostrophe, upon which Weber bases his argument, does not sound ominous, even if one were to ignore what has gone before: ". . . now the boat seems to float along peacefully beneath the water, making music" (*op. cit.*).

The qualifiedly more realistic basis of this apostrophe when compared to Simon's dream of Paris (also utilizing the metaphor of motion, a more decisive muse in Klara, and the utopistic image of the union of

---

* Steige, hebe dich, Tiefe! Ja, sie steigt aus der Wasserfläche singend empor und macht einen neuen großen See aus dem Raum zwischen Himmel und See. Sie hat keine Gestalt, und dafür, was sie darstellt, gibt es kein Auge. Auch singt sie, aber in Tönen, die kein Ohr zu hören vermag. Sie streckt ihre feuchten, langen Hände aus, aber es gibt keine Hand, die ihr die Hand zu reichen vermöchte. Zu beiden Seiten des nächtlichen Schiffes sträubt sie sich hoch empor, aber kein irgendwie vor-handenes Wissen weiß das. Kein Auge sieht in das Auge der Tiefe. Das Wasser verliert sich, der gläserne Abgrund tut sich auf, und das Schiff scheint jetzt unter dem Wasser ruhig und musizierend und sicher fortzuschwimmen (*G*, 54ff.).

heaven and earth) is consistent with Marti's more realistically secured contact with the world. In the depiction of Marti's encounter with Villa Abendstern, Walser still hesitates to give authority to the reliance on imagination, but he has taken a step in the direction of *Jakob von Gunten*. The parallel sentence structure in the apostrophe that anticipates the style of Jakob's entries is nothing less than an insistence on the validity of non-rational perception, expressed most clearly in the statement that the shape of the lake's ascent is limited to what no eye can see and to what "no knowledge present in any way" can know (*op. cit.*).[12]

In their everyday meetings Frau Tobler remains "an incomprehensible woman" (*G*, 207) for Marti while she raises him from the approbation in her original judgement of him as "peculiar" (*G*, 27–28) to the prideful indulgence of "a curious person" (*G*, 165). She cannot reconcile his diligent execution of household chores with what she regards as an exaggerated fear of her husband. "I still haven't been able to make you out," she says to Marti; "Are you magnanimous? Are you a base person?" (*G*, 202).

It is typical of the scenes between them, in which the feelings elicited carry over and color following scenes, that shortly after this open abuse Marti accidentally sees Frau Tobler in her negligee while on his way to the attic. Arrived there, he forgets what he had come for. "Instead of what he was looking for, he found an old pair of Tobler's Wellingtons, which obviously weren't being used any more. He looked at the top boots for a disproportionately long time, until he broke out in laughter at his absent-mindedness" (*G*, 202). What subsequently occupies Marti's conscious thoughts, however, are not the "glorious arms" (*G*, 202) he remembers seeing before Frau Tobler hurriedly shut the door, but his diversionary rejoinder to himself to even the score by criticizing her mistreatment of her daughter Silvi (*G*, 203). That he does not do so attests to his attempt to transform suppressed sensuality into self-vindication and hurt.[13]

Suppressed eroticism also underlies sequences of scenes such as the one in which Frau Tobler asks for Marti's honest appraisal of Tobler's prospects (*G*, 174–181). At his deferential answer she challenges him to prove himself a man, capable of thinking for himself. Shortly after ordering him to leave she appears in the office to invite him to coffee. He "escapes" from the violent reaction this causes in him—when "life itself flickered before his eyes" (*G*, 176)—by going for a swim. But he does then rejoin her for coffee. Afterwards she asks to be pushed in the swing, hoping to "profit" from the garden while the weather is still pleasant. Marti is sufficiently moved by her presence and intoxicated by the fragrance of her body to be momentarily tempted to kiss her. When they resume their conversation she ingenuously relates how a young man once became enamoured of her and stole into her bedroom, only to be apprehended by Tobler and thrashed. Marti's reaction is dry but knowing: " 'So I had better take care,' Joseph said. 'You?' she said with a completely blank look on her face" (G, 180). This sequence of scenes ends when the guileless Frau Tobler displays a new gown to Marti, and is radiant at his compliments (G, 181).

To the extent that their relation has at its base the "curious person" and the muse of the gondola ride, the psychological acuity of such scenes allows for the inclusion in them of comic elements. Their tension devolves from another aspect of the tenuousness of their relation; the imminence of a fateful misunderstanding is always present where so much is left unarticulated. Such a misunderstanding underlies the last of such private encounters between the two, when a climatic argument terminates the evening after Frau Tobler's return from the visit to her mother-in-law to beg for more money (G, 273–274). While Frau Tobler is trying to relax at cards, Marti is preoccupied, trying to fathom her behavior. His happiness that they are together again is so great that he laughs out loud. She asks him to explain. He answers evasively, saying: "Oh nothing! Just nonsense." They fall to arguing about the propriety of expecting an employee to play cards late into the night; she misses the distinction he is making between his employment and his devotion to her and he soon leaves the room angry and trembling, vainly hoping to be called back. What remains with Marti of the nocturnal boat ride is probably most evident in his projections and idealizations of Frau Tobler. Marti would wish for a change in her personality towards mildness, a sensitivity bespeaking a more vital imagination, and a reliance on the simplicity he recognizes as her strength. Yet characteristically for a book whose perceptual nexus lies at the point where description of appearance becomes an investigation of the reality behind the appearance, when such description of a change in Frau Tobler does come, it is illusory and evanescent. When she appears to have discarded "a certain complicatedness of the heart" and her countenance reflects sorrow and friendliness, composure "and something almost majestically maternal" (G, 242), it proves to be only the sign of an incomplete convalescence. Marti can think of her as an "angel" (G, 50) or later as "splendorous" (G, 254), but when the long-postponed discussion of her treatment of Silvi finally comes (G, 248–249) he has to accept the fact of her admission that she hates her child.

Similarly, the author does not permit Marti's imaginatively directed image of Frau Tobler to compromise the contradictory aspects of the lawgiver who emerges in the final sections of the book. Marti's initial temptation to see Frau Tobler's departure by train to her mother-in-law (*G,* 266–267) as "the departure of a queen" (*G,* 266), with Tobler in the role of "gloomy heroic figure" and Marti "the afflicted servant and vassal" is invalidated and ironically righted: "This wasn't a matter of perpetual banishment to a bleak rocky island," the family dog "was no dragon," "he might possibly have even snapped at such a malicious medieval presumption. All in all it was an image of the twentieth century" (*G,* 266–267).

By the time Marti leaves the Toblers at the end of the book, his loyalty to this two-sided house is limited to its familial, feminine half. This is clear from the doubts he has about his respect for the inventor Tobler immediately after having told his wife "I love this house, I have the desire to be useful here" (*G,* 205). When he therefore bows before her in the final scene of the novel, kissing her hands as they say good bye, he does so before the central force of what will remain of the Tobler home in the twentieth century. Frau Tobler's domain is more modest than her husband's and her image is blemished, but her vision is clearer because it is intuitive.

> . . . we women, continually tied to the narrowness and the confines of the home, we think about quite a number of things and we see things and feel things. We have something of a gift for divining things, since the legitimate sciences are really our sworn enemies. We know how to read glances and how to construe behaviour. Curiously enough we never say anything, we are silent . . . *

Marti's act of submissiveness at the end is the tangible expression of his love for the man Tobler and his acknowledgment that the sustenance offered by the subrational fundament of their society in the person of his wife precludes its transferral into the actuality of their lives. During the ride on the lake Marti had raised the conflict between imagination and self-restriction. But the muse of the lake ride is unpromising and ultimately recalcitrant in the real life of Villa Abendstern; she is unwilling to acknowledge a spiritual love that offers the humility of service, let alone offer any assurance that this love is reciprocated.

* . . . wir Frauen, beständig in die Enge und an die Beschränktheit des Hauses gebunden, wir denken über mancherlei nach, und wir sehen auch manches und fühlen manches. Es ist uns gegeben, die Dinge ein bißchen zu erraten, da einmal die korrekten Wissenschaften unsere geschworenen Feindinnen sind. Wir verstehen es, in den Blicken und im Betragen zu lesen. Wir sagen seltsamerweise nie etwas; wir schweigen . . . (*G,* 262–263).

In counselling Marti to continued silent adherence to the laws which govern "domestic life"—which she equates with those governing "Weltleben"—the creative gift Marti exhibited in the lake scene is effectively banned from the mercantile, public facade of the house, where it has no nurturing soil. The liberating promise of the humanity at the root of Marti's "double vision" is unimpaired. He leaves in the company of Wirsich, a man whose failures make him less self-reliant than Marti ultimately is, and to whom he has given more assistance than it was possible to give the Toblers. Following Marti's muted exit it is left to the hero of the next novel to inquire further and more aggressively into the role of the creative imagination which Marti left undeveloped.

Notes

1. The modulated register of the novel as a whole seemed to a contemporary book reviewer a proof that the book was a waste of talent. Hans Nordack admitted to Walser's "technical skill," but insisted that Walser had nothing to say: "On nearly four hundred pages nothing really happens. . . . all of it commonplace, not to say boredom, admittedly narrated so impressively that its effect is finally hypnotic . . ." (*Hochland*, 7. Jg., Bd. I [Oct., 1909–March, 1910]), 744–745.

2. Greven claims that, "excepting for some insignificant details" (*Greven*, 207), the narrative perspective is uniformly that of Marti himself, "as soon as Marti's vision . . . takes command." The proximity of author point of view and the hero's perception is indeed frequently obvious, but the retention of author irony toward Marti in isolated remarks and the treatment of his defeats at the hands of Frau Tobler (e.g., G, 283) does maintain a distinction between them that is necessary to the statement made by the novel (cf. Chapter Five).

3. Werner Weber, "Das unheimliche Idyll: zu Robert Walsers *Der Gehülfe*," *Neue Zürcher Zeitung*, July 24, 1955.

4. Greven cautions not to mistake this "general idea" (*G*, 222), which Marti feels he ought to have defined, "for a definite concept of a profession . . . for which one 'exchanges' his own life. The idea must be general enough to replace or complement the 'total reference,' without signifying falsified termination of free existence" (*Greven*, 72).

5. Greven views Marti's return at the end of the book to the anonymity of the unemployed from which he came as the resumption of "poverty and lowliness," as the "truer form of existence" (*Greven*, 73f.).

6. The perception of this unified duality in *Der Gehülfe* may have been the impetus behind Max Brod's claim that Walser was the first author to write at three levels. In an extraordinarily enthusiastic essay written in 1911, Brod identifies naïveté and irony as the first two levels before continuing as follows: "Der Verstehende aber sieht unter dieser wirklichen Naivität und wirklichen Ironie. . . . eine ganz inwendige Seelen-Unbekümmertheit, eine über allen

Mitteln stehende und deshalb in den Mitteln mit Fug wahllose Dichter-Urkraft"
(Max Brod, "Kommentar zu Robert Walser," *Pan*, II, Nr. 2 [October 15, 1911],
55).

7. Cf. the two sketches on the small town Bärensweil (*G*, 71–73; 167–169).
As ironic vignettes of a "safe" society these are only matched by their stylistic
antecedent, the sketches in Keller's second volume of *Die Leute von Seldwyla*
(1874).

8. Werner Weber regards these words from the narrator as "principal motif"
and "key word" for his interpretation of *Der Gehülfe* as a "Zeitroman" related
in theme to Mann's *Buddenbrooks* (Werner Weber, "Das unheimliche Idyll,"
Neue Zürcher Zeitung, July 24, 1955). Weber appropriately stresses the novel's
symbolism, but his remarks disregard the comic scenes, Tobler's romantic disregard of the economic portents of ruin, and the irony within the novel toward
the hero, all of which suggest a greater affinity with "Felix Krull" than with
Buddenbrooks.

9. The author's comic portraiture of Tobler is also at work when Marti does
once protest against his employer's assumption that generosity excuses his lack
of civility toward Marti. Taken aback by Marti's speech the narrator says: "Tobler
felt the most sensible thing to do was to laugh out loud" (*G*, 155). As soon
as Tobler regains his "moral" equilibrium, his face darkens and he scolds Marti
for the meager benefits his assistance has brought.

10. The boat scene with its concluding visionary apostrophe fits Friedman's statement
on the applicability of Henri Bergson's philosophy to literature: "The entire
Bergsonian philosophy depends on these special moments of introspective vision
which are determined aesthetically by an art form, preferably music, that relies
more on pattern than on representation, which are determined philosophically
by a parallel passage of time and space, and which are determined psychologically
by an abstract view of consciousness, caught up in an uninterrupted flow of
movement" (*Friedman*, 91).

11. "Das unheimliche Idyll," *Neue Zürcher Zeitung*, July 24, 1955.

12. Greven comments on the above scene as follows: "The magic nature of the
deep in its absolving delimitation represents an antithesis far removed from
human-societal reality of the novel—there is however no bridge between the
two spheres and Joseph Marti's existence as well is related to everyday reality"
(*Greven*, 71).

13. Middleton stresses the sight of Frau Tobler and the ensuing attic scene as
an example of the "averted vision" found in *Der Gehülfe*. Felix Poppenberg,
the book's earliest commentator, was prompted by a similar perception when
he wrote: "Der feine dichterische Reiz des Buches kommt aus der unmerklichen
wie natürlich und selbstverständlich wirkenden Kunst, mit der denn das äußere
Leben eine tönende Gefühlsbegleitung, eine beziehungsvolle innerliche Spiegelung
empfängt" (*Die Neue Rundschau*, 19 [1908], 4, 1548–49).

4

JAKOB VON GUNTEN

The complex and elusive personality of the eponymous hero of *Jakob von Gunten* (1909) can best be introduced by quoting part of the *curriculum vitae* he writes at the request of the school principal shortly after entering the Institute Benjamenta, a training school for servants. After running away from home he had entered the school in order to prepare himself to fulfill "the dreams of a career in life achieved through my own exertions" (*JvG*, 397) and to satisfy "these ardently burning plans for self-education" (*op. cit.*). As a document of self-analysis and self-identification it is both more secretive and more audience-directed than anything written by the two previous heroes. The first half of the *vita* reads:

Curriculum Vitae

The undersigned, Jakob von Gunten, son of respectable parents, born on such and such a day, raised in such and such a place, has enrolled as a pupil in the Institute Benjamenta in order to acquire the few skills that are needed to enter somebody's service. The selfsame person has absolutely no hopes for life. He desires to be dealt with firmly, so as to find out what it means to have to pull oneself together. Jakob von Gunten does not promise much, but he intends to behave himself honestly and well. The von Guntens are an old family. In earlier times they were warriors, but their pugnacity has diminished and nowadays they are board chairmen and merchants and the scion of this house, subject of this report, has resolved to foreswear all haughty tradition entirely. He wants life to educate him, not inherited, or in some way aristocratic principles. He is proud, to be sure, for it's not possible for him to deny the nature he was born with, but he means by pride something quite new, something which, in a certain sense, corresponds to the time in which he lives. He hopes that he is modern, not altogether useless and stupid and that he is relatively skilled at rendering service. But he is lying, he not only hopes this, he knows and avers it. He has a hard head, some of his predecessors' unbridled spirits are still alive in him, but he begs to be admonished whenever he is defiant, and if that doesn't help, to be chastized. For that, he believes, will help. Beyond that, one will have to know how to deal with him.*

The ostensible purpose of the *vita*, to help Jakob find employment, is hardly a consideration in his own mind; for him it is part of a calculated plan to elicit a human response in the grim, brooding giant who runs the school by means of an intentional provocation. Noting that Benjamenta is smiling "quite slyly and craftily" (*JvG*, 381) as he reads it, Jakob rejoices and thinks: "An outpost skirmish has been won" (*JvG*, 381). The *vita* represents the single public document in a novel consisting of a journal kept by Jakob during his stay at the school. That the *vita* undergoes several drafts (*JvG*, 376f.) before a satisfactory version is written points to something more than a symbolic reduction of perspective inherent in the novel's journal form. Taking a double jump from the expository introspections Simon Tanner and Joseph Marti write only to destroy immediately, Jakob writes what the very first sentence reveals to be a parody of a *vita*, which at the same time bridges the gap across the inarticulate and unrealized creative forces in the two previous novel

---

* Lebenslauf.

Unterzeichneter, Jakob von Gunten, Sohn rechtschaffener Eltern, den und den Tag geboren, da und da aufgewachsen, ist als Eleve in das Institut Benjamenta eingetreten, um sich die paar Kenntnisse anzueignen, die nötig sind, in irgend jemandes Dienste zu treten. Eben derselbe macht sich durchaus vom Leben keine Hoffnungen. Er wünscht, streng behandelt zu werden, um zu erfahren, was es heißt, sich zusammenraffen müssen. Jakob von Gunten verspricht nicht viel, aber er nimmt sich vor, sich brav und redlich zu verhalten. Die von Gunten sind ein altes Geschlecht. In früheren Zeiten waren sie Krieger, aber die Rauflust hat nachgelassen, und heute sind sie Großräte und Handelsleute, und der Jüngste des Hauses, Gegenstand dieses Berichtes, hat sich entschlossen, gänzlich von aller hochmütigen Tradition abzufallen. Er will, daß das Leben ihn erziehe, nicht erbliche oder irgend adlige Grundsätze. Allerdings ist er stolz, denn es ist ihm unmöglich, die angeborene Natur zu verleugnen, aber er versteht unter Stolz etwas ganz Neues, gewissermaßen der Zeit, in der er lebt, Entsprechendes. Er hofft, daß er modern, einigermaßen geschickt zu Dienstleistungen und nicht ganz dumm und unbrauchbar ist, aber er lügt, er hofft das nicht nur, sondern er behauptet und weiß es. Er hat einen Trotzkopf, in ihm leben eben noch ein wenig die ungebändigten Geister seiner Vorfahren, doch er bittet, ihn zu ermahnen, wenn er trotzt, und wenn das nichts nützt, zu züchtigen, denn dann glaubt er, nützt es. Im übrigen wird man ihn zu behandeln wissen müssen (*JvG*, 378–379).

heroes. This articulated creativity is gained by the employment of a self-irony pointing towards disguise and by a naïveté underlying his self-assurance. The distancing effect between narrator and self which this achieves is more conscious than that found in *Der Gehülfe;* it takes verbal form largely from the yoking together of contradictions of tone, diction, or attitude, as in the remark "his modesty knows no bounds" (*op. cit.*). The intermingling of the serious with the humorous makes the *vita* an intellectual balancing act that charges the theme of humility and service found in the two earlier novels with a tension of uncertainty. The provocative, but self-cancelling verbal energy of the *vita* has its intellectual counterpart in the contradiction inherent in a hero whose background is only fragmentarily sketched and who is willing to become anonymous by foreswearing his noble name, aspiring to the estate of a servant. Behind the elusiveness of the personal identification in Jakob's unsparing plan to present himself to life is this hero's heightened explicitness of intention to make his encounter with life a reevaluation of values.

As the novel begins the nature of this confrontation is unclear. There is little exposition on the hero. His presentiments that on entering the school he had fallen into the hands of swindlers, his suspicion regarding the rationale behind the teaching, and the suspension of chronological sequence in the journal entries all are factors that combine to create the first instance of the mystification that is so integral a part of the tone and the meaning of the novel. Prime importance is given to Jakob's interior life and his reflections through the journal form. The time and place of the novel are ambiguous; only told is the information that the school is situated in the upper story of a building behind a courtyard in a metropolis and that Jakob is conscious of living in a modern age. More than in the two previous novels, the locale of the novel is not a geographical, but a spiritual terrain. The first journal entry, remarkable in its entirety, concludes with a statement that summarizes the meanness and insignificance of the life all pupils at the school share in common. It expresses too the bleakness of Jakob's prospects for the future in cadences that anticipate the dark humor that punctuates the melancholy of Kafka's stories:

> . . . one thing I know for certain: Later in life I shall be a charming, roly-poly cipher. As an old man I will have to wait on self-confident, badly mannered boors, or I'll go begging, or I'll perish.*

* . . . das Eine weiß ich bestimmt: Ich werde eine reizende, kugelrunde Null im späteren Leben sein. Ich werde als alter Mann junge, selbstbewußte, schlecht erzogene Grobiane bedienen müssen, oder ich werde betteln, oder ich werde zugrunde gehen (*JvG,* 336).

Jakob's journal entries describe his confrontation with three segments of reality: the world outside the school, to which he has access through his painter-brother Johann; the world of Institute Benjamenta as seen in the brother and sister who run the school and Jakob's fellow pupils; the world within Jakob as it is seen in his fantasies and dreams. Consistent with the use of a form that elevates the private stratum of life to the narrative surface, the emphasis is most consistently on Jakob's interior life. The technique and, to a large extent, the dissociative plot of the novel consist of the narrator-hero's attempts to discover the meaning of the nature of the school through descriptions and analyses of life within and without the school against the background of his own ambiguous involvement. As such it is a work unique in German literature before Kafka in the creation of a hermetic cosmos through a masterful manipulation of light and dark tones of style. In this sense *Jakob von Gunten* is the most overtly modern of the three novels in theme, and the one most influential on Walser's future writing.

As journal narrator Jakob monopolizes the created space of the novel. He contributes to the hermeticity of the novel through his own cellularity. We learn even less about Jakob's past life than we do about Simon's and Marti's. He ran away from home and from his father, an industrialist and privy councillor, because he feared "being suffocated by his excellence" (*JvG*, 340).[1] Having found at the Institute Benjamenta the isolation and incubation he senses he needed, Jakob is at a loss to explain to himself the completeness of the break from his family. "Yes, I think about Mama," he admits, when he tries to explain why he never writes: "That's it: I don't like to give information. It seems too stupid. I don't want to be loved and hankered after. Let them get used to not having a son any more" (*JvG*, 350).

Jakob needs this cellularity to investigate the possibility of personal freedom within the self-restriction which in this novel takes the concrete form of the precepts and regulations of the school he has entered. The pendant to his cellularity is his defiance and irony. Here we note the sharpening and abstraction of themes and motifs from the two previous novels. In *Jakob von Gunten* the hero's isolation is self-imposed. The hope all three heroes nurture of establishing a claim to a home in the world by their adherence to "laws" has been refined from Simon's "Weltgesetze" (his fateful identification of nature and society) and "the laws of day-to-day existence" Marti acknowledges when he bows before Frau Tobler, into the more confining and immediate "regulations" at the Institute Benjamenta, which Jakob alternately glorifies and defies. This defiance may appear as arrogance, spitefulness, or masochism. It is often as conscious a form of "childishness" as is his naïveté, since it too is premeditated. One of Jakob's earliest instances of obstinate resistance to authority is directed against having to join three other pupils in a warren-like bedroom. He falls to his knees, clutches the school teacher's legs and refuses to get up until she promises him what he calls a "place to sleep worthy of a human being" (*JvG*, 344). Pathetically protesting he does not want to insult his fellows, he continues imploring Fräulein Benjamenta for another room, "for all I care a hole in the wall." He presses his advantage as the teacher begins to weaken: "She was smiling already. I noted it, so I pressed myself still closer to her and quickly added: 'I want to be good . . . '" (*JvG*, 344).

The pattern of defiance is present throughout the book. It begins with Jakob's nominal acceptance of what he initially calls the "worse than foolish regulations" (*JvG*, 347), when he admits: "Schacht likes to do whatever slights the rules, and if I tell the truth, I not any less, unfortunately" (*JvG*, 341). The pattern continues into the last scene, a death watch Jakob and Benjamenta keep beside the corpse of Fräulein Benjamenta. Here Jakob intimidates Benjamenta by suggesting that he would prefer to leave the school without him. His only explanation for thus discouraging Benjamenta—"this all too confident person" (*JvG*, 488)—supports the manifest symbolism of the entire scene by divorcing his words from mere eccentricity: "Devilments really are the neatest thing about life" (*JvG*, 489). What gradually emerges from the pattern of defiance is a consuming passion to contact the human being behind his role. Something of the strength of this passion can be felt as Jakob considers the pleasure he derives from teasing his beloved Kraus, the ideal pupil at the Institute Benjamenta. The light this unsparing self-revelation casts is unsteady, since it includes the ironic and disheartening knowledge that Jakob too has to be comprehended through his role.

> I find nothing more pleasing than to give people whom I have taken into my heart a completely false picture of myself. Perhaps that is injust, but it is bold, and so it's fitting. Moreover, with me this gets to be a little sick. Thus, for ex. I imagine it as inexpressibly beautiful to die in the terrible knowledge of having hurt the thing I love more than anything in the world and filled it with bad opinions about myself. No one will understand that, or only the person who can feel the shudder of beauty in defiance.*

---

* Nichts ist mir angenehmer, als Menschen, die ich in mein Herz geschlossen habe, ein ganz falsches Bild von mir zu geben. Das ist vielleicht ungerecht, aber es ist kühn, also ziemt es sich. Übrigens geht das bei mir ein wenig ins Krankhafte. So z.B. stelle ich es mir als unsagbar schön vor, zu sterben, im furchtbaren Bewußtsein, das Liebste, was ich auf der Welt habe, gekränkt und mit schlechten Meinungen über mich erfüllt zu haben. Das wird niemand verstehen, oder nur der, der im Trotz Schönheitsschauer empfinden kann (*JvG*, 354).

The transformed ancestral pride that Jakob describes to Benjamenta in his *vita* as "something quite new" (*JvG*, 379) is the absoluteness of commitment to the riddle of existence. In his willingness to submit to corporal punishment from Benjamenta in order to breach the barrier erected between men by custom, Jakob sacrifices his nobility of station for the birthright of individuality. The irony that permits Jakob the boldness to attempt to break down the established order or to figuratively goad God to prove His existence by a display of might is a transparent device for communicating his knowledge of the separation between men brought about by idols man himself has created. Jakob's irony no longer permits him to view the world with anything like Simon's wonder or Marti's quizzical hope. Consequently, Jakob's ironic awareness of the disillusions of reality expresses a spirit that defiantly demands of itself a sprightly watchfulness as an ironic counterpart to the stolidity of self-importance. At a point when he is still baffled by the opaque human relations he finds at the school, he says: "It amuses me to put my ear to something that won't make any sound. I pay close attention, and that embellishes life, for if you're not obliged to pay attention life doesn't really exist" (*JvG*, 378). Jakob's insistent profession of light-heartedness amidst the renunciations and strictures of the Institute Benjamenta may at times have the appearance of play-acting. But this is a pose disguising a foreknowledge of human pain that Jakob—almost unbeknownst to himself—brings with him to the school. A reference by Jakob to a youthful memory of primitive brutality, comparable to traumatic memories of brutality in Simon and Marti (cf. *T*, 119–120 and *G*, 138f.) reveals his irony to be an annulment of ineffectual moral imperatives. Jakob comments on the memory of a murdered French-Swiss factory worker whom he saw lying in a pool of blood: "To know that the good, the pure, the sublime is hidden some, somewhere in the mists and to venerate it and idolize it softly, very, very quietly, so to speak with positively cool and shadow-like ardor, that's what I'm used to" (*JvG*, 369).

Jakob is the spiritual relative of both Simon Tanner and Joseph Marti in his ultimate belief in ideals that have no valid currency. Jakob's acknowledgement of a disappointment that Simon and Marti experience but do not admit underlies the range of Jakob's inimitable "voice" in the journal entries. The language of the entries drops from the glossy-surfaced self-assurance of Jakob's wit and humor to the riddle of an adamantly depersonalized and selfless view of life expressed in Jakob's reflection about teasing Kraus (above, p. 88). It is not surprising that as a journal writer Jakob can explicitly adduce themes that occur in the earlier novels. What is noteworthy about him—and apparently antithetical to this depersonalization—is that as he reasserts Simon Tanner's aggressiveness, encountering life at closer quarters than Simon was able to do, his figure as a hero undergoes a heightening of traits found in the earlier heroes, adding to his durability. He is younger than either Simon or Marti and more "childish," but his ethical sense is closer to the surface; he is both more defiant and yet more submissive than either of them. "Yes, yes," he admits, "I like being subjugated" (*JvG*, 432). Jakob places greater emphasis on experience than they did. ("My desire to gain experience," he says, "is getting to be a dominant passion" [*JvG*, 373].) But he is more patently the non-participant whose suspension of belief lies in his "cool shadow-like ardor."

This radicalization of elements from the two earlier novels[2] will be discussed in this chapter and the one following. The thematic and stylistic implications of the use of a journal form allow the emergence of a fictional personality only implicit in the two earlier novels. The world encompassed in Simon's soliloquies is now seen in the person of the narrator-hero as he writes his journal. The journal entries are private, but as they are written with the intensity of Simon's public rhetoric they nevertheless cast expansive rings of meaning. The outward manifestation of the reduction of the hero imposed by the form is his youthfulness. Similarly, Jakob's entrance into a school to prepare for life, in contrast to the nominal participation in life by both Simon and Marti represents an analogous "regression" in plot complexity. The effect of such reductions permits the artistic realization of a figure whose emotional nexus is at what might be called ground level.[3] The symbolism inherent in the ultimately indeterminate perspective of the two earlier books has here been channeled into the figure of the narrator-hero, principally in the irony which is Jakob's only intellectual expression of hope.

In *Jakob von Gunten* the contrast between the interior and exterior world found in the two earlier novels is given a new, internalized focus. In place of the tangible reality of the inaccessible worlds Simon and Marti confront, Jakob confronts in the Institute Benjamenta an amorphous and indeed dreamlike exterior world. In this novel the riddle of being is given a more overt and dominant role than in the two earlier novels. This is achieved through the narrative formal "reductions" mentioned above, as well as through the reactions—expressed in Jakob's personality and thoughts—that are loosed by the experience of the school and its inhabitants. More explicitly than in the case of either of the two earlier heroes, Jakob's world lacks a base to provide perspective against which the questions the hero poses can be viewed. As a result Jakob's recurrent questions about himself reveal a much more extreme disorientation of spiritual locale. In his function as first-person narrator,

Jakob is also the first of the novel heroes whose creativity is allowed a certain sanction from the author. Further discussion of the novel will show that this is related to still another radicalization in relation to the first two novels: the license to write is contingent on the heightened explicitness of life's condition of submission as the price for a free existence. Thus, the Institute Benjamenta provides an opportunity to resolve the contradictory demands of creativity and self-restriction linking all three novels.

The Institute Benjamenta

The school which Jakob enters for the purpose of furthering his self-education is ideally suited to act as a foil for his own erratic and fragmentarily portrayed personality. The school shares in and, indeed, is largely the source of the mystery and ambiguity objectified in the narrator-subject of the novel.

The question of the character of the school is an integral part of Jakob's self-portrayal. The shifting time perspective in this expository material initially makes it difficult to decide whether the surreal school is a travesty of education reflecting Nietzsche's attacks on the moribund character of German education, a parody of the secret leagues that furnished stock plots for the German popular novel through the beginning of the nineteenth century, or a projection of a norm for conduct in society, ironically distorted to represent the hopelessness of its realization.[4]

The pedagogic rationale of the school—at least as regards the transmission of a traditional, intellectual corpus of knowledge—is compromised in the first sentence of the novel. The verbal and syntactic intensity of this idiomatically-shaped sentence results in a bi-directional force that is characteristic of the entire work: "One learns very little here, there is a shortage of teachers, and we lads of the Institute Benjamenta will get nowhere, that is, all of us will be small and subordinate in later life" (*JvG*, 335).

Specific comments concerning the teaching at the school are limited; only seven of the book's seventy-nine journal entries deal with instruction. We learn that formal instruction is apparently limited to memorization of "many implacable regulations" that are mainly proscriptive in nature: "We aren't allowed to let our thoughts wander, not allowed to daydream, we are forbidden to be farsighted . . . " (*JvG*, 392). This emphasis on memorization is appropriate to the school since memorization is only incidentally intellectual. The pupil must finish all the food on his plate (*JvG*, 358). The only classroom instruction offered is on the subject "How is the lad to comport himself?" (*JvG*, 337). This one subject, constantly repeated, forms the basis of the entire instruction; "Instruction in subjects we do not get," Jakob says. The only reading matter assigned the pupils is a descriptive catalog entitled "What are the aims of Benjamenta's School for Boys?" There are other teachers than Fräulein Benjamenta at the school, but Jakob reports that they are "sleeping, or they are dead, or only in a trance, or they are petrified . . ." (*JvG*, 337). In a fantasy Jakob later enters in his journal, he describes a room especially set up for people in need of quiet, where the moribund teachers sit or crouch against the walls (*JvG*, 386–387). There he castigates their remoteness from life. In place of the missing intellectual disciplines, the school demands of its pupils an adherence to the external formalities such as comportment and polite, proper greeting. The required drills and exercises in obedience are intended to compel the pupils "to get to know the exact composition of our own souls and our own bodies" (*JvG*, 391). Precise rules prescribe the "kind of precursory attestation of respect" (*JvG*, 417) required as the pupils sit— "completely attentive and expectant"—waiting for the teacher to appear in the morning. "Like real dumb bunnies," Jakob comments, "we pupils are supposed to prepare ten minutes long for getting up from our places" (*JvG*, 417). The pupils are to be prepared for life by uncompromising, unquestioning submission, by exterior depersonalization, by energetic and unflinching embrace of failure, and by a reliance on intuition and innate character in place of intellect. "The law that commands, the compulsion that obligates, and the many implacable regulations which specify bent and taste: that is what is great and not we, we *élèves*" (*JvG*, 392).

Despite the primacy and the absoluteness of this supreme law and "the regulations that think of everything" (*JvG*, 383), the non-intellectual character of the law makes it impossible for Jakob to articulate it. The pupils are educated by "being given clearly to understand that compulsion and privation are formative, in and of themselves, and that a greater blessing and more real knowledge reside in a perfectly simple, so to speak stupid exercise than in the mastery of diverse concepts and interpretations" (*JvG*, 391). The rest of the students lack Jakob's critical curiosity, nor are they oppressed by the restrictions at Institute Benjamenta. Jakob describes them as "completely placid and cheerful" (*JvG*, 420). The rigorous inculcation of the law and its complementary regulations impose a mode of existence on the pupils reminiscent of an ascetic order, but, as Greven correctly points out, "any sort of content in the strict rules of belief, any expectation of salvation and any outline for reform, regardless of whether directed toward this life or to a tran-

scendent realm is lacking" (*Greven*, 83). The school engenders an atmosphere of a kinetic morality suspended in a social vacuum, a latter-day
Kierkegaardian church without a faith. As such, the school is an excellently integrated symbol of the imposition on modern man of a life
in abeyance: the recognition that while values of a previous age are
insufficient, they have yet to be replaced by new ones.

The absurdly limited "curriculum" only occupies the students through
mid-afternoon; then they are free to do as they choose—or to do nothing.
But the rules forbid restlessness, sighing, or squirming during periods of
inactivity. "We boys don't do such things. We press our lips together and
are immobile" (*JvG*, 399). In one passage Jakob accurately conveys
this allusory nature of the school, recreating the boredom of the afternoon torpor in the classroom that compounds the aimless vitality of the
classes. His combination of earnestness and flippancy while practising
comportment in the odium of inactivity has the same borderline effect
as the reputed ability of Rabbi Hillel to recite the entire law while
standing on one foot.

> . . . tedium rules the classroom, a tedium that almost makes one
> ill. No noise is allowed. . . . Kraus is memorizing by mumbling
> lessons to himself. There is a graveyard stillness everywhere. The
> courtyard lies there deserted like a rectangular eternity and I am
> usually erect and practise standing on one leg. For variety I often
> hold my breath for a long time.*

The most detailed information on instruction at the school is found
in the account of the "calesthenic, etiquette, and dancing classes" (*JvG*,
438–441), which describes practice scenes from life and impromptu comedies that "degenerate into buffoonery." Under Fräulein Benjamenta's
direction the pupils play voraciously at adult life, imagining themselves
in a bewildering variety of situations in life, "in everything possible."
When they finally tire "from all these stupidities," their teacher raps
the desk with her white staff and calls: "*Allons*, forward, boys. Work!"
Once more they hurl themselves into new imaginary activities until they
tire again. Now their teacher calls: "What? Have you already tired
of public life? Move, move! Show us what life is like. It is easy, but
you have to be sprightly, otherwise life will crush you." Again they
busy themselves with still other aspects of life until: " 'Stop. Enough

* . . . im Schulzimmer herrscht Oede, eine Oede, die einen beinahe krank macht.
Lärm soll nicht vorkommen. . . . Kraus lernt auswendig, indem er Lektionen vor
sich hinmurmelt. Eine Grabesstille herrscht überall. Der Hof liegt verlassen da wie
eine viereckige Ewigkeit, und ich stehe meist aufrecht und übe mich, auf einem Bein
zu stehn. Oft halte ich zur Abwechslung den Atem lange an (*JvG*, 399).

for today,' the teacher says. Then life is extinguished, and the dream which people call human life takes a different course" (*JvG*, 440).

Jakob does not come to terms with the Institute Benjamenta and its ideals as they have been so far described. Although he is necessarily the source of our knowledge about the school, certain features in the novel itself dictate a postponement of an analysis of his relation to it at this time. Jakob's meaningful encounter with the school comes in his experience of Kraus, the model student at the school, in the vision of his "initiatory" admission into the secret "inner chambers" he imagines the Benjamentas inhabit, and his subsequent experience of their real rooms. Although these experiences are intimately related to the precepts the school seeks to inculcate, their quality as personal experience and their specific literary and emotional conception help in setting Jakob apart from the Institute Benjamenta's formalism. Another factor now limiting our discussion is the ambiguity with which Jakob's acceptance of the teaching of the school is presented. He nominally accepts the precepts early in the book. Yet it is more than Jakob's penchant for paradox and his irrepressible defiance that make it difficult for the reader to honor this acceptance and turn his attention to other enigmas. In the very first entry Jakob indicates that he has come to terms with the school, notwithstanding his doubts and his earlier views. He makes this statement after saying "I have managed to become a riddle to myself" (*JvG*, 335). In fact Jakob sustains a retreating holding action against the school, while seeking such "experience" as Simon and Marti also valued so highly. He only becomes ready to engage himself with significant experiences in the school after his forays into the city and contact with his brother's circle have exhausted the possibilities of meaningful experience outside the school.

The intellectual rationale of the school is compromised through the insistence on a concentration of the pupils' efforts in the absence of a specific goal, even though the efforts are categorically devoid of hope. Shortly after entering the school, Jakob tries unsuccessfully to withdraw, complaining to Benjamenta that "nothing is here" (*JvG*, 347), no "plan" of any sort, no organizing "thought" behind the school. But Jakob's narration of his initial fears that the school is a fraud, that he is being deceived, and the fright which, at first, made him think of "slow strangulation" (*JvG*, 340) must be related to his subsequent nominal acceptance. For its part, this acceptance is constantly at odds with a defiance that posits proscriptive regulations: ". . . . not to be allowed to do something means doing it somewhere else twice as much" (*JvG*, 432). Jakob indicates that his initial fears were misplaced: "How really stupidly I behaved when I first got here" (*JvG*, 339); "On the first day I was horribly prim and behaved like Mommy's boy" (*JvG*, 343). He subjects this acceptance to criticism in the rationale he gives in the first entry for agreeing to wear the Institute Benjamenta uniform. He ultimately accepts the demeaning it implies, only to cancel it out through a submerged pun, the intent of which is to ridicule any and every theory of clothes, be it that of the Carlylean clothes that make the intellectual man in *Sartor Resartus* or the emotional security a uniform provides for both father and son in Kafka's *Metamorphosis*: "For me, for example, wearing the uniform is very pleasant, because I never properly knew what to put on" (*JvG*, 336).

The feeling of the unreality of the school never abandons Jakob. It begins early when he says "God knows, the whole of my stay here sometimes seems like an incomprehensible dream to me" (*JvG*, 337f.). It is still at work when he says of the two parts of the instruction, the theoretical and "the practical or physical part" (*JvG*, 391): "both departments even now still impress me as a dream, as a senseless and at the same time very meaningful fairy tale" (*JvG*, 390). As long as Jakob is prey to the mystifications of the school and of the brother and sister who run the school, he looks to the world outside the Institute Benjamenta for relief or as the arena where his hunger for experience—an ambition forbidden by the school's ethic—will be tested and satisfied. His statement: "The only thing I esteem are experiences" (*JvG*, 418) is the brusque credo of his plan for a resolutely anti-idealistic life apart from the Institute Benjamenta. Although Jakob never comprehends the meaning of the school in intellectual terms and never identifies the physical instruction as an interim safeguard against the corrosiveness of intellectualism, he is the only one to test the ethics of the school in the experience of reality and thus—through his apprehension of the common denominator of humanity—to complement and comment on the teaching and the practise of the school.

His forays into the metropolis provide Jakob with the raw data he later refines into insight in his role as sentient observer and journal writer. Jakob's integrity as observer is evident. The insight he gains through outwardly unrelated particulars as a private, unabsorbed being, observing from the outer edge, and the exaltation he feels at the fulcrum his understanding of trivia gives him, is best illustrated from his notes written after attending an afternoon tea-room concert. As an extrapolation of the momentous from the insignificant it illustrates a new formulation of Simon's and Marti's less explicit ambitions as wanderer-observers.

O, sometimes I feel as if I had the power to play with the earth and all the things on it however I choose. All at once I understand the lovely nature of women. Their coquetries amuse me and I perceive profundity in their trivial movements and the way they talk. If you don't understand them when they lift a cup of tea to their lips or gather their skirts, then you'll never understand them. Their souls trip along with the high, curved heels of their sweet little boots and their smile is a two-fold thing: a silly habit and a part of universal history.*

While Jakob still regards himself as a free agent, the bufferline of moral demarcation he draws here between himself and the outside world already forms a mirror reflection of the moral vacuum in the school itself. Shortly thereafter he applies his defiant lightness to an analogous perception of the world outside the school. "There are no more masters who can do what they please," he reflects, "and there are long since no more regal mistresses. Should that make me sad? Wouldn't think of it. . . . I take the times as they are, and merely reserve for myself the right to make observations on the quiet" (*JvG*, 398).

In other descriptions of experiences in the city Jakob peculiarly relates their intimations and imitations of life to those found in the practice games and comedies put on at the school. He thereby further disembodies the reality of the school, and, through the mirror reflection, the outside world he is describing. This relation is based on the roles Jakob himself assumes in the external world. The memorable, verbally economic description of Jakob's piquant erotic adventure with a Polish barmaid shows such a role. This passage stresses the pungent pleasure he felt in being a silent partner while being duped by the girl. The following selection from this episode illustrates Jakob's instinctive reliance on disguise and on a humility that in its equivocation contravenes the principles of the school: "Now I kissed her. She said: 'Tell me, what do you do? You act like a nobleman.' I couldn't take in enough of the fragrance that came from her. She noticed that and felt it was refined . . . I told her a lie and said I was a stable hand" (*JvG*, 355).

Jakob's reference to the walks he says it is his habit to take after the conclusion of the plays in the school attentuates the reality of the knowledge gained through the "life games" in the school. On these walks he regularly encounters a salesgirl whose yearning glances remain un-

---

* O mir ist manchmal, als hätte ich es in der Gewalt, mit der Erde und all den Dingen darauf beliebig spielen zu können. Ich verstehe mit einemmal das liebliche Wesen der Frauen. Ihre Koketterien amüsieren mich, und ich erblicke Tiefsinn in ihren trivialen Bewegungen und Redensarten. Wenn man sie nicht versteht, wenn sie eine Tasse zum Mund führen oder den Rock raffen, so versteht man sie nie. Ihre Seelen trippeln mit den hochaufgeschweiften Absätzen ihrer süßen Stiefelchen, und ihr Lächeln ist beiderlei: eine alberne Angewohnheit und ein Stück Weltgeschichte (*JvG*, 388).

answered—in part, no doubt, because of a combination of arrogance and reticence in Jakob. His own explanation, however, singles out the girl's reliance on an uncritical emotional response. She mistakes him for a man of settled circumstances. "She errs," he concludes, "and that's why I ignore her" (*JvG*, 440).

The occurrence of the metaphors of dream and fairy tale in both the plays imitative of the life for which the pupils are ostensibly being prepared and in the life Jakob encounters on the street suggests a relation between the two that transcends Jakob's play-acting. This life was described as "the dream which people call human life." The uncertain reality of the model becomes still more ambiguous through Jakob's remark that the instruction still seemed to him a "senseless and at the same time very meaningful fairy tale." The external world's irreality as seen from the perspective of the games at the Institute Benjamenta is added to what Jakob denominates a "dance" that acts as prelude to a period of play or the transition from one play period to another. What he designates as dance, however, is more appropriately a description of human affairs: "Then we dance. We hop around, followed by our teacher's smiling glances, and suddenly we race to the assistance of someone who has been injured . . . on the street. . . . We give imaginary beggars a little pittance, write letters, scream at our lackeys . . . and just do everything that happens in life" (*JvG*, 439). Jakob had just said that during these periods of instruction the classroom is transformed into a "street filled with human traffic." This phrase immediately brings to mind a generalizing description of a street scene Jakob had written (*JvG*, 365–367). In this entry the sheer amplitude of activity and vitality made Jakob think he was living in "what seems a tempestuous fairy tale" (*JvG*, 365)—the street scene seeming alternately humorous and infernal. The end of the entry acknowledges the double unreality of the plays, both in their imitation of life, and in the uncertain reality of the model. It too is a dance, but a macabre one. When Jakob "corrects" himself in the second half of the quotation, he sublimates his perception of the human energy in the streets thereby making the scene more haunting by demonizing it.

> And when it is grey and is raining? Then all of these figures, myself included, go off swiftly beneath the gloomy veil, swiftly and like dream figures, seeking something, and, so it seems, almost never finding anything beautiful and right. Everybody here is searching, everybody longs for riches and fabulous fortunes. They walk hastily. No, they all control themselves, but haste, longing, torment, and disquiet shine forth from their covetous eyes with a faint glimmer.

Then it all becomes a bathing in the hot, midday sun. Everything appears to be asleep, even the carriages, the horses, the wheels, the noises. And people gaze so incomprehendingly.*

The Cushions of Middle-Class Comfort

Jakob continues to act as observer in the entries that depict his meetings with his brother Johann, a successful artist. He penetrates a society furthest removed from the permanently inferior world of Institute Benjamenta, revealing the existence of a brother and his presence in the same city relatively late in the novel. His seeming reticence points out the riddle of Jakob's own existence, an exaggerated sense of his own insignificance—"What am I and what is he?" (*JvG*, 381). Jakob rejects the thought of contacting his brother: "I shall not go to him. If we run into one another accidentally on the street and he recognizes me, and comes toward me, fine . . ." (*op. cit.*). These words are clearly a psychological masking of his own ambition and a masking of a lack of self-reliance as pride. More important to the theme of the novel, however, is the fact that Jakob does not think of Johann as a brother but as "the well-situated man." Jakob's most pronounced trepidation, that his brother would be condescending, is a thought that is intolerable to him: "In any case," Jakob says, "I wouldn't let him bestow any good precepts on me, and that is just what I fear he will do . . ." (*JvG*, 382).

Curiously enough, the chance meeting comes. Johann is solicitous, and Jakob's initial fears are borne out in the counsel Johann gives his younger brother (*JvG*, 393–396). Commentators refer to Johann's statement at the first meeting of the brothers as profoundly Walserian. While this is true, it must be added that Johann's remarks have no greater authority than the precepts of the Institute Benjamenta, which they resemble in their disdain of the world and their support of the morality of insignificance. Johann himself is presented more as a bourgeois than as an artist, or, at best, as an artist whose disdain of his own commercial success is the source of the existential advice he gives Jakob. Jakob's accurate anticipation of his brother's behavior compels us to read

* Und wenn es grau ist und regnet? Dann gehen all diese Figuren, und ich selber mit, wie Traumfiguren rasch unter dem trüben Flor dahin, etwas suchend, und wie es scheint, fast nie etwas Schönes und Rechtes findend. Es sucht hier alles, alles sehnt sich nach Reichtümern und fabelhaften Glücksgütern. Hastig geht man. Nein, sie beherrschen sich alle, aber die Hast, das Sehnen, die Qual und die Unruhe glänzen schimmernd zu den begehrlichen Augen heraus. Dann ist wieder alles ein Baden in der heißen, mittäglichen Sonne. Alles scheint zu schlafen, auch die Wagen, die Pferde, die Räder, die Geräusche. Und die Menschen blicken so verständnislos (*JvG*, 366–367).

Johann's words first of all as the fulfillment of Jakob's presentiment: "I nodded vigorously," Jakob reports, "for even before he said it, I agreed with him . . . ; but I asked him to continue." Similarly Jakob's facile agreement compromises the apodictic nature of Johann's advice: "I nodded again. It's true, I consent to everything very easily" (*JvG*, 396).

Johann encourages his brother to begin "down deep," since in the upper strata of society "an atmosphere of having done enough prevails and that is deadening and confining." He assures Jakob that there is no such thing as rejection, since "there is perhaps absolutely nothing in this whole world that is honestly worth striving for. And yet you ought to strive, with passion." Johann sees modern society as a degradation and caricature of genuine culture. Excellence and beauty have disappeared and "you have to dream the beautiful, the good and what is honorable." In summation, his advice to Jakob is to remain poor and disregarded. "The rich people of today," Johann says, "no longer have anything. They are the truly starved . . . You must hope and yet not hope for anything . . . Look up to something, sure, that suits you . . . but always admit to yourself that you disdain what you look up to with respect" (*JvG*, 396).

In subsequent contacts with Johann's world the patronizing advice is missing. The fear, however, of finding his brother, as Jakob had anticipated, "lying on the cushions and rugs of middle-class comfort" (*JvG*, 382) becomes a reality. Jakob visits Johann's elegant apartment, where, surrounded by "serene worldly manners" (*JvG*, 382) he reacts ironically, submitting to the comportment prescribed by the surroundings: "Brother came towards me in a very friendly manner and we stood facing one another like distinguished men of the world who know what pleasure can lie in decorum. We chatted. Then a tall, slim, snow-white dog bounded towards us in graceful, happy leaps. Well, I naturally petted the animal" (*JvG*, 419).

The rejection of Johann's world, implicit from the outset, becomes more explicit in an entry recounting Jakob's attendance at a theater performance and an elegant dinner as his brother's guest. Disguised in a borrowed frock coat, and behaving "like a man with an income of twenty thousand a year" (*JvG*, 424), he is not impressed by the world he has entered in moral incognito: "Women who would scorn me completely, if I were to tell them I was a boarding school pupil smiled across to me, and, as it were, made signs to encourage me . . . I noticed little that could be called elegant manners. On the other hand I noticed that people took me for a bashful youth, while in fact (in my own view) I was bursting with impudence" (*JvG*, 424f.).

The express rejection, and the final contact in the novel with this sphere of reality is seen in the reflections Jakob writes after meeting intellectuals and artists at a last visit to his brother's (*JvG*, 443–444). He characterizes the people he meets there as undifferentiated worshipers of the myth of reputation with identical faces and despising no one for fear of behaving imprudently, although perhaps they are genuinely scorning everything. Yearning for the testimony of success, they all fear the successor that will ultimately displace them. Jakob concludes his dissection of reputation in a permissive intellectual society: "In these circles of progressive culture there prevails a weariness that can hardly be overlooked or misunderstood. Not the formalized blasé attitude say, of nobility of old extraction, no, a real, a quite genuine weariness, based on deeper and more vital feeling, the weariness of healthy-unhealthy human beings" (*JvG*, 444).

Jakob had entered this world in his search for experience and not as a prospective participant. This is established in Jakob's efforts to see his brother "whole, not just half" (*JvG*, 425). Similarly, the somewhat programmatic nature of Jakob's reckoning with intellectuals and artists proceeds under the aegis of Jakob's transformed concept of pride. In the entry immediately preceding the one characterizing the intellectuals, Jakob says that he has the Benjamentas to thank for the fact that he is no longer the previous Jakob von Gunten, "the descendant, the offspring of my house." Now seeing himself as "an ordinary human being" he says: "I have replaced my pride, the species of honor" (*JvG*, 442). The brother whom he had tried to see whole was himself the embodiment of "the healthy-unhealthy human being" found in Johann's society. Taking off "the elegant coat" of his disguise he "crawled back to the Institute" in his "boarding-school suit" (*JvG*, 425). Finished with Johann's world, the search for a breadth of experience is more consistently focused inward on the unresolved mystery of the school as Jakob uninterruptedly faces the oppression of what to him still seems absurd and yet contains "a deeply hidden meaning" (*JvG*, 391).

Kraus

Kraus, the exemplary Benjamenta pupil embodying all the principles of the school, personifies for Jakob the depersonalization imbued by the school. The ostensible model for Jakob's development at the school, Kraus is the one true celebrant of the faith, or, as Jakob puts it, "the representative of all the existing regulations in Institute Benjamenta" (*JvG*, 356). Kraus enjoys a favorite position in the eyes of both principal and teacher. He is privy to the secret "inner chambers" exerting so strong an attraction for Jakob. Kraus' diligence is unflagging. Having "mastered the knack of rushing obligingly, head over heels, in the direction of commands" (*JvG*, 335), he "hates, persecutes, and despises idleness" (*JvG*, 353), and foreswears any claim to success in the world, acceding willingly to the prohibitions and humiliations his present (and foreseeably future) low station will entail, as the ideal expression of selfless service. He embraces poverty, hard work, and ingratitude without rancor. Thus Jakob describes the horizons of Kraus' world: "Kraus sees first of all human beings, secondly duties, and, thirdly, at best, savings, which he intends to put on the side, in order to send to his mother" (*JvG*, 375f.). Jakob's characterization of the pupils' behavior as "humble but extremely confident" applies perfectly to Kraus. Kraus has no time for exploratory ventures into the city such as Jakob's for "the bustle of the big city . . . leaves him absolutely cold" (*JvG*, 376). He smiles contemptuously when Jakob returns to the school insisting that one is obliged to learn what the world is like (*JvG*, 367). Kraus constantly looks askance at Jakob's behavior, whether it be Jakob's irrepressible curiosity about the school and the Benjamentas, or his malingering at chores (*JvG*, 356–357).

Jakob responds, both to the ostensible model and the school, with ambiguity. Assuming great disparity in the characters of Jakob and Kraus, the distinction between them is expanded by the narrative device of double perspective. Within the entries indications of the affection Jakob has come to feel for Kraus abut on "regressive" statements reminiscent of his original judgment of Kraus as the "stupid monkey" (*JvG*, 340) who opened the door for Jakob when he first came to the school and for whom he once felt "a violent dislike" (*JvG*, 358). Actually, Jakob learns to understand and esteem Kraus' virtues, although his behavior toward him continues to give Kraus cause for "Abraham-like reproaches" (*JvG*, 415). The enumeration and analysis of Kraus' virtues present a problem to the journal writer-narrator; the form of the novel meshes inextricably with its content. Thus the comprehension of the Kraus riddle and its transmission to paper is for Jakob far and away the most difficult problem with his student portraitures, and it is one that Jakob postpones. He is able to write witty, incisive, unobtrusively intelligent character sketches of his fellow pupils Schacht (*JvG*, 341), Heinrich (*JvG*, 338f.), Schilinski (*JvG*, 352f.), tall Peter (*JvG*, 369f.), and Hans (*JvG*, 367f.) because their models, like Jakob himself, have flaws; the subjects lend themselves to verbalizations by one who refers to himself as "the cleverest among them" (*JvG*, 352). But Kraus is different; he is complete. Jakob later describes him as "an image of scrupulous, quite, quite monotonous, monosyllabic, unequivocal being" (*JvG*, 410), and as a "rock" unaffected by life's "stormy wave" (*JvG*, 468). Rooted in and permanently bound to a world Jakob is too conscious ever to be a part of, Kraus defies description even in a form as flexible as the journal and even given Jakob's use of it as an anti-idealistic, a-rational medium for the discovery and transmission of truth.

The "firm, good whole [Kraus] represents" (*JvG*, 407) strikes Jakob first of all in the limitation of Kraus' intellect: "Wherever little is taught, that's where a Kraus belongs, accordingly he fits in the Institute Benjamenta excellently." Kraus, "who came into the world provided with a rather thick skull" (*JvG*, 391), is safe from boredom as Jakob never can be. When asked whether he too is ever bored, he heatedly rebukes Jakob for the "naive as well as sinful" question, and suggests that Jakob follow his own prescription for keeping the spirit occupied: ". . . one can mumble Jakob . . . do you even know what I mumble? Words, dear Jakob. I keep mumbling and repeating words" (*JvG*, 414).

To speak only of Jakob's rejection of Kraus and to stress, as does a recent critic,[6] the patronizing air in contrast to Jakob's affection for Kraus, is to overlook the complexity of their relationship and to ignore the symbolism of their confrontation. Even though Jakob's old, indestructible pride is at pains to maintain a distance in their relationship, the humaneness of Jakob's perception of Kraus' being as recorded in the characterization that Jakob is finally able to write attests to his ultimate respect, indeed, to a longing for what Kraus represents. Kraus fascinates and attracts Jakob. But as the embodiment of the question of the viability of goodness as seen from Jakob's consciously modern perspective, Kraus' portrait long eludes Jakob's literary skill. One commentator has suggested[7] that Walser was constitutionally incapable of admitting evil into his world. In view of the intimation of evil and the threat of extinction that alternate with a defiant lightness of tone in *Jakob von Gunten,* and the undefined but ominous realms that frequently loom immediately beyond the ring of language in Walser's short prose, this appears academic. Jakob's struggle to give expression to an evanescent good in the "broken" literary form of a journal shows Walser expressing the moral heritage derived from his perception of cultural problems that started toward the end of the nineteenth century, while his literary style is indelibly part of the twentieth. If the Enlightenment's obsession with moral goodness could be transferred into modern terms, it would have to be in terms such as those Jakob uses as he begins the extended confrontation with Kraus:

> Nothing can excite me as profoundly as the sight and the odor of what is good and decent. You're soon enough through feeling anything for what is common and evil, but figuring out something fine

and noble is so hard and at the same time so alluring. No, vices interest me much less than virtues. Now I'm going to have to depict Kraus, and I almost dread doing it.[*]

Several inconclusive assaults on Kraus' goodness follow in Jakob's journal. Unsuccessful parries, they bring Jakob's intelligence into play to secure insight clothed in bemused humor. "Kraus only wants what is right and good," he notes at one point. But Kraus' very goodness makes him seem like an anachronism—appropriately the star pupil at the school. "His eyes are frighteningly good," Jakob continues. "This human being, what is he doing, really, in a world given over and trained to slogans, lies, and vanity?" "He properly belongs in the Middle Ages, and it's a terrible shame that he doesn't have a twelfth century at his disposal" (*JvG*, 337). Kraus is "forlorn" in this world, but "firm," "unapproachable . . . like a demi-god" (*JvG*, 469).

Only after Jakob embraces Kraus' external ugliness can he proceed beyond his intellectual insights and penetrate the riddle of Kraus' being. In contemplating Kraus as a lowly servant, Jakob paradoxically elevates Kraus beyond his own intelligence. "I no longer see the indelicate sores that disfigure him," he says in an entry devoted to Kraus' qualities as a servant, "I don't even notice that he looks ugly. I see his soul on his face, and his soul, that is what is caressable" (*JvG*, 360).

The broadened prospect of this double vision makes possible the climactic characterization of Kraus. The three entries make up the longest of the student portraitures (*JvG*, 405–411). These entries, together with the descent to the so-called passageways of poverty and privation, communicate the meaning of the school to Jakob in non-intellectual terms. The Kraus entries utilize fully the discursive narrative technique possible in the journal form: starting with alogical, aphoristic speculation at the beginning, they rise to dithyrambic language that feverishly communicates the transport of non-intellectual revelation.

The progress of Jakob's thoughts and images is diffuse and tangential, resulting in circuitous verbal and conceptual probings. Jakob first sees Kraus as a Joseph-in-Egypt figure: sold into servitude in Potiphar's house, tempted by Mut-em-enet's sensuality, but resolute, pedantic and unbending in his duty. "Kraus would act just like his ancient Egyptian image. He would lift his hands imploringly, and, with a half-beseeching

---

[*] Nichts kann mich so tief aufregen wie der Anblick und der Geruch des Guten und Rechtschaffenen. Etwas Gemeines und Böses ist bald ausempfunden, aber aus etwas Bravem und Edlem klug zu werden, das ist so schwer und doch zugleich so reizvoll. Nein, die Laster interessieren mich viel, viel weniger als die Tugenden. Nun werde ich Kraus schildern müssen, und davor ist mir direkt bange (*JvG*, 353).

mien, half reproachfully, say: 'No, no, I won't do that and so on' " (*JvG*, 407).[8] This image of Kraus as a slave—a heightening of the motif of all the pupils' insignificance—establishes Kraus as submissive to the still inarticulated law in force at the Institute Benjamenta. The second entry is not so diffuse in its imagery. Proceeding from Jakob's paradoxical aperçu of Kraus as a perfect example of cultivation (a pun is involved: in speaking of *Bildung*, Jakob is stressing the integrity of Kraus' being and not the product of education and culture usually implied by the term) the entry locates the authority of this law within the person. "Kraus knows little," Jakob writes, "but he is never, never thoughtless, he always submits to certain self-imposed commandments, and that I call cultivation" (*JvG*, 408).

The third Kraus entry continues the revelatory and probing character of the previous two in occasional uncertainties, and in returning to an idea and finding that it has not yielded all it contains. For example, Jakob finally accepts the improbable masterpiece of Nature, the unsightly Kraus, as a measure to protect him from the cancer of fame. The sporadic development of thoughts and images from the first two entries is balanced by an increase in the biblical cast of the language. This reaches a high point in a transport of insight so precise in its formulation that we are persuaded of the credibility of seers' visions. Jakob only stops writing when he senses a near paroxysm: "I must stop, for today, writing. It's too overpowering. I'm running wild; and the letters are flickering and dancing before my eyes" (*JvG*, 411).

In reading the following selection from the final Kraus entry one must bear in mind that the solution of the riddle posed by Kraus' unprepossessing existence is an achievement in the activation of the imagination comparable to Simon Tanner's Paris dream and Joseph Marti's reverie during the lake ride. It differs from them in the consciousness of the human and literary task it involves. Kraus' mystery is penetrated, but his impregnability is not. Jakob perceives the imperturbable vitality of Kraus' being in his realization that Kraus will "live on that way." The psychology in Jakob that exults in the promise of exploitation in God's hands attests to the reality of Jakob's humility here, but it is humility before an image embodying being rather than before an individual.

> No, Kraus will never be a success, neither with women, who will find him dull and ugly, nor anywhere else in the outside world, which will carelessly pass him by. Carelessly? Yes, Kraus will never be esteemed, and the very fact that he will live on without enjoying any respect is just what is wonderful and purposeful, is what reminds us of the Creator. God sends a Kraus into the world in order, so to speak, to assign it a deep, insoluble riddle. Well, and then the riddle

isn't comprehended, for you see, no one even takes the trouble to solve it, and this is the very reason this Kraus-riddle is so splendid and profound: because no one craves to solve it; because no living person whatsoever will suspect any task, any riddle, or a finer meaning behind this unutterably insignificant Kraus. Kraus is a genuine God-creation, a nothing, a servant. To everybody he'll seem uncultivated, just barely good enough to perform the hardest work. . . . Kraus, modesty itself, the crown, the palace of humility, why he wants to perform trivial jobs, he knows how to and he wants to. He has nothing on his mind but to help, obey, and serve and . . . he will be taken advantage of, and the fact that he is taken advantage of—therein lies a resplendent, golden, divine justice . . . he will absolutely remain unsuccessful. I find that delightful, delightful, and delightful all over again. Oh, what God creates is so benevolent, so attractive, draped over and over with delights and ideas. . . . No, no success, no fame, for successes merely bring distraction and cheap conceptions about the world as unavoidable escorts. . . . Gratitude, yes. Gratitude is quite something else. But Kraus won't even be thanked, and even that is absolutely not necessary. Every ten years someone may perhaps say to Kraus: "Thanks, Kraus," and then he will smile stupidly, horribly stupidly. My Kraus will never become a bum, for he will always be confronted by great, loveless difficulties.*

---

* Nein, Erfolg wird Kraus nie haben, weder bei den Frauen, die ihn trocken und häßlich finden werden, noch sonst im Weltleben, das an ihm achtlos vorübergehen wird. Achtlos? Ja, man wird Kraus nie achten, und gerade das, daß er, ohne Achtung zu genießen, dahinleben wird, das ist ja das Wundervolle und Planvolle, das An-den-Schöpfer-Mahnende. Gott gibt der Welt einen Kraus, um ihr gleichsam ein tiefes unauflösbares Rätsel aufzugeben. Nun, und das Rätsel wird nie begriffen werden, denn siehe: man gibt sich ja gar nicht einmal Mühe, es zu lösen, und gerade deshalb ist ja dieses Kraus-Rätsel ein so Herrliches und Tiefes: weil niemand begehrt, es zu lösen, weil überhaupt gar kein lebendiger Mensch hinter diesem namenlos unscheinbaren Kraus irgend eine Aufgabe, irgend ein Rätsel oder eine zartere Bedeutung vermuten wird. Kraus ist ein echtes Gottes-Werk, ein Nichts, ein Diener. Ungebildet, gut genug gerade, die sauerste Arbeit zu verrichten, wird er jedermann vorkommen. . . . Kraus, die Bescheidenheit selber, die Krone, der Palast der Demut, er will ja geringe Arbeiten verrichten, er kann's und er will's. Er hat nichts anderes im Sinn, als zu helfen, zu gehorchen und zu dienen, und . . . [man] wird ihn ausnutzen, und darin, daß man ihn ausnutzt, liegt eine so strahlende, goldene, göttliche Gerechtigkeit. . . . er wird durchaus erfolglos bleiben. Reizend, reizend, dreimal reizend finde ich das. Oh, was Gott schafft, ist so gnädig, so reizvoll, mit Reizen und Gedanken über und über behangen . . . Nein, kein Erfolg, kein Ruhm, denn die Erfolge haben nur die Zerfahrenheit und einige billige Weltanschauungen zur unabstreifbaren Begleitschaft . . . Dank, ja. Dank ist etwas ganz anderes. Doch einem Kraus wird man nicht einmal danken, und auch das ist durchaus nicht nötig. Alle zehn Jahre wird jemand vielleicht einmal zu Kraus sagen: "Danke, Kraus", und dann wird er ganz dumm, gräßlich dumm lächeln. Verliederlichen wird mein Kraus nie, denn es werden sich ihm immer große, lieblose Schwierigkeiten entgegenstellen (*JvG*, 409–411).

This is Kraus' gospel. It is Jakob's imagination that gives him the light to decipher it in these brief moments thereby resolving the mystery of the school in his intellectual life. Jakob's resolution, particularly the reverence for God's creation in its unobtrusive forms, is the basis for a commitment to life that is at odds with the Jakob von Gunten that entered the school. But just as the knowledge Simon Tanner and Joseph Marti gain through the imagination becomes a secret part of the subconscious, Jakob "forgets" the insight gained here through the medium of "disorganized" journal entries.

Kraus is the personification of one aspect of Walser's two earlier novel heroes: he embodies their self-sacrificing service and their reverence for God's creation. The self-negating traits in Simon Tanner which made him offer himself to Klara Agappaia and insist on a fate of lovelessness ("I out and out hate being given a gift," Simon says to Klara. "That too is the reason destiny ordains that no one love me . . . I wouldn't be able to bear love, for I can bear lovelessness" [*T*, 86].) reappear in Kraus' renunciation of gratitude and the certainty of his own loneliness. Kraus is also the development to perfection of Simon Tanner's fantasy of himself as servant to mankind in the snow-child fairy tale, which is later modulated into Marti's complaisance and compliance in his role as servant at Villa Abendstern. It is precisely Kraus' selflessness and depersonalization in service that Fräulein Benjamenta praises in her repeated urgings to Jakob not to tease Kraus. "Yes, Kraus isn't at all like other people," she once tells Jakob. "He sits there until you have need of him; if he is called, then he starts to move and comes running. . . . And one hardly senses that one has been served. And how perfectly! . . . Kraus the person is absolutely nothing, only the hard worker, the doer Kraus is something, but him you don't even notice . . ." (*JvG*, 449).

To what extent does the discovery of Kraus' significance through writing about him, the first of the two central imaginative experiences in the novel, effect the vanity and arrogance Jakob brought with him (*JvG*, 358f.), the defiant spirit he later claims he has renounced (*JvG*, 421–423), and the exchange of "pride," of "the species of honor" (*JvG*, 442)? The same questions might be asked about Jakob's descent to "the passageways of poverty and privation," although the confrontation with Kraus provides a ready vantage point from which to view the emphasis on and ultimate idealization of the interior life implicit in the two earlier novels.

From the Kraus experience Jakob learns that as an image for the secrets of nature, "a genuinely divine creation, a nothing, a servant"

(*JvG*, 409), Kraus will endure, no matter how maligned and exploited. The comprehension of Kraus' integrity of being cannot necessarily be equated with Jakob's own development, precisely because the function of imagination is discrete and personal. The narrative development of Jakob's acceptance of Kraus, however, includes contradictory strands interwoven through journal entries, that, lacking causal integration, vary within individual entries in which subject matter and perspective may alternate from one sentence to the next. Thus the schematization necessary to sum up their relationship unavoidably ignores the intentional complexity and interrelation of the entire work.

Fräulein Benjamenta's remonstrances in defense of Kraus are justified, since Jakob never entirely abandons his intellectual irony toward Kraus. An aura of guilt in the presence of Kraus results in his wishing to be scolded and reprimanded by him. ("How nice it would be, if my good Kraus were to come and, as so often, would rebuke me again a little bit" [*JvG*, 471]); in a masochistic contemplation of Kraus' perfection ("At times I should like this Kraus to thrash me" [*JvG*, 377]); and in his willingness to embrace what will always remain his opposite when he humbles himself before Kraus' soul. The closest point of Jakob's rapport with Kraus is described in the entry in which Jakob speaks of his "double-life" as "Croesus-Kraus." This begins: "I lead a strange double-life, a regulated one and an unregulated one, a controlled one and an uncontrollable one, a simple one and a highly complicated one" (*JvG*, 468). Basing this entry on the "illumination" that the mighty are weak, he experiences an intimation that he is a "Croesus, that is . . . Kraus. Kraus loves and hates nothing, that's why he is Croesus, something in him touches on the incontrovertible" (*JvG*, 468). But even these words are not a true identification with Kraus, since the oxymoronic pun that Jakob uses to serve as link between them has its source in Jakob's final renunciation of the temptation of money. The basis for the apparent identification is narrowed further when he suddenly thinks of Benjamenta, thus transmuting the reflection on Kraus' semi-divine impregnability (cf. *JvG*, 469) into Jakob's perception of his own fallibility, as it refers specifically to his affection for his master, Benjamenta. Hardly indicating a delusion on Jakob's part that he could become a Kraus, his words signify that with his awareness of a double, irreconcilable life comes the recognition that Kraus, the God-directed being, offers a refuge and a respite from the wakefulness of his intellect and humane sensitivity. For Jakob, Kraus has meant facing the problem of individuation. The double-life that Jakob speaks of is the outgrowth of the dichotomy between Kraus—who remains the paradigm for his education at the Institute Benjamenta—and the transformation and absorption of the tenets of the school on his own terms so that Kraus will not become the image for his own future existence. This disquieting fear, accentuated by Kraus' perfection, explains in part Jakob's difficulty in describing Kraus. Finally, as the dichotomy becomes more pressing, Jakob's situation symbolizes the dilemma the intellect faces in the modern novel. He can now contemplate and almost welcome the impersonal resolution of "a truly crushing blow" (*JvG*, 425). Then the designation for his intellectual life, "these lies and self-deceptions, this imagining one knows and yet never really knowing anything" (*JvG*, 425), "this reaching out for a meaning" (*JvG*, 470), will have come to an end.

Shortly thereafter the sufferance of and even covert desire for the limited rewards of a Kraus-like life finds its most moving expression in a memorable, if disconcerting prayer for life—an outgrowth of the Kraus experience in its emphasis on physical indestructability at whatever spiritual cost.

> Perhaps I shall never spread out branches and boughs. One day an exhalation of some sort will come forth from my being and my endeavors. I shall be in bloom and give off a bit of fragrance—as if for my own pleasure—and then I'll bow my head, the head that Kraus calls a dumb, arrogant, stubborn one. My arms and my legs will grow strangely limp, my spirit, my pride, my character, everything, everything will crumble and wither and I shall be dead; not really dead, just dead in a certain way and then perhaps for sixty years I shall live on this way and die. I will have gotten old. Still, I'm not afraid for myself.*

Occurring almost at the end of the book, these reflections set forth a somber fall into the shadows as a way of existence. The entry begins with Jakob's assertion that there will always be something childish about him because he "was never actually a child." He takes the same pleasure now that he did then in stupid pranks: "but that's just it, I never really played stupid pranks." He was always interested in the idea and he "sensed profundities" even in the pranks. When Jakob adds, "I'm not developing," he anticipates the penitent tone of the quotation above.

---

* Vielleicht werde ich nie Äste und Zweige ausbreiten. Eines Tages wird von meinem Wesen und Beginnen irgend ein Duft ausgehen, ich werde Blüte sein und ein wenig, wie zu meinem eigenen Vergnügen, duften, und dann werde ich den Kopf, den Kraus einen dummen, hochmütigen Trotzkopf nennt, neigen. Die Arme und Beine werden mir seltsam erschlaffen, der Geist, der Stolz, der Charakter, alles, alles wird brechen und welken, und ich werde tot sein, nicht wirklich tot, nur so auf eine gewisse Art tot, und dann werde ich vielleicht sechzig Jahre so dahinleben und sterben. Ich werde alt werden. Doch ich habe kein Bangen vor mir (*JvG*, 472).

For Jakob, youthfulness guarantees an intimation of infinite relation and significance. The prayer speaks of a promise that is part of Jakob's vision of reality beyond youth; it speaks also of an aging to follow, a willing forfeiture of distinction as the price for the emergence from youth. Thus the outcome of this engagement with life indicates that all three novel heroes interrelate psychological with ontological elements.

Although Kraus represents the furthest development of the integrality of inner life that provided both Simon Tanner and Joseph Marti with the counterbalance for a non-integral public life, he lacks the creative imagination which this inner life comprehended and secretly nourished in the two earlier heroes. Kraus is pure, indestructible, and self-reliant as a servant, but he is divorced from the risk and responsibility of life that Jakob symbolically undertakes in each new journal entry. When Jakob explains away Kraus' pimples, "the unelegant sores" (*JvG*, 360), he is at the same time commenting on the inadequacy of Kraus' naive idealism and momentarily yearning for the refuge provided in Kraus' self-negation. Kraus incorporates the inadequacy of both the psychology and the ideals of the nineteenth century. When Jakob's education has progressed enough to permit him to recognize the traits they share in common, Jakob says of them "I am almost a little ashamed" (*JvG*, 445). When Kraus leaves the school, thereby depriving it of its last rationale, Jakob says: "A light, a sun has vanished" (*JvG*, 481), and "Half of life left with Kraus" (*JvG*, 483). If Jakob's metaphor is precise, then it refers to the undifferentiated identity of human existence, since it would never be possible to say of Jakob, as Fräulein Benjamenta previously says of Kraus: "Kraus the person is absolutely nothing . . ." (*JvG*, 449).

The narrative method of the book, making both Jakob's situation in the plot and his symbolic situation paradoxical, may tempt the reader to broaden the significance of the Kraus figure to include Jakob. However, it is erroneous to assume—on the basis of an inoperative psychology of realistic character development—that Kraus has more than symbolic value, the function of which is to underline the rootlessness of the world Jakob ultimately accepts, albeit with trepidation. Reacting in a pluralistic manner, Jakob initially rejects "the dumb monkey" Kraus, praises him as the exemplary student, investigates Kraus' meaning to him and to the school through the inquiry into his being, rejects the implications of a freedom based on social servitude for the sake of his own integrity, and, finally, eulogizes and laments what he senses as an anachronism in Kraus' idealism. Jakob's own attitude to individualism can only be judged from the perspective gained with the final resolution of the plot. In his role as journal writer, however, it is now enough to say that

Jakob is willing to support his claim to complete freedom of the imagination at the price of social anonymity. Jakob expresses this only indirectly, through his knowledge that his defiance makes him a marked man who perhaps may not escape. "Strange," Jakob says early in the book, "how much pleasure I get from provoking outbursts of rage in people with power. Do I actually yearn to be whipped by this Herr Benjamenta? Do I harbor frivolous instincts in me?" (*JvG*, 372).

The Passageways of Poverty and Privation

Another of Jakob's imaginative confrontations with the Institute Benjamenta's tenets of self-denial and self-restriction occurs in his visionary descent to the lower depths, the "passageways of poverty and privation" (*JvG*, 425–431). With Fräulein Benjamenta as his guide, Jakob is admitted to the "heretofore secret world" of the "inner chambers" to which only Kraus has had access and behind whose doors Jakob has assured himself he would indeed find "wondrous things." He is not led into the real inner chambers where the Benjamentas live—these he visits later. Nevertheless, these entries constitute Jakob's symbolic initiation into the renunciations and disillusions inherent in the Institute Benjamenta in a form dictated by his own imagination.

The vision Jakob introduces simply as "something incomprehensible to me" occurs as he sits alone in the semi-darkened schoolroom. Its structure is reminiscent of Simon Tanner's dream of Paris as are some of its details. As in the Paris dream a revered female figure acts as guide to revelatory scenes of the mysteries of life; one scene fades into another; music bubbles down the walls in one of the scenes; the unreality is heightened by the intimation that a dream occurs within the original waking-dream or vision; just as does Klara Agappaia in Simon's dream, the guide here retires before the termination of the vision, in this case leaving the initiate to try to swim for himself in "a viscid . . . river of doubt."

The teacher and her student reach some passages along stone steps after a brief, blinding celestial light which Jakob describes as "splendorous and latent with meaning." Fräulein Benjamenta tells him that the light represents, even in its brevity, the joy of future happiness. His teacher urges him on—to "traverse and thrill through" what awaits them in the subterranean passages. Jakob now experiences apotheoses of freedom (". . . one must dance in this freedom," the teacher says. "It is cold and beautiful."); enervating material comfort; and tribulation of the soul. Jakob, asked to give a tangible sign of his willing submission "to the oppressiveness and to the affliction" that will mark his life, does so. Further on, the teacher asks Jakob to embrace the wailing wall before them, as "one has to try to move whatever is rigid and irreconcilable." Jakob obeys, flinging himself at the wall, speaking "friendly, almost jocular words" to it. Again, as with the "Croesus-Kraus" reflective association of symbolic relations, several levels of the novel coalesce. As a response to his teacher's request to try to animate an all-too-obvious symbol of misfortune within a vision by means of symbolic gesture, it illustrates both the cultural remoteness of the school's ideals as well as the elusiveness of Jakob's commitment. Yet Jakob's own words at the wailing wall are an instructive example of how Jakob can, through a liberating and apparently negative irony, indicate private idealism beneath levels of irony. Jakob modifies his words to the wailing wall by saying that he was playing "comedy" for his teacher's sake, only to admit, in the same sentence: "yet on the other hand what I was doing, was anything but comedy" (*JvG*, 429). Play-acting is thereby associated with its apparent antithesis, life's earnestness.

This latent derision in Jakob's description of the initiatory descent provides an illuminating perspective for understanding Jakob's educative experience at the Institute Benjamenta. A journal—necessarily produced by intellectual ability—here serves the speaker-writer by articulating for him his non-rational knowledge. Thus in Jakob's journal entry of his descent to the passageways of poverty the reader senses narrative irony as Jakob attributes the "lesson" of the vision to the teacher and not to the dreamer. This sense is added to when Jakob shifts perspective as he terminates the description. After the rest of the pupils return from a visit to the city and Fräulein Benjamenta leaves him to prepare supper, Jakob notes, in conclusion, how "terribly much" he likes to eat at certain times: "Then I can dig into the most unpleasant dishes like a hungry young craftsman; then I live like in a fairy tale and no longer like a civilized person in a civilized age" (*JvG*, 431). To Jakob the vision is an epiphany, realizing for him the dichotomy inherent in modern civilization. While the episode remains "incomprehensible" to Jakob, he discredits his teacher's resigned negation of modern civilization when he transmutes the vitality produced by the experience into a non-intellectual physical appetite. The visit corresponds to the Kraus divination. Both help define the encounter with reality, though their medium is the imagination.

It is impossible to construe the meaning of a life suspended between pride, moral scruples, ambition, and intelligence on the one hand and, on the other, the prohibition of ambition and individuality as instilled by the Institute Benjamenta in its trainees that bespeaks the school's implicit condemnation of society's norms and values. Even the change in himself that Jakob refers to early in the book is subject to new, or continuing mysteries. This is not surprising as Jakob's perception of the change in him transpires in the realm of dream and fantasy. Tangible only in the final entry, Jakob's consciousness then enables him to decide to no longer follow the "intellectual life" (*JvG*, 492). Between the descent discussed here and the final entry, we see Jakob absorbing and transforming the school's teaching.

The change that occurs in Jakob shifts his perspective as narrator toward subjectivity as expressed in imagination. The pattern of fitful revelations, false starts, and unresolved enigmas that had defined the tone of the book earlier is now redefined. The renewed sense of aristocracy that Jakob referred to before resulted from his imaginative experience of the teaching of the school. He now imputes a double meaning to "descendant," and, borrowing from Kraus' pathos, foreswears the prospect and desire for fame. "Never now and never ever," Jakob says, "is one ever going to achieve great things with feelings of the kind with which I face the world, excepting if one lets the greatness that glitters go hang, and designates as great whatever is wholly gray, silent, hard, and lowly" (*JvG*, 445).

Jakob actualizes the precepts of the Institute Benjamenta in his acceptance of insignificance. This is one outcome of the isolation and incubation he entered upon in the school. The material form of the subservient role for which the school trains its pupils is reflected in the change in Jakob's attitude toward money. Initially he craves money as a symbol of power (*JvG*, 335) and as the medium for satisfying his hunger for experience (*JvG*, 355). Thus he complains of the strictures imposed by poverty and pleads with Benjamenta for a job that will enable him to earn money; he promises always to revere him if he will thereby alleviate the aridity of life at the school. "God himself," he says, "commands me to go out into life. But what is God? You are my God, Head Master, if you allow me to go earn money and esteem" (*JvG*, 390). Shortly thereafter and immediately before the Kraus entries, Jakob reports a revery of himself as a rich man (*JvG*, 403–405). The first of the dreams and fantasies characteristic of the second half of the novel, it shows Jakob beginning to accept poverty, and reflects his changing apprehension of reality outside the school. In the revery Jakob encounters a man whom he recognizes as an impoverished artist during a night walk through the city. He gives him a princely sum. Then, rejecting the thought of spending his wealth on extensive travels, he imagines taking walks through the fog-filled streets and enjoying climactic squandering of his fortune on "an insanely rich and pleasure-laden banquet . . . and orgies of a kind never before seen" (*JvG*, 404). The spiritual conflict awakened in Jakob as the precepts of the school begin to "take" is indicated in a dream sequence described in the entry before Jakob's account of his visit to his brother's luxurious apartment (*JvG*, 418–420). The sense of the dream repudiates ambition furthered by money. Jakob has become "a completely bad, bad human being" by the unscrupulous destruction of whoever might impede his acquisition of great wealth. The dream objectifies the moral scruples of Jakob's realization that he cannot achieve the success he envisages for himself through disregard of ideals or through others' suffering. Embodiments of "wisdom of life," "child-like innocence," "zeal," and "virtue" that anticipate the dramatization of internal conflict in Expressionism—all of them cowed and debased—make obeisance to a haughty, lustful Jakob, while he feasts at a sumptuous table. Awakening in fear and perspiration after the dream had reached "the border of madness" in the appearance of God, Jakob concludes the entry by asking: "Good God, can't I even hope that some day I'll turn out to be something?" (*JvG*, 417).

The final abandonment of the atavistic force represented by money occurs in the conscious suppression of the thought of money at the beginning of the Croesus-Kraus entry, where the intimation of the traits shared with Kraus underlie the dichotomy of the "regulated" and "uncontrollable" life. "Now I am a Croesus," he says. "To be sure, as regards that precious money—quiet, don't talk about money" (*JvG*, 468). The outcome of this reversal of hope that comes from the acceptance of poverty as well as from the experience of his descent to the passageways of poverty is made clear shortly thereafter. Perhaps more than being a complete sacrifice of the hope for distinction, the passage expresses a denial of worldly power for reliance on the inner resources developed at the Institute Benjamenta. The impassioned tone of this declaration of faith in an undistinguished life marks it as the highest point of Jakob's acceptance.

> How happy I am not to find anything in me that's estimable and remarkable. To be small, to stay small. And if a hand, some circumstance, a wave were to lift me and carry me up to where power and influence rule, I would demolish the circumstances that favored me and myself I would cast down into lowly, meaningless obscurity. I can breathe only in the lower regions.

* Wie glücklich bin ich, daß ich in mir nichts Achtens- and Sehenswertes zu erblicken vermag! Klein sein und bleiben. Und höbe und trüge mich eine Hand, ein Umstand, eine Welle bis hinauf, wo Macht und Einfluß gebieten, ich würde die Verhältnisse, die mich bevorzugten, zerschlagen, und mich selber würde ich hinabwerfen ins niedrige nichtssagende Dunkel. Ich kann nur in den untern Regionen atmen (*JvG*, 472f.).

The final fourteen journal entries in the novel achieve a climax and a provisional resolution that emphasize the symbolic implications of Jakob's existence. The remainder of this chapter will stress the role occupied by the imagination in this conclusion and leave a more detailed discussion of Jakob's relationship to the Benjamentas for the following chapter. We should, however, note now that the dismantling and disappearance of the purgatory of the school is precipitated by the resolution of his personal relationship to the Benjamentas. Jakob sees the two not so much as the advocates and the supporters of the school they claim to be than as its victims. In resolution, Benjamenta recognizes and accepts Jakob as a revivifying force and subsequently proposes that they leave the school and re-enter the world together. For Fräulein Benjamenta, it means her abandonment by Jakob to the death she prophesied for herself. Both of these relationships remain uncrystallized until the resolution of the plot, when Jakob's long-awaited entrance into the real inner chambers inhabited by the brother and sister reveals them as unexpectedly real passageways of poverty.

Jakob was persuaded that, having once penetrated the mystery-laden private apartment of the Benjamentas, he would clarify their mystery too (*JvG*, 373). But his imagination has far outdone what he finds there. Instead of the palatial rooms, the ancient library, the park, the wintry courtyard under falling snow, and the luxurious dinners where elegance and good breeding prevail that he imagined he would find, nothing more than two sparsely furnished rooms, a goldfish bowl in one of them, await him. He wonders what made him expect "anything even remotely magical" in place of a typical Prussian civil servant's dwelling. He scolds "niggardly reality" for having "quasi-stolen" the inner chambers from him. But he acknowledges and accepts this anti-climactic disenchantment and thereby partakes of the knowledge that lay behind Simon Tanner's praise of misfortune as the natural obverse of happiness: the reality of the world resides in the incontrovertible vitality of its insignificant features. Jakob goes beyond Simon Tanner as an artificer, however, since he can integrate a single experience of disenchantment into a bi-polar, self-correcting insight that acknowledges the integrality of the Benjamentas and yet remains personally allusive enough to underline what distinguishes Jakob from both brother and sister. "Niggardly reality," he muses, "what a rascal it sometimes is. . . . It seems that it just plain amuses reality to spread melancholy. It's true, on the other hand, that melancholy is very dear to me, very, very estimable. It's formative" (*JvG*, 461).

Immediately thereafter Jakob's presentiments about the dissolution of the school materialize with dreamlike swiftness. At the time of his undifferentiated acceptance of the school he had termed it "the ante-room to the living rooms and stately halls of expansive life" (*JvG*, 392f.), now there is a feeling "as if one were standing in mid-air, not on firm ground" (*JvG*, 454). "This continual composure and conscious-ness" demanded at the school makes Jakob speak of "the not quite healthy and natural" atmosphere there. "It's as if, any more, we were eating, sleeping, standing alert, giving instruction and receiving it here only temporarily" (*JvG*, 455). Jakob takes the decisive step to free Benja-menta from his self-imposed imprisonment in the school; the principal's sister dies and Kraus eulogizes her before the assembled students; Kraus takes gruff farewell of Jakob, scolding him one last time and warning him to "better yourself, change" (*JvG*, 482); the Head Master effectively pronounces a death sentence on the school by finding employment for the remaining pupils. The tempo of the plot accelerates noticeably after Jakob has experienced the unity in Kraus' sacrifice of self, the ontological permanence of poverty, and the de-poetization of both teacher and prin-cipal in "reality." This acceleration anticipates the resumption of normal time that will follow the resolution of the crisis whose portrayal presup-posed a "timelessness" such as that in the Institute Benjamenta. It is also a narrative device for underlining the force of the decision taking form in Jakob.

As the internal tensions that supported the surreal school dissipate, Jakob is left with the knowledge that the ideals of the school cannot have for him the monistic character they had for Kraus, since for Jakob they represent a part of a personal moral code and not, as for Kraus, historically sanctioned conservative values adhered to as a determined last resort to avoid social extinction. Aware of the anachronism of Kraus' ethics and aware too of the pseudo-mysticism of Kraus' soul-deadening mumbled memorization exercises, to safeguard his imagination, Jakob accepts the school's dicta in a world that rejects Kraus' values except when they are limited as they are at the dilapidated Institute Benja-menta. Thus, aware of and accepting his modernity as Kraus never does, Jakob ultimately sets himself free from Kraus. Yet this separa-tion—an undefined, intuitive act—points to Jakob's symbolic defense of Kraus, specifically, to his defense of a dimension of being under attack from various quarters, among them the traditional defenders of the spirit. Jakob's conditional acceptance of the law at the school remains valid. "If no command, no 'thou shalt' were to rule in the world," he says, "I would die, starve, deform for boredom. Me they really ought to urge on, compel, tutor. That's absolutely the way I like it. In the last analysis I decide after all, I alone" (*JvG*, 356).

Jakob balks when the school presumes to dictate to the imagination.

Although he agrees with the emphasis the school places on social bearing, he struggles unsuccessfully to accommodate himself to the inner rewards promised for good behavior in the pamphlet "What are the aims of the Benjamenta School for Boys." In the entry immediately following the Kraus divination Jakob contemplates the abandoned garden behind their building. Pupils are forbidden to enter it and encouraged instead to cultivate the "flowering garden" of "good conduct" prescribed in the pamphlet. The impulse Jakob feels—and rejects—to tend the real, overgrown garden is the spark and the license for the imaginative extension of the pamphlet's dicta that reveals them as empty rhetoric. The imputed riches available to the pupils in this manner is the object of the parody of the rules of the Institute Benjamenta that result from Jakob's ironic acceptance of them: "And in my paltry school-boy opinion there is some truth in the tidy precept" (*JvG*, 412).

Two further fantasies from the final third of the book, one showing Jakob in the role of a victorious mercenary in northern Italy in the fifteenth century (*JvG*, 436–438), the other a projection of what the life of a foot soldier under Napoleon would have been like (*JvG*, 463–466), reveal the gradual acclimatization of his ambitions to the precepts of the school. They also illustrate the belief nurtured by this imagination until the end of the novel: "I can still make anything at all of myself" (*JvG*, 469). The increasing reliance on subjective imagination thus expressed supplants the attainment of a rationally directed life. This process parallels the sacrifice of individuation that the writer of the journal associates with knowledge won intellectually. Early in the book this motif is expressed in Jakob's words: "What good are thoughts and ideas to a person, if he feels, as I do, that he doesn't know what to do with them"(*JvG*, 352). Later, between the Kraus entries and the visit to the passageways of poverty he says: ". . . basically I despise all my powers of reasoning. I esteem only experiences, and as a rule these are totally independent of all reasoning and comparisons" (*JvG*, 417f.). The subordination of this intellectual individuation is achieved in the entry contemplating the prospect of a Kraus-life: ". . . I feel no anxiety about myself . . . I don't even respect my own ego at all, I merely see it, and it leaves me quite cold" (*JvG*,472).

Yet it is in the realm of imagination that Jakob is exposed to the most profound disappointments. As with the real "inner chambers," he nearly always senses mystery, magic, and enchantment in what he does not know. Shortly after arriving at the school he says: "But perhaps I will indeed one time penetrate into these inner chambers . . . I know, somewhere here there are wondrous things" (*JvG*, 348). Similarly he is inclined to make a sorceress of Fräulein Benjamenta (*JvG*, 427) and to believe Benjamenta "a deposed king" (*JvG*, 435). His initial enchant-ment with the world is a continuation in Jakob of "the viewing of the world as a continuous miracle" that Christian Morgenstern singles out as a characteristic element in what was probably Walser's second novel (See Chapter Two, Note 1.). It is an enchantment necessary to break through the protective and isolating private imagination that, in varying degrees, distinguishes all three novel protagonists and facilitates their entry into or—more accurately—their encounter with the world. Jakob's development at the Institute Benjamenta shifts the focus of his disen-chantment. Through the impact of "trivial" realities such as the interior of the Benjamentas' apartment and the repeated, insistent premonitions of defeats to come, Jakob is deprived of a magic that distorts reality. He is forced to sacrifice a glorious dominion so he can secure in this world the being that owes its existence to the original enchantment. Jakob, proceeding through the reality of disillusions, discovers the magic of the vitality inherent in the lowly, the unpretentious, the real, and the diurnal. This process requires a humanizing of mythic forces, which when used by Walser takes the form of the apprehension of man's dispossession in a modern society. The unabating concentration on the hero in Walser's novels is the literary expression of this apprehen-sion. The poetic vision of the novel does not terminate in the blind alley of the Institute Benjamenta; it goes on to delineate the prospect of transition in a morally ambivalent age. For this Jakob abandons his noble heritage and insists steadfastly on his cultural and intellectual minority: "I hold licentiously fast to this one thing, one thing, that I am petty, petty and worthless" (*JvG*, 469). The single liberating factor in this disavowal of modern society is an irrepressible imagination that continues to work after Jakob's disillusions. Even as Jakob relates his disenchantment at the reality of the Benjamentas' apartment, he sponta-neously enlarges on what he supposed lay behind the doors he has since passed through. The final, conclusive act of imagination in the novel is the dream in the penultimate entry of the book. It envisions Jakob's acceptance of Benjamenta's proposal that he and Jakob leave the school together. As an analysis of the past and prophecy of the future it verifies the primacy of imagination in Jakob.

The dream occurs while Jakob and Benjamenta watch at the dead teacher's side. The vision casts rays of illumination on Jakob. Time and place are dissolved, scene follows scene, "now the dream rolled on," Jakob writes, "as if it were a carriage, section by section" (*JvG*, 490).

Benjamenta has not only been lifted from the self-imposed isolation of the Institute Benjamenta, he has also regained his lost human nobility, appearing to be a knight who leads Jakob through the deserts of the Near East to India, where they initiate a successful revolution and Benjamenta is made a prince. Jakob is conscious of how "horribly exaggerated" the dream is, but he also senses a joy in living that fills his whole body. "Life," he says, "shone before our far-reaching gaze like a tree with branches and boughs" (*op. cit.*). For "both of us had disappeared forever, or at least for a very, very long time from what one calls European culture" (*JvG*, 490). This insight into the need for a new life divorced from the anachronism of European culture and based on an imaginatively secured human relationship is clear to Jakob's dream consciousness but defies articulation: "'Aha' I thought involuntarily, and, as it seemed to me, rather stupidly: 'So that was it, that!'—But what it was I was thinking then, I couldn't make out. We wandered on" (*JvG*, 490f.).

The knowledge gained in the extra-rational experience of the dream is decisive for Jakob. On awakening from the dream he nudges the sleeping Benjamenta and tells him that he has decided to leave the school with him. Jakob presents in the final entry new, unresolved doubts that arise from his "intellectual capacity." But he suppresses them in the conviction that his future encounter with life will sustain the vigor of his imagination. "This person [Benjamenta] suits me, and I'm no longer going to ask myself why. I feel that life demands agitated flow, and not deliberations" (*JvG*, 492). This decision means that the hero who showed himself so capable of incisive reflection must foreswear intellect as the medium for the comprehension of life. Consequently the journal and the unfathomable riddles brought on by its composition are at an end. In an act of literary irony Jakob cuts himself off from the articulated, literary, and therefore ultimately conscious recreation of his imaginative life to accept the risk of life, and the possibility that hardship and even disaster await him in the world his disillusion has transformed into a wilderness. He enters this ambiguous and imaginary promised land armed only with the hope that this act of self-restriction may point a way toward man's liberation from the sham values of a spiritually ossified society.

> And if I shatter and decay, what is broken and undone? A nothing. The single human being I is only a cipher. But anyway, throw the pen aside now! Enough now of the reflective life. I am going into the wilderness with Mr. Benjamenta. Let's see if you can't live, breathe, be, desire genuine good and do it, then sleep and dream at

night in the desert as well. Aw shoot! Now I want to think about nothing at all any more. Not even God? No! God will be with me. Then why think about him? God goes with the thoughtless.*

Notes

1. The emphasis in Jakob's explanation for leaving his family is more on personal freedom than the vindictiveness often found in the more vehement revolt of the son in Expressionist dramas. Generalizing to Seelig from his memory of a Berlin production of Walter Hasenclever's *The Son* he had attended, Walser said: "Wanting to do battle with eternal laws is a sign of intellectual immaturity" (*Wdgg*, 27).

2. Joachim Benn, writing in 1914, recognized the abstraction of themes from the earlier novels and *Fritz Kochers Aufsätze* to be found in *Jakob von Gunten* (cf. *Benn*, 133). The reaction of J. V. Widmann, the editor who had launched Walser's literary career by publishing his first poems and prose pieces in *Der Bund*, was principally perplexity and annoyance. In a three-part feuilleton on the latest work of his former protégé (*Der Bund*, May 10–11; 11–12; 12–13; 1909), he wrote off what he called an "Institute impossible to begin with," and balked at what seemed the stylistic excesses of "Wildlife, Dreamgod, Luckyboy Walser."

3. Middleton's keen sense of Walser's gift for associative word groups led him to suggest that Jakob's noble name might be a pun on "von unten" (*Middleton*, 416). This conjecture is, however, not supported by Swiss German linguistic usage, where the stress in titled names is on the preposition "von." In standard High German, the stresses would read Jàkob von Gúnten. Walser may, too, have gotten the name from Gunten, a small town near the city of Thun, where he was twice employed for short periods during the Zurich years.

4. Bänziger's remarks on the school appear to be based on a view of the school as a travesty of education. In the context of his presentation (cf. *Bänziger*, 80–83), the references to Pestalozzi and Goethe's *Wilhelm Meister* are makeshift and misleading. But in fact, Walser seems to have acquainted himself with Goethe's *pädagogische Provinz* before undertaking to create his own. According to a journal entry recording a visit to Walser in Berlin on October 30, 1907 by the Swiss author Albert Steffen, Walser was reading *Wilhelm Meister* when Steffen entered. Walser's remarks on Goethe's style in their conversation together persuaded Steffen that Walser was familiar with both the form and the content of *Wilhelm Meisters Wanderjahre* (Steffen's journal entry quoted in *Mächler*, 104–105). In one of the prose pieces written in Biel, the wanderer-narrator refers to the statue of Philipp Emanuel von Fellenberg, the founder of the

---

* Und wenn ich zerschelle und verderbe, was bricht und verdirbt dann? Eine Null. Ich einzelner Mensch bin nur eine Null. Aber weg jetzt mit der Feder! Weg jetzt mit dem Gedankenleben! Ich gehe mit Herrn Benjamenta in die Wüste. Will doch sehen, ob es sich in der Wildnis nicht auch leben, atmen, sein, aufrichtig Gutes wollen und tun und nachts schlafen und träumen läßt. Ach was. Jetzt will ich an gar nichts mehr denken. Auch an Gott nicht? Nein! Gott wird mit mir sein. Was brauche ich da an ihn zu denken? Gott geht mit den Gedankenlosen (*JvG*, 492).

school in Hofwil (Canton Bern) which provided the model for the "pedagogical province" in Goethe's novel.

5. Greven's analysis of the function of this street scene and a later one (*JvG,* 374–376) stresses Jakob's acclimatization to the ideals of the school by ascribing to both street scenes the experience of "humanity in the masses" (*Greven,* 85f., cf. also 74). It seemed more appropriate in a discussion of Jakob's reaction to the school to present the affective frame in which this experience takes hold in him.

6. H. M. Waidson, "Robert Walser," in *German Men of Letters,* ed. Alex Natan (London: Oswald Wolff, 1963), Vol. II, 173–196.

7. Alex Natan, in his introduction to *German Men of Letters,* Vol. II (London: Oswald Wolff, 1963), 8.

8. Thomas Mann's treatment of the same episode in *Joseph and His Brothers* is a persiflage of the Biblical story in Mann's development of the growth of the concept of individuality, whereas Walser uses the Old Testament story to underline Kraus' anomaly in modern society. There is, however, a coincidence of purpose in the attempt by both writers to humanize a myth, principally through linguistic means. Jakob interrupts his thoughts on Kraus to say: "How strange that today one still knows all about such ancient slow-burn and backdoor stories" (*Treppen- und Türensachen*) (*JvG,* 406).

5

THEMES AND VARIATIONS

The discussion of the individual novels has concentrated on the heroes as characters and on their reaction to the spiritual situations in which they appear. In the present chapter we want to amplify the presentation of the novels by comparing the treatment in them of three recurrent motifs—the family, nature, and art—in order to illustrate the specific development in the novels of a theme that is contemporary with their writing, the redefined liberation of the artist.

The recurrence of these motifs in the novels illustrates Walser's preoccupation, from his earliest to his latest work, with a limited range of themes. Middleton mentions the limited objective reference in Walser's work (*Middleton,* 419). Occasionally, the similarity in motif and theme in much of Walser's prose has given readers the mistaken impression of creative lassitude. Walser himself, investigating the range of possibilities and freedom within the thematic limitations of his personal poetic vision, properly emphasized the uniqueness of each work and the independence of its inspiration. Recently, Friedhelm Kemp, the critic and translator, has broadened the perspective from which to view Walser's repetition of theme, referring to what he calls the figurativeness of Walser's language. In a group of essays dealing with linguistic transformations in modern poetry, Kemp says: "Robert Walser's entire work seems to me an actualized proof that one can only extricate oneself from historical or personally inflicted linguistic difficulties by means of a continually active reflection on used, hackneyed language, and not by means of renunciations and reductions."[1] The repetitiousness that Walser defended (cf. "Luise" [*KP*] and "Naturstudie" [*S*]) as a consequence of the unchanging nature of the world, Kemp has thus, by implication, put into historical perspective by relating the thematic and verbal repetitions in Walser's short prose to the nature and justification of art. Our consideration of the three motifs will also show how the novels anticipate Walser's untiring investigation, analysis, destruction, and reconstruction of the esthetic possibility of creativity as well as its ethical implications.

Although the theme of art and the artist is important for Walser's writing in Biel and Bern, it is subsidiary, and in large measure an anti-theme to the theme of nature in the novels. In *Geschwister Tanner* it is a frequent, but marginal motif; it is implied in the theme of nature, but its emergence is impeded by the inconsistently executed but constitutive irony of the narrative mode. In *Der Gehülfe* art is subsumed entirely by the ironic narrative mode, the achievement of which clears the way for Jakob von Gunten's personalized irony. Under cover of Jakob's irony, art reappears in terms that divorce it both from nature and from the family. In illustrating the use of nature as both theme and motif in the first two novels and in suggesting a reason for its near total disappearance in *Jakob von Gunten,* we also prepare for the later discussion of Walser's use of nature in the shorter prose works.

The development of the motif of the family parallels the emergence of art. A significant number of the minor figures in the novels are members of a family to whom the hero is related or with whom he establishes contact. With the single qualified exception of Klara Agappaia's prospective remarriage (*T,* 298), the family is implicitly represented as a disintegrating social unit.[2]

The fragmented depiction of the Tanner siblings in Walser's first novel stands at a considerable remove from conventional, causal narrative exposition and thereby underlines, in the narrative mode, the separate isolation in which all the siblings live. The siblings have no reality as a family; either because of their own insufficiency or because of individual pride that calls the world insufficient, they all purchase whatever happiness they enjoy at the price of social and cultural estrangement. In the quiescent family the siblings represent, they seem unwittingly to ironize the family novel. In Simon's characterization of them, it is their separateness that he emphasizes:

> We live scattered over this round, wide world and that is very good, for we all have the kind of dispositions . . . that aren't much good together for long. We all have a rather difficult manner that would be an impediment if we were to appear among people united. . . . But we love one another as we should.[*]

[*] Wir leben zerstreut auf dieser runden, weiten Welt, und das ist sehr gut, denn wir haben alle solche Köpfe . . . die nicht lange zueinander taugen. Wir haben alle eine etwas schwere Art, die hinderlich sein würde, wenn wir verbunden unter den Menschen aufträten. . . . Doch lieben wir uns, wie es sich geziemt (*T,* 27f.).

The oldest of the siblings and the one with the most tenuous relationship to Simon is the scholar Klaus. Of all the characters in the book, only he and the lady who employs Simon as servant—as the two outspoken adherents of the existing social order—try to persuade Simon of their vision of the world. Behind Klaus' sincere concern for Simon's future is the burdensome presence (*T*, 156f.) all the siblings feel in the face of the older brother's ever-foundering compulsion to effect a bond of dependence with his siblings. In his infrequent meetings with Simon their relationship remains at best an acknowledgement of their incapacity to share one another's world. For Simon, Klaus remains a victim of his own pedantry. Thus he discounts Klaus' admission in a letter to Simon of his loneliness and unhappiness as self pity (*T*, 18). When Simon realizes the futility of writing his brother, he ironically explains this quality in him: "He was one of those people, who out of a need to fulfill duties, hurl themselves into a huge tottering edifice full of disagreeable duties out of fear that a secret, hardly noticeable duty might conceivably get away from them" (*T*, 11).

Simon's relation to his brother Kaspar, the painter, is quite different; he regards his attachment to him as a meaningful substitute for the formalized, impersonal obligations of the ties of blood. Simon respects the painter's resolve to spare his affective energies for his art by calculatedly ignoring the demands imposed in social intercourse by human imperfection. "He didn't like turning his head back to past matters," the narrator says of Kaspar, ". . . he felt looking back on old relationships was harmful" (*T*, 74). Kaspar's inflexibility is apparent in his single long monolog in the novel, in which he tells the excruciating story of his former friend, the unsuccessful painter Erwin (*T*, 51–54). It is seen again in Kaspar's mockery of Sebastian's plan to write a long poem on his own life (*T*, 80), then in his harsh rebuttal of Klaus' well-intended but gauche suggestion that Kaspar study in Italy (*T*, 74–75), in his failure to indicate how, if at all, his emotions are involved in his affair with Klara Agappaia, and, finally, in his decision to sacrifice this liaison out of fear that it might endanger his art (*T*, 93).[3]

The latent hero worship in Simon's relation to Kaspar tells us something of the emotional climate in which the novel was conceived. The source of the affection that eventually overcame Kaspar's hostility to his brother is Simon's sensitivity to the fright and melancholy he once saw in Kaspar's eyes (*T*, 212). Simon acknowledges their separateness and defines their relation in a letter inviting Kaspar to join him at the Agappaias' house. He says: "Actually we are strange birds, we two. We chase around on the face of the earth as if only we lived here and no other people at all . . . we are not brothers at all, but friends

. . . I tell you that it's not at all unlikely that our hearts basically aspire to get away from each other, but simply can't" (*T*, 30). The author's apparent intention to provide Simon with more of the unpremeditated aggressiveness that motivates Kaspar—of whom the author says: "He lacked completely any understanding whatsoever for tragic human beings, or more accurately, he paid them no attention because he understood them too well and too easily" (*T*, 81)—suggests that when Simon imitates Kaspar's moral utilitarianism he reflects the author's portrayal of the struggle, in all three heroes, to release themselves from their inward sensitivity.[4] Simon's admiration for Kaspar's Stendhalian single-mindedness is the basis for the feeling of brutality that the uninhibited enjoyment of nature calls forth in him (*T*, 59); it explains his unsparing resolve that his leavetaking from Hedwig be final (*T*, 180–181) as well as the tenacity of his determination to trample his own memories so he might advance his prospects for service (cf. p. 57). But this is an aspect and not the basic element of his being. A more rudimentary characteristic is described by Hedwig when she says of Simon: ". . . You hardly give the impression of cleverness, much more that of love, and you are aware of how this feeling is judged. . . . Only people who know you will regard you as capable of deeper feeling and bold thoughts, not the rest. That is your center of gravity and the reason you very probably will remain unsuccessful in life . . ." (*T*, 176).

By way of emphasizing the siblings' separate, unshared lives, all of them have disappeared by the end of the novel. Klaus' brief appearance at the beginning of the final chapter only points to the distance between him and Simon by providing an antithesis to the snow-child fairy tale that follows. The failure to portray on the plot level a vital connection between Kaspar and Simon is more apparent following the fifth chapter, when Kaspar disappears from the narrative level of the book. His later whereabouts are revealed only incidentally and confusedly (*T*, 212f.). In the Paris dream, he is seen through the double lens implicit in the dream narrative and the revelations ascribed to Klara Agappaia—as an artist and former lover of Klara, but neither as brother nor as friend.[5]

The tendency in *Geschwister Tanner* to use the motif of a disintegrating family as a basic form of symbolic alienation as well as a backdrop for the hero's search for an order, is nowhere more evident than in the depiction of Hedwig. Typical of the unevenly paced narrative rhythm of the book, the sister's role is confined to two appearances: her participation in the lakeside conversations and Simon's visit to the village where she teaches. Her single long monolog near the end of Simon's visit (*T*, 164–180) depicts a crisis of feeling and identification that establishes her as the Tanner most resembling Simon. Sensing that she is "as if separated from life by a thin but opaque partition" (*T*, 164) and ascribing her unhappiness to the gap between her idealism and the reality of her life as a teacher, she is planning to take work as a governess in a foreign land. Her letter of application, containing what she calls "a view of service that is fervent and at the same time composed" (*T*, 169), is a striking anticipation, in its sacrifice of individualism,[6] of Jakob's analysis of Kraus' fate as a servant. Hedwig's response to the moral dilemma she feels in the contradiction between her pride and her weaknesses (*T*, 165 *passim*) is resignation. She plans, as a last resort if she is not hired as a governess, a loveless marriage to a farmer. In such a union she would hope to find the solitude gradually to stifle the loss of real love along with her own sensibility and humanity. She foresees that one day, as the outcome of this projected emotional and spiritual suicide, she would no longer be able to emotionally tolerate women of the sort she herself had been before, "because I should regard them as dangerous and harmful . . . I should have become like the others and would have understood life the way the others understand it" (*T*, 173).

Simon provides little direct comment on their developing relationship beyond gratitude for the respite the stay in the country gives him and the recognition that he and Hedwig "are no longer living together like blood relatives, but like comrades" (*T*, 147).[7] That the two are distinct, however, is borne out by Hedwig's "death" in the Paris dream. What the brother and sister share is the courage to risk misfortune in the search for personal realization (cf. *T*, 171f.). Underlying Hedwig's dream death are the unstated characteristics that distinguish them. Hedwig accedes to dictates that thwart the process of self-identification. The rigidity and renunciation in her notion of service lacks the spiritual leavening of Simon's wish to "please my fellow men" (*T*, 257). When Simon ironically denies ideals in himself, he privately nurtures the hope that acceptance will not mean self-betrayal; at the same time he attempts, unsuccessfully, to define a bond to the world that will leave him spiritually self-sufficient. The radical isolation of the siblings in the Paris dream explains Simon's description of the dream as "melancholy." And too it accentuates the wistful acknowledgement seen in all the novel heroes that the reassurances a Fritz Kocher receives from his family and milieu are indeed empty.

Whereas Simon's isolation from his siblings and, in particular, the resultant dream death of Hedwig provide Simon with the same freedom which Jakob von Gunten's abandonment of Fräulein Benjamenta secures for this later hero, the figure of Klara Agappaia in *Geschwister Tanner* personifies the promise and the possibilities of freedom as an alternative to the separation of the siblings. Klara is the source and the object of love in the novel. As a central participant in the first phase of the novel; as the solitary inhabitant of the Agappaia house on the edge of the forest in the narrative calm following the lakeside scene until Simon leaves the city to stay with Hedwig; as the sorceress of the dream of Paris whose spectre haunts Simon until he finds her again at the end of an outwardly aimless walk through the city; and as the lodestar that leads him back to what used to be her home in the final scene, she is the most important figure in the novel after Simon Tanner. She is the first of a succession of idealized women in Walser's novels. Found first in the early dramolet "Die Knaben" and in Fritz Kocher's shy ministrations to a countess in the essay "Aus der Phantasie" (*FKR*) that are reminiscent of the early Werfel's "troubador" love, and extending through the ironically etherealized figure in "Ein Flaubert-Prosastück" (*GKW*), the involuted satire of "Ophelia,"[8] and the comic surrealism of "Olympia" (*UP*), they are found as well in numerous further examples from the uncollected prose works of the Bern years.

The amorphousness characteristic of this figure has several sources. At the point of her probable literary conception, she was invested with the mystery and langorous sensuality that defines her as the product of an imagination still under the influence of *art nouveau*. Her development within the novel contrasts with this figure.[9] Initially enjoying economic security as the wife of a scholar, by the time she and Simon meet for the last time she is an unwed mother living in a working-class neighborhood, the spiritual instructress of the poor. Simon's imaginative projection of this present situation in his dream of Paris reflects the widespread desire in pre-World War I Europe for a "reform of life" that followed the less conclusive spirit of reform contemporary with *art nouveau* and that anticipated modern art's more radical statement of the need to effect a revitalization of European culture. A use of lyric exposition as pronounced as that used for Simon, but not including the fantasies and dreams that fill out his character, makes an explanation of Klara's physical movement within the novel unnecessary as the emphasis is on the idealized inner portraiture of her and her relations to the Tanners. There is no explanation of why she fears her husband (*T*, 30), the mysterious scholar, half bugbear, more cuckold, with the "bestial expression in his eyes" (*T*, 45), whom Simon thinks of as "the stupid devil" (*T*, 59). Likewise there is no indication of how her seizure following an agitated evening at the theater (*T*, 94–95) is to be read. Both its resemblance to an epileptic attack and Klara's statements in the comatose state following the seizure invite interpreting the passage as an instance of clairvoyance associated with the "royal illness." Her words are described as incoherent, "curt, fragmented sentences, half sung, half spoken . . . which came up like bells from a far distance, clear and yet hardly audible" (*T*, 94). Finally there is a discrepancy between the figure Simon idealizes and the woman who loved Kaspar. The connecting link is Klara's physical beauty. Simon etherealizes this beauty, associating it with her compassion (cf. *T*, 29, 55, 73) and her magnanimity of sacrifice. Early in the book as Klara enters a restaurant for the poor looking for Simon (*T*, 66–68) is seen the idealization that anticipates and sanctions her later role in Simon's perception. He makes her beauty the testament of a nobility of spirit and the countersign for her entry into this bleak world of the "expelled, hungry and homeless," likening her to a transcendental vision of absolute beauty so far removed from the lives of the people in the restaurant that they grimace at the shock and mythical memory "the noble woman" (*T*, 68) awakens in them. The resultant novel figure lies outside the limits of the novel's realism, and indicates the complexity and interrelatedness of the physical world Walser set out to redefine in his novels without the application of psychological characterization.

Just as the figure of Klara in Simon's dream of Paris looks forward to her as "queen of the poor" rather than back to Kaspar's lover, Klara is more important to the author (and to Simon) as the recipient of the gift of his spiritual love (*T*, 84–86). She is the alternately grateful and repentant author of the letter to Hedwig, which underscores her desire to make good in the gift of her love for Hedwig what she transgressed through her love for Kaspar (*T*, 88–92) and as the "sublimer, distant being, descended from different regions, from a stratum and world different from ours" (*T*, 67) in the restaurant scene, as well as the soliloquistic communicant with nature on the morning following her seizure (*T*, 95–98).

The plot presents three incidents that figuratively describe the process of spiritualization and liberation in Klara. The first is a modern ballet she and her husband attend with Kaspar and Simon. She identifies the art and culture of theater as a part of nature: "But perhaps everything is nature . . . culture can become ever so refined, it still remains nature, for it is, after all, the gradual invention through the ages by beings who will always be dependent on nature" (*T*, 50). The second is the "violent attack" (*T*, 94), a rather too obvious Ophelia-borrowing that is mixed with an overweighted emphasis on the symbolism of Klara's words. Her words are a soliloquy such as a newly harmonized personality conducts after an ascent from the "deep, deep waters" of unconsciousness with a former self. She had languished in her union with Agappaia (the husband's only remark as he and the brothers watch Klara recover from the convulsions, is: "It is not the first time" [*T*, 94].) and suffered guilt in her association with the brothers.

The description of Klara's gradual recovery of speech uses synesthesia to convey the psychic character of the change of personality the attack signifies. For Klara the sonorous violet on her lips is an emblem of an ethic rooted in nature, assuring her a new faith in herself: "Do you hear me ringing?" she asks herself. "It is my violet that is ringing . . . I have always known it. Just don't say it" (*T*, 95). The corroboration of the rejuvenation of her soul through the seizure is given expression in the monolog she addresses to the forest the following morning. Klara feels "new-born"; she says a joyous, grateful prayer to a deistic, indulgent, and modest God who has forgotten his creation. Klara perceives this deity as one that is easily lost to man "if one thinks about him"; he is perceptibly near only in the forest. In the reappearance in her monolog of images from the night before although she is unaware of her attack, she transposes the self-realization incoherently expressed in the "fragmented sentences, half-sung, half-spoken" into her waking life.

Klara is made the visionary medium for a new apperception of the total world as an infinite miracle; Simon's adventures before he promises the manageress to settle accounts with "maternal earth" offer the practical, imperfect example of the apperception. It is Klara's unwitting anticipation of such a role that permits her to say: "One would find everything wondrous, if one sensed everything, for one thing alone can't be wondrous and the next thing not" (*T*, 98). To this woman Simon gives his spiritual love during the evening on the lake shore, but only with the condition that it not be reciprocated. The source of this paradox, the self-fulfilling, selfless love of God's creation that inspires Klara's monolog with nature, remains, for Simon a contradiction in terms because of the still undefined freedom he seeks. Thus, before making his gift to Klara he owns that after growing up "I took the bit of freedom, but I dreamed of experiencing love." Still, he knows that he will never experience this love: "I believe life wants something else of me, has other plans for me. It lets me love every phenomenon that it sends my way" (*T*, 84). To Klara, Simon can make this declaration of absolute allegiance to life since he is willing to invest his own life totally. We see how Walser's vision modified the Renaissance model for his hero. "I place no value on my own life," Simon adds, "only on others' lives, and nevertheless I love life, but I love it because I hope that it will provide me the opportunity to throw it away in a decent manner" (*T*, 85).

One device used to portray Simon's (and, thus, the author's) idealization of Klara is that she is never seen as the young, sensual woman she must be; she is never seen experiencing the force of her own desires, except as they are sublimated during her communion with the forest. For Simon she represents the direction his own path to freedom will follow as he, separated from a family, sacrifices the possibility of personal love to replace it with the love of creation.[10]

Klara disappears temporarily from the action of the novel after an idyllic period in which Simon is able continually to contemplate her beauty and share with her the loss of Kaspar. When Simon finds Klara again after the passage of more than a year, she has fulfilled the role defined by his early idealization of her, as well as her role as prophetess in the Paris dream. As queen of the poor she practises the brotherhood of man (*T*, 294–295). Simon is guided to Klara by sensory affinities that lie beneath the cognitive level of consciousness. After having been reminded of her by a black-clad woman passing beneath his window, Simon wanders through the city streets until—as a sign of their emotional and symbolic bond—he unerringly finds her rooms. Simon's waking sleep-walking is the narrative projection of this bond; Klara's words to Simon provide its verbal correlative. In her welcome to Simon she echoes his own thoughts of her earlier in the day (cf. *T*, 286f., 290f.); when she chides him for ever having tried to forget her she employs similes drawn from the Paris dream. Klara's monolog to Simon in this scene (*T*, 292–298) details the progressive social descent she has experienced since the dissolution of her home following her husband's reversal of fortune. Revealing to Simon that she plans to make a marriage that will enable her to continue to devote herself to the poor, she also reveals the fulfillment of her prayer of gratitude following her liberating attack. Her work among the poor actualizes the reverence of the wonder of all creation in that prayer, and simultaneously carries out the dictum for the conduct of life she had formulated following the theater performance: "If we now love what is closest to us, then we've made a gain that will drive our centuries forward more impetuously, one that allows us to circle along with the earth, filled with thoughts, a gain which will make us live more quickly and sense more blissfully, and one that we therefore have to seize and make use of, a thousandfold, in a thousand moments . . ." (*T*, 50).

As Simon leaves Klara, he is "deep in thought" (*T*, 299); he is preoccupied with her thereafter (*T*, 302), but he never sees her again. He only thinks of her as the "dear, strange woman" when he returns to the Waldhaus. The manageress he finds there, however, is remarkably similar to Klara in the humane dictates she follows. The manageress foreshadows the cointeraction of religion, nature, and art to create "a dizzying, arched, free bridge into a still inexplicable future" (*T*, 313f.), as she fulfills the role in society that Simon ascribed to Klara as muse of the Paris dream. Still more clearly than Klara, she articulates a hope for a utopistic future that will rest on the devotion of humans to the present, but, like Klara, a free agent, she achieves her self-realization in ministering to the needs of what the author has chosen to depict as diverse lower-class family groups (cf. *T*, 310–318). As a surrogate Klara figure, she shows Simon empathetic understanding climaxed by her returning him to nature. What emerges from Simon's contact with both these women and what explains the role they fill as guides, is a pattern of experience analogous to the musical method of retardation. Simon's inability to see himself—even in a dream—as the author of the revelations and the promise of brotherhood in the Paris dream is an early expression by Walser of the moral dubiousness of an avowedly creative career, but it is also a corroboration from the subcognitive level within the novel's narrative of the hero's foredoomed attempt to achieve a freedom that can be put to the service of man. Throughout the first novel it is only a feminine intuitive force, personified as a woman standing above and free of society, that achieves such a synthesis.

Walser's achievement in writing *Der Gehülfe* was a disengagement of his theme of the irresolvable opposition between what Simon terms "the world" and interior being from the realm of symbolic dream and fantasy. He does so by transposing this theme to the realistic world of Swiss middle-class society at the turn of the century. What Walser sacrificed in abandoning the panoramic canvas and private symbolism of *Geschwister Tanner* he more than regained through the art of creative omission and the infusion into *Der Gehülfe* of what the German Romantic literary critic and theoretician, Friedrich Schlegel, termed the irony of love (quoted in *Allemann*, 75). The realistic setting and the uninterrupted development of the spare plot of the novel makes *Der Gehülfe* the most accessible of Walser's novels—even as consistently generous an advocate of Walser as Max Brod referred to it as Walser's most beautiful novel (*Brod*, 386)—yet, it is at the same time the necessary link in Walser's development as the ironist who wrote *Jakob von Gunten* and as the author of the prose pieces that ended the testimony of what Greven has referred to as Walser's "difficult love"* by choosing silence. *Der Gehülfe* stands as an artistic watershed in Walser's early work. It raises the elusiveness of Simon's commitment to a pervasive irony that comprehends the public and the private spheres of the first novel. The correlatives of the "hovering effect" achieved by this irony

* "Die Rekonstruktion eines Werkes," *Neue Zürcher Zeitung*, Nr. 291, October 23, 1965.

are found in the breadth of verbal reference in the language, in the amalgamation in the hero's personality of surface and depth, comedy and earnestness, and, finally, in the theme of attraction to and repudiation of bourgeois society—in the attempt to become part of it and the repeated unmasking of its moribundity.

At the physical and symbolic center of this world stands the family inhabiting the Villa Abendstern, the symbol of the larger family of man that Simon encountered in his final visit to the forest house. When Marti enters the Villa Abendstern he is seeking a spiritual home in this large family united in their common humanity. As discussed earlier, his success is limited to his comprehension of the humanity of the Toblers as it is distinguished from the exterior image of the family, the facade of Villa Abendstern. Only toward the end of the novel is the implication of Marti's search given explicit statement (cf. *Middleton,* 413). While Marti and Frau Tobler sit in the living room, the author transcribes Marti's thoughts: "That was something; that resembled a home. And how often in his earlier years had he walked through busy streets and empty lanes with the cold, evil sense of abandonment in his heart. . . . How the consciousness of not having a home anywhere had been capable of crippling him and suffocating him within! . . . and how barren was the thought of being allowed to participate only in the meager, hardly perceptible reflection of this anciently beautiful goldenness! This beautiful prerogative of the bourgeoisie!" Besides revealing the allegorical significance of Marti's search, these words also reveal the illusion of this hope, for Marti's recognition of his responsibility both to live in and illuminate both sides of the house (*G,* 26) results in his realization of the fateful portent signified by the illusory liaison of two component parts.

Although Marti's "double vision" can penetrate the visual image of this family to discover its redeeming humanity and thereby justify his ultimate acceptance and love of the Toblers, Marti himself is disqualified as an objective commentator on events at Villa Abendstern through the author's use of him as an antithesis to the Toblers for the creation of irony. Marti's moral judgment is, perhaps, more pointed than Simon's, but the silent complaisance deriving from what the author ironically describes as "the obligation . . . to become a familiar part of the strange, cozy scene . . . and favorably disposed as quickly as possible" (*G,* 11), is the price the realism of the novel pays for the disengagement of this new, more wittingly estranged hero from the world of *Geschwister Tanner.* As long as Marti sees the contrast between the Toblers' carefree indulgence in genteel lakeside luxury and his own inability to advance his employer's prospects as an indication of his own personal failure of will or character, or even as unintentional deception (*G*, 6, 10, 57), there are elements for comic irony. This author-directed irony distinguishes the author's involvement with the family from the hero's, from the "assistant conductor" who is "too modest, too satisfied a nature" (*G*, 207). Marti's vision of the heart and the eye safeguards his humanity amid the illusions and the disappointments of Villa Abendstern; it enables him to love the inhabitants of a society which he rejects ethically and which excludes him socially. But it is the author's distance from the events at Villa Abendstern that permits him the freedom for the literary objectification of the ambivalences inherent in the world the novel depicts.

In subordinating himself to the non-valid norms that support the Villa Abendstern, Marti can subjectively perceive the discrepancy between his failure to help Tobler and his more willing performance of services for Frau Tobler. But the sincerity of his commitment and the ironically employed "muddle-headedness" that he laments make it difficult for him to objectify this contrast. Max Brod says Marti "does not want to lead a rationally regulated life, he wants to be ruled over, wants to serve—driven from without and within—wants to do what is inevitable and beautiful" (*Brod*, 386).

Deprived of the ironist's insight, Marti continually criticizes his preference of small familial tasks to what he calls his "duties" to the husband. He fails to realize that those tasks are related to the lives of the Toblers while his employer's inventions—which are presented in a language emphasizing a deception of the public for which they are intended—or even the questionable utility of his employment, are not (cf. *G*, 187). After throwing away the gloss on his "bad habit" (*G*, 197), Marti goes about cleaning the storm windows preparatory to hanging them. While Frau Tobler anxiously watches his daring "hanging-out motions," the narrator ironically notes Marti's view: " 'How very becoming the expression of fear is to this woman' the window-worker thought, and was very satisfied with himself" (*G*, 198). For Marti, these small tasks metaphorically represent his unquestioned identification with this one half of the Tobler home. The narrator of *Der Gehülfe* must supply for Marti the differentiations Jakob does through his self-irony. Jakob's elegant, provocative irony that is akin to Marti's preferment of undeliberated activity is seen from a radically different perspective: "For example what I esteem in myself is the way I open a door. More life lies hidden in the opening of a door than in a question" (*JvG*, 418). A description of Marti's first few hours on a lovely Sunday morning (*G*, 92–94) illustrates the difference between Marti's repeated, hopeful confusion of the two sides of Villa Abendstern and Jakob's unabating, wakeful irony.

Marti's perspective remains distinct from that of the narrator. Marti is shown savouring the Sunday respite from workaday uncertainties. He succumbs to this Sunday "thoughtlessness," dulls his scruples with the sensual pleasure of the attractively prepared Sunday breakfast table set out on the lawn, writes a few business letters after breakfast, is reassured by a feeling of "catching up" and the knowledge that Sunday doesn't count, allows himself to interrupt this "work" while he undertakes a casual inspection of the garden, and thinks to himself that "this evening one would have to give the garden a really good watering once again." "Thinking about that, Joseph felt he was the ideal assistant. Now he carried the glass globe out into the open" (*G*, 94).

This narrative irony is based on the author's knowledge of the transitory nature of Marti's encounter with the bourgois world.[11] Thus Marti sees the lack of a precisely defined area of responsibility as assistant, and the informality of the salary arrangement, less as the condition of his employment, than as the token of his acceptance by the Toblers. The clearest sign of his desire to become a part of the family is his failure to demand the salary that is owed him and that distinguishes him from the family. Significantly, he never thinks of money until he senses estrangement from the Toblers (*G*, 285), and insists on his wages only when he is certain that he will leave (*G*, 310).

At the source of the narrator's ironical objectivity at the expense of the "dumb" hero lies the author's desire to underline the incompatibility of the moral orders represented by Marti and the Toblers.[12] The bond between them is based not in the area of Marti's employment as assistant nor in the hardly more secure social and mercantile premises Tobler himself follows, but on their relation as human beings. On the Monday morning after Marti's Sunday walk through the city, his unacknowledged emotional refractoriness and resistance to a return to a meaningless employment has assumed severe form. Marti himself is aware only of a veritable plague of complications obstructing his arrival at work: uncombable hair, a bar of soap lost under the farthest corner of the bed, a collar that suddenly doesn't fit. The author drily describes these real and fancied perplexities as similar "collar-stories, coat-stories and shoe-stories" (*G*, 151) that had occurred before in Marti's life. Marti turned to his last emotional resort when "He betook himself down to the living room in order to breakfast. He ate immoderately: it was practically indecent. . . . What ever made him so hungry? Because it was Monday? No, he plain lacked character, that was it" (*G*, 151).

Walser is concerned with the paradigmatic hero at the mercy of the uncertainty of his acceptance as it is reflected in his reliance on the heart. He assumes an ironic position of neutrality, as he shows Marti uncertainly pitting his superior moral weight against the presumptive superiority of the "two sided" Villa Abendstern. Marti tears up his "memoires" when he understands how incapable of intellectual dissection his situation is. But the narrator chooses to refer to him as "the assistant so poorly qualified to keep a journal" (G, 98). When the skill Marti has acquired in the manipulation of evasive business terminology fails him in an interview with a prospective investor visiting Villa Abendstern in Tobler's absence, the author feigns surprise: "Was that Joseph who couldn't speak better?" (G, 83). He even examines Marti's "muddlehead-edness" when he rhetorically asks: "Did he then really so dislike his mind, a human being's better half? Was he born to be a woodcutter or a coachman?" (G, 198). This pose of quizzical stand-offishness "diminishes" the hero by consciously separating the narrator from Marti's "poetic" cognition and thus divesting him of "heroic" qualities, but, using the ironic indirection emerging from authorial objectivity it does interpolate in Marti's behalf:

> No, he was not at all without intelligence, as after all no healthy, normal human being is anyway. But there was something in him that preferred physical activity. He liked cross-country walks, climbing mountains, washing dishes. . . . He liked to sweat; on occasion that could be quite revealing. Was he a born brick carrier? Ought he have been hitched up to a cart? In any case he was no Hercules.
>
> Yes, he had mind well enough, if he wanted, but he liked too much to take breaks in his thinking. One day, when he saw a man in the middle of the village who was lugging sacks he right away thought: he would do that too, as soon as Tobler got rid of him. That was in mid-summer.*

Walser does not maintain the position of ironic chronicler through the entire book. He becomes sympathetic observer as Marti's separation from the Toblers approaches. At the same time, paralleling Simon Tanner's retreat to nature, Marti, in a different form and context, becomes allegorically uncommunicative. The greater identification between hero

---

* Nein, geistlos war er vielleicht keineswegs, das ist übrigens nicht so rasch irgendein gesundgeborener Mensch. Aber er hatte so etwas Körperbevorzugendes an sich . . . Er liebte das Gehen über Land, das Steigen auf Berge, das Abwaschen von Küchengeschirr . . . Er schwitzte gern, das ließ unter Umständen tief blicken. War er der geborene Ziegelsteinträger? Hätte man ihn an einen Karren spannen sollen? Herkules war er jedenfalls nicht.

Ja, er hatte schon Geist, wenn er nur wollte; aber er machte zu gern Pausen im Denken. Als er eines Tages mitten im Dorf . . . einen Mann sah, der Säcke schleppte, dachte er sogleich, das tue er auch, sobald Tobler ihn fortjage. Das war im Hochsommer gewesen (G, 198–199).

and author that results from an author-sanctioned "flight to nature," the sort that had previously been ironized (cf. *G*, 166), coincides with a shift of narrative perspective and a decrease in verbal irony. Walser thereby sacrifices some of the crispness of the genre study he implied was part of his intention when he defended the realism of *Der Gehülfe* to Seelig.

The use of irony in the novel extends beyond the amplification of Marti's insufficient insight into his relations to the Toblers. Its function in the novel as a whole anticipates the use of irony in *Jakob von Gunten*, although the semi-omniscient narrator in *Der Gehülfe* works from a broader narrative base. At its affective inception, the critical attitude presumes separation in time from subjective experience. Its apparent re-objectification as verbal irony in *Der Gehülfe* represents an attempt in a literary mode to release society from iron-clad, invalidated conventions and thereby rescue its human rationale. Such a verbal mode of irony is pre-eminently suited to Walser's use since it expresses love and hope in a transparently disoriented world.

The Toblers are viewed not only in their relation to Marti but as representatives of their class and their society. Comic scenes related to the depiction of both Tobler and his wife (e.g. the résumé of the incidents leading to the firing of Marti's predecessor Wirsich [*G*, 33–35], Tobler's celebration of Swiss Independence Day [*G*, 67–71], and the episode of Frau Tobler's reaction to a threatening letter from a former maid [*G*, 121–128]) aim as much at showing the social and psychological milieu which the Toblers inhabit as at character portrayal. The same can be said of a large number of details, such as the impersonal lavishness of the table at the Toblers that Marti inclines to mistake for personal interest (cf. *G*, 27), the description of how Tobler irrevocably terminates Wirsich's unsuccessful pleas to be reinstated to his former position (*G*, 45), or the set pieces on the village on the lake below the Villa, whose inhabitants the narrator calls "the Bärenweilers or Bärenwilers" (*G*, 71–73; 167–169).

The representation of Frau Tobler is somewhat more ambitious and more complex. As a self-proclaimed "dependent woman" (*G*, 86), she tries to reassure Marti (*G*, 85), although neither recognizes that the basis for their relationship lies in the fact that each remains a riddle to the other. Marti unsuccessfully tries to make her the Egeria of his stay at the Villa Abendstern, yet her parting words to him counsel him to continued silence and adherence to the laws of *Weltleben*—her extrapolation from the conduct of domestic life (*G*, 286). At the termination of their relationship, the long drawn-out leave taking from the Villa Abendstern, during which both Marti and Frau Tobler are subject to a shift in narrative focus, Walser's irony reaches its highest, most sovereign form. The two principal figures have each become esthetically and psychologically whole by the very process of irrevocably separating them.

Thus in the laconism of the concluding episodes of the novel, Marti's earlier hesitancy and silence is expanded into the fictional representation of a timeless dialog between the customs and the character of a people and the hearts and minds of its individual members.[13] From this perspective *Der Gehülfe* must be accounted as a literary representation of Walser's Swiss homeland that merits being classified with Gottfried Keller's writings.

Underlying and subsuming the tonal variations in the mixture of comedy and lyricism in *Der Gehülfe* is an irony deriving from the author's effort to represent the ineffable distinctiveness of the elements of the world he is fictionally recreating. The narrator irony, although similar in its awareness of an existential incommensurability, stands in contrast to Marti's "double vision" as it is expressed in his perceptions during the Sunday walk through the city and is more active and manipulative than Marti's passivity. Due to the formal and verbal reconciliation of opposites achieved in the book, it is also more abstract and synthetic than Marti's. The quality of this irony is perhaps more immediately perceptible in the author's depiction of the Toblers' children than it is in the unresolved encounter between Marti and Frau Tobler that concludes the book.

The narrator's extended reflective characterization of the children (*G*, 114–119) describes the distinguishing traits of the two daughters and two sons with an ostensible objectivity whose aim it is to report the inevitable injustice in treatment caused by the fact of the children's individual personalities. Silvi, the black-sheep daughter whose maltreatment is the repeated object of Marti's concern, is the child to whom the author here gives his most incisive attention. She is described as unattractive, a badly-formed image of her mother. She is the most frequent victim of the perverse "training" inflicted by the maid Pauline, "this female from the broader ranks of the folk" (*G*, 119), "who, due to a speech defect, is incapable of articulating an 'l'" (*G*, 114) and calls after her little charge: "Si-vi, Si-vi." Even Marti is more attracted by Silvi's sister Dora, who is "charmingly forthright in her whole personality" (*G*, 115). By contrast, Silvi's character "—if one can speak of such a thing in a child—seems distrusting, and in her soul she seems to be false and mendacious" (*op. cit.*). The narrator is aware of the fact that her chronic bed-wetting is a desparate device to insure herself attention and that the fear silencing and feeding on the child's heart makes it impossible for her to ask for a favor with Dora's irresistible manner, since "in order to be able to request something, one must possess an unbounded, strong confidence in oneself and in others" (*op. cit.*). Ironically aware too of the absence of any familial reassurance—"The child's own mother can't stand her, so it seems natural enough that everybody detests her a little bit" (*G*, 114)—the narrator shows the labyrinth maneuvers that the child will follow as long as there is no recourse to natural affection.

> An abused little urchin like Silvi easily gets to be more and more disagreeable and uglier to look at and put up with from day to day, because a little person like she not only no longer watches her p's and q's, but from a concealed, pained spitefulness that no one at all would think an undeveloped child capable of—even keeps trying to incite the loathing and disgust of people around her by her steadily worsening behavior.*

The culminating image in the section, describing the children as "a very irregular rectangle" (*G*, 118), repeats the nominally objective descriptive style in order to represent the dissolution of this quadrilateral relationship. It also intimates that the separate, distinctive, and irreconcilable fates of the children are metaphorically significant for the Tobler domain. The speculative, ironically abstracting quality in the narrator's description is stressed in the conclusion of the passage: "Now the irregular rectangle shifts, the children disperse, each into its own way and kind, into hours and days and into a child's secret feelings and into the universe all around the Tobler house. . . . Perhaps they even exert a certain weight on the helm steering the Toblers' ship 'Enterprize': Who can know!" (*G*, 119).

Of all the children, it is Silvi to whom Marti's relation is most instructive. Despite his sympathy, he only musters the courage to advocate her case before her mother after interminable postponements, and then is ineffectual. Yet this relation is sustained less by the demands of character psychology or by Marti's incapacity to transform thought into action than by the ironist's manipulation of the hero in order to sustain the theme of irreconcilability. For the author, Marti occupies one pole in the panorama of images that constitute the book. The same basic

---

* Ein verprügeltes Hudelgeschöpfchen wie Silvi wird leicht von Tag zu Tag unliebenswürdiger und häßlicher zum Anschauen und Ertragen, weil sich ein solch kleiner Mensch nicht nur nicht mehr in Acht und Zucht nimmt, sondern sogar aus einem geheimen, schmerzlichen Trotz, den nur niemand einem unentwickelten Kind zutraut, bemüht, durch ein immer schlechteres Betragen den Abscheu und den Ekel der Nebenmenschen stets höher zu reizen (*G*, 116).

narrator perspective utilizes distancing "objectivity" in the description of Marti's meal with Pauline and Silvi, where the narrator ironically assumes the point of view of the maid, as she attempts to "amuse" Marti by heartlessly censuring Silvi's table manners (*G*, 98–101). Despite Marti's relatively early insight into the nature of the Tobler household, the submersion of the hero through narrator irony permits the emergence in Marti of tender and loyal familial bonds to the Tobler home (See *G*, 195, 270), reflecting in him the fundamental ambivalence the book portrays.

The line that traces the hero's withdrawal from the family in the quest for individual freedom parallels the development of irony in the novels from the dichotomy created between Simon's public speeches and his interior life, through Marti's confrontation with the family of man in an intransigent social order, to the relation between Jakob von Gunten and the Benjamentas, where the decisive step to relate freedom of the creative imagination to separation from the family is accomplished. Consistent with the heightened intellectuality and irony in *Jakob von Gunten*, the figures of the brother and the sister who run the school fulfill roles that transcend their development as fictional characters. Yet Jakob's preoccupation with them from early in his stay at the school (*JvG*, 348) until he makes the final entry is shown by the journal's extended articulation of their changing significance for Jakob as both archetypal and private symbols rather than as individuals.

The contrast between brother and sister is a further antithesis in a novel whose unique tone derives from the antithesis between the extreme individualism of the central figure and the theme of depersonalization as it effects the practising artist. Both brother and sister contend for Jakob's affection and loyalty. In this contest Fräulein Benjamenta gains only a temporary victory because Jakob finally sees in her an ideal too far removed from his goal of participation in life. In the resultant abandonment of the sister, Jakob von Gunten accomplishes for himself the release of those forces that in the earlier novel heroes had only partially and intermittently been freed—first through the guidance and inspiration of Klara Agappaia and later through Frau Tobler. The emergence of service as a creative energy is developed in Simon's snow-child fantasy and Marti's employment as assistant and now in the Kraus role. Kraus embodies the perfection of service and thereby affords Jakob a vision of the divine, although it is left to Jakob to investigate and seek to utilize the freedom service can comprehend. Appropriately enough, Lisa Benjamenta is Kraus' consistent advocate with Jakob, yet it is Kraus who steps forth from the circle of pupils surrounding Lisa's corpse to deliver the rhetorical eulogy on the teacher who always told the pupils they "should remain modest and docile" (*JvG*, 480). Jakob promises never to forget either brother or sister (*JvG*, 393), but he leaves the Institute Benjamenta with the brother after the dissolution brought on by Lisa's death and Kraus' departure.

The only active teacher in the school, Lisa Benjamenta unites narrative and ideational elements of Hedwig Tanner, Klara Agappaia, and Frau Tobler. She is not only sister, but the mainstay of a radically fragmented family whose existence depends upon her presence and the reliance of others on her sacrifices. Her beauty is even more ethereal than Klara Agappaia's; it is a beauty which the contrasting figures of speech used to describe it reveal as beauty born of sorrow and separation from the disfiguring vissicitudes of life. When Jakob looks into her eyes he sees "something fearsomely precipitous and profound." "These eyes," he continues, "impress you as so familiar and at the same time so unknown that their gleaming blackness seems to say nothing and at the same time to tell all that is ineffable" (*JvG*, 400). Her eyebrows "are like crescents of a moon against a morbidly pale evening sky, like wounds that pierce all the more for being fine, wounds that cut within."

Jakob, sensitive to the pain of her unhappiness, feels an inner pain while listening to Lisa's prophecy of her own death, although he maintains the exterior composure prescribed by the school (*JvG*, 473). At the same time, he perceives the purity of her spirituality as an estranging quality even within the Institute Benjamenta. Appearing among the pupils during the lethargy of the empty afternoons, she strikes Jakob "as a spirit." "Then," he adds, "it's as if someone were coming from far, far away" (*JvG*, 399f.). Lisa re-introduces the motif of female guide for the hero when she leads Jakob through the passageways of poverty and privation. She carries the magic wand with which Klara Agappaia opens the French windows to show Simon Tanner his siblings. This motif can be traced back beyond the Paris dream to the figure of the remote but erotically alive queen in "Schneewittchen," one of Walser's first works. Jakob's imagination still invests the guide with the staff, as the ensign of royalty and authority, although there still is a decisive difference between this scene and the dream of Klara Agappaia. Having accepted Lisa's guidance and having tried to mollify the wailing wall by his earnest play-acting, Jakob's spirit returns from the passageways undaunted; it is the teacher whose response to the vision is one of disheartedness. As the vision ends Jakob and the teacher are back in the darkened classroom. Jakob writes that she was standing behind him "and she stroked my cheeks, but she did so not as if it were me she had to console but herself" (*JvG*, 431).

For Jakob, the teacher remains the sorceress of the lower passageways and princess of the inner chambers until Jakob undergoes the disillusion of the Benjamentas' real rooms and until he learns that an unhappy love causes Lisa's uncontrolled tears in the classroom (*JvG*, 461f., 473–474). Thus Jakob suffers another disillusion that enables him to redirect his imagination to the perception of the diurnal and the humanly commonplace. "And now?" Jakob concludes after the "princess" has told him of her love, "Fräulein Benjamenta is a delicate, suffering woman" (*JvG*, 475). Yet this "realistic" explanation of her sorrow only subjects Jakob to disillusions necessary for his re-education. It is the symbolic portraiture of Jakob's independence and imaginative self-reliance that dictates his relationship to the sister more than realistic psychology. More important to the structure of the novel is the sense of their separate identities. This is what Jakob himself insistently reaffirms as he begins to relate his descent to the lower passageways, after admitting to himself that he and his guide belonged together: "To sense this, that Fräulein Benjamenta and I were two very differently disposed and situated beings, therein lay happiness for me" (*JvG*, 426). This conscious knowledge in Jakob terminates a process of separation of the novel heroes from female figures whose sexual attractiveness was not acknowledged but who served as muses and regal guides in dreams and fantasies and as spokesman for infallible nature. By the time of the composition of *Der Gehülfe* this motif had left the realm of private symbolism it occupied in *Geschwister Tanner* to be transposed into the divided narrative focus existing between the narrator as ironic observer and the narrator as sympathetic chronicler in the final third of that novel. It is here advanced to the plot level, the most accessible component of any novel.

In the absence of any evidence of intimacy or mutual reliance between brother and sister, Jakob accedes to the role of perceptive confidant Lisa wishes him to fill. But his reserve toward her appeals for sympathy and affection is dictated by his discernment that "the virgin purity of inwardness which is given form in Lisa Benjamenta" (*Greven*, 92) includes an element of evasiveness towards the reality of the world. And it is the purpose of Jakob's journal to demonstrate his successful resolve to forswear this evasiveness. When Lisa unburdens herself to Jakob, his response is calm (*JvG*, 449f., 462f.). She repeatedly wants to be reassured of Jakob's devotion: "Tell me, Jakob," she asks having first hinted at her early death, "are you a little fond of me? Do I signify anything to your feelings, to your young heart." "Do you esteem me?" she asks in a voice so high that it was "already almost stifled, dead" (*JvG*, 448). Before the disillusion that divests Lisa of her magic and her imagined royalty, as well as in his reaction to her death, Jakob's

Robert Walser in about 1898, while he was living in Zurich.
Photographed on a visit to Biel.

The villa *Zum Abendstern* near Wädenswil on the lake of Zurich.
Walser worked here for the engineer Karl Dubler in 1903.

Robert Walser in 1905, shortly before
he wrote *Geschwister Tanner*.

Robert Walser in Berlin in 1909.

Robert's brother, the artist and stage designer Karl Walser.
The photograph, taken during Karl's stay in Berlin,
first appeared in a Swiss magazine in 1912.

Lisa Walser, Robert's older sister. A Christmas
photograph made in Biel in 1901.

Robert Walser on a walking tour with Carl Seelig
in Eastern Switzerland.

Robert Walser as a patient in the sanatorium
at Herisau in 1949.

words to her and his thoughts about her indicate that his experience of and reaction to Lisa closely parallel his experience of Kraus. That is, as an acknowledgement of a subconscious stratum of idealism that does not bear overt expression and that is protected by irony when it is articulated. Jakob's single declaration of devotion and loyalty to Lisa Benjamenta, along with his self-incriminating admission to her of sins of commission and omission and his expression of gratitude to her for deflating his earlier arrogance (*JvG*, 452–454), is marked by a slight inflation of diction that identifies it as the declaration of an inveterate ironist. Jakob himself says when he records the experience, that if Lisa's thoughts hadn't been elsewhere he would never have ventured to make the speech. It is probably accurate to say that this credo is by its nature not meant to be heard. Certainly Jakob's denunciation of "hateful life" in this speech (*JvG*, 453) and his claim to "despise life" (*op. cit.*) show a complaisance not evident in Jakob's character and convictions. While the speech acknowledges woman's ideal didactic role, her confident reliance on her instincts, and her unwillingness to face life alone, the recklessness of Jakob's rhetoric is the ironic expression of Jakob's awareness that he has to sustain himself in life as a woman is unable to do. Jakob's irony as he expresses it toward Lisa, shows that a clearer vision and a broader range of experience than that accessible to the teacher, comes from insisting on self-awareness. His speech to Lisa represents a thematically consistent realization that his own path will be determined by the irrevocability of his commitment to replace the "illusions" of the idealism of inwardness with the need to respond to the infinite complexities of a world divorced from ideals.

The metaphoric character of Jakob's decision to favor Herr Benjamenta over Lisa Benjamenta is prepared for in his own repeated juxtaposition of the brother and sister. He undermines his own joy at the response his *curriculum vitae* elicits in Benjamenta by wondering whether he is insane to feel so happy while his teacher is in tears (*JvG*, 381). (Actually the *vita* contains an implied denial of Lisa in Jakob's resolve to face life at whatever cost.) After Lisa tells him that she will die and urges him not to tell her brother anything, Jakob says: ". . . I'll obey teacher and will keep silent about her story. To be allowed to obey her! As long as I obey her, she'll be alive" (*JvG*, 463). The brother and sister are most clearly presented as alternatives as Jakob, leaving Lisa after having listened to her tell why she will die, enters Herr Benjamenta's office, even though he considers his principal a starving beast of prey. "On the one hand a maiden's lament and corpse," Jakob notes, "on the other hand her brother, who doesn't seem to have lived yet at all." The contrast is stressed again in the final words of the same entry: "Now into the business office. The poor teacher!" (*JvG*, 475).

The relegation of Lisa Benjamenta to an area of safety and innocence separate from life is also evident in the sections describing her death and the reaction to it (*JvG*, 478, 481, 486). Viewing her corpse, Jakob says: "Something like smiling forgiveness for every sort of fault seemed to hover and resound quietly in the living room" (*JvG*, 486). Because of her remoteness from life, Jakob felt there was "nothing, nothing at all uncanny" about her death (*op. cit.*). The final reference to her occurs in the climactic dream related in the penultimate entry, the event that persuades Jakob to leave with Benjamenta. Here her symbolic portrayal is consolidated by distinguishing her from the rational intellect. Greven identifies the beautifully naked girl in an Alpine setting that Jakob sees in the dream as a personification of the "innocent unity of 'art' and 'nature'" (*Greven*, 95). The happiness engendered in Jakob by the girl's beauty in the natural setting is inhibited until he finally bans the memory and knowledge of Lisa Benjamenta from the realm of speculative thought: "We have no teacher any more," Jakob reflects. "Well, then it was just somebody else, and I saw, as it were, how I consoled myself . . . : 'Ah bah, stop the analysing'" (*JvG*, 490).

Just as the irony presented by Jakob's more precise knowledge of the divergency of life leads to the inevitability of Lisa Benjamenta's death, it is the irony clothing Jakob's indomitable affection for Benjamenta that leads toward a revival for this slumbering giant and encourages him to wrest back his birthright of human nobility that he "abdicated" when he came to the Institute Benjamenta (*JvG*, 487). In contrast to the fragile beauty of the sister, which "almost forces one to gaze into something so difficult and so threatening" (*JvG*, 400), Benjamenta presents more of a challenge to Jakob as he trains himself to master problems in the world outside the school. He presents a perplexing mixture of a fairy-tale ogre of frightening power and an abject human being whose rescue through a return to life it is Jakob's mission to effect. Initially, Benjamenta presents Jakob with a human mystery as intractable as Lisa's. Despite the gruff, peremptory treatment he shows Jakob (*JvG*, 340, 346–347, 364f.), his withdrawal into the business office to brood behind a newspaper, and his repeated representation as fearsome giant ("Herr Benjamenta is a giant, and we pupils are dwarfs compared to this giant . . ." [*JvG*, 345; cf. 470–471].), Jakob is soon inspired by the ambition "to possess this man's nascent confidence" (*JvG*, 373). While Jakob's rather formalized adulation of Fräulein Benjamenta has its source in the ambivalence of his reaction to his own somewhat abstracted representation of the teacher as the personification of feminine soulfulness, he almost immediately (*JvG*, 346) senses in Benjamenta unused human capacities that spur him to elicit a human response from him. Even though early in the journal he notes a physical threat from Benjamenta after only limited experience of the school, Jakob undertakes an exploratory entry on Benjamenta—this self-styled former king—to discover what it is that attracts him about this "certainly noble and clever man," whose life is so "horribly lonely" (*JvG*, 373). Jakob writes that "one senses this man has behind him severe misfortunes and reverses, and it is this humanness, this near divineness that makes him handsome" (*JvG*, 372). Jakob effects a bond with Benjamenta through his effrontery in the *curriculum vitae*, then through the relentlessness of foolhardy provocations such as the demand that Benjamenta find him a job (*JvG*, 389–390), and finally through "trifling questions" (*JvG*, 373) to him. All show Jakob instinctively rebelling against the solipsism of the Institute Benjamenta. But whereas Jakob bases his bond with Fräulein Benjamenta on their dream-like descent to the lower passageways, he achieves his bond with Benjamenta by withstanding a realistically depicted test of character that comes when his principal admits his preferment of Jakob (*JvG*, 421–422). Describing the conclusion of this test, Jakob writes "Both of us, the bearded man and I, the boy, looked one another in the eye. It was like an internal contest . . . And now I noticed that the massively built Principal was trembling slightly, ever so slightly" (*JvG*, 422).

This relation, ensuing after Jakob thus demonstrated his courage before life's incalculability, retains paradoxical features until the end. Jakob's private reaction to the breakthrough the "outpost skirmish" had promised is a paroxysm of emotion in which he feels a pre-cognitive communion with a fellow man: "I felt as if I were at home. No, I felt as if I weren't yet born, as if I were swimming in something prenatal. My eyes got hot and my gaze became marine-blurry" (*JvG*, 423). Although Jakob thereby completes a phase of his education, he continues to treat Benjamenta with coldness (*JvG*, 423), with the irony of a reserve whose function it is to remind his master to respect his own dignity as well as Jakob's (*JvG*, 476–477, 488f.), and with a sovereign comedy that makes of Benjamenta "this lion in the cage" (*JvG*, 485) whom he fears and whom he will liberate. Yet the irony and the comedy only complement the precarious nature of Jakob's commitment to Benjamenta and his abandonment of the teacher. Jakob himself senses the risk he has assumed when he says that he reveres Benjamenta "more than anything, to my regret, to my regret" (*JvG*, 381). Jakob thereby realizes the wish of the two previous heroes to serve their fellows with what he has learned from Kraus. The simultaneity of fear and affection that Marti felt towards Tobler has been heightened in Jakob's reaction to the more schematic figure of Benjamenta. Likewise, the actualization of Simon Tanner's snow-child fantasy through the rescue of Benjamenta illustrates the transmutation of symbolic images in the novels by amplifying an irony in which humanity is the constant behind the heroes' subjective individualism.

Whereas the correlative in Jakob of a reality composed of complementary elements is his ironic perception of fear and affection, in Benjamenta it takes the form of the sudden alternation between omnipotence and tenderness. After Benjamenta's admission—in the critical interview with Jakob—that "there is something significant about you, Jakob" (*JvG*, 422), his affection grows apace. He regards Jakob as if he were a "younger brother or something else naturally-close" (*JvG*, 435). At the same time he warns Jakob of the savageries that seize him; he admits that he is dependent on Jakob and that his loss would be a mortal loss to him, since, "for the first time I love some one" (*JvG*, 457). But Benjamenta reminds Jakob that he could, were he so inclined, crush him like a worm. The emergence of the force of love in Benjamenta is too sudden an alchemy for his soul to dissolve the hate (*JvG*, 484) that caused him to withdraw to the Institute Benjamenta. Jakob is both the medium and the object of his love—a gift, in Benjamenta's words, sent "from heaven" "by an omniscient God" (*JvG*, 484); but he is also the victim of this residue of hatred when he is attacked and nearly strangled by Benjamenta (*JvG*, 470–471).

The dream during the death watch with Benjamenta—a dream described as falling from the heights—resolves the novel as a disillusion of disillusion. Following the appearance in the dream of a naked girl who is "mistaken" for the teacher, the dream projects Jakob and Benjamenta's re-entry into the world through a journey to biblical lands and hence to India with Jakob as vassal to Benjamenta. In the dream the "noble" Benjamenta is seen utilizing his human capacities as he had not done during the somnolence of his directorship of the school (cf. *JvG*, 346). The flight from "European culture" is consistent with the training of the school for unreflective service, as a safeguard for existence in a society whose nominal values are inimical to being. The resolution of the novel in a dream, rather than in an identifiable society, and the simultaneous fulfillment of Benjamenta's hope that together he and Jakob could "do well in something like a bold, adventurous, exploratory undertaking" (*JvG*, 477) reiterate the ontological truth ascribed to the insight of a dream life. Jakob's resolve to terminate completely the interregnum of the Institute Benjamenta by putting aside his pen and with it the primacy of intellect suspends the intelligence responsible for the journal. This decision complements the resolution of the plot in dream at an abstract, conscious level. Putting a stop to writing corroborates for Jakob the primacy of unpremeditated existence in contrast to the denaturalization Jakob identifies as the result of intellectualism. It also shows that the liberated creative imagination had finally become articulate in Jakob von Gunten who sought a vehicle for this imagination separate from traditional literary forms and expression.

As the most radically fragmented family group in the three novels, the Benjamentas are isolated within the Institute Benjamenta and from each other. This isolation is a result of the contrast between the feminine idealism and the male vitalism they symbolize. At the same time the suspension of their reality as related persons is illustrative of a shift within the novels in the role of the family. Primarily a symbol of confinement and of the ineffectuality of the past in *Geschwister Tanner*, in *Der Gehülfe* the sociological family is ironically dissolved in order to preserve the identity of its individual members in the larger family of man. In *Jakob von Gunten* the family is reduced to one motif among others, against which the hero tests himself and, though less overtly, tests as well the possibility of creativity, by the practise of an art that is unburdened by the odium Walser attached to art as the agency of cultural exclusiveness. Through the novels the motif of the fragmented family becomes more and more clearly the symbol of cultural suspension, the acceptance of the alienation that is the precondition for the re-evaluation of values.

Art and Nature

The themes of art and nature and their antitheses figure importantly in Walser's entire oeuvre. The development of their relationship within the novels anticipates his preoccupation with nature in the years in Biel from 1913 to the end of 1920 as well as the marked diminution of nature as motif during the final phase of Walser's career. Both themes also provide the basis for some of the work written before the novels. The prose piece "Der Wald" in *Fritz Kochers Aufsätze* (*FKR*) serves as a paradigm for the perception and celebration of nature. The description of the forest as a living organism which antedates European civilization and which, in a relatively short time, could re-cover Central Europe "if civilization receded" (*FKR*, 100), symbolizes the destructive antagonism between nature and civilization. As a catalyst for a paean to a lost unity, the writer concludes his description of the character of the forest with the hope that he will at least once be able to reproduce the forest's tranquility in his own writing: "I can't quite describe what I love as tranquilly as is necessary. Perhaps I shall yet learn to master this conflict of feelings" (*FKR*, 119). A story from the same collection entitled "Der Maler" tells of a Nietzschean conflict between the demands of life and of art. Typical of Walser's work to the end of the Berlin period, the figure of the painter permits a more straightforward treatment of the problem of art than do the novel heroes. Filling out the view of nature in "Der Wald" as a model for a writer's prose, the painter says that his landscapes and portraits have no representational aim, but instead seek "to render truest nature" (*FKR*, 79). The artist of the story avoids excessive contact with external nature since, as he says, it "would positively cripple my desire to produce" (*FKR*, 80. For another contemporary use of this motif, see the figure of Adalbert, the artist in Thomas Mann's *Tonio Kröger*). Instead he creates "a second nature" in his memory, from which he paints. These two instances selected from a great variety of treatments of both art and nature in the work preceding the novels indicate an interrelation between the two spheres that somewhat alters their traditional antithesis. In the novels this interrelation takes the form of the relegation of the creative capacities to the realm of nature as a medium which incorporates a visible transcendence. None of the heroes is permitted the development of creative gifts, although all three possess the artist's discriminating analysis that can organize the vision of the mind, the heart, and the eye into language. These talents are ignored, suppressed, or, in Jakob's case, disavowed.

The uniquely personal cast of the treatment of the ambivalence toward art as it develops in the novels, in contrast to "Der Maler," relates Walser to the widespread ambivalence toward the calling of the artist in European writing after the turn of the century. Indeed, the figure of the sentient observer as creator and the question of the possibility of creativity lie at the core of Walser's writing and unify it as no other theme does. Max Brod is very likely correct in his belief that it was the absoluteness of Walser's calling as an artist that ruined the man (cf. *Brod*, 384). Historically the beginning of Walser's career coincides with the beginning of an intellectual and cultural epoch in which the dominance of industrialized society was great enough to force on writers an acknowledgment of their cultural isolation, whether it was expressed through the defensiveness of a regionally-oriented literature, the presumptive cultural leadership that emerged as Expressionism, or the isolation of the self-proclaimed elect. As an artist Walser accepted this isolation as a pre-condition of his own creation. His pre-novel artist figures are subject to a similar isolation—be it the figure of Oskar, whose longing for the medium to express his sense of communion with the universe in the early dramolet "Dichter" (*KGS*) lacks an immediate social context, or the parodistically viewed poets in two of the "Sechs kleine Geschichten" (*KGS*), originally published in 1901 (*Die Insel,* II, Bd. 4, 217–233). In the remainder of his career Walser's abiding anthropological concern was to inquire whether an artistic existence in which isolation was equated with freedom was still viable in human terms and whether such an existence had meaning beyond the realm of the culturally elect. With the creation of the novels and their subordinate heroes Walser goes beyond the historically conditioned awareness of the vulnerability of the artist by positing an existence all the more vulnerable for the absence of art. This distinguishes Walser from the more general reaction of a literary generation that transformed their experience of the despoilment of nineteenth-century ideals into classical statements on the ambivalence of art such as we find in Hofmannsthal's "Lord Chandos Letter" (1900), Thomas Mann's *Tonio Kröger* (1903), and Arthur Schnitzler's *The Green Cockatoo* (1899). Walser sought to find an alternative for the invalidated idealism in a broadly understood concept of the nature he regarded as the common denominator in all epochs of civilization. Taken as a whole, his work represents a courageous inquiry into contemporary man's inability to effect such a substitution. Post-Nietzschean expressionistic literature in Germany promulgates a New Man rooted in his stark humanity and inimical to the persona of the artist. While the occurrence of such a protagonist in German Expressionism was frequent enough to assume the proportions of a sociological phenomenon, such figures are distinguished from those in Walser's novels by his thematic reiteration of the vulnerability of the central figures.

The presentation of nature in the novels correlates with the emergence of the heroes' freedom. The depiction, the reliance on, and the definition of nature alters as does the degree and the utilization of this freedom. In *Geschwister Tanner* nature represents a supporting and sustaining universal that subsumes mankind, his civilization, and his art as a guarantor of their durability and continuity. When Klara is moved by the symbolism of the modern dancer, she uses a figure of nature as the touchstone for the comprehension of a new age and its demands. Simon explains his admiration for painting as an art form by the immediacy of the wellsprings of nature in painting (*T,* 112–113). The Paris dream "explains" Kaspar's abandonment of Klara as the fulfillment of his inevitable obligation to nature. The manageress' prophecy of a better future for mankind is based on the proposition that nature be taken as a model.

The most important functions of nature in this novel, however, are to communicate by analogy the amplitude of Simon's character, to provide an objective correlative for the alternation of speeches and reflection with dreams and fantasies, and to objectify symbolically the realm to which he returns at the conclusion of the novel. Both the range of the author's descriptions of nature and Simon's perceptions and musings on nature sketch a broad, stylistically pluralist nature that reflects the catholicity of Simon's ambition for experience. The correlatives of his ambition are found in features such as the interplay of light and dark, of colors, or of sky and water; the double perspective that includes distant and nearby scenes; the outlining of a space filled with unseen objects by noting sounds from widely separated sources; and descriptions of woodlands.

The organizing perception of nature in Simon that permits its expansion to include human beings is the paradox of nature perceived as energy and peace. This conceit may be found as early as "Der Wald," but it is refined in the novels into such details as the projection of Benjamenta as restless adventurer in the tranquility of Jakob's dream. In *Geschwister Tanner* repose in nature is expressed in the descriptions of nature which are intermingled with reflections about time. For Simon the passage of time in nature is the paradoxical proof of its permanence. The degree of his identification with nature (cf. *T*, 113, 158f.) attests to his hopeful trust in his own subsistence. In his first conversation with the male nurse he compares his own reluctance to leave his homeland with nature's eternal return. In his refusal to imitate the nurse's concept of freedom as symbolized in travel and in his reiteration of the freedom to be found within the mobile permanence of nature, Simon evinces the defiance that in the person and writing of Jakob become the objectification of art as his own "second nature."

> Well then, does nature go abroad? Do trees travel, so as to outfit themselves with greener leaves somewhere else and then come home and boastfully make a show of themselves? Rivers and clouds move, but that is a different, deeper going off that doesn't ever return. And it isn't a going but only a flying, flowing repose.*

A similar perception is expressed in the introduction to the snow-child fantasy, where the passage of time in nature suspends Simon's consciousness of his failures.

> Winter came. Strange: time left behind all one's good intentions just as easily as the bad qualities that one couldn't master. In this

---

* Geht denn die Natur etwa ins Ausland? Wandern Bäume, um sich anderswo grünere Blätter anzuschaffen und dann heimzukommen und sich prahlend zu zeigen? Die Flüsse und die Wolken gehen, aber das ist ein anderes, tieferes Davongehen, das kommt nie mehr wieder. Es ist auch kein Gehen sondern nur ein fliegendes und fließendes Ruhen (*T*, 255).

movement of time lay something beautiful, something dispossessing, something forgiving. . . . Simon loved the seasons' swift movement above him and when, one day, snow fell onto the dark, black alley, the forward movement of eternally glowing nature gladdened him.[*]

This expansion of the perception of nature can be seen in the description of the arrival of spring (*T*, 33–34), in the languorous and self-enclosed description of evening that introduces the conversations on the lakewide (*T*, 70–71), and—anticipating the scenic narrative technique of *Der Gehülfe* and the fragmented imagism of the single entries in *Jakob von Gunten*—in the panoramic, cartoon-like description of the Sunday morning when Simon encounters the male nurse (*T*, 251–253). Each of these three descriptions reproduces the energy of nature by activating the scene with passersby or strollers. This transposition of the energy and rhythm of nature into the activation of street scenes recurs in both *Der Gehülfe* and *Jakob von Gunten;* it represents the earliest instance in Walser's work of the synthesis of movement and imagination. In the work following the novels, in Biel and in Bern, an unusually large number of prose works take as their subject matter a walk narrated by the walker himself. In them an increasing abstraction of nature is discernible to the point where the wanderings have become interior perambulations, recordings of interior movement at varying tempos. Although the motif of the solitary walker is only implicit in the novels as a metaphor for the three heroes' isolation, the symbiosis of imagination and energy patterned after nature occurs in the fantasies of each of the three heroes. While the central fantasies or dreams of the "subordinate" heroes are inspired or guided by idealized female figures whose presence comments on the meaning of their subordination (Klara in the Paris dream, Frau Tobler in the lake reverie, and Fräulein Benjamenta in the lower passageways), this more rudimentary symbiosis issues from the dreamers themselves and symbolizes a hope for the exercise of creativity outside the formal realm of art. This correlates the successfully elicited animation found in the opening scene of the Paris dream before Klara appears in it, in the nocturnal movement of the boat on the lake that Marti transposes into the climactic apotheosis, in Jakob's dream of himself as a soldier in Napoleon's army (*JvG*,

---

[*] Es wurde Winter. Merkwürdig: die Zeit ging über alle guten Vorsätze ebenso sicher hinweg wie über die schlechten Eigenschaften, deren man nicht Herr werden konnte. Es lag etwas Schönes, Hinwegnehmendes und Verzeihendes in diesem Gehen der Zeit . . . Simon liebte dieses Rauschen der Jahreszeiten über seinem Kopf, und als eines Tages Schnee in die dunkle, schwärzliche Gasse hinabflog, freute er sich des Fortschrittes der ewigen, erwärmenden Natur (*T*, 306).

463–466), and in Jakob's commentary on the mobility of fantasy in the concluding dream: "Apparently to please me, the dream now rolled on, section by section, as if it were a wagon" (*JvG*, 490). Similarly an emotional and structural link exists in the minimal distinction between interior and exterior vitality in Simon's dreams and his experience of life in the streets, in Marti's Sunday walk in the city, and in the reflection of Jakob's earlier perception of life on the streets of the metropolis to be found in the form apprehension takes in the sequence of scenes in the lower passageways.

Conversely, the climate in *Geschwister Tanner* and *Jakob von Gunten* is not congenial for artists. The unrealized synthesis between art and nature in *Geschwister Tanner* is reflected in the fact that the artists in the book are marked men whose common bond is the experience of pain that underlies their artistry. When, as in Kaspar's case, the relation to nature has become the objectivized one of the creator rather than the symbiosis with nature of Klara and Simon, the tendency is to minimize Kaspar's resolution in favor of a perspective that emphasizes the symbolism of irresolution. This seems generally to be the case both with regard to the original deletions in the manuscript and those made before publication of the novel. It is specifically the case in a deleted letter Kaspar wrote Simon after the painter had left the city and Klara. Again, Walser seems here to have been guided by a sure instinct for having the novel as a whole reflect the dominance of nature over art. In this deleted letter Kaspar writes of himself: "Nature, and you, and Klara as well are now everything to me." This may indeed have corresponded to an earlier conception of Kaspar, but the statement is inconsistent with the figure in the published novel. When Klara looks into Kaspar's eyes, she feels sudden pain, as if she "saw them wounded by splinters" (*T*, 74). Kaspar says of his friend Erwin, the painter with a "birthmark across his entire face" (*T*, 54): "To love nature the way he does must be anguish, and it is a disgrace; for a reasonable man won't let any object fool, dupe, and torment him for long, even if it be nature" (*T*, 51). The young, dissolute poet Sebastian,[14] who retreats to a forest hut to uninterruptedly "worship nature" (*T*, 113), is found by Simon on his way to Hedwig's as a frozen corpse lying in the snow. Simon, who admires the immediacy to nature in Sebastian's death, sees it as the result of the poet's misjudgment of his own character and the resulting groundless belief in his strength to create while scorning his fellow men (*T*, 132).

Not having achieved Jakob's synthesis of art and nature in an "artless" creativity, Simon is unaware how near is the vulnerability he acknowledges as a pre-condition to his search for relation (*T*, 242f.) to the vulnerability that Jakob masks with irony in order to equitably contest for the life he seeks. Aware only of his own dangerous sensitivity as a child (*T*, 328) and the proximity of pain and artistry in his brother Emil (*T*, 239, 322), Simon disavows art, as he knows it, as unrelated to nature. He only intimates what would constitute meaningful art. Castigating "the seekers of beauty" as he once contemplates the failure of new buildings to fit "ornamentally" with their surroundings, he says that "snooty art" seems to him "the most irrelevant thing in the world" (*T*, 289). "Just think," he tells himself, "what is it, indeed, compared to dying and eternally re-awakening nature" (*op. cit.*). He finds it more fitting that the minds of men occupy themselves with "problems of life" before those of art. "Now, to be sure," he adds, "problems of life are on occasion problems of art as well, but problems of life are in a much higher and nobler sense problems of art" (*op. cit.*). Two remarks by the narrator in Chapter Seven of *Geschwister Tanner* deleted before publication, one immediately preceding, the second following Simon's "purposeless" reminiscences of his childhood, corroborate this portrayal of Simon as an unpotentialized creator. In the first deleted passage the narrator speaks of Simon's wish to write "something like a novel. That is," the narrator explains, "he was trying to write one, or more accurately, it wasn't a question of the novel, but of passing the time, since . . . no one was concerned about him, no one felt a desire for him, and he knew no one whom he could have done a service." In the novel, Simon destroys his reminiscences immediately "because [they] no longer had any value for him" (*T*, 124). Originally this sentence preceded the following clause: "he was decidedly too young and too immature to write novels." In this sense it is appropriate that Simon localize his dream identifying nature and subordination in a humane society where the artist Kaspar has gone to work—in Paris.

Art or the artist does not play a part in *Der Gehülfe*. As a way-station to the creation and definition of an art related to nature, the theme of art is absorbed into the author's irony toward the contrast of irreconcilables distinguishing his "directed" hero Marti and the Villa Abendstern and also absorbed into the depiction of nature. The principal function of the descriptions of nature in the second half of the novel is to provide Marti with a counterbalance to and a respite in his encounter with the world of Villa Abendstern while defining nature as the antithesis to Villa Abendstern that permits Marti his double vision. Since it is the author whose ironic juxtaposition creates the commentary on the cultural and human situation—leaving to Marti the ironic apperception of the baselessness of Tobler's adamant optimism—the perception of nature as a permanent counterweight to society is divided between hero and author.

The nature descriptions and the reflections on nature in *Der Gehülfe* parallel the revelation of the fate of the house and the certainty of Marti's homelessness in it. As long as the summer lasts, as long as the false idyll of Villa Abendstern's image is most bewitching, the narrator ironizes Marti's frequent walks down to the post office, his solitary swims, and his daydreaming in the summer forest after the unpleasantness of the meal with Pauline and Silvi (*G*, 101–107) as makeshift attempts by Marti to ignore the uneasiness of his position. As indicated above, this perspective of direct irony begins to give way to the impersonal irony of love that dominates the conclusion and the reiteration of Marti's isolation in nature there. This shift is prepared for by the increase in the number and length of descriptions of nature that provide a new level of relief for the hero as the fate of the house is fixed. The corresponding descriptions of nature begin shortly after the middle of the book (*G*, 169) with the mute, almost imperceptible cessation in nature that anticipates the onset of autumn. For a day or two the continued warmth and mildness effects an unintended deception. Autumn then settles as a wet, blanketing greyness, accentuating the silences and showing Marti in its unchanging "pale and rounded image" a visage at once earnest and tender.

> And there were days, genuinely autumnal ones, neither lovely nor ugly, neither especially bright nor particularly gloomy, neither sunny nor dark days, but instead the kind that remained uniformly light and dark from morning until evening, where four o'clock in the afternoon showed the identical image of the world as eleven in the morning, where everything lay there quietly, a quiescent gold, somewhat melancholy, where colors silently withdrew into themselves, as if they were sorrowfully dreaming.*

Marti's reaction to the passage of time is the uncertainty born of his realization of how little he has changed (*G*, 210). The author's amplification of Marti's thoughts equates Marti with nature in a majestic description of the four seasons as movement in permanence, part of which reads:

---

* Und Tage gab es, echt herbstliche, weder schöne noch wüste, weder besonders freundliche, noch besonders trübe, weder sonnige, noch dunkle Tage, sondern solche, die ganz gleichmäßig licht und dunkel blieben von morgens bis abends, wo vier Uhr nachmittags das selbe Weltbild bot wie elf Uhr vormittags, wo alles ruhig und mattgolden und ein bißchen betrübt dalag, wo die Farben still in sich selber zurücktraten, gleichsam für sich sorgenvoll träumend (*G*, 188–189).

And the world, does it change? No. A winter image can cast itself across the world of summer; spring can come from winter; but the face of the earth has remained the same. It puts on masks and takes them off, its great lovely forehead wrinkles and brightens, it smiles or is wrathful, but it is always the same. . . . Rivers and streams flow the courses they have for thousands of years. . . . Flows and eddies are its primeval law. . . . Everything in and on the earth obeys strict, beautiful laws, as does man.*

In Marti's more frequent communion with nature he experiences a norm missing in the public image of Villa Abendstern. The fullness and variety of these descriptions contrast with the spiritual impoverishment of the house. This is made clear in the description of the appearance of winter (G, 288–289); in the contrast between the forlorn celebration of Christmas at Villa Abendstern (G, 291–293) and the sense of the promise of Christmas in Marti's solitary celebration on the lakeside hill immediately before; and in the contrast between his laconic departure from the Toblers and his reverential leave-taking from the surrounding nature (G, 304, 311). That this reintroduction into nature is the reassurance of Marti's unimpaired humanity is seen when Marti realizes that he can "suddenly fit" his image of the drinker Wirsich into the surrounding landscape (G, 304). This perceptual integration sparks Marti's announcement to Frau Tobler that he will put Wirsich up in his room after the two celebrate New Year's Eve in the village taverns (G, 304–305).

Concurrently the author attempts to make the nature descriptions the medium of his ideational purpose. With the arrival of the winter that signifies the death of the house, the narrator says: "Something spectral seemed to have taken up residence around the beautiful Tobler house, and fortune and the elegance of this home, in fact even its justification seemed to have been lost in a pale, tired, lusterless and bottomless dream" (G, 232). In the rarification of time and increasingly abstractive use made of nature by the author during the gradual dissolution of the house, nature even seems to promise a temporary reprieve (G, 245). What the author does finally foresee for the home is expressed in a perception of the house which Marti has on returning from a walk

---

* Und die Welt, verändert sie sich? Nein. Das Winterbild kann sich über die Sommerwelt werfen; aus dem Winter kann Frühling werden; aber das Gesicht der Erde ist dasselbe geblieben. Es legt Masken an und ab, es runzelt und lichtet die große schöne Stirne, es lächelt oder es zürnt, aber bleibt immer dasselbe. . . . Die Ströme und Flüsse fließen dieselbe Bahn wie seit Jahrtausenden. . . . Das Strömen und Wühlen ist sein [des Wassers] uraltes Gesetz. . . . Alles in und auf der Erde gehorcht schönen, strengen Gesetzen, wie die Menschen (G, 210–211).

through the winter landscape. Here Marti's perception accords with
the symbolic role given Frau Tobler in the preservation of the family
after the dissolution of the home.

> And then suddenly he was standing again in front of the Tobler
> house, was looking up to it from below, and saw how the cold moon
> enchanted it while semi-darkened clouds flew around it, resembling
> tall women, mourning yet lovely, apparently to draw it to the heights,
> so that it might dissolve in a beautiful way.

The interrelation between art and nature in *Jakob von Gunten* is made
more radical by juxtaposing an almost completely internalized nature
(which is equated with human nature, "stupidity," or "sleep") with
Jakob's manifest artistry and the disavowal of art that is climaxed by
his abandonment of writing in the final entry. When, early in the book,
Jakob says: "One thing is true, nature is missing here" (*JvG*, 349),
he is referring to a representational nature that had already begun to
be replaced by the symbolic "second nature" of *Der Gehülfe*. Even as
a child, Jakob notes, "Nature . . . seemed like something divinely distant.
So I can do without nature" (*JvG*, 368f.). The single instance of repre-
sensational nature in the novel is in Jakob's memory of his homeland
(*JvG*, 349). It is replaced by the imagined nature with which Jakob
furbishes his vision of the world of the inner chambers, which he is
subsequently forced to acknowledge as unreal.[15] A double disavowal
of representational nature may be found in Jakob's final dream. In the
first section of the dream, where Jakob sees the buxom naked beauty,
the journal writer says of the scene: "It was nature and yet is wasn't,
portrait and at the same time substance" (*JvG*, 489). The rhythmically
animated, predominantly metaphoric quality of this nature is replaced
later in the dream by the "desert" scenes. These dissolve time and space
more radically than in comparable dreams in either *Geschwister Tanner*
or *Der Gehülfe*.

Jakob's art is created against the greater explicitness of an anti-literary
bias that represents the actualization of Simon's intimation of an art
dealing with "problems of life." The revision of esthetic criteria for fictional prose implied in the writing of this journal is evident despite
the infrequency with which Jakob takes account of himself as a writer.[16]

---

* Und dann stand er plötzlich wieder vor dem Toblerschen Haus, schaute von
unten zu ihm hinauf und sah, wie der kalte Mond es verzauberte, während die
halbdunklen Nachtwolken um dasselbe herumflogen, großen, trauernden, aber
lieblichen Frauen ähnlich, um es scheinbar in die Höhe zu ziehen, damit es sich
auflöse in schöner Weise (*G*, 295–296).

An awareness of the uniqueness of the novel's "insignificant" theme is evident in Jakob's musings on the unlikely possibility that a writer would visit the Institute to gather source material. Jakob is persuaded that in such a case the writer would only be amused by the spit-and-polish exterior similarity of the pupils (*JvG*, 385). When he speaks of himself as a journal-writer he speaks ironically. He concludes one entry because he is out of breath (*JvG*, 426); he excuses a slip into sententiousness, saying that the pages have somehow to be filled (*JvG*, 433); he contemplates how severely Fräulein Benjamenta would reprimand him were she to read a "very poetic" phrase he writes (*JvG*, 375); and he disparages trenchant polish by the conscious persiflage of: "How I hate such clever turns of phrases" (*JvG*, 455). As an author Jakob contravenes usual connotations of "belles lettres" by his disinterest in the esthetic quality of what he writes. Thus, even an esthetically and thematically unsuccessful entry such as his fruitless attempt to organize his reflections in a form that will mirror the self-sufficiency of ignorance and experience (in contrast to knowledge and thought) is finally dismissed as "prattle" (*JvG*, 418). But it is left unaltered in the text. The denial of art set forth in the last entry should not be read as irrevocable (cf. *Greven*, 111), but rather in the light of this programmatic criticism of conventional art. The vitality and activation of imagination that Jakob manifests even after the disillusions taught by the Institute Benjamenta reveals one of the themes of the novel to be the processes of imaginative writing. The novel itself is the proof of Jakob's participation in the two poles of existence in their most rudimentary form: sleep and waking. The aristocracy Jakob foreswears on entering the school must likewise be seen in the context of Jakob's writing. As a sacrifice of the privilege and prerogative of talent and intelligence it resolves the anomaly of the Romantic vision of the artist's nobility and the contrast to this vision in the pessimism expressed towards the artist in the work written before the novels. Related to this sacrifice is the depersonalization Jakob is taught at the school. Together, the images and the language of Jakob's journal indicate that this depersonalization carries over his subversion of normative literature to the social station of the artist. Dissociating himself from the self-confident "nobility" of art, he accepts as part of the freedom which he retains through his irony the esthetic diffidence and isolation of the artist as amateur.[17] Walser utilized the literary freedom thus secured throughout the remainder of his career. The esthetic concomitant of this freedom is given shape in *Jakob von Gunten* where disregard for the conventions of plot and logically consistent narrative technique risks, at each entry's survey of the riddle of existence, the suspension of integrality. Thus the themes of freedom and self-sacrifice in all three novels—freedom vouchsafed by nature, self-sacrifice as depersonalization in the world—are combined in the realm of art, where self-sacrifice becomes the price for freedom of creation.

Notes

1. Friedhelm Kemp, *Dichtung als Sprache. Wandlungen der modernen Poesie* (Munich: Kösel, 1965), p. 61.

2. The experience of life sought by all three heroes brings them face to face with the paradox that the implementation of this ideal of commitment can only be realized by a sacrifice of the self, by the adherence to invalidated laws, or by a separation from society. The impossibility of encompassing and resolving this antithesis underlies the elusiveness of the heroes' commitment and the irony of situation that frequently finds them incapable or unwilling to fulfill their ideal of service in their search for meaningful human relations. Simon's employment as a servant in Chapters Eleven and Twelve is an obvious example. The symbolic value Simon himself attributes to his role as servant is clear from his pleasure in imagining a provocation that would cause his mistress to strike him in anger and thereby refute her image of herself as a paragon of matronhood. Simon is objective enough to be able to identify this wish in himself as "a genuinely middle-class feeling" (*T*, 211). Greven accurately identifies several such instances as "sacrifice of the Ego to what is unknown" (*Greven,* 235). This is precisely the symbolic expression of the search undertaken by Simon after having freed himself from what are for him the confines of his family.

3. In a long letter from Kaspar to Simon which originally stood in Chapter Six but was deleted before publication, Kaspar reveals that he is writing Klara very frequently. Had this letter been included in the final text, it would have provided some details regarding Kaspar's whereabouts but would not have complemented his characterization, since Kaspar has—despite the conflict in his feelings—already decided in favor of his art, which he calls "the infuriated enemy of my love." (Cf. the section Art and Nature.)

4. In an article entitled "Die Brüder Walser" (*Schweizerland,* I. Jg., Hft. 11–12 [August–September], 1915), Hans Trog asserts that in a conversation Walser had explained the choice of the name Simon by referring to the section in the second chapter of Burckhardt's *Renaissance Culture in Italy,* on the tyranny of the Bagliones in fifteenth-century Perugia. Before finally being murdered in an intra-family strife following a partial settlement of an older feud with the Oddi family, Simonetto had distinguished himself by leading a small band of defenders against several hundred attackers. Wounded more than twenty times in this battle, he was helped back on his steed and—as Burckhardt's source puts it—resembling Mars, led the counterattack. He was even heroic in death. The chronicler speaks of the bold defiance witnesses claimed to see in his face after death, as if not even death had been able to contain him.

5. The frequent appearance in Walser's work of a painter figure biographically resembling Karl Walser (see "Der Maler" [*FKR*], "Brief eines Malers an einen Dichter" [*P*], "Leben eines Malers" [*S*], "Die Brüder" [*PS*]) has been the source of questionable comparisons of the brother's art (e.g., *Bänziger,*

99). Walser's justified reluctance to have his brother illustrate the four long prose pieces published by Rascher in Zurich in 1919, because the entire volume was "too prevailingly intellectual-reflective" for illustrations (cf. Fritz Huber-Renfer, "Robert Walser-Ausgaben," *Der kleine Bund,* February 8, 1957), as well as the ironic depiction of an essential difference between himself and his brother in prose pieces like "Koffermann und Zimmermann" (*PS*) are an indication that the frequency of a painter-figure is most likely an exercise in the manipulation of a double figure as a reflex of the protagonist's antipathy toward art.

6. Without specifically mentioning Hedwig, Greven carries this thought further by relating Kraus and Fräulein Benjamenta. He speaks of the "tragedy of pure inwardness" (*Greven,* 176) in the teacher.

7. A commentary by the author goes beyond Simon's remark to associate this personal bond with the encounter with life: "They had long since forgotten that they were only brother and sister; to themselves they appeared to be related more through destiny than through the same blood and they lived together much like two prisoners in confinement who are endeavoring to forget life through their friendship" (*T,* 162).

8. *Wissen und Leben—Neue Schweizer Rundschau,* XVII (1924), 25, 1515–1527.

9. All that is known of one of the stories that originally stood where the Paris dream does now, "Gräfin Kirke," is that in a letter to the Insel Verlag in November, 1903 Walser included a work with this title in a list of prose works and poetry that he was offering for a contemplated volume of selections from his work. The implications of the title of this story, the consuming love of a countess for a painter in the story "Der Maler" (*FKR*), and the representation of an early model for the Klara figure in the story "Simon, Eine Liebesgeschichte" (*KGS*) as a demon lover support the assumption of a modification of her figure in *Geschwister Tanner*. As originally written, both "Gräfin Kirke" and "Mein Leben" ("Ein Jüngling") were the literary products of a young clerk who had lived in Simon's room before him. The removal of the Paris dream from its original location in Chapter Seventeen, where it followed Simon's final meeting with Klara, can be understood as a calculated artistic decision on Walser's part and not as a disinterested concession to Cassirer, since the material deleted here (as in the case of the deletion of Kaspar's long letter to Simon from the village where he is decorating a dance hall), belongs to an earlier, more immediately autobiographical conception of the material of the novel.

10. That Simon is not referring to physical love is clear from the paradigmatic quality of his search in the novel. While it is accurate to refer to the infinite quality of his gift to Klara, as does Greven (*Greven,* 55), to read the section as a crisis in intrapersonal relations, as does Bänziger (*Bänziger,* 73), is to overlook the meaning of the speech as an article of faith to a person Simon regards as a guide to an extra-familial ethic. This view of Klara is clear from his projection of her in the Paris dream as a woman whose self-denial takes the form of her willingness to surrender Kaspar to his "voluptuous-beloved" nature, rather than accede to norms of society. Bänziger's view also disregards the personal bond between Simon and Klara as they live together in the house until it is sold (Chapter Six) and the later meeting between them (Chapter Seventeen), that is possible only on the strength of this intimacy.

11. In contrasting Joseph Marti's "still more certain knowledge regarding the true locus of existence" to Simon Tanner, Greven asserts: "Joseph Marti can still accomodate himself to the bourgeois idyll of the Tobler house—to be sure, precisely because [the idyll] is in the process of dissolution . . ." (*Greven*, 73). Lacking any amplification, this statement seems to ascribe to Marti the intellectual autonomy vis-à-vis the Tobler home that the author denies, using this ironic device, in part, to permit Marti to develop a loyalty to the Toblers which each of the participants in the novel understands differently. As the statement stands it is also inconsistent with Marti's explicit desire to find a home. Although Greven ascribes to Marti more intellectual cognition than is warranted, he does accurately describe Marti's experience of the Tobler's world as an image, "in the glittering surface of which appearance and reality are blended, as a totality of experience . . . outside the province of true objectivity" (*Greven*, 56).

12. The author does not ironize the interior manifestations of Marti's compassion, since these need not be "de-poeticized." Thus in the narration of Marti's acquaintance with a cigar store saleslady (*G*, 24–25), in his thoughts as he watches the Wirsichs leave after the disastrous visit with the Toblers (*G*, 46), and in his identification with the downtrodden in his dream of the Wirsichs (*G*, 57–59), the perspective is that of Marti.

13. Hermann Hesse's review of the republication of *Der Gehülfe* in 1936 points to certain poetic qualities of the novel as the reason for its effectiveness nearly thirty years after its original publication. He says in part: ". . . we recognize much more clearly than . . . thirty years ago [that] it is not at all the problems and their interpretation which have made this work of art endearing, but its atmosphere, its poetic substance, what it contains of the fairy tale, of timelessness and play" (Hermann Hesse, "Robert Walsers 'Gehülfe' in neuer Ausgabe," *Neue Zürcher Zeitung*, Nr. 1361, August 8, 1936).

14. Walser, whose care in the choice of names for his figures is evident even where the intention is parodistic, used the name Sebastian for one of the youthful literati in the dramolet "Dichter" (*KGS*), for the title figure in a parody of a detective story that Walser himself titled a novella, and again as a title for a still unpublished work. The so-called novella (originally in *Der Neue Merkur* [1914–1915], now in *GW* VI, 200–216), tells of a spoiled young man who robs and then murders a man he encounters on the street. Sebastian is apprehended by a famous detective, who subsequently marries Sebastian's fiancée.

15. That is, the real inner chambers and not the lower passageways. Jakob's confusion of the two as he is about to make the descent with Lisa in his vision touches on the sexual overtones implicit in his relation to both the brother and the sister. Jakob recognizes as real the experience of the lower passageways in the "inner chambers" of himself as the deprivations life comprehends; he denominates as unreal the initial associations he had had of the Benjamentas' rooms as bedrooms. Middleton correctly assumes that the constable's sword and helmet that hang above the door leading to the Benjamentas' rooms are sexual symbols, but Jakob sees them only as superannuated emblems of the authority in force at the school, which he "wouldn't want as a gift" (*JvG*, 363).

16. No one knows that Jakob keeps a journal, but the only one of Kraus' scoldings Jakob reports in detail is an attack and repudiation of what Kraus calls Jakob's

"leaping and dancing frivolousness" (*JvG*, 466). He derisively calls Jakob a "lord of existence" (*JvG*, 467), and tells Jakob that he scorns his "pitiful playing of roles" (*loc. cit.*). The burden of his condemnation—which is the single, indirect evidence of a feeling of guilt as an artist in the novel—is directed at the ontological neutrality of art: "The elegance (*Grazie*) of you artists—which is what you people are—certainly doesn't all of a sudden lessen hardships for a worker or for any living being for that matter" (*JvG*, 466).

17. Walser's pose as a literary amateur is one of the many useful points made by Michael Hamburger in a section devoted to Walser in his *From Prophecy to Exorcism: The Premisses of Modern German Literature* (London: Longmans, 1965), pp. 104–111. The article originally appeared in *The Times Literary Supplement* of July 21, 1961, under the title "A Miniaturist in Prose."

6

STYLE

Walser is most elusive when an attempt is made to relate the elements of his style to the statement of his prose works. In the present chapter we shall describe and enumerate the configuration of salient stylistic features that contribute to the effect, the articulation of meaning, and the realization of the novels as works of art.[1] The divergency of style in the novels suggests this as the necessary first step towards analyzing the cohesiveness they achieve despite their prevailingly linear composition. The individual elements are varied enough. Walser's style is broad in its range and registers; it is a style of daring and verve, a style at times crude, at times excessively refined; a style alternately vexing and delightful. Walser can be impassioned or indifferent, romantic or unperturbedly pedantic, long-winded or terse, brilliantly incisive or fatuous. Middleton speaks of a style in *Jakob von Gunten* in which no one thing has any single meaning (*Middleton*, 414). We can perhaps more accurately describe Walser's style if we recognize the equipoise of antitheses as the formal principle that makes the style the medium for the content of the novels.

Contemporary reviewers and later commentators on the novels frequently praise the somewhat unexpected effectiveness of Walser's prose while cautioning against too hurried an attempt to identify the factors contributing to the style.[2] In view of the subordinate role of plot in Walser's short prose it is understandable that other commentators on Walser's style have concentrated their attention on his language. Thus, without any knowledge of the importance Walser himself ascribed to language (cf. above Chapter One, p. 27) Walter Benjamin's essay on Walser deals almost entirely with the interpretation of Walser's use of language. In touching on the vexing question of intention in Walser,

Benjamin felt it would be wise to give credence to reports that Walser never corrected his work. "For then one can take comfort from this insight," he continues, "that the complete interpenetration of the most radical lack of intention and the greatest intention is in fact to write and never correct what one has written" (*Benjamin*, 149).[3] Benjamin's formulation fairly approximates the exterior texture of Walser's style: in all three novels a combination of strong emotion and reflection is given verbal form by an "amateur" literary artist whose most profound presentiments are the certainty of oblivion in the death of the spirit and the emancipating vitality of creation.

Since our emphasis here is on the novels as works in their own right and as the stylistic anticipations of Walser's subsequent concentration on short prose, this chapter will proceed from the larger compositional elements of narrative prose to the more specific. Since, by the standards of their time, the novels require either a loose definition of their form or a generously expanded one, the emphasis here is less on the identification of the genre than on the application of specific novelistic elements, and concludes with an attempt to identify a common structural pattern in Walser's novels.

Composition

A necessary premise to a discussion of the elements of composition is the relative insignificance of the story line compared to other compositional elements. The tendency in all three novels is to reduce the function and meaning of exterior action as a means of highlighting the primacy of the inner life. The quality of Simon's speeches, and the alternation between author narration and any variant of indirect discourse in *Der Gehülfe* culminate in the immediacy of Jakob's "monologist" journal entries. Yet just as the subordination of story or plot elements results in the heightened importance of narrative elements that slow the action and give the first two novels the dominant tonal qualities that support their themes, the greater immediacy and directness of Jakob's journal entries are realized by their autonomous form. An examination of some of the novels' elements of composition will illustrate how intimately the style of the novels is integrated with the personality of the respective heroes.

The division of narrated time in *Geschwister Tanner* patently reflects the structuring of the novel's forward movement according to the rhythms of Simon's existence. The events of the novel cover a period of nearly two years, from the end of winter through Christmas of the following year. In the first segment of the novel, Chapters One through

Six, the identifications of (seasonal) time, beginning only with the arrival of spring, accompany the events of the action until the end of autumn. Coincident with the termination of the first segment of the novel we find both the arrival of winter (*T*, 115) and the first report on Simon's youth as a retrospection Simon himself writes at the beginning of the transitional Chapter Seven. This chapter, serving as a bridge both with regard to time and to season by restricting the action in it to Simon's walk through the winter landscape to Hedwig's, describes only the events of two consecutive days in winter. Yet at least three months transpire before the action is resumed in Chapter Eight. Thus the action is retarded and the dynamism inherent in the narrative bridge itself, Simon's walk with the supporting contrast between Sebastian's death in the forest and Simon's vitality, creates a tension that only partially fills the hiatus in the action itself. In contrast to the contractions in narrated time and narrated events that parallel winter here, the two following chapters distend spring and summer through a more detailed narration of events occurring in those seasons. Chapters Nine and Ten cover Simon's three months in the country; Chapters Eleven and Twelve, his four weeks' summer employment as a servant after his return to the city; Chapters Thirteen through Fifteen, the two days in mid-summer during which the dream of Paris, the conversation in the tavern concerning Simon's brother Emil, and his first encounter with the male nurse occur. The two penultimate chapters, described as "several weeks" at the end of summer, are spent with the male nurse. The autumn and winter-related retardation of action is again apparent in the final chapter. There a relatively long time span is telescoped into scenes (the fall meeting with Klaus, the snow-child fantasy) that prepare for Simon's figurative return to nature, a thematic echo of Sebastian's death the winter before.

Despite the arrangement of chapters in groups emphasizing the principal segments of Simon's public life, a contrast between the formal function of the chapters and the rarefication of time in the fantasies, dreams, and descriptions of nature contravenes the logic of chapter divisions. This contrast contributes to the often remarked "fairy-tale" atmosphere in Walser's novels.[4] The more obvious rarefication of time in *Der Gehülfe* results first of all in the complete omission of chapter divisions. In their place are forty-five scenes and episodes. Although these generally closely follow a single story line, they permit the author to set the accents and emphases in his work through the selection of detail, through the determination of which episodes shall be amplified and indirectly commented upon by their proximity to reflection by the narrator or by Marti, and through the location of reminiscences.

The individual sections of *Der Gehülfe* clearly represent an intermediary stage between the chapter divisions of "Tanner" and the single journal entries of *Jakob von Gunten,* many of which exhibit a radical and outwardly unmotivated change of topic from entry to entry or within single entries. Before illustrating the use of sections in *Der Gehülfe,* it should be noted that over a third of the chapters in *Geschwister Tanner* end either with sleep, night, fantasy, or dream; thus neither book has genuine narrative transitions but both sustain a physical sense of continuity. Indeed geographical and topical transitions in the first novel are more frequent within chapters and, not infrequently occur within paragraphs.

A central passage from *Der Gehülfe* that extends over two sections will illustrate some of the narrative devices used to support the ironic juxtaposition of Marti and the Toblers. The rhythm of a seasonal cycle in nature is expectedly the background against which the precarious stability of Villa Abendstern and Marti's subsequent watchfulness are presented in highly distinct time segments. The first section deals with the milder appearance of Frau Tobler during her convalescence from a sudden illness, and the social isolation of the family. The author describes the attenuation of time in the villa and the complementary telescoping of all other time as follows:

> Several days passed. During these days one felt every hour of the day. They were counted, they were counted on; for it did make a difference whether they passed by quickly or slowly since the existence of the house of Tobler was only a matter of days. One had forgotten how to think of months or years, or one abbreviated the imagined months and years; this caused memories to comprehend more rapidly, and one lived on in this manner and waited for the signs the days brought . . .*

He then concentrates, in describing "these, as it seemed, final days" of Villa Abendstern, on the perception of sounds and colors and thereby adds to the scenic diffusion. These perceptions corroborate Frau Tobler's seeming change for the better, her casting off "a certain complexity of the heart" (G, 242). Yet even the narrator's foreshadowing of a resolution in the term "final days" is mitigated by a reference to the incessant

---

* Es vergingen einige Tage. Sie wurden in allen ihren Stunden empfunden, diese Tage. Man zählte sie, man rechnete mit ihnen, denn es war nicht gleichgültig, ob sie rasch oder langsam dahingingen, hing doch das Bestehen des Hauses Tobler nur noch von Tagen ab. Man verlernte es, an Monate oder Jahre zu denken, oder man verkürzte die Gedanken-Monate und -jahre und veranlaßte die Erinnerungen zu einem rascheren Erfassen, und man lebte so und wartete auf die Zeichen, die die Tage gaben . . . (G, 244).

motion of time. He follows with a change of tone, a "correction," the purpose of which is to soberly deny the illusion of a change of heart in Frau Tobler. He reports that the healthier she became the more she began to resemble her old self and concludes with an ironic self-reminder of how unlikely the hoped for change was. "No," the narrator seems to be reminding Marti, "a living human creature didn't leap out of its own nature that quickly" (*G*, 245). Here he is less involved than in the paragraph on the passage of time. The complementary change in narrative perspective could be described as *style indirect libre* (see Chapter Six, Note 23) were it not for the authority the author maintains in relation to his hero. Finally it is important to note that the chilling effect of this final paragraph is lessened by its internalized statement. The lyricism of the passage-of-time paragraph is carried forth by a different device. The total effect resembles the more pronounced "disillusions" experienced by Jakob von Gunten, where the disillusioning "correction" itself is refuted at a different level of literary discourse.

The next section (*G*, 246–253) has two narrative climaxes: Marti's long-postponed conversation with Frau Tobler about her mistreatment of Silvi, and the more emotional exchange between Tobler and Marti after Frau Tobler has gone to bed, when the subconsciously jealous employer wants to shout "robber" and "dog" at his assistant. It provides an excellent example of Walser's skill in utilizing frequent, often hardly discernible shifts of narrator perspective and motif repetition for a concise representation of complex human emotions, of which the first paragraph is an example. As the narrator begins his description of "an evening during this period," he purposefully distinguishes a new tone, an aftermath of the disillusion regarding Frau Tobler. The suppleness of diction and receptivity for nuances is gone; in its place a factual tone containing a slight, yet discernable note of condescension toward the two card players prevails. His involvement in the description of the gentle, but irrevocable passage of time is gone, as are the emendations and shifts of emphasis that permitted a sharper focus on the characters' sensibilities allowing the narrator to amass particularized evidence for the passage of time. However, the narrator is able to rekindle the suppressed excitement that is characteristic of *Der Gehülfe* and part of the source of Jakob's "naive" pleasure. Despite the contrast in tone, the narrator by restricting his perspective to Marti's re-introduces the recently subdued tone of emotion as the assistant gazes fixedly at Frau Tobler while she reads a novel. Except for several isolated sentences employing *style indirect libre*, however, the narrator remains distinct from Marti. The empathetic tone of this scene with Frau Tobler has in fact been prepared for by an account of similar evenings Marti spent alone with Frau Tobler described just before the time passage (cf. *G*, 244, 246). Thus the repetition of situation contains an emotional echo that works against the author's distancing tone here by utilizing an emotional equivalent of musical counterpoint.

The choice of a fictive journal for *Jakob von Gunten* concretizes formal and thematic tensions inherent in the two previous novels' division of exterior and interior life. A consequence of the use of the journal is a furtherance of the tension which the discrepancy between the external divisions of the work and the phases of internal rhythm imply. While the near standardization of the length of the individual entries goes even further than do the variously long sections of *Der Gehülfe* towards external uniformity and balance, the flexibility within the divisions themselves is all the greater. First, a journal may, and in this case does, dictate its own time scheme by beginning in *media res* with an authority not possible in the earlier novels, and not to be possible in any but the stream-of-consciousness novel or the so-called *roman nouveau*. From the first entry, this "free" narration adduces a state of suspension that is dilated or momentarily reduced, but never abandoned. The suspended quality is due in part to the diminished significance of real occurrences compared with the reflections, descriptions, dreams, fantasies, and flashbacks that interrupt and retard the meager action. A second contributory factor to the tension is the indefiniteness of time in single entries and in the novel as a whole. Not only is it impossible to specify the duration of the events of the novel, but the few reminiscences from Jakob's earlier life lie within an undifferentiated time mass, even less subject to time than the expository episodes in *Der Gehülfe*. Moreover, the more important episodes of the novel (the Kraus entries, the vision of the lower passageways, Jakob's entry into the real inner chambers, Fräulein Benjamenta's death, and Jakob's final dream) have, at best, only a nominal relation to calendar time.[5] As the novel with the fewest time determinants and the one in which narrated time most often coincides with time required for narration, the immediacy of the latter and indefiniteness of the former combine to increase the paradigmatic quality of the whole.

Narrative devices

The narrative method common to the three novels is that of addition and parataxis. The cohesiveness of the works depends on the variation and reintroduction of unifying themes in the separate parts. In this sense the novels increasingly anticipate Walser's later work. An obvious use of addition and parataxis is found in the characterizations of the figures in the novels. Even examples chosen from *Geschwister Tanner,* the novel in which traditional exposition occurs most frequently, are instructive. Only two of the figures in *Geschwister Tanner,* Klaus and the poet Sebastian, are introduced through narrator exposition. The characterizations of the other figures are defined by events or by the meaning of the scenes in which they appear. Commentaries and connectives between scenes and figures in the novel are usually omitted. This suppression of narrative commentary means that subsidiary figures like Rosa remain unrealized, although her being emphasizes the difference between Kaspar and Simon and anticipates Klara's dual role toward the brothers as mistress and friend. Similarly, the depiction of Klara's husband is so fragmentary that the irony intended by his departure from the scene of the novel "to hunt for a lost Greek city" (*T,* 105) is easily overlooked. The advantage of the method is the possibility of vari-levelled creation of character consistent with the integrality and uniqueness of personality. This succeeds with most figures, particularly when the briefness of their participation would leave them "flat" by the standards of realistic fiction. Typical of Walser is the sharp, narrow focus in the segments of characterization that readjusts as different levels of personality come into view. Thus, it is a misunderstanding of the respective weight of Simon's experiences in the novel to speak of their interchangeability and allow them significance only as a totality (*Greven,* 54). Such a view disregards the links between Simon and his siblings and Klara that are attested to in the Paris dream and the waking somnambulism of Simon's later discovery of Klara. The "shortsightedness" of narrative résumés, the omission of commentary, and the curt, unmotivated transitions are evidence of the preponderant weight given in the characterizations to the characters' own words in specific situations.[6] Because of the broader canvas of *Geschwister Tanner* Walser was unable to have scenes within this novel fulfill the sophisticated function they do in *Der Gehülfe,* yet the novel demonstrates how crucial human relationships and thematic development can be shown through addition and narrative parataxis. This may be seen in the successful characterizations of the briefly-seen Klaus and Hedwig, in the insight achieved by the location of individual scenes, such as the emotionally, physically, and intellectually transposed sequence in the vicarious utopia of the Paris dream and in the scene climaxed by Simon's celebration of misfortune.

Retardation

The theme of the primacy and cohesiveness of the interior life of all three heroes has been referred to as a factor in the formal realization of the incompatibility of the exterior world and interior being.[7] Walser employs an array of devices ranging from large narrative elements to phrases to give form to an emotional counterpart for the heroes' symbolic failure to attain an external goal. The majority of these devices interrupt or divert the forward motion of the action; they are retarding moments whose structural function it is to stress the polarity of the two worlds present in each of the novels. These retarding moments bind together the heroes' desire for the experience of life and their imaginative existences. Predominantly lyric in tone, these devices provide the machinery for an inner form—the *drauflosmusizieren* of the novels that Walser himself later dejectedly censured (*Wdgg*, 14). This inner form gives unity to the esthetic effect of an externally additive form whose individual components became progressively smaller from the first to the last novel.[8]

The most obvious of such retarding moments, the dreams and fantasies of the heroes, have been discussed in earlier chapters. Viewed as plot inserts, they are "freer"—that is, neither introduced as plot nor outwardly dependent on the action—than other narrative elements. Nevertheless they not only provide the commentary and the transitions omitted by the nominally objective narrator, but are so situated that their symbolic force as recapitulation and anticipation permeates each work.

Numerically more frequent than the dreams and fantasies are the inserts whose character is primarily expressive or paradigmatic. Among these are the letters in *Geschwister Tanner* and *Der Gehülfe*. Simon's awareness of the expressive and revelatory nature of letters is made clear as he decides not to answer Klaus' letter: "One's soul always wants to speak out in letters and as a rule it makes a fool of itself" (*T*, 18). Simon's readiness to reveal his thoughts and feelings in his speeches is evidence enough of his willingness to expose his soul. Thus, the progressively greater reluctance of all three heroes to communicate through letters might be viewed as one of Walser's devices to refashion traditional narrative components of the novel to his own needs. Both Marti and Jakob sense the artifice that letter-writing demands. Within the novels however, Klara's overwrought letter to Hedwig immediately preceeding her attack, Simon's two letters to Kaspar, Klaus' letter to Simon, Marti's letter to his former landlady, Frau Tobler's letter to her former maid's mother, and the letter Tobler dictates to Marti all emphasize characterological or thematic elements in the novels. As resting points in the narrative they corroborate the events of the novel and anticipate plot, but as subjective, ephemeral, and free—because unanswered—utterances they add only minimally to the action.

A preponderance of "monologist" narrative in the novels, together with the progressively more varied stylization in the diction of narrator "voice," anticipate what Walser later spoke of as "crawling back into the snail shell of the short story and feuilleton" (*Wdgg*, 72). Still more monologist in character than the letters are the many speeches in *Geschwister Tanner*. Occurring in dialog situations, they are more accurately termed speeches since they function primarily as individual and mimetic colloquy, secondarily for emotional reciprocity between the figures involved, and only nominally in intellectual reciprocity. Whether it be Simon's opening speech to the bookdealer, his critical analysis of the business world to the bank director, the recapitulative apologues to the rich lady after his return to the city, his speeches to the male nurse or to the manageress—all of which are emotionally "new starts"— or the speeches of Hedwig, Kaspar, or Klara as queen of the poor, the effect is that of a monolog spoken past the listener. As esthetically autonomous, self-expository verbalizations of character they are comparable to Simon's dreams and fantasies but for their fore-shortened view into the future. The facility of expression and the extensiveness of affective response in them represents a risk undertaken by the speakers that the prolixity of detail offers the medium for explaining these spiritual monologists to the world from which they are estranged. The speeches often show unquestionable wisdom and insight, yet there inheres in all of them an unmistakeable narrative irony based on the fact that, despite their attempted completeness,[9] they remain imperfect, fragmentary reflections of interior integrality. We have discussed this thematic dichotomy in Simon's final speech; in Hedwig's speeches in the country and Klara's speech in her final meeting with Simon we find an analogous double plot amplification through both location and the statement of the speeches themselves, that is, a double and not necessarily coincident integration of plot.

The characterization of the novels as Walser's experiments to find a literary form appropriate to his heroes is intimately related to his use of speeches in the novels. The freedom of form gained through their disproportionate weight in *Geschwister Tanner* anticipates certain narrative advantages that are utilized in the two later novels. The high correlation in speeches between narrated time and time required for narration guarantees the immediacy that was always an aim of Walser's writing and one that plays a dominant role in his short prose. The speeches necessarily emphasize human reactions and thereby permit Walser to highlight the uniqueness of individual being; they reduce the narrator's role as storyteller while simultaneously amplifying and personalizing the fictional world of the novel. They also serve to integrate the chronology of the plot. They do so traditionally by providing a form for relating the speaker to the action through active participation in speech, connective description, or abstract statement; by stressing both durative and iterative time aspects they can also, as they do in Walser's novels, transcend chronological limits and contribute to their character as paradigm or fairy tale. Simon's dominance in *Geschwister Tanner* is in large measure due to the frequency and significance of his action-retarding participation. The result is a reduction of the conventional bi-dimensionality achieved by creating one dimension for narrator statement and another for that of a figure in a novel. This bi-dimensionality is, however, introduced into *Der Gehülfe*. Used to represent the silent seeker Marti in the Villa Abendstern world, it explains the more conventional ratio between author-narrated segments and retarding inserts such as fantasies, dreams, speeches, and reflections from the hero. Marti's verbal passivity illustrates just how significant a part of the action in both *Geschwister Tanner* and *Jakob von Gunten* is the act of speaking as distinguished from statement itself (Lämmert's distinction between speech as *Aktstruktur* and *Aussagestruktur*). Jakob's journal, on the other hand, can be classified as a radical stylistic consequence, an extension of the relation between retarding elements and theme in *Geschwister Tanner* and Marti's ironically utilized silence in *Der Gehülfe*. Walser uses Marti's silence to create the uncertainty in the hero and ironic suspension characteristic of the novel, while in *Geschwister Tanner,* it is the vociferousness and autonomy of the speeches that encompass Simon's uncertainty. The consequences for *Jakob von Gunten* are clear: the journal form makes possible a literary discourse deriving from the speeches that is expansive enough to tolerate the related introspection and reflection as parts of the hero's attempts at self-definition, while the exploratory aspect of Simon's speeches is combined with the irony and hero uncertainty of *Der Gehülfe*. The integration of these elements is facilitated by the increased use in *Jakob von Gunten* of the retractions and attempts to temper the finality of articulation present in all three novels. As evidences of a narrative equivalent of hypothetical statement, such retractions or cancellations overlay the self-knowledge gained by the heroes with the symbolism of their permanent alienation. Or, stated differently, the lack of resolution in all three novels is sustained by contrasting the varieties of mimetic speech with the indivisibility of the inner life—from the irony of love that contrasts irreconcilables in *Der Gehülfe* either by the evasion of statement or by the manipulation of indirect discourse, through the development of Simon's self-exposure in his speeches to the *parlando* tone of Jakob's journal entries.

In Walser's use of traditional action-retarding narrative devices such as retrospective reminiscences, introspective reflection, and descriptions, a stress on iterative-durative aspects consistent with the emphasis on interior life can be noted. Even descriptions of non-repeating situations assume iterative-durative value. Both the description of the old man seated next to Simon in the restaurant (*T*, 65f.) and the description of the copying office for the unemployed (*T*, 271f.) respectively predict and substantiate Simon's own material poverty. In the more traditional composition of *Der Gehülfe*, descriptions such as those of Tobler's inventions and the Bärenwilers are pure chronological retardation, since they are altogether outside of narrated time. Reports that fill out the plot—such as the events leading to Wirsich's dismissal, Tobler's first of August celebration, and Frau Tobler's reaction to the calumnious letter from Wirsich's paramour—bear little chronological relation to the story. Because they are ironic and relatively autonomous, they contribute rather to the pronounced scenic quality of the whole. This tendency, even more discernible in the dissolution of calendric time in *Jakob von Gunten*, reflects the dominance given to Jakob's personality. The descriptions in the journal (those of the sleeping teachers, the classes at the school, the street scenes) are retardations, but because they are filtered through Jakob's consciousness their integration with the plot is complete and they lose their narrative relevance and work rather as variations on the motif of bright and dark, past time and present Benjamenta time.

References to the past lives of the heroes in the form of narrator flashbacks are relatively infrequent. The heroes' action-retarding reminiscences accentuate the inadequacy of the past to their present being and recall events that are regarded by the heroes as obstacles in their present lives. Narrator flashbacks occur most often in *Der Gehülfe*. Except for the narrator's explanation of Marti's relation to Klara (see below, p. 189, Note 19) and the expository passages, the only express linking of the past and the present is the revelation of Marti's desire for a home (*G*, 285). The absence of measurable time referents in *Jakob von Gunten* subsumes even the events predating the time of the actual journal entry so long as the particular entry does not come under the basic then-now division. The uncertainty characteristic of Jakob's own present-time entries is a sophistication of the use in *Der Gehülfe* of *vision avec* in narrative irony toward Marti (cf. Lämmert, "Bauformen," pp. 70–71, 142–143).

The tension between intelligence and nature (in its manifestations as imagination, intuition, and the subconscious) is typical of Walser's writing. Viewing Walser's career as a whole, this tension is present in the fullness of style utilized within the discipline and inherent in the choice of a small form. For the novel heroes, the tension is reflected in their penchant for reflection and their proclivity toward aphorism.

The quality and the effectiveness of the heroes' reflections and maxims within the novels differ in their degree of integration with the plot and the theme, but they all derive from the persuasion that the diurnal and the obvious provide a source of knowledge and insight. As such the reflections are always of "phylogenetic" interest in comparing and comprehending the heroes, since their thoughts are passive counterparts of the acts of human witness and testimony that are emphasized in the speeches. Simon's sententious reflections resemble the narrator's summarizing maxims in a conventional novel, but are more programmatic than is customary in the speech of central figures.[10] Marti's preoccupation with the anomaly of his own uncertain external identification and the illusory security of Villa Abendstern inhibit his generalized reflections. His few speeches are somewhat self-conscious reactions to specific moral challenges (cf. *G*, 128, 154, 251); his reflections—excepting the "memoires" and the gloss he destroys—are restricted to his thoughts.[11] *Jakob von Gunten* utilizes the journal form to the full as the ideal medium for reflection and sententious discourse. As Jakob himself notes in a late entry on the relation in his own being between childishness and old age: ". . . I was always more interested in the thought than in the thing itself. I started feeling out profound things early, everywhere, even in stupid pranks" (*JvG*, 472). The overlapping thematic, character-portraying, and narrative functions of the reflections with which Jakob tries to ascribe meaning to his existence lead to the heart of the novel's statement.

Many of Jakob's reflections and maxims illustrate the asceticism, the conscious anachronism, the resignation, and the criticism of the contemporary world which the school propounds.[12] A larger, broader-ranging group, of a more immediately personal cast, extends from observations confirming the school's code to anomalies reiterating Jakob's personal transformation of his experience at Institute Benjamenta. The emphasis here is more on humor, exaggeration, exploratory puns, or experiments in parody of maxims such as: "Whatever moves forward incessantly, enforces propriety" (*JvG*, 374). There are contradictions in both groups; to view them as the expression by Jakob of a nihilism of values (*Greven*, 89) would give too little consideration to their metaphoric use in the novel. As verbal derivatives of Simon Tanner's assuredness that he can fill any role in life, the contradictions represent a stylistic correlative to two spheres of the novel that are only partially concentric: first, to the gradations possible within Jakob's "voice" between his unreflected and his intellectual life and, second, to the double mystery of the school and its chronicler. Regardless of whether or not we relate these products of Jakob's journalistic activity to the writer whose development we witness, as the most frequent instances of time retardation in the novel, the reflections enforce the requirement imposed by both the theme and the plot that the reader separate the two principal strands of the novel. As the principal deterrent to the presumed development Jakob will undergo at the school, they parody the German *Entwicklungsroman*. To the extent that they contribute to the "broken form" of the journal novel and the simultaneous search for linguistic means adequate for the portrayal of the hero's complexity, they also indicate a possibility for the fusion of the novel of development with the picaresque novel.

Acceleration

Each of the three novels reflects the conviction Walser illustrated in his short prose that for a contemporary writer, a gripping narrative is a distracting irrelevance. Notwithstanding the pre-eminence of action-retarding elements that concentrate on the depiction of a symbolically creative personality whose energies are channelled away from creativity, certain narrative devices in the novels support what Middleton referred to in *Geschwister Tanner* as "this suspense of unknowing" (*Middleton*, 410). These create the literary illusion of forward motion. Most obvious are the narrator omissions that excite reader anticipation concerning situations and characters. Some of these expectations that thus create suspense have already been referred to. This suspense devolves not only from elliptical treatment of subsidiary figures such as Rosa or of more important figures such as Agappaia[13] and the manageress, but from the relations between Simon and Klara, Hedwig and Kaspar, Marti and Frau Tobler, and Jakob and the Benjamentas—particularly to the sexual overtones in his relation to brother and sister. The effect of ellipsis in the portrayal of relationships leaving unsatisfied the expectation of more detail or rational psychological motivation, and the limitation of scenes and episodes largely to the vision of the participants, incorporates these relations into a larger narrative frame whose rhythm works contrapuntally to that of the action-retarding elements. The elliptical contractions necessary for narrative actualization of a counter rhythm extend in *Geschwister Tanner* from the chronological ellisions at the beginnings of chapters or sections ("It became winter" [*T*, 114]; "Thus several weeks passed in that wonderful summer" [*T*, 281]; "Autumn came" [*T*, 303]; "It became winter" [*T*, 306]; "Around Christmas time . . ." [*T*, 309]) through the abrupt but effortless transition from *Geschwister Tanner*'s highly stylized beginning in *medias res* to the characterization of Klaus within the space of four pages, and to the concentration that follows on and contrasts to the extended digression of Simon's reminiscences of his youth. In one sentence an omniscient narrator relates the destruction of what Simon had written and rationalizes it from Simon's point of view. In the next the narrator accomplishes a physical, situational, and tonal transition: "Then he went out to the suburb, to Rosa, and said to her: 'Perhaps now I may soon get a position in a small town in the country . . . '" (*T*, 124).

The principal devices in *Der Gehülfe* that accelerate the narrative are concentration on the figure of Marti and the subordination of events at some remove from Marti through indirect discourse. Both of these related devices, however, are no more than counter-rhythmic adjuncts to the more pervasive illusion of timelessness, and strengthen this illusion through contrast. Relating the content to the style, they are the verbal counterpart of Tobler's confusion between permanence in nature and his evanescent social status. The acceleration possible through contraction is carried still farther in the narrative of *Jakob von Gunten*. Restricting the point of view to the first person is thematically justified as an actualization of the symbolic crisis of individuality in the central figure but it also serves to heighten suspense and mystery. Whereas the narrator of *Der Gehülfe* complements the illusory aspect of Villa Abendstern by referring to the uneventful passage of time between narrated episodes (e.g. "Everything went along quietly until Sunday. Could anything have happened?" [*G*, 31]; "In the course of the week, which otherwise passed quietly . . . " [*G*, 119].), the disjointedness of Benjamenta time is accentuated by the omission of time between entries. The basic then-now time scheme projected against the certainty of an uncertain future is amplified by the distension of inner time in the dreams and fantasies (most notably in the vision of the descent to the passageways of poverty) from their actual fleeting measure to the time required for their narration. At the same time the typically correlative form of connective employed in the digressive vision of the lower passageways illustrates how the disordering of causal relationships between episodes is decisive for plot. An analogous use is made in *Geshwister Tanner* and *Jakob von Gunten* of the narrative contraction attained by advancing the action through coincidence (cf. Simon's meeting with Kaspar, his chance first meeting with Agappaia, his overhearing two men discussing Emil, his last meeting with Klara, the unexplained presence of all the Tanners in Chapters Four and Five, the discovery of Sebastian's frozen corpse, and Jakob's meeting on the street with his brother Johann).

Walser's employment of a conventional device, plot anticipation, for ordering the movement and direction of literary prose also sustains his characteristic movement toward suspense directed at the unknown or inarticulable. Anticipations are numerically infrequent in the first two novels. In *Geschwister Tanner* Klara's attack, Simon's Paris dream, his snow-child fantasy, and the tacit relation between the street scenes and nature anticipate and foreshadow. Anticipatory images, such as that of Simon as a beggar (*T*, 25), the "Teufelsjungen" in the first section of the Paris dream, and the anticipation of the snow-child's insensibility to the cold (*T*, 282) are the tokens of the development of anticipation and foreshadowing later used in *Jakob von Gunten* to forecast imagination rather than plot. Walser's use of foreshadowing within the work to terminate a phase of the story, such as the description in the penultimate paragraph of Simon's visit to his sister (*T*, 180) of Simon's thoughts as he preoccupies himself with a novel, clearly evading his knowledge that he must resume a solitary life in the city, Jakob's abandonment of Fräulein Benjamenta, or the pupil Schacht's difficulty in holding a job (*JvG*, 450f.), is conventional. In *Der Gehülfe* it is the constancy of the author's concentration on the deceptively slow transition from one day into the next, the limits of Marti's perspective in his position at Villa Abendstern, and the author's ironic accents that limit the opportunity and need for foreshadowing. Aside from isolated conventional foreshadowings (e.g. Marti's anticipation of clashes with Tobler in his letter to Frau Weiss [*G*, 18] and Frau Tobler's projection of what life will be like after the loss of the villa [*G*, 312]), the author's infrequent foreshadowings help him sustain his ironic distance from events in the novel such as Tobler's defense of the preparations for August 1, reproduced in indirect discourse (*G*, 62f.), or the ostensibly reassuring report on the condition of Tobler's credit, that in fact anticipates his financial collapse (*G*, 112f.). The more effective narrative foreshadowing of the demise of the house is found in the many intimations of the polarity existing between nature and Villa Abendstern. Instances of conventional foreshadowing in *Jakob von Gunten* underline the significance of the Kraus entries and Jakob's *curriculum vitae*. Other anticipations in the novel are blind—that is, although they provide insight into the meaning of the work as a whole, their value as anticipations of plot is limited or is diverted in unexpected directions. Such is the case with Lisa's prophecy of her own death, Benjamenta's promise to tell Jakob the story of his deposition from royalty, Jakob's question about why Benjamenta founded the school (*JvG*, 346), Jakob's certainty that his penetration into the inner chambers and into the mystery of the Benjamentas will reveal wonders to him, or his conviction that he somehow must get money to finance his longing for experience (*JvG*, 403). Anticipations extending beyond the events of the novel, such as Kraus' future employment as a servant (*JvG*, 360, 424), are undercut and compromised by diversionary words or thoughts—in this case Jakob's employment of school jargon for getting a job. Many of the anticipations, like the one concluding the first entry, predict uncertainty. This is not a narrative ruse but rather a transposition of a theme of the book into discrete narrative elements. Two significant instances of somewhat conjectural prophecy that are linked with thematically synoptic statements help explain the relation of the school's teaching to Jakob's own career and role at the school. In the first, Jakob reflects on the termination of his childishness by old age (*JvG*, 472–473) and commits himself to a life of anonymity by his resolve to prevent any circumstances which might result in social distinction. "I can only breathe in the lower regions," he concludes. Two entries later Benjamenta foresees a meaningful life— either a bold adventurous one or a fine moral one—if Jakob accompanies him, for he assures Jakob that "both tender and fearless blood runs in you" (*JvG*, 478).

A stylistic projection of the conflict in Jakob between intelligence and "stupidity" uses the rhetorical device of aposiopesis and is found at the end of certain entries[14] in the form of intentional suppression of unanswered questions or a shift to a neutral topic. Within entries, aposiopesis appears as the fragmentation of description or analysis (e.g., *JvG*, 447, 468). Jakob's conscious truncation of thought is an outgrowth of his hatred of "all those precise phrases" (*JvG*, 378). At the school he is constantly beset by questions. By thus dwelling on a rhetorical form of uncertainty, Jakob echoes the spiritual uncertainty that is symptomatic for the fictional representation of modern consciousness. As narrator Jakob suppresses the resolution of the opposition between his creative imagination and the precepts of the school to the extent that the narrative aposiopesis contrasts with the projections of himself without the aid of intellect—the dreams and fantasies. The contrast between the intellectual life and the imaginative life underlined and activated by aposiopesis conveys more directly than was conveyed in either of the two previous novels a life suspended between a forsaken and amorphous past and a utopistic future. The possibility of fulfillment of these hopes in the world is unique to *Jakob von Gunten;* paradoxically the realization of such a promise for this third novel hero rests on his acknowledgment of imagination, or in the terms of the book, sleep. In this sense, Jakob's awareness of the dichotomy between sleeping and waking life underlies the symbolic aposiopesis which concludes the final entry. In this way the journal bridges the separation between narrator and hero previously formalized as Simon's interior life and Marti's silence.

The narrative and the syntactic rhythm of Walser's prose is sustained by the alternation between narrative intelligence and intuition, between the radical contractions and ellipses in chronology and character portrayal, and between the detail and the verbal kinesis in the action-retarding elements, which Walser himself gave its most inclusive expression when he characterized nature as energy and peace. The pervasiveness of a concomitant world view—one we might call spiritually concessive—extends from the themes and the form to the imagery and diction of Walser's prose.[15] The perception of this organizing energy induced both Hermann Hesse and Oskar Loerke to speak of a conscious art that had found its way back to nature.[16]

Language and Tone

The distinctive tone of each of the novels is based less on qualitatively different language than on the utilization of specific ranges of language by the narrator and the figures in the works and a common idiom increasingly reliant on conversational rhythms but always distinctly literary. We now turn to some of the linguistic features and the mode of their articulation that gives each of the novels its own tonal balance. Walser's consciousness of language stands out in the few remarks he made on his own work. (See pp. 13 and 27). When Walser justified his "spontaneous" style as an experiment in search of an "unknown vivacity" latent in language (*GKW*, 198), he thus complemented the words attributed to Fritz Kocher when he emphasizes the "how" of writing—which attracts him—in contrast to the "what" of writing, which is "altogether a matter of indifference" to him (*FKR*, 27). A critic has referred to the stylistic sophistication of Walser's first prose work, *Fritz Kochers Aufsätze*, as "admirable and at the same time frightening."[17] In each of the novels, the spirit of play implicit in Fritz Kocher's essays assumes a successively greater role in the attempt to extend the possibilities of language by shedding unaccustomed light on the worlds in which the peripatetic heroes move. The artistry found in the resultant combination of verbal play, syntactical resourcefulness, and moral sensibility does not encourage an easy labelling of Walser's talents. In Walser one finds, concurrent with the manifest literary intelligence, the subordination by the narrators and the heroes of the consciously artful and artistic. Part of Walser's contribution to modern German prose is the skilled use in his short prose of the conversational tone he had developed by the time of his third novel. Jakob is the protagonist with the greatest self-awareness, with the most stylistically radical locutions. He constantly skirmishes against "such clever expressions" (*JvG*, 455) as he repeatedly strives to actualize a more colloquial and more quintessential mode of written discourse.[18]

Taken as a whole the language of the novels moves in the direction of a heightened consciousness and heightened ambivalence. At its best in *Jakob von Gunten,* Walser's language can draw together disparate emotive catalysts, propel them in unexpected directions and leave an unresolved question in the reader's mind about the formulator of an ostensibly didactic observation such as Jakob's "I like earning everything, learning everything, and, for example, even a laugh requires its complete experience " (*JvG,* 432).

The role occupied by the narrator is crucial. The least obtrusive narrator is found in *Geschwister Tanner.* There he generously marks out a peaceable literary kingdom in which the pathos and the irony of the speeches, the fresh wonder Simon brings to his encounters, and the dynamism of his dreams and his wanderings live side by side with his lethargy and self-recriminations. On the one hand the amplitude of the language is the vehicle for the multi-faceted view of nature to which Simon subscribes, on the other hand it sanctions the forthrightness between the Tanners that neutralizes the thematic, imagistic, and linguistic residues of *art nouveau.* A certain narrator lassitude anticipating *Jakob von Gunten* can be discerned in details such as the casualness of the first mention of Simon's name (*T,* 10), in the remark that Klaus' letter to Simon read "approximately as follows" (*T,* 12), in the abrupt, sometimes unmotivated references to Simon's sensitivity (e.g., *T,* 18), and in several instances where a self-indulgent verbal play that is extraneous to the novel can be seen. More symptomatic of the narrator's language is the unprepossessing honesty, the directness, and the unaffected attention to detail that may gradually veer into gentle irony, as it is used in the description of the evening Simon and the male nurse spend in several taverns (*T,* 260–262). The introduction to the evening on the lake shore (*T,* 70–71) shows a gradual alternation of tonal accents. It is predominantly euphoric and poetical; at first rich in abstract metaphor and simile, it is then naive, and finally colloquially ironic. One of the seven of the seventeen chapters that end with night or dream concludes with the narrator's description of Simon's walk home through what is described as "a deep, black, oppressive night" (*T,* 245) after the inkeeper had "gently" escorted Simon out of the tavern in which he had spoken about misfortune. Like so many of Walser's night scenes, the enveloping night is a literary relief symbolizing balance and equilibrium. While the narrator's range is broad, emotional high points such as Simon's spiritual gift to Klara are rare. The narrator is more disposed toward the obvious and the apparently insignificant. With painstaking accuracy he describes how Simon sets a table (*T,* 199–200); in a description of the arrival of spring, he can successfully integrate "Many coats were taken off by many people" (*T,* 34); and he describes in unlikely detail Simon jumping over muddy puddles in Hedwig's village (*T*, 138). This early insistence by Walser on the validity of the obvious and the trivial further attenuates action in the novel. It also enhances the role of Simon's imaginative life in filling out the plot. In terms of style, such passages demonstrate Walser's instinctive response to the realization he shared with contemporaries like Rilke and Hofmannsthal that literature had to be enlarged to encompass the diurnal and the miniscule.

The narrator's use of language in *Der Gehülfe* is more complex than that in *Geschwister Tanner* and contributes more consistently to the creation of tone in the novel.[19] As has been indicated above, the expansion of ironic statement within the novel is based on the control exercised by the narrator. Some of the narrative aspects of this control have been noted earlier in this chapter; the more memorable ones are primarily of a linguistic nature. The parenthetical humorous touches referred to in Chapter Three have already indicated that narrator and hero are nowhere as distinctly separate as in the employment of humor. The longer set pieces that describe episodes and comment on events are distinctly set off from the action. They belong to the masterpieces of German comic writing. The first of them is the report that identifies Wirsich (*G*, 33–38). It describes his situation at the Villa Abendstern until his violent expulsion from the house one night when, after a relapse into heavy drinking, he nearly succeeded in breaking through the grillwork on the door with a crowbar and threatened "to set fire to the whole place." Among the more notable devices in the piece is its consistent tone of dispassionate punctiliousness. The language is choice, momentarily even officious; the epithets and relative clauses intimate a moral repugnance at Wirsich's sorry figure which only the good breeding of the language manages to regulate. The wise, tempered insights, the lavish, yet deserving praise given Wirsich at the outset corroborate the narrator's resolve to be just, despite Wirsich's disloyal behavior. In the manner of a true ironist,[20] the narrator sustains his unruffled tone as the described events become grotesque, thereby increasing the effectiveness of the puns and variations in diction. The communication of the narrator's own attitude is prepared for by quotes illustrating Tobler's clemency toward Wirsich in the past. From ostensible agreement the narrator subtly, but decisively castigates Tobler's paternalism. The entire passage firmly establishes the authority of the narrator and permanently distinguishes him from both Marti and the Toblers. The somewhat more indulgently written description of the first of August celebration and the initial description of Bärenweil immediately following it (*G*, 67–73) reveal themselves as ironic variations on the motif of the insecurity of Villa Abendstern in the homeland whose independence Tobler has so vaingloriously celebrated.

An outstanding example of verbal and narrative irony in *Der Gehülfe* is the passage introduced by the narrator as "a minor incident of moral and cultural character" (G, 121–131). The episode relates Frau Tobler's response to a calumnious letter from Pauline's predecessor who, while at Villa Abendstern, had carried on a provocatively brazen affair with Wirsich. Her letter—a little masterpiece of vulgar insult—is described in indirect discourse. Marti's reluctance to comply with Frau Tobler's insistent request that he assist her in the composition of a letter to the girl's mother leads to a series of successively discharged taunts that end in her intentional humiliation of Marti; these insults emphasize the latent eroticism between them and illustrate Walser's use of psychological irony to comment on "moral" acts. The high point of the verbal irony here is the reproduction of the letter Frau Tobler finally writes which begins: "Esteemed Madame!" At the same time the revealing emotional and stylistic *non sequiturs* of the letter parody the pretense of late nineteenth-century upper middle-class diction.

Similarly the ironic descriptions of Tobler's advertising clock (G, 15–16, 30) and the coin-operated machine dispensing live ammunition for Swiss sharpshooters (G, 75–77), as well as the transcription of Marti's self-administered pep talk (G, 147–149)—all of which transpire in Marti's thoughts—illustrate the source of Marti's "failure" as assistant to be other than an anomaly caught between the unreflective life and Tobler's attempt to secure social station by trading on the inflated verbal coinage of commerce. Thus in each instance Marti unsuccessfully seeks a subjective, personal basis for his professional relation to Tobler by trying to humanize the combination of commercial German and the transparent enthusiasm of the advertising prospectuses used to describe the inventions. How the author conveys the distance between ironic narrator and Marti is seen in the narrator's parenthetical note explaining the transition to direct speech at the end of the description of the ammunition vending machine. The narrator says that Marti was so absorbed in his thoughts about the machine that he began to talk to himself (G, 76–77).

In *Der Gehülfe* an ironic narrative mode penetrates even the smallest segments of the novel,[21] and perhaps offers a better case for demonstrating the positive intention of Walser's irony than does the more apparent irony in *Jakob von Gunten*. The irony separating narrator and hero in *Der Gehülfe*, as in all three novels, permits us to comprehend the real as well as the imagined or projected assumption of a different role as Walser's attempt to expand narrative techniques by using these roles not as an expression of cultural nihilism[22] but as an earnest intimation of the possibilities inherent in his concessive view of the world. As the development of the idea of nature in the three novels shows, and as a large part of the work of the Biel period confirms, nature itself is not utilized in the esthetics of the novels as experience to be translated into literature but—to refer to Jakob's achievement—as the ironic symbol of plurality and continuation.

An example of narrative verbal organization that buttresses narrator control of the story while adding to the tone by suggesting more than is articulated is the narrator's extensive use of indirect discourse and the narrative mode referred to, in French, as *style indirect libre* or, in German, *erlebte Rede*.[23] The emotional ambivalence characteristic of the language of *Der Gehülfe* is related to the flexibility with which the narrator employs a verbal expression as fluid as *style indirect libre*. A case in point is the situation of the narrator in the description of Marti's walk through the forest following the dinner with Pauline and Silvi (*G*, 101–107). Until the climactic section of the walk, in which *style indirect libre* is used for Marti's reminiscence of his youth, the narrator holds in check the inherent lyricism of this narrative mode by repeatedly inserting himself between Marti and his thoughts by expressing reservations about Marti's thoughts, by isolated sentences from a more distant perspective, by ironical responses to some of Marti's questions, and by the narrator's reappearance in interspersed sentences in present tense.

The description of the nocturnal boat ride is an instructive example of the integration of *style indirect libre*, indirect discourse, and the attempt to separate narrator objectivity from hero lyricism. The overall lyric tone of the passage (*G*, 50–55) depends on the verbal and imagistic parallels and repetitions which are climaxed in the *style indirect libre* of Marti's apostrophe to the lake. Yet the entire passage is permeated and made memorable through the frequent shifts of perspective in it. Certain elements of the paragraph preceding the apostrophe anticipate it emotionally, while reinforcing its meaning. The strains of music from different points on the shore anticipate the inaudible interior music of the apostrophe; the near collision with another boat which seems to come "from far-away, or from out of the deep" foreshadows the descent into the subconscious; and the words "everything seemed possessed of a peculiar satisfaction, gratification and significance" anticipate the harmonious vision Marti's imagination will shortly project. This entire paragraph is a bridge between the apostrophe and the preceding assertive and self-confident analysis of Frau Tobler's emotional lineage and personality. The analysis, in historical present tense, is still nominally the

point of view of the narrator. The transitional paragraph is in the imperfect tense, and although the narrator has clearly made the shift of tenses
at the beginning of the paragraph, his perspective coalesces with Marti's
in the course of the paragraph. The dominance of Marti's imagination
at the end of this transitional paragraph is attested to by the remark
that Frau Tobler seemed to Marti to be smiling, although it is too dark
for him to tell, and by the short exchange in direct discourse between
Frau Tobler and her son, which is, however, not set off in quotation
marks, which are omitted both at the end of this paragraph and in
the apostrophe that follows, providing a contrast between indirect discourse and indirect *interior* statement.[24] The shift back to present tense
in the apostrophe itself also suggests Marti as the author of the analysis
of Frau Tobler. By filtering all but one of the spoken remarks made
during the preparations for the outing, the embarkation, and the ride
itself through the narrator into indirect discourse these remarks sacrifice
their substantiality compared with Marti's apostrophe and—as indirect
discourse—sustain the atmosphere.[25]

After this single demonstration of the vitality of Marti's imagination,
identifying it with the factual, objective language the narrator uses until
the boat is in the water, Marti is never again allowed so direct or immediate a voice. The reassertion of the narrator's authority in fact terminates the scene. Immediately following the apostrophe, as the boat jars
into a pile off the dock, the narrator says: "It must be admitted that
Joseph had given way to his imagination a bit too much" (*G*, 55).

Throughout the rest of the book, indirect discourse contributes significantly to the tone of the novel, explaining a recent critic's suggestion
that Marti was a source for the figure of Josef K. in Kafka's *The Trial*.[26]
Yet it is impossible to designate a consistent situation or attitude for
its use other than to say that it permits the narrator to test alternate
perspectives in plot-related situations without ever sacrificing his ultimate authority. Given the very large number of Marti's interior monologs
and reflections which are presented in quotation marks and the fact
that the diction of some speeches reported in indirect discourse makes
it inconceivable that they ever could have existed as direct discourse
(cf. *G*, 250, 297), the only consistency discernible is the alternation
to indirect discourse to sustain the informational nature of the narrator's
level of discourse and his role as chronicler of illusion. With the free
alternation of narrative voice and the ensuing ironic retardation in the
action, the narrator is provided with a symbolic verbal counterpart to
the incommensurability of vision that rests on Marti's idealistic love
of existence.

The stylistic consequences of the amalgamation of hero and narrator

in *Jakob von Gunten* reflect the central theme of restriction and freedom
in a linguistic mode serving as a single common denominator in the
attempt to secure a positive relation between existence and imagination
through irony. In the following description of some of the stylistic features of the novel, the liberating aim of Jakob's unrelenting spirit of
play must be borne in mind. A reflection of this spirit of play in the
plot is the actualization at the Institute Benjamenta itself of the motif
of disuse of talents. Simon opposes on principle a sacrifice of talents
as inimical to life, Marti provisionally accepts a social order embodying
such a sacrifice, but Jakob constantly contravenes it in the sprightliness
and latent intellect of his speech, in his masquerades, in his perception
of the power available in play (*JvG*, 388), and in his belief that every
road in life is still open to him (*JvG*, 469).

The formal explanation for the development of ambivalence and variety of tone into a stylistic principle in *Jakob von Gunten* is the disjoint-
ment of time and the coalescing of subject and object in the novel by
a narrator—a narrator who alternately disavows the intellectual element
in speech and thought and who sets as his aim the reproduction in
his journal of lucid, immediate perception. A primary result of this is
extensive contrast in the language, as well as in the motifs and themes.
Contrasts in the two previous novels derive essentially from the presentation of the heroes' confrontation with an external reality; here, however,
it is Jakob's inability to warrant the validity of a solitary law that underlies his idiom of contrasts.

Constrasts find their way into the fabric of the language. Jakob says
of the pupil Heinrich that "he has the bearing of a major and is so
small" (*JvG*, 338), thus combining a connotative and denotative contrast.
When Jakob inquires into his own cosmopolitanism, he states that he
grew up in a "very, very small metropolis" (*JvG*, 368). What distinguishes the verbal and tonal contrasts in *Jakob von Gunten* from those
in *Geschwister Tanner* and *Der Gehülfe* is the drastic telescoping of
intervals between them that may result from the immediacy of Jakob's
speech or from his role as narrator. Contrasting attitudes toward Kraus,
for example, abut on one another in the same entry, as do Jakob's fear
and ridicule of Benjamenta: "I fear him and at the same time something
in me laughs at him" (*JvG*, 475). Similarly the alternation between
somberness and joy and light and dark overlap, as in the laughter
and the tears in the passageways of poverty, or the "inexpressible, simultaneously cold and hot shudder" (*JvG*, 428), or the rays of light that
illuminate the final dream. Similar overlapping of tones is discernible
in individual sentences. Spontaneity and vividness describe the humiliations imposed by the school: "Our faith in ourselves is our modesty"

(*JvG*, 392). It is seen too in sentences in which the school's strictures on hopes for the future are in contrast to the spirited cadence of the sentence itself (cf. *JvG*, 420).

Underlying and articulating all these contrasts is Jakob himself, the pupil of undetermined age, the literary crossbreed between the adolescent hero of German Neo-Romanticism and the more mature protagonist in the modern novel of spiritual crisis, whose ambivalent language mixes the naïveté of the child with the wisdom of age. Jakob himself speaks only of his minority; this is given verbal coherence in the leit-motif of stupidity. Jakob's penchant for analysis, his hunger for enlightening experience, and the native intelligence in his formulations are not enough to make clear the distinction between rational thought and imagination; as his own commentator Jakob refers to his "lack of thoughts" (*Gedankenlosigkeiten*) and his "stupidities." Over forty-five instances of "stupid" or compounds of it, not including related concepts such as "foolish" or "nonsense," occur in the novel, usually in reference to Jakob. Jakob's "stupidity," in contrast to the probing reflections and analyses usually concomitant with the journal form, reflects first of all, his perception of the antithetical constitution of a negatively analyzed society and the Institute Benjamenta, where the pupils can "sparkle" "with delicious stupidities" (*JvG*, 370). This leit-motif represents the narrator-hero's cognition of what the composition and the narrator communicate in the earlier novels: the repudiation of the primacy of the rational intellect where it does not discover being or meaning.

A still more frequent symbolic metaphor used as a contrast to Jakob's intelligence is the conceit of smallness, underlining the consciousness of permanent insignificance instilled by the school. The recurrence of smallness in Walser's subsequent writing as a formal and thematic element, together with the liberation of the artistic impetus in the safety of "insignificance," as described in the previous chapter, help clarify both this metaphor and the related one of stupidity. Behind both Jakob's acceptance of his "descent" from nobility and his "stupidity" is an attitude whose aim is to safeguard against the intellectual determinism of the contemporary age. Jakob is himself, of course, too much a vehicle for the author's theme to perceive the symbiosis he represents. He does however recognize that he is now stupid in a different, "in a finer, more amiable way" (*JvG*, 359). Using the discursive style of the Kraus entries in two entries on the mental capacities of the pupils (*JvG*, 417–418, 420–421), he works through to his own "stupid" presentiment of their lack of intelligence as a manifestation of their humanity. Both the "stupidity" and the "smallness,"[27] however, seem also to indicate that a central function of Walser's irony is to convey through the moral relativism of his heroes and the verbal playfulness found in all three novels a historical awareness of modern man's need to reexamine the relation between consciousness and being. "For people as small and humble as we scholars are," Jakob says when describing the school plays, "nothing is comical. A degraded person takes everything seriously, but he also takes everything lightly, almost frivolously" (*JvG*, 438).

Jakob's language is the most tangible evidence of the novel's experiment in using the diction of irony as an imperfect substitute for hope. Jakob's is a language that takes apart clichés like "a man of principle" by pursuing the connotation of the phrase through expanding it associatively (cf. *JvG*, 335). Or he may parlay his own combination of back-handed compliment and proclivity for verbal play into a curiously apt *non sequitur*. Whenever by dint of application and will Kraus finally manages to learn something, according to Jakob, it seems as if it were engraved in metal. "There is no chance of his sweating it out again or anything of that sort," he adds (*JvG*, 391). Whether Jakob be willful, self-indulgent, frivolous, sentimental, or obvious, he finds verbal shape for the sentiment. The fine gradations of tone that give *Der Gehülfe* its beauty are missing here; the humor depends on the verbal agility of the language and on hyperbolic images that are sometimes drily presented, sometimes with discernible gusto, as in the case of Schilinski's electric tie pin (*JvG*, 352) or the predicted effect on Jakob's pride were he to ask his brother for money (*JvG*, 397). The finer tones are achieved in slight shifts of syntax, usage, or point of view. For example, Jakob's formulation of a simple question at the beginning of an entry transcribing a conversation with Fräulein Benjamenta ("'And are you still striving sincerely,' the teacher asked me" [*JvG*, 447]) presents a problem of narrator point of view that suggests a hidden level of discourse throughout the entire entry. An uncertainty emerges in Jakob's ironic wonderment at the end of the entry: "Am I living in a house of the dead or in a celestial joyhouse [*Freudenhaus*] and house of raptures?" (*JvG*, 448). At the conclusion of his mock-serious consideration of the promises made in the school pamphlet concerning the garden of good behavior, he signifies his doubt that the bliss waiting at the end of this garden could ever mean anything to the pupils, because, as he says: "I don't quite know, whether, say, Schilinski and Tall Peter are really the people for sacrifices" (*JvG*, 413).

Unquestionably a high degree of self-consciousness and self-indulgence inheres in this prose. This is shown in the development of the adjective—from its use in *Geschwister Tanner* for somewhat mannerized sarcasm (*T*, 36), to express the amorphousness engendered in Simon by the arrival of spring (*T*, 160), for the composition of contradictory abstracts (*T*, 64), through its more chastened use in *Der Gehülfe*, to the frequent use of double or triple adjectives in series in *Jakob von Gunten*, where Walser simultaneously shows himself highly conscious of choice for effect but threatens to make the attribute more important than the object itself. Similarly the "corrections" nominally adduced for the sake of accuracy in all three novels are most frequent here. They combine with Jakob's frequent exhortatory prods to himself to stress the "personal" cast of the language. These are the blemishes Walser chose not to remove. They give credibility to the process of creativity Jakob exemplifies in the pleasure his language tries to capture. No less than his irony, his language depicts "the intimation of the utopistic in all existence" that Beda Allemann has identified in the irony of Robert Musil's *The Man Without Qualities*.[28] The impelling force for the dynamism of this language is heard in Jakob's words "In me dwells a strange energy to get to know life from the ground up and an indomitable desire to prick things and people so that they reveal themselves to me" (*JvG*, 442). Although the language of *Jakob von Gunten* presumes the alternating narrative voices of *Der Gehülfe* as a preparatory stage, it is self-contained, radically variegated, particularized, and personal, and shows only a minimal reliance on a supra-individual, literary mode of speech. Jakob's persuasion that reality cannot be reproduced in conjectural terms makes him sound like a bright, but erratic pupil of Bergson. His language is the most "modern" of the idioms in the novels, because it moves under cover of its enthusiasm toward hope and existence through its own efforts to secure a terrain against the spectre of silence. In its literary naïveté, it attempts to articulate the absoluteness of phenomena without regard for the conventions dictated by subject matter, exposition, or unity of point of view. Conversely, Jakob, as the reflective journal-author, projects not an absolute, but a potential reality. As a writer Jakob assumes the risk of imperfect art in order to reunite art with being.

Structure

The aim of this chapter has been to illustrate how the themes and motifs in the novels are supported by style. Inevitably, where style and content are so interrelated and so interdependent, a complete separation is not possible. To wish them so, even in the abstract, is to distort in the name of pedantry. I would like, however, to venture a speculation on the inner form of the novels in terms broad enough to reconcile themes and style with the rudiments of plot which are common to the works under discussion. In so doing I wish also to unburden the developmental presentation in this chapter by placing the emphasis where it belongs—on literary variations of a fundamental imaginative configuration.

The novels follow a pattern of situations. These situations are residually developmental, but they are not interchangeable. In general terms the patterns are: arrival at a vaguely specified scene from a generally indeterminate past (at this point the language fosters ambiguity); an initial hero orientation in which fear (Jakob), suspicion and uncertainty (Marti), and conflict with established codes (Simon) are critical; reassertion of a suppressed idealism that encourages illusion (Simon's gift of himself to Klara, Marti's provisional complaisance with the false idyll, Jacob's analysis of Kraus as an exemplum and his descent to the lower passageways); disenchantment (Simon's return to the city, his work in the addressing office, Marti's realization of his permanent separateness from the Toblers, Christmas at the Tobler's, Jakob's visit to the real "inner chambers," his denial of Lisa, his repudiation of a double life as Croesus-Kraus); the re-introduction of imaginative forces that assure a link to nature (Simon's snow-child fantasy, the author-sanctioned frequency with which Marti "flees" to nature, Jakob's final dream); a departure of the hero in a setting that emphasizes the durability of his being, but which is indeterminate in its intellectual commitment.[29]

This pattern seems weakest when applied to *Geschwister Tanner*, yet the discrepancies, such as they are, occur only if the pattern is applied to the work as a whole. Single episodes such as Simon's walk to his sister's, the stay in the country, his employment as a servant, even the speech about his brother Emil and the final speech to the manageress substantiate it.

The basic alternation that underlies the rhythm of Walser's work, whether in the depiction of character through contradictory traits, in narrative method largely independent of logical progression, or in the effect of adjoining sentences, is universal enough to permit the literary expression of a specific reality and the pretense of artlessness in the novels. The alternation takes the shape of Simon's periods of passivity and seclusion followed by the eagerness of his street encounters. Marti flees to his room as long as the author ironizes his flights into nature. Later he seeks out an increasingly unpeopled landscape. Even the modulation of *Der Gehülfe* as a whole adheres to a pattern of quiescence followed by perplexities, outbursts, and antagonisms. The alternations are at their most extreme in *Jakob von Gunten*. Marking the onset of silence at the end of an entry after Jakob had consciously transgressed against the rules of conduct by his overbearing insistence that Benjamenta find him work, he writes: "I stood still in the corridor and listened at the keyhole. Inside in the office everything was quiet as a mouse. I went into the schoolroom and buried myself in the book 'What are the Aims of the School for Boys' " (*JvG*, 390).

None of the heroes sees the world with the eyes of convention; it is always their ("literary") task to reconstitute a world according to their own vision. The isolation from which they come and the hope they take with them upon their departure basically relate these novels to the fairy tale. As long as the three heroes are sustained by the possibility of fruitful intercourse with the individual members of society—even in the form of an Institute Benjamenta—they are willing to refute and "correct" their imaginative propensity for "fairy-tale" fancies. Yet it is Jakob's singular achievement at the Institute Benjamenta that permits him to dream of Benjamenta as a knight following his disillusionment at the school, whereas Marti rejects a similar perception of Tobler (*G*, 266).

Notes

1. The criteria employed in the discussion of style are in part based on Eberhard Lämmert's *Bauformen des Erzählens* (Stuttgart: Metzler, 1955).

2. Notably Poppenberg's review of *Geschwister Tanner* in *Die Neue Rundschau;* J. V. Widmann's review of *Der Gehülfe* in *Der Bund;* Albin Zollinger's article on the same novel at the time of its republication in 1936 (*Die Zeit*, Bern, December, 1936); Werner Weber in his essay "In Sachen Robert Walser," (*Neue Zürcher Zeitung*, Fernausgabe, June 24, 1962); Heinz Weder in his radio-essay "Bericht über Robert Walser" (Süddeutscher Rundfunk, February 11, 1963); and, most recently, an article by the contemporary novelist Martin Walser entitled "Alleinstehender Dichter. Über Robert Walser" (*Der Monat*, 17 (1964), Hft. 195, 37–39).

3. A related question, posed in more general terms, occupied two contemporary reviewers of *Der Gehülfe*. Both Auguste Hauschner (*Das literarische Echo*, 10. Jahr, Hft. 21–22 [July 1, 1908], Columns 1580–82) and Wilhelm Schäfer (*Die Rheinlande*, 8. Jg. [1908], 16. Bd., 168) praise the technique of the novel while admitting their inability to decide whether the artistry is naive or intentional.

4. Although the failure to specify time in an initial narrative segment is not unusual in prose fiction, Walser in all three novels omits any specific subsequent chronological identification. The pattern for creating an individual time scheme, which applies basically to the other two novels, is most notable in the time references in the first two chapters of *Geschwister Tanner*. The only time orientation given there is in phrases such as "one morning," "around this time . . . ," "one day Simon . . . ," "several weeks had passed . . . ;" and "One evening, as he was going home . . . " The third chapter then proceeds with relative definiteness from within this time outline with the phrase "on the next morning . . ." (*T*, 41). Regardless of whether or not one is willing to characterize

the time sense in the first two chapters by speaking of musical repeats, their overall effect is undoubtedly to strengthen the lyric tone of the novel.

The near-mathematical exactitude in the composition of the original manuscript—before deletions or corrections—makes the contrast between the externally imposed form of the novel and its internal logic all the more striking. The unmodified manuscript consisted of two books, nearly equal in length, each containing ten chapters, the chapters in the first book each approximately ten pages long, the length of the entire manuscript coming to just over two hundred pages.

5. The emphasis in the first seven entries on events following Jakob's arrival at the school constitutes a kind of exposition. Although Jakob subsequently returns to this past time within the Institute Benjamenta, the present time of the novel begins with the eighth entry (*JvG*, 353). The only meaningful time discrimination within the novel is the one between the class activity in the mornings and the emptiness of the afternoons. But this is clearly an artificial discrimination inserted for motif variation, since the afternoons are in fact an ironic mirror image of the uselessness of the instruction in the mornings.

6. The scenes in Chapters Four and Five on the lake shore and Klara's attack offer a familiar example of Walser's method of thematically energizing a chronological and geographical "resting place" by integrating additive narrative elements. A contrast to the scenic character of the two chapters is made through the repeated reference to "strolling people." None of the scenes from the evening through to the next morning is commented on. But all the scenes (Hedwig's introduction of Sebastian, Simon's gift to Klara, Klara's thoughts on Kaspar, Klara's attack and her subsequent communion with nature) have the common theme of the irreconcilability of nature and art.

7. Speaking of the "homelessness" of the first two heroes, Greven says: ". . . the flow of time in which the single episodes of external happenings move past does not produce a unity of the inner meaning, does not of necessity determine esthetic realization, but is rather a fortuitous element" (*Greven*, 71).

8. Joachim Benn's essay on Walser speaks of such a unity of disparate parts in *Geschwister Tanner:* "In many ways the form is very free, the action compounded of speeches, letters, essays, and reports; and yet the whole has the unassailable compactness and lightness of a soap bubble" (*Benn*, 134).

9. In his long monolog to the manageress, Simon reassures himself that she wants to be spared no detail, "to learn it all according to the truth, otherwise not at all, isn't that so?" (*T*, 322).

10. Typical examples are Simon's distinction between the behavior of man and youth in affairs of the heart (*G*, 130); his observation on why a woman can bring unhappiness but never dishonor (*T*, 194); his repudiation of the suggestion that his defense of misfortune sounded like a poet's: "Respect for people is always subordinate to our love for them" (*T*, 243); his differentiation of hatred between unrelated people and siblings (*T*, 213); and the distinction between censure and rebuke of an office worker and a servant, respectively (*T*, 193).

11. An exploratory and occasionally playful language that mixes the abstract and the concrete (cf. *G*, 20, 47, 53, 134–135) indicates both the stylistic proximity of Marti's introspective discourse to Jakob's voice in his journal and a greater

degree of identification between hero and author than is evident from the shifting perspectives the narrator employs.

12. Examples are Jakob's judgment of his parents' paternalistic treatment of the family servant Fehlmann (*JvG*, 398); his criticism of the permissiveness allowed contemporary youth (*JvG*, 393); the dimunition of vitality resulting from excessive learning (*JvG*, 418); his "Foregoing something, that also has aroma and strength" (*JvG*, 349); his guying of self esteem (*JvG*, 420f.); and the safety in anonymity that Jakob formulates when he denies his double life (*JvG*, 469).

13. In the story that in all likelihood was the nucleus of the later novel, "Simon, Eine Liebesgeschichte" (published in *Freistatt*, 6. Jg., Nr. 14 [April 2, 1904], 266–267, but, to judge from a letter to the Insel Verlag, written by the end of 1902), Aggapaia, the "very stupid, betrayed, horned devil" (*KGS*, 138) does play a more central role. The variant spellings of the name in the story and in the novel suggests his figure represents a caricature of what Walser understood as the abstraction of Pauline *agapé*. The relationship between Klara and Simon in this story is more clearly *fin-de-siècle* eroticism. Only the narrative irony suggests Walser's later attempt to overcome and transmute this original Klara's demonic beauty.

14. Cf. *JvG*, 359, 362, 373, 389, 413, 448, 475, 492.

15. The attempt to reproduce a perceived totality through an alternation within a whole is heard in this sentence from the end of the narrator's ironic projection of Villa Abendstern's future prospects, where the irony momentarily abates: "In the way in which it is built and in the place in which it is built this house expresses two sorts of feelings, that of vivacity and that of repose" (*G*, 113).

16. In his review of the republication of *Der Gehülfe* Hesse wrote: "Language is Walser's great love, a love he sometimes admits, sometimes ironizes. He writes out of pleasure in the language, a pure musician, and this gives each of his poetic works the magic of an art that has almost become nature again" (Hermann Hesse, "Robert Walsers 'Gehülfe' in neuer Ausgabe," *Neue Zürcher Zeitung*, August 9, 1936). A review of Walser's *Poetenleben* in 1918 by the poet Oskar Loerke spoke of the great control behind Walser's chatty style and attempted to define the quality of a writer who "so to speak, invented narration *per se*, without an object," as follows: "A naïveté so starkly natural that even following its shattering through consciousness it still depicts itself so assuredly and entire, as if it were nature" (*Die Neue Rundschau*, 29 [1918], Bd. 2, 1238).

17. Paul Müller, in: "Aufbruch, Einfahrt, Zerfall: Bemerkungen zu Robert Walsers Prosa," *Neue Zürcher Zeitung*, June 17, 1962.

18. The beginning of the entry on *Jakob von Gunten*, p. 455 is an illustrative instance. From the formulation and immediate disavowal of individually colored precepts, he works through to the real concern and intention of the entry.

19. In his "Exkurs über Robert Walser" (*Deutsche Literatur im 20. Jahrhundert*, 4th ed. [Heidelberg: Wolfgang Rothe, 1961], I, 99–110) Bernhard Rang singles out as a characteristic use of language in the novel the meeting between Marti and Klara (*G*, 139–147). Of this section Rang says: "The natural recall that Proust makes the principle of his search for *temps perdue*, Walser formulates in the image of his abstract metaphors" (*ibid.*, 107). The formulation applies to the long (*G*, 140–144) narrator flashback that explains Marti's and Klara's

relation and still more specifically to the narrator apostrophe to the past. Certain observations must precede the quotation of the apostrophe. The undoubted mastery at work in this entire section harnesses a two-fold climactic tension: the first is the termination of Marti's Sunday walk through the city with the arrival at Klara's. The second is the echo of Marti's perceptions during the walk in the relatively brief direct discourse conversation between them, where Klara, in her disproportionate part of the conversation, suggests that Marti's humanity is related to his being "overlooked by life." That the flashback is indeed acting as a long transition from the paragraph describing Marti's arrival at Klara's to their conversation becomes clear when we note that even after the narrator has returned to the present time of the novel ("Und nun saß er da am Fenster . . ." [G, 144]), he controls the emphases by résumeéing the conversation between them before the apostrophe in indirect discourse. Yet the heart of the visit is the narrator's success (in the flashback using what Jean Pouillon calls *vision par derrière*) in characterizing an epoch of enthusiasm for socialism and cross-hatching it with intimations of the inevitability of human shortcomings that no dogma can expunge. The inevitability of this soberly ironic narrator-recall anticipates the remainder of the scene and suggests the wide applicability of the past that Rang suggests in his mention of Proust.

In his further discussion of this section, Rang pointedly denies the metaphors any dynamism. In fact, however, a dynamism inheres first in the narrator shifts within the flashback, in the relation of the walk to the second half of the Sunday, in the sense and in the rhythm of the narrator's observation that introduces the apostrophe—in which he generalizes on the harmony of such meeting and the "musical sense" of their confrontation—and last in the apostrophe that concludes the involvement with the past in the section:

> Ja, das Vergangene kam über sie, und rauschte um sie herum, und machte sie die Welt rückwärts, gleichsam treppab, überschauen. Sie brauchten ihre Gedächtnisse gar nicht zu zwingen, dieselben bogen von selber ihre feinen Arme und Schlingen nach den Gegenden des Erinnernswerten, um es spürbar näher zu bringen und zu tragen (G, 146).

20. Following Beda Allemann's article on irony (in *Literatur II*, ed. Wolf-Hartmut Friedrich and Walther Killy, Das Fischer Lexikon, 35–1 [Frankfurt a. M.: S. Fischer, 1965], 309), we understand irony as a subdivision of the comic. From Walser's early fairy-tale dramolets through *Jakob von Gunten* and into the last prose works, his most successful examples of irony are distinguished by the characteristics Allemann uses to distinguish comic irony from tragic or bitter irony: the "intellectual sharpness" separating it from humor and its ability to intimate "at any time a dark, resigned, tragic, and nihilistic reverse side" (*loc. cit.*). There is indeed no basis for tragedy in *Der Gehülfe* and Marti is only able to "fit" Wirsich into the landscape at the end of the novel, but after their first meeting he incongruously thinks of him as "the man with the face of sorrows" (*Leidensantlitz*) (G, 43).

21. Examples are the effect of the sequence of adjectives "light, laughing, rich" in the résumé of Wirsich's relations to the Toblers (G, 35); the use of the conjunction "or" at the beginning of the section in which "the dependent woman" encourages the assistant (G, 83); or the laconism towards Marti when his emotional involvement with Frau Tobler reduces his articulateness (cf. G, 236, 273).

22. The difficulty of identifying Walser with a reassuringly monistic moral position

has been a source of uneasiness on the part of some commentators. A recent essay which concentrates on the artistry in *Jakob von Gunten* ultimately faults Walser for an imputed moral obliqueness (Gerhard Piniel, "Robert Walsers Roman *Jakob von Gunten*," *Schweizer Monatshefte*, 43, 11 [February 1964], 1175–86). Piniel's essay does not credit the artistic achievement that produced so composite a reflection of the crisis in the German novel, the untapped resources of the language Walser had worked out before the advent of Expressionism, nor his representative depiction of the crisis of values and ideals that characterizes the beginning of the new century. Instead it attempts to resolve the esthetic problem the novel presents in its contradictions, contrasts, and irresolution by resorting to moral judgments. The implication of the essay that the very perfection of the art of *Jakob von Gunten* underlines Walser's ineptitude as a Swiss citizen, besides being extraneous, overlooks Walser's insights and the significance of the novel as a historical phenomenon.

23. In his discussion of Flaubert's narrative method Friedman defines *style indirect libre* as "one variety of monologue which assumes a mid-point between the reverie in the first person and the indirect discourse of internal analysis." Because of its participation in the "tonal scales of poetry" Friedman regards *style indirect libre* as "admirably suited as a model for what we might call the indirect interior monologue" in the stream-of-consciousness novel (*Friedman*, 21). Lämmert's discussion of the terminological problem that has plagued critics indicates the limitations of terms that have been suggested as substitutes for Bally's formulation. Lämmert defines the device as "the unintroduced (*libre*) but indirect *Wortkundgabe* of spoken, thought, or perceived narrative elements." Properly stressing the role of the narrator, he suggests as a way out of the terminological impasse that one speak of "free transmission of speech" (*freie Redevermittlung*) (Lämmert, *Bauformen*, 281). In a lucidly presented contribution to the theory of literature Dorrit Cohn has recently argued for the adoption of the term "narrated monologue" in English. See Dorrit Cohn, "Narrated Monologue: Definition of a Fictional Style," *Comparative Literature*, Vol. XIII, No. 2 (Spring 1966), 97–112.

24. Indirect interior monologue would seem a misnomer due to the tense and the visionary quality of the apostrophe. For another thing the apostrophe is too clearly a triggering of the subconscious by the character analysis in the second paragraph preceding, the emotional and structural center of the entire passage.

25. All the examples of indirect discourse have a modulating effect. The following shows how Walser can wrest a muffled yet strongly emotive climax from minor shifts of tone. The first sentence of the quotation represents a shift within the entire section from a relatively dry and straightforward description that begins the third paragraph of the section.

> Etwas wie eine schöne, glückliche Naturträumerei schien [Frau Tobler] die gewöhnlichen Tagesdinge und deren umfangreiches Gerede unwichtig und unwert gemacht zu haben. Ihre großen Augen leuchteten ruhig und schön mit dem Gleiten des Schiffes dahin. Ob Joseph nicht müde werde vom Rudern, fragte sie. O nein, was sie denke, antwortete er (*G*, 52).

Even the single direct quotation in the entire section—of part of Frau Tobler's suggestion to go on a lake ride (*G*, 50)—is syntactically subordinated to the narrator's point of view; thus its directness is circumvented.

26. M. Robert, introducing her translation, *L'Institut Benjamenta*, p. 27.

27. The conceit of smallness also occurs together with an occasional biblical cast in the language for faintly sounded foreshadowings of the utopistic journey to the East. The biblical note is first evident when Johann praises Jakob at their first meeting: "You're absolutely a tree laden with understanding" (*JvG*, 396); when Jakob considers the possibility that Benjamenta may want to become friends with him he speaks of this as "something like" a "visible, forbidden fruit" (*JvG*, 433); later Jakob makes a somewhat cryptic prophecy regarding the tree of life when considering the prospect of a Kraus existence (*JvG*, 472); the biblical flavor of the Kraus divination and the wailing wall in the passage-ways is quite clear. The further references deal with Benjamenta, the man who once uses Pascal's concept of a "deposed king" to characterize himself. Benjamenta's physical size is repeatedly contrasted to the dwarf-like pupils. The epithets used for Benjamenta—giant and Hercules (*JvG*, 345), Samson (*JvG*, 470), Goliath (*JvG*, 470)—bear on his character: Hercules was subject to madness, tried to strangle his beloved nephew Iolaus, and on regaining his sanity secluded himself from all human contact; the Biblical Samson, although physically powerful, was impotent as a moralist (Judges, 16), and the giant Goliath was vanquished by a youth (I. Sam., 17).

28. Beda Allemann, *Ironie und Dichtung*, p. 208.

29. None of the novels employs a climactic ending. In the return of the heroes to nature there is instead a parallel to what has been described as "the slow dissolution into sleep" (*Friedman*, 187) of the epiphanies of stream-of-consciousness novels such as Larbaud's *Mon plus secrèt conseil*, Dorothy Richardon's *Honeycomb*, and Joyce's *Ulysses*. Similarly the compromise of Simon's final affirmation achieved by the preceding snow-child fantasy parallels the "vague affirmation of Molly Bloom's final monolog" (*Friedman*, 239).

7

SHORTER PROSE WORKS

Within a writing career that began with the publication of Walser's
first poems in 1898 and ended in 1933 with Walser's removal from
Waldau to the mental institution in Herisau, in the Canton of his legal
residence, the novels are no more than a short and relatively early interlude in Walser's production of over a thousand shorter prose pieces.
Had Walser's five other novels (the three he claims to have destroyed
in Berlin,[1] "Tobold," and "Theodor") been published, it might be possible to say with more certainty that Walser abandoned the novel because
of his dissatisfaction with the critical response to his experiments to
renew the form. In retrospect, Walser associated the crisis of his final
years in Berlin with a definite decision to abandon the novel.[2] However,
his asserted persuasion that his talents lay in other directions does not accurately convey Walser's continued concern with the novel. Self-ironic
references to publishers' disappointed expectations of a new novel[3] and
the fact that he wrote a novel in Biel and another in Bern after the
failure of the first three to gain so much as a *succès d'estime* are signs
of this concern. That the second of these, "Theodor," reflected an uncertainty among contemporary novelists about the province of the novel
is suggested by a plot dealing (in part) with the search for material
for a novel. That, conversely, the novel's scope of statement remained
a norm for Walser as miniaturist can be seen from the remark in
the Bern piece "Schaufenster": "For me every essay is something like
a novel . . ." (*UP*, 144).

This chapter discusses selected works from the short prose that illustrate Walser's motif variation of the themes of isolation and attraction
found in the novel heroes. In limiting the selection largely to the motifs
of the commercial world, the youthful personality, the wanderer, the

ironist as "lover" and as amateur artist, certain thematic and stylistic aspects of Walser's short prose must be overlooked entirely or summarily treated. It is necessary to treat only tangentially problems related specifically to the short prose, first because our concentration has been on the novels and secondly because of the discovery, principally by Jochen Greven, of nearly again as many short prose pieces as had heretofore been published in book form.

It is therefore not our intention to rehabilitate Walser's late prose. It is, however, hoped that an indication of the quality of some of the unpublished work written during the Bern years will serve to counteract the misinterpretation of this period of Walser's career. It is true that the stylistic idiosyncracies resulting from Walser's masquerading of his art as non-art, his unabating concentration on figures transparently based on himself, and a language only too often on the verge of becoming the mannerized victim of a refusal to take language for granted, makes Walser's eccentric artistic course a difficult one for us to follow. Yet to designate the ironic self-portrayals in *Die Rose* as a disintegration of style forecasting Walser's mental illness is an unfortunate misrepresentation based on an incomplete knowledge of the production of the final twelve years of his career.[4] Walser himself was conscious of the extremity of style he employed in *Die Rose*. In a letter to Resy Breitbach in 1925 he questions why she purchased this, "one of my finest books," rather than more of his earlier work. He finds it more suitable reading for more mature women, since "in this book there is a great deal to understand and to forgive." Walser's contributions to the *Prager Presse* in the same year that *Die Rose* was published, further indicate his manifest control of style. Since the most instructive developments of the themes and motifs in the novels are to be found in the late prose, the loosely chronological sections in this chapter emphasize this period whenever possible. In concentrating on the motifs that demonstrate investigations of creativity outside the normative definition of art in a writer whose prose is conditioned by the sensitivity of a miniaturist, we are well advised to take note of Walser's assertion in a late piece when he speaks of a prose piece resting "entirely on the most refined attentiveness conceivable" (*UP*, 138).

Es gibt viele, viele Schicksale

The mysterious and fugitive plurality of life underlying the novel heroes' desire for experience gives the novels a thematic contrast in the relation between subject and world. Walser's comparably sensed attraction led him to seek to portray his own experience of life in an extensive variety of forms. His ability to use only those forms where a subject (subjective or metaphoric) replaces the "epic connectives" Walser complained of in the novel is clearest in his failure to write successful novellas. During the years in Biel Walser repeatedly tried his hand at the novella. Instead of using the genre's restriction to a dramatic sequence of events in a single plot, Walser's narrator stresses the exemplary and paradigmatic quality of the tale. The narrator thus preempts the "story" while the ostensible novella is left hanging.[5] "Ophelia. Eine Novelle," published at the beginning of the Bern period, is a striking example of the prescription Walser drew for the remainder of his work. Here story is repeatedly relegated to a severely limited element within the work. The termination of the attempt to use story for poetic statement in Bern denotes Walser's concentration of his efforts on the prose miniature. His frequent intimation in Bern that his work was being misunderstood stemmed from what Walser regarded as the failure of the critics to comprehend his attempt to expand the statement of his work with the stylistic means available to the minaturist. Aware as he was of the external narrowing of the range of his work, he ironically cautions the reader that he is fixing his mind's eye on nuances, tenuous connections and, above all, possibilities.

> May I request placing confidence in this prose piece. I am calling attention to the fact that I am always only capable of offering something to those who wish to strive to discover possibilities, to cherish—to some extent—what is proferred.
>
> For me there exist circumstances, connections of a peculiar kind. Perhaps there exist consequences and effects that no one can perceive.*

In his late prose Walser turned to advantage the shortcomings of his middle-period novellas. By putting the narrator's time and the narrator's observations and reflections alongside the subject's perceptions, Walser succeeded in a characteristically modern combination of essayism and lyricism. The antecedents of the bold and willful integration in his late prose of a lyrical mood in the non-lyrical form of the essay can be

---

* Darf ich in dieses Prosastück Vertrauen zu setzen bitten? Ich mache auf die Tatsache aufmerksam, ich sei immer nur denjenigen irgendetwas darzubieten imstande, die bestrebt zu sein wünschen, Möglichkeiten zu entdecken, das Dargebotene einigermaßen zu schätzen (*UP*, 42).

Es gibt für mich Umstände, Zusammenhänge seltsamer Art. Vielleicht existieren Folgerungen, Auswirkungen, die niemand wahrzunehmen vermag (*UP*, 214).

found from Walser's earliest prose pieces on. It exists in the novels as the level of discourse that separates narrator and hero; it is most clearly discernible in the more overtly "poetical" pieces disguised as reports, written in the Biel period (e.g., "Poetenleben," P). Walser's innate penchant for lyric detail and his essayism of sententious observations that are "timeless" as regards narrative progression create an expanded narrator space in a small form where in place of a conventional story the narrator conveys insights to the reader through the variety of levels possible with ironic dissimulation.[6]

With rare exceptions Walser relies on his own experiences for the subject matter of his short prose. His employment as a clerk before devoting himself entirely to writing provided the basis for stories and prose pieces dealing with figures from the world of commerce. The earliest of these, "Der Commis. Eine Art Illustration," appeared in the volume *Fritz Kochers Aufsätze*. These ten essays describing the life of a commercial clerk are casual in tone, the humor is conversational. By virtue of a preface, an epilog and frequent insertions, the narrator is at least as dominant as the clerk. The benevolent irony shown toward the limitations, disappointments, and strictures of the clerk's life is paralleled by the self-indulgences and the ironic apologies of the narrator. He modestly excuses the narrowness of his subject matter but also justifies it by claiming that the clerk had heretofore been overlooked by writers. "For me," however, the narrator says in the preface, "he is just right. It was a pleasure for me to look into his small, fresh, unmowed world and to find corners in it which the gentle sun bathes with close shadows" (*FKR*, 54–55). As an idyll harboring the possibility of the comic in its self-conscious irony, "Der Commis" anticipates the intentional flexibility of tone in *Der Gehülfe* and in *Jakob von Gunten*. The narrator of "Der Commis" shares with Jakob the difficulty of convincingly portraying a figure whose goodness makes him uninteresting (*FKR*, 61–62) as he verbally surveys and prods the subject until an opening is found. Also, in anticipation of the novels, the withdrawal of the narrator in three of the episodes of "Der Commis" (the clerk's letter to his mother, a surrealistic stage-fantasy, and a dream of love) creates a narrative anomaly that contradicts the rather carefully developed tone of witty causerie, since these episodes—each of which adds significantly to the portrayal of the clerk—introduces an autonomous subject lyricism at variance with the author-imposed narrative perspective.

While the irony in "Der Commis" is such that its soft-pedaled social criticism reminds us of the clerical world from which Marti came, this imitative satire, based on anaphora and expressive variation in later vignettes of business offices, is closer to Simon's criticism of the system (cf. *T*, 42–44). Common to all these pieces is the meanness, the senseless, perverse jealousy, and the welcome tyranny in which the employees work.[7] Helbling, a figure found in all of the rest of them, is the antipode of the hard-working, conscientious idealist in "Der Commis." "Ein Vormittag," ("One Morning," *KGS*, 248–257; originally in *Simplicissimus* [1907/08]) is a macabre portrayal of Helbling's Monday morning boredom and the near-maddening agony he endures by wasting the morning without working. A reportorial tone is varied in the direction of the grotesque through verbal anomalies that succinctly capture the extremity of Helbling's boredom. "Helblings Geschichte" (*AKD*, 263–284; originally in *März* [1913]) is the best of the studies of the clerical world, but it is also a character study of the sort Walser excelled in. It is an outstanding example of Walser's Berlin prose at a time when his ability could infuse a calculatedly unemotive, sober, and, in this case, even disillusioned language with emotive tension. Narrated in the first person, Helbling himself unwittingly portrays his stultified heart and moribund soul. With frightening self-hatred, with the willful crippling of his inner resources that makes the forthrightness of his address uncanny, and, with the dishonesty towards, the fear and hatred of himself and his fellow men that twist his expressions of disdain into emasculating time-serving, Helbling summarizes his life, his office work, and his sordid love affair. The discrepancy between the "lyricism" of the discourse and Helbling's perversion of sensation reaches a high point in the dolefully repressed, sterile rage of a conclusion that makes him absurd as none of the novel heroes are.[8] After the Berlin period the commercial world only rarely provides a background for Walser's work. When it does (principally within lyrical autobiographical reminiscences), it is no longer the reflection of an encounter with exterior reality it was earlier.

The youthful personality is a motif that antedates the novels, recurs during the Berlin period and then undergoes a metaphoric transformation in the Biel period and after. This motif, current at the turn of the century, is given symbolic import in its first decade in the refutation of "*a priori* forms" by members of the *Charon* group around Otto zur Linde and Rudolf Pannwitz. Walser's own use, as a symbol for the rejection of a self-deceptive positivist society, of a soliloquistic "youth" who accepts man's sorrow in an uncertain journey in the direction of belief, can be viewed as pre–expressionistic to the extent that it anticipates Expressionism's remodelling of the "young person" by divesting him of estheticism. Walser, however, does not actualize the prophecy of youth as revolt. The novels have shown that Walser's own interest in youthful figures is related to his metaphoric representation of the creative personality. But only Jakob's figure foreshadows the relationship between this personality and the play found in the late work. There, the element of playfulness is a central one, to which we shall return. Here, it is enough to indicate the importance Walser attached to it by referring to his "Hamlet-Essay" (*Stille Freuden*, 71–77; originally in *Prager Presse*, May 11, 1926). Walser sees Hamlet's "ripeness is all" as one of the many pranks his great intelligence played on him. Wishing a society cleansed "of the male and female Hamlet-esque" Walser suggests we "need mirth and credulity" rather than Hamlet's intellectually arrogant "spleen," together with a flexible morality that tolerates play, since "only those who like to play possess genuine responsibility." In a much earlier prose piece ("Aus Stendhal," originally published in *Rheinlande* [1912]) devoted to a section in Stendhal's *De l'amour*, Walser comments on Stendhal's anecdote by saying: "They experience the pinnacle of life at the moment when they gambol (*spielen*) with their lives, and this is the only possible way to reach the pinnacle" (*AKD*, 137).

The clearest anticipation of the metaphoric interrelation of youthfulness and play in the style of *Jakob von Gunten* is found in *Fritz Kochers Aufsätze* (originally in *Der Bund* [Summer, 1902]). Using the ironic artifice of an "editor" who introduces the essays as a mixture of childish naïveté and insight into the narrow world of a schoolboy, Walser repeats the consciously limited prospectus of the preface to "Der Commis." The essays (typical titles are: "Die Schulklasse" ("The Classroom"), "Der Mensch" ("Man"), "Die Natur" ("Nature"), "Das Vaterland" ("My Country"), "Höflichkeit" ("Politeness")) report observations on a still-nascent world in a style that parodies the innocence of the "themes." Separating both Fritz Kocher's essays and "Der Commis" from Walser's somewhat opaque symbolism in his early verse fairy tales is a post-symbolistic reaction to art. This reaction is evident in the (partly ironic) narrator modesty of these two prose works just as it is later in the novel heroes' antipathy to art. It culminates in the knowledge established in *Jakob von Gunten* of the "significance of the element of play in all art" (*Kayser*, 439) that indicates Walser's conclusive disengagement from literary Symbolism.

In addition to the obvious formal, thematic, and narrative antecedents of *Jakob von Gunten* in *Fritz Kochers Aufsätze*, the schoolboy resembles the boy that Jakob may have been before entering the Institute Benjamenta. He is aware of the nuances in the world around him, enjoys longing for something he cannot identify, reveals a penchant for the superlative and the enthusiastic in his appreciation of art and nature, but is firmly reliant on bourgeois ethics. He anticipates Jakob in his self-admonition "to be casually and naturally nice" (*FKR*, 24); in his view of the classroom as the reproduction in miniature of the outside world (*FKR*, 52) in which he ardently wishes to test his ambition. He has Jakob's predilection for investing reality with the added dimension of fantasy and dream (cf. *FKR*, 25, 29–31), and he relies on judgments of the heart and the veracity of unselfconscious naturalness (cf. *FKR*, 10, 48–49). His expression of the search for insight is, like Jakob's, paradoxical: "I don't wish to know everything," he says in one essay; "I possess little thirst for knowledge" (*FKR*, 48). In an earlier essay, however, he says "One must know everything" (*FKR*, 37).

Stylistically the essays show an accomplished miniaturist at work; they contain an early form of the aposiopetic termination of journal entries (cf. *FKR*, 9, 10, 26, 29, 46, 54) and the penchant for "naive" reflection from an unusual verbal focus found in *Jakob von Gunten* (cf. *FKR*, 23, 28, 54). Fritz Kocher also illustrates in incipient form Jakob's proclivity for burlesque and self-irony.

> I want to be famous. I want to meet beautiful women and love them and be loved and pampered by them. Notwithstanding I shall suffer no loss of basic strength (creative force), but rather I shall and will, from day to day, become stronger, freer, nobler, richer, more famous, bolder and madly bolder. For this style I earned a flunk. But I proclaim: this is nevertheless my best essay, which I have ever written.*

"Die kleine Berlinerin" ("A Young Girl from Berlin," *AKD*, originally in *Die Neue Rundschau* [1909]), the secret diary of the twelve-year old daughter of an influential art dealer, repeats the theme of youth as a seeker of ethical definitions. The diary reveals a personality whose directness of vision is about to be submerged under the conventions of the life her social station will impose upon her. The breadth of statement in so potentially sentimental a story is quite impressive. Sustaining throughout a tone that balances self-deprecations of what are genuine discoveries of the self as "stupid and immature," "stupid nonsense," etc. with childish prattle and not-so-childish reveries, and echos of the dicta governing her parents' world, the diary is an unwitting indictment of her society generally, as well as of her parents' failure to satisfy her need for spiritual and emotional growth. Her attempt to rationalize her

---

* Ich will berühmt werden. Ich will schöne Frauen kennen lernen und sie lieben und von ihnen geliebt und gehätschelt sein. Nichtsdestoweniger werde ich nichts von elementarer Kraft (Schöpfungskraft) einbüßen, vielmehr werde und will ich von Tag zu Tag stärker werden, freier, edler, reicher, berühmter, kühner und tollkühner. Für diesen Stil habe ich eine Fünf verdient. Aber ich erkläre: Dies ist dennoch mein bester Aufsatz, den ich jemals geschrieben habe (*FKR*, 9).

200 Inquiry and Testament

loneliness and accept "reality" so she might dispense with the sustenance she has gotten from reflective imagination reminds us of Jakob's acceptance and enlargement of his minority through his actual and intellectual explorations. The story's completely persuasive tone and diction elevates it above the sociological and psychological insights it contains. In a coda of questions at the "fragmentary" conclusion of the work (*AKD,* 127–128), Walser actually unifies the portrayal of a human being who has attained the maturity to submit to the uncertainty and promise of life.

The next significant portrayal of youth in Walser's work, the title figure of the long story "Tobold" (*KP,* 148–201; originally in *Die Neue Rundschau* [1917]), depicts a metaphoric youthfulness in a setting characteristic of the Biel period. As with Fritz Kocher, Jakob, and "Die kleine Berlinerin," however, it presumes youth's capacity for metamorphoses and awareness of the variety of relationships implicit in reality. The reappearance of a figure named Tobold in several other works[9] as well as the use of the name for the title of the lost novel from the end of the Biel period indicates Walser's recurrent imaginative preoccupation with this youth. The story is based on Walser's service as a butler in Dambrau castle in Silesia in 1905. The first-person narrator of the enclosing story is the product of successive metamorphoses which—through death and transfiguration—have allowed Tobold to emerge from his earlier forms of Peter, Oskar, and Wenzel as Walser's equivalent of Expressionism's New Man, for whom death is the unequivocal proof of life (cf. *KP,* 150). The ambiguous relationship between aristocracy and lowly service in *Jakob von Gunten* is repeated here in the spiritual and imaginative freedom Tobold finds as a ducal servant. In Tobold's more limited encounter with reality Jakob's persistent uncertainty is replaced by Tobold's indefatigable joy and voraciousness of perception. They do resemble one another when Tobold praises Don Quixote as a man who "in his infamy and ridiculousness" is a happy man, and in Tobold's understanding of man's insufficiency as an attestation of the richness of experience to which he is heir.

The Tobold figure is of interest in its positive realization of Jakob's entry into the world and, as well, in its relation to the Biel period—in which both Middleton and Greven note a marked diminution of creative power from the Berlin years. Middleton finds it difficult to explain "the lapse into 'Kitsch', the stylistic enervation which affects some of [Walser's] work during the Biel period" (*Middleton,* 420). In a chapter on the work of the entire Biel period, Greven undertakes to relate what he views as artistically highly problematic work in relation to the whole of Walser's career (*Greven,* 112–135). Citing instances of mannerism,

formalism, and stereotyped formulations and images in analyses of
Walser's depictions of nature, the artist, the wanderer, and the humane,
Greven characterizes "the harmonic image of the world" found in this
"literature of pure illusion" as a consistent consequence of the separation
between art and being found in the work of the Berlin period. In
Greven's view, the Biel period "bursts the limits of traditional esthetics,"
indicating "transformed ontological thinking" that requires the reader
to intellectually perceive the dualism between them in his own thinking
"so as to comprehend the one-sided creation of an art of pure subjectivity
in its meta-esthetic function." "The literature of pure illusion," he explains, "is not only thereby negatively justified by virtue of the impossibility of having pure being appear in quasi-real, perceptual shape, but
positively as well, as the reconstitution of the dualism of inwardness
and being. [In this reconstitution] both move from their estrangement
within culture back into their genuine positions, in which they truly
correspond to one another" (*Greven*, 134–135).

"Tobold," however, stands out from Greven's persuasive general
analysis because it achieves a harmonious world view that is free of
the stylistic shortcomings he scores in other work from this period. While
the metropolitan flavor of the social criticism implicit in the Berlin work
is lacking, the criticism itself is present in the parodistic "Studie über
den Adel" that Tobold writes only to have rejected by a daily newspaper
(*KP*, 170–173, 174). The story does not—as is often the case in other
works from this period—end in night, in the forest (cf. "Naturstudie,"
S), or in vague hopes for the future (cf. "Leben eines Dichters," *KP*
or "Poetenleben," *P*), but with an enthusiastic return to life outside
the castle. As in possibly no other work of the Biel period, the variety
of style and tone here symbolically résumés Walser's literary career:
from the mixture of symbolism and *fin-de-siècle* resignation in the earliest
works (where Greven says the alternatives are withdrawal to an inner
life or death), through Walser's experience of his failure as a "man
of letters" in Berlin, to the ironic illumination from within a world that
Jakob is only about to enter. Tobold's style after his metamorphosis
is reportorial, masterfully controlled in its gentle irony, communicative
when he uses the language of pathos, and discreetly humorous in the
speeches characterizing the Danish ducal secretary or the office-proud
Polish steward. His seemingly effortless transformation of reality into
an unobtrusively individualized vision, is indeed a metaphoric use of
the role of youth as double for the artist. "Tobold" has the transitional
character that Greven himself stresses in his description of the work
of the Biel period; yet as a successful metaphor it suggests an earlier
inception for the transformation of the artist to save art and culture,

which Greven sees as characteristic of the Bern period (*Greven*, 155). Before considering the walks and the fairy-tale tone associated with work from the Biel period, we shall discuss two works from the Berlin period that are related to the novels and have further consequences for the later short prose.

The historical study "Die Schlacht bei Sempach" ("The Battle of Sempach," *KGS*, orginally in *Die Zukunft* [1908])[10] has been referred to as Walser's single artistically realized work in which "a completely objectivized substantial, world-reality with valid, active figures" (*Greven*, 28) appears. Yet the "objectivity" is not as far removed from Walser's later ironized factual reporter as it might seem. Behind it is a style that corrupts the nominal "historicity" of the piece to make of it an extremely personal and at times elementally impassioned vision in celebration of simplicity. A series of fine hatch drawings describes the approach of the Austrian army toward Sempach, the lassitude and luxury of the armored noblemen as they await the Swiss foot soldiers in the summer dust, the joining of the battle that is decided after Winkelried's sacrifice—"the noble thought," as it is abstractly paraphrased—effects the breach in the Austrians ranks, the cool cruelty of the ensuing massacre of the Austrians, the bloody, profane work of cleaning the battlefield, and the return of the Swiss to their villages. The discharges of electric tension that transfigure the objective prose are effected with devices encountered in the novels: a fetish for sometimes improbable detail, "corrections" that are not erasures but amplifications uncovering illusion, anachronistic similes, compound similes—the willfulness of which seems to destroy the effect of an otherwise opalescent description, but which in fact verbalize the spiritual condition of the Austrians for the "naturalistically" objective narrator—abstract metaphors, and parataxis. Unique to the story are the verbal anachronisms in contemporary locutions combined with a leit-motif of theatrical images and similes. These elements burst forth in the description of the battle, where they jar and reverberate against the "naïveté" of the narrator in revealing a demonic vitality successfully conjuring up an infernal, theatricalized, sometimes primeval struggle (cf. *KGS*, 230–234). In the severely restrained style of the concluding page and a half, one sentence—not limited to description of the burial of the dead—indicates the profane battle fought: "No priests were there, what would they have done with priests?" (*KGS*, 236).

Walser's perspective here was not a historical one, but the same ontological and humanistic one that links his novels to the rest of his work. The testament of this particular "report" is a vision of man's liberation in Walser's own time from the tyranny of convention and social illusion. The "moral" of the story, articulated well before the pianissimo conclusion, comments indirectly on the theatrical similes in the story and indicates that Walser still foresaw a proud future victory: "The Battle of Sempach shows, really, how terribly stupid it is to put on too much clothing" (*KGS*, 234).

Despite the fascination the motif and theme of the artist held for Walser from his earliest writing through to his final works, both as self-identification and as a symbolic fate, it was only in his depiction of the artist as ironist during his Bern years that he was able to purge him of the ambivalence he held toward art. In "Kleist in Thun" (*KGS*, originally in *Die Schaubühne* [1907]) the artist-hero is the victim of the dichotomy between his art and the "naturalness" he vainly seeks in Switzerland.

Of thematic interest in the depiction of this artist is the ambivalence of his relation to nature (Kleist's longing for a family is reduced to the sexual erethism of many of the similes, and his desire to accomplish "a great deed" to: "His whole being itches for physical exertion" [*KGS*, 199]). Kleist's creative intellect and his demand that his writing be absolute literature divides his response to the majestic nature before him into perceived beauty latent with ominous danger. Kleist's submission to his artistry and his abandonment of his hopes for a "normal" life are depicted as a rock slide. "He even helps," the narrator continues, "now it is decided. He wants to sink totally into the catastrophe of being a poet: the best thing is for me to perish as quickly as possible" (*KGS*, 105). It also serves as an early example of the literary portraits that critics praised as a new form or as a view of an author unobstructed by the clichés of literary history.[11]

Yet the emphasis properly belongs on the style. The startling effectiveness of the literary portraits that achieve the mimesis of psychologically variegated human personality through a varied style rather than through "psychological" narrator analysis depends on an empathy occasioned by a real or imagined shared trait. This applies to Walser's literary portraits of Brentano, Lenz, and Büchner, as well as to later studies devoted to Dickens, Jean Paul, and Hölderlin. The struggle in "Kleist in Thun" between artistic ambition, the longing for a "natural" life as father of a family, and the wish to accomplish a heroic deed links it to the halting, metaphoric liberation of the heroes' artistic potential in the novels. The language here is fluid and mobile; it externalizes the extremity of the hectically emotional states that torment Kleist during his stay in the lake-side city with the same "cool ardor" with which Jakob regards his distant ideals. A proximity to *Der Gehülfe* can be seen in the uniquely Walserian employment of present tense to create and fill narrative space. Beginning the study as an imaginary recreation of Kleist's life at that time, the narrator mentions only "Der 'Zerbrochene' Krug" but neither *Die Familie Schroffenstein* nor "Robert Guiskard" (*KGS*, 196). From this historical present he shifts to a near identification with Kleist (a variant of *style indirect libre*) by using direct speech indirectly (without quotation marks) yet, in the same sentence, still maintains narrator perspective. He re-emerges at the conclusion of the story as a reportorial narrator, distant and laconic, directing a finale that is a perspectivistic marvel (*KGS*, 206–209).[12]

The Artist Wanderer

Walser develops still another analogue of man's creative potential in his descriptions of walks that are characteristic of the period[13] following his return to Switzerland in 1913. More explicitly than in the novels, these walks link the themes of wandering and imagination by having one act as catalyst for the other. Now it is on the walks, in the real and imaginary encounters, that we find the alternation of momentary disorientation with reflection and also the awe that was formerly set in street scenes. The walks provide an interim solution for the figurative representation of interior reality being supplanted by Walser's much more conscious use of masks for the same purpose in the twenties. Although the structure of Walser's work supports the logic of denominating the walks as "the basic scheme in Robert Walser's poetic world,"[14] the applicability of Bänziger's emphasis on the personal civic hazard in a wanderer's mode of existence (cf. Bänziger's section "Der Spaziergänger, Der Schweizer") is questionable in the light of Walser's use, in the twenties, of the "walks" to comment on Swiss life. In fact the novels anticipate two related elements found in the most effective of the walks—the poetry of described motion and the dynamic use of abstractions as the imaginative bases for walks. On the other hand, the depiction of nature itself in the walks cautions one to read nature as the conscious amplification of the concept of being it had become in *Jakob von Gunten*, a symbol of plurality and continuation. The natural settings become increasingly abstract and assume the stage-scenery quality that intermittently oppressed the poet in "Kleist in Thun." Walser himself said that one of the reasons for his move to Bern in 1921 was that "the motifs and the decorative props that I had drawn from Biel and its environs gradually began to run dry" (*Wdgg*, 21). The progressive disappearance of scenery reaches its apex in *Die Rose*, in the late prose pieces collected in *UP*, and in much of the work in the *Prager*

Presse, at a time when Walser can say: "In this prose piece I am going to hold myself aloof from descriptions of landscape on principle" (*UP*, 62), or: "It's boring to hear talk of landscape and such" (*FKR*, 202). When, in the twenties, the framework of the walks is retained but the scenery that formerly catalyzed insights and relations is dispensed with, the walks become skeletalized, metaphysical wanderings.[15]

The most representative of these walks is "Der Spaziergang" (*KGS*, 261–343). It catalogs Walser's gifts and it parades his weaknesses. It makes a lasting impression despite its stylistic peculiarities, in part because of its representation of the "immersion in the minimal" (*Middleton*, 414, on *Geschwister Tanner*) with a forceful array of ironic devices. The plot is most simple: the narrator-poet wanders through a city until nightfall. Both a dinner with a Frau Äbi and several errands interrupt the walk. As though it were a parody of a story the narrator intimates traces of plot only to demolish them, while revealing that he will presently recount the events of the walk in a work to be titled "Der Spaziergang." The thread of the narrative serves only to mark a large number of soliloquizing speeches by the narrator. Whether imaginary or real, real but addressed to imaginary figures or to the reader, self-ironic, or bombastically "literary," they parody the convention of plot foreshadowing.

Although nearly all of the monologs in "Der Spaziergang" exhibit mercurial transitions and verbal tightrope walking, the problematic intention of the work as a whole stems from the earnest concerns these speeches express—Walser's exclusion from popular success (*KGS*, 264–266),[16] his instinctive distrust of ostentation (*KGS*, 271–273, 335–339), and his attempts to reestablish roots after his return to his homeland (*KGS*, 279–281).

The longest of the speeches is an *apologia pro sua vita* as wanderer-artist (*KGS*, 309–316). The verbal symmetry of the entire speech parallels the intellectual progression in it from the diurnal needs satisfied by the walks to the spiritual and subjective needs dictated by a conception of reality dependent on a unity outside civilization. As a human rationale it anticipates the series of often simultaneously self-critical and ironic self-depictions that form a decisive part of Walser's work in Bern.[17]

The climactic moment of dematerialization in the walk occurs after the narrator passes a grade crossing. The scene he then describes had been ironically foreshadowed four times and yet, a new, pathetic style is introduced to describe this vision of Jesus' descent onto the street, the disappearance of suffering, and the transformation of objects into "soul." It is clearly intended to convey in graphic terms an emotional justification for the narrator's wandering (*KGS*, 319–320). The images of the vision reflect the motif of recuperation found in other walks published with "Der Spaziergang" ("Hans," "Naturstudie," "Reisebericht," *S*): they are abstract and yet stress the safety of a dream-like security; they emphasize the primacy of inner existence, but they hold out the promise of identity in change. The vision, which is sparked by the narrator's external perception of only "the smallest and most modest things," is characteristic in its portrayal of nature. The thematic antitheses are nature and reflection. But a particular, perceptible nature gives way to an imagined, symbolic nature that becomes a landscape of the soul, since "what we suppose we contemplate and take into ourselves pours forth out of our own interior" ("Naturstudie," *S*, 73). The strongly reflective character of the walks themselves (often explicitly referred to as "the intellectual" or as "mind") is often shown by Walser's terminology for the imaginative perception of the distinction between spirit and intellect, even as perceived within the bliss of "pure being."

> Pure being became my happiness, for which I found neither words nor thoughts. I would have liked to compare myself with trees, which are silent. . . . At times I forgot myself and all other people entirely . . . thought nothing, was like an unthinking, struggling growth, but the contemplative approached me of itself, and involuntarily I had to murmur to myself: "Poor, forlorn earth."*

The anomalies of the verbal and narrative irony in "Der Spaziergang" are most evident in the explicit expression of moralistic judgments (*KGS*, 270, 277, 325, 326) and the undeniable sentimentalities (*KGS*, 275, 320). How are these anomalies to be weighted in a work where, but for the final scene, the illusion of fictional reality is replaced by badinage with the reader, parodied plot anticipations (e.g., *KGS*, 282), the parodying of conventional narrative time flow, the refraction of nature descriptions through narrator interruptions, and a comic scene with Frau Äbi in which the narrator's irony is matched in a humorous speech based on expressive variation (*KGS*, 297–298)?

More than any work so far discussed, "Der Spaziergang" is consciously suspended between intention and realization. It is a philosophically more conservative, stylistically more eclectic, literarily more self-conscious re-

---

* Das reine Sein wurde mir zu einem Glück, wofür ich weder Worte noch Gedanken fand. Ich hätte Lust, mich mit den Bäumen zu vergleichen, die stumm sind. . . . Mich selbst und alle andern Menschen vergass ich zeitweise völlig . . . dachte nichts, war wie gedankenlos strebendes Gewächs, doch das Gedankliche kam von selber wieder zu mir heran, und unwillkürlich musste ich vor mich hin murmeln: "Arme, verlorene Erde" ("Naturstudie," *S*, 84–85).

production of Jakob's willingness to let his journal entries stand as written, as the imperfect mirror of his own "nature." The structurally unin-
tegrated lists of objects in "Der Spaziergang" (*KGS*, 285, 335) that
are typical of the Biel period are perceptually a segment of "pure being";
historically they are a part of the attempt by writers in the first decades
of this century to demonstrate the unlimited poetic potential of reality
in the wake of Poetic Realism's selectivity. (By contrast, an example
of a stylistically integrated "list" can be found in a three-page long
sentence in "Tobold" [*KP*, 188–191].) If Walser's pose of artistic modesty
has meaning and conceptual integrity it can be found in his preference
for "reporting" his lyric perception of the individual reality of objects
(cf. *S*, 56, 80–82) instead of consuming them in art. ("If you tell a
story then its contents disappear" ["Rodja," *GW*, VII, 211–213; originally
in "Prosastücke," *Der Neue Merkur*, 8. Jg. (1925), Hft. 6, 467–479].)
Beyond its willfulness, baroquely florid speeches, and various parodies,
the earnestness of "Der Spaziergang" emerges in the two final sections
of the piece. One is an officious-ironic defense of the repetitions in
"Der Spaziergang" that are a parallel to nature and human life and
a denial that "the serious writer feels himself called upon to provide
accumulations of story material" (*KGS*, 339), revealing the speeches
as an extreme use by an ironically lyrical narrator to attempt—without
a story—to pierce the autonomy of existence and the multifariousness
of the individual objects that compose it. In his chapter on the Biel
period Greven correctly points to repetitions of earlier locutions that
have a self-parodistic effect and indicate a less vital relationship to language. Yet it is necessary to bear in mind Walser's awareness of repetition, the presence throughout his work of both an elliptical style and
parodistically employed periodic sentence constructions, and his subsequent ability to creatively modify this style. Given Walser's commitment
as an artist and his unabating inquiry into the limitations of art, the
instances of self-parody in Biel and later are best understood as a variant
expression of the ineffability of existence through art. This too is the
sense of the final scene in "Der Spaziergang"—a change of mood and
tone that occurs as the approach of night concludes the walk. As the
narrator strolls along the river in what is the first credible nature scene
in the work, he muses both on his failings as a human being and on
"two sorts of human figures"—a girl whose love he frivolously forfeited
and an aged, weary man once encountered in the forest. The sombreness
of this scene and the refraction of the unitary narrator perspective
through the two sorts of figures achieves a degree of tone contrast which
only a modern author committed to a view of man as an elemental
force ultimately defying analysis would risk. The conclusion effects a

retroactive tension similar to that found in the novels. The *esprit* of art is contrasted to the existential certainty of death. During this final scene the narrator had been gathering flowers, a graphic counterpart to the verbal bouquet assembled in the walk. At the end he drops the bouquet and muses: "Then why the flowers? 'Was I collecting flowers to place them on my own unhappiness,' I asked myself, and the bouquet fell from my hand. I had gotten up to go home; for it was already late, and all was dark" (*KGS*, 343).

Fairy tales

The quality of suspension in so much of Walser's prose was refined in "Der Spaziergang" into a narrative method that rarely had to touch ground. A most profoundly ironic source of this suspension was Walser's "a-literary," bald insistence on seemingly insignificant detail. Instances such as those referred to in the novels occur throughout the works. Middleton accurately describes an example of "the deliberate ironic elaboration of the obvious" he cites from the late prose as a "kind of inverted form of caricature as word play" (*Middleton,* 422). But Walser's penchant for this detail should also be viewed as part of an irony inherent in the narrator dominance of the short prose. He seems to say: this is the writing ego that describes itself to inquire into the composition of the world.

Throughout his career Walser was capable of conveying a perceivable, but difficult-to-specify dimension in his writing. This perception of suspension that has been described as "fairy-tale-like" (cf. the early reviewers of the novels; *Greven,* 24, Note 28; *Middleton,* 423) inheres in the emotional effect of the narrator's language in "Die Schlacht bei Sempach," in the complexity of the novels' naive heroes, and in the "pure illusion" of a large part of the work in Biel. The use of fairy tale is warranted since it is an apt term that characterizes the stylistically lucid evocation of uncertainty some of Walser's work shares with the fairy tale. His work on the whole justifies the use of the term by describing his gift for simultaneously exciting pleasure and puzzlement in the reader.

Now we shall discuss some of the alternations of traditional fairy tales, fairy-tale-like stories, and fantasies to which this tone has been ascribed, beginning with résumés of two of Walser's early works, even though they are dialogs in iambic verse. "Schneewittchen" and "Aschenbrödel" both ante-date *Fritz Kochers Aufsätze* and "Der Commis." "Schneewittchen," the more distinctive of the two, was singled out in Walter Benjamin's essay as "one of the most profound creations of recent poetry—which of itself would suffice to have us comprehend why this apparently most dissipated of all poets was a favorite of the implacable Franz Kafka" (*Benjamin,* 151). He further states that only in "Schneewittchen" can one observe the process of recovery that gives Walser's "superficial" figures their mixture of blessedness and the uncanny.[18] Walser's version of this fairy tale begins only after the Prince's kiss reawakens Snow White at the conclusion of that of the Brothers Grimm. Snow White is "sick" as the playlet begins and must decide whether her mother did in fact try to poison her after sending her paramour, the hunter, out into the forest with her to kill her, or whether the queen's protestations are true and these suspicions are all childish "fairy tales." The complexity of the work is achieved by intertwining strands of fairy-tale plot, post fairy-tale "reality," and illusionary theatricality in which masks alternately hide and create reality. After Snow White initially accepts her mother's version of the fairy tale as a superstitious fancy, the queen insists Snow White and the hunter re-enact the attempted murder so she may prove that her hatred and envy of Snow White's beauty are past. When Snow White defends herself against a raised dagger, the enraged queen shouts to the hunter to cut out Snow White's heart; the prince intervenes, at which moment the queen declares: "Why, it is nothing but a play" (*KGS,* 102). Snow White, unsettled by this test, is still ultimately willing to be persuaded of the truth of the queen's version by the hunter's rhetoric. The dramolet ends with the reconciliation of Snow White and the queen, although Snow White, the symbol of naive beauty, must first assuage her mother's fears that one day Snow White's fate will be that of her mother, her sensuality making her fall victim to another "hunter."

The work is clearly a keystone in Walser's writing. Its themes are the need and difficulty of love, the healing, even redemptive power of the believing child, and reliance on the judgment of the heart. Behind the interplay of motifs that create a fairy-tale aura quite different from that of the original is found an acute psychological insight into man's adamant refusal to substitute good for evil and into the passions aroused with the uncovering of human failings. Finally there is created the intimation only precariously suppressed that evil is never banished but only intermittently subdued.

"Aschenbrödel" (*KGS,* 32–76) was also written in 1899, and, if Walser's repeated suggestions to Insel Verlag regarding the possibility of its publication are an indication, he esteemed it more than "Schneewittchen." Here the traditional fairy tale provides the plot, although omissions of episodes such as the ball scene and Cinderella's rediscovery by means of the lost shoe, and transformation of the prince's character and the inclusion of a fool and a figure called "Märchen" alter the tone. This work sheds light on the cellularity of the novel heroes and the ahistorical world from which they appear. At the same time it is important to note that Cinderella's awareness of her prince's "by-gone personality" "that no longer fits our times" (*KGS*, 44) and Snow White's reference to the "misery of the age" posit a contemporary consciousness, later seen in the novel heroes, along with the inward consciousness of the heroines within the fairy tales.

The action-retarding speeches and reflections of both heroines antici-pate the novels in their lyric portrayal of an inner existence unable to accept what is here a fairy-tale reality. The climax of this verse dramo-let occurs as Cinderella decides not to follow the prince. She is unwilling to submit to the urging of "Märchen" to follow the "reality" of the plot. To do so would mean sacrificing the "roaring pleasure" she derives from accepting her role as Cinderella in a life of humiliation and drudg-ery where she has "yet/ to dream to the end of the good/ that hovers all about me here . . ." (*KGS*, 90). When she does consent to leave with the prince, and thus live out the fairy tale, it is on the condition that she will continue to dream after the end of the fairy tale. Cinderella clearly anticipates Jakob although she lacks his compulsion to investigate the world and the people in it; for her the dream is exclusively a refuge from the world.

The theme of service in its relation to freedom and the conflict be-tween imagination and creativity in the novels are foretold in these two works amidst the private symbolism of the individual figures. Some of the factors contributing to Walser's interest in a form he modified so radically from the outset are the *fin-de-siècle* trappings in the diction and imagery (e.g., the "scene" of the queen and the hunter embracing on a bench under a willow tree) that point to the renewed interest in the fairy tale at the turn of the century, and Walser's own reading. Seelig reports that at the time Walser was "intensively occupied" with Büchner and Shakespeare (*KGS*, 351). One critic has recently identified the model for the world-weary Prince and the fool in "Aschenbrödel" as the Prince and his fool in Büchner's comedy of romantic irony *Leonce und Lena*.[19] Walser, later in his career, made rather extensive use of narrative elements associated with the fairy tale and variants of "simple forms" such as moral tales, anecdotal grotesques, and ironic humoresques and fantasies. Here too the impetus may have come from an integration of his reading with his own literary talents and his personality. His interest in a variety of forms, even in their negative aspects, is part of the modern redefinition of literature that parallels what one critic has called the "avowed campaign against 'innocent' story-telling" of the fairy tale in German Romanticism, an attempt to portray the world in "degrees of reality beyond representational realism" (*Thalmann,* 22).

The stylistic influence of the Romantic poet Clemens Brentano is highly probable. Walser's proclivity for lyrical structuring, the mixture of neologisms, accumulations of adjectives, the tight-rope exercises between a tragic destiny and comedy of situation in the fairy-tale-like moralities and in the scenes from clerical offices, the conscious theatricality he associated with the fairy tale from the outset, and the pleasure in a primarily linguistic idea that is emotionally related to it bespeak Walser's early knowledge of Brentano's works.[20] The starkly reduced perspective of the fairy tale, its inherent tendency to narrative reduction and concentration on rationalistically unmotivated "highpoints," its dispersion of the cognitive levels of fiction into a single action that allows for a parabolic increment, and, finally, its universalist tendency in the indefiniteness of time and place all complemented Walser's own creative personality.

In Walser's knowledge of Ludwig Tieck[21] we find a likely link to the art fairy tale of German Romanticism. Stylistic correspondence between them lies in the uncertainty of mood in Tieck's fairy tales and in the sequence in Tieck's texts of causally unconnected, heterogeneous material taken from everyday life using a minimum of fairy-tale appurtenances. A thematic relationship inheres in the amorality seen in the work of both authors with their recognition that the inner person embraces good and evil[22] and in the "thrust forwards toward the person" in works depicting the "dynamic levitation of salubrious life" (*Thalmann,* 39). More specifically the fairy-tale mood of the animal story "Katzentheater" (*KGS,* 179–187; originally in *Die Schaubühne* [1907]), the surrealism of "Entwurf zu einem Vorspiel" (*AKD*), and the purposeful elimination of the distinction between theater and life in "Zwei kleine Märchen" (*AKD*) suggest strongly the influence of Tieck's fairy-tale comedies.

Walser's moralities are often concerned with purposely undeveloped figures who are incapable of responding to the variety and riddle of life and who consequently actualize their non-life through death.[23] Related to these are the ironic moralities that focus on a single shortcoming that the figures described have allowed to distort their lives.[24] Walser's principal use of the device of stock phrases as it occurs in the folk fairy tale was for anaphoric variation in his ironic humoresques.[25] A distinguishing characteristic between the folk fairy tale and the art fairy tale, the use of miracles in contrast to the symbolic projection of the interior life or the "inner reality" of the world, is limited in Walser to anti-Märchen that are in fact parables.[26]

Walser's fairy-tale quality is perhaps best described by noting the effect of his technique of unmediated narration from a consciously restricted perspective in combination with an affectively complex language that emphasizes the narrator's consciousness even when he is nominally only a transmitting medium for the story. This can best be seen in fantasies of a harmonious world (e.g., "Phantasieren" [*GW*, VI, 167f.; originally in *Literarisches-Echo. Ein Kriegsbuch der Dichter, 1914–1915*.]; "Träumen," *GW*, VII, 77–79; originally in *Schweizerland*, 6. Jg., Hft. 7 [July, 1920], pp. 485–486), fantasies of such a world that are ironized as unreal (e.g., "Seltsame Stadt" [*KGS*, originally in *Freistatt*, 7. Jg., Nr. 4 (January 28, 1905).]), in the many prose pieces that lyrically review the beginning of Walser's writing career or the transparent transformations of his own figure ("Der Student" [*KP*], "Der Arbeiter" [*P*], and "Hans" [*S*]). Across this bridge of narrative and linguistic devices Walser moves from the infallible sureness of touch in early prose such as "Kleist in Thun" and "Die Schlacht bei Sempach" to the extensive reference of late works such as "Ophelia," "Olympia," "Die Ruine," "Eine Stadt," and "Ein Flaubert-Prosastück."

In the rare instances when Walser uses the term fairy tale in a title, it is the initial element of an ironically poised study of contrasts and has no relation to the folk fairy tale, just as he uses Märchen in "Aschenbrödel" as the only player with an objective view of events. "Märchen" (*GW*, VI, 107f.; originally in *Pan*, I [1910], Nr. 1), a short piece thematically related to *Jakob von Gunten*, tells of an emperor who is sick, as is the age in which he reigns, because profiteers have made the land "resemble a desert." The fairy tale in "Märchen" (*UP*) stems from transformations of self which the narrator regards as positive, but which, because of their autism, are a source of disinterest or misunderstandings by others. "Mehlmann. Ein Märchen" (*KGS*) assumes the narrative naïveté of a fairy tale to present a comedy of human limitations and illusions on both sides of a cabaret stage.

A prose story from approximately mid-career that exemplifies the tangibility of true fairy-tale plots[27] and using a figure related to the orphans of Walser's earliest work (cf. *Greven*, 45), is as close as Walser ever came to writing a bona fide fairy tale. In "Das Ende der Welt" ("End of the World"), "a child that had neither father nor mother, nor brother and sister, belonged to no one, and had no home of its own hit upon the idea of walking continuously until it came to the end of the world" (*KP*, 37). In the single-mindedness of its search the child is deterred neither by mankind nor by passing events, and it gives no heed to day or night, to sun or moon. Its thoughts are always occupied with what the end of the world must be like.[28] After more than sixteen years, a farmer on the way tells the nearly exhausted child that the end of the world is only half an hour's walk away. A farm named "End of the World," a paradise of tranquil growth and beauty, is the unwitting child's goal. Taken in, the child promises to serve "and now the child didn't run away again, for it was like at home" (*KP*, 41).

Using the wanderer motif common to fairy tales and a rationally unmotivated central figure that undergoes no development, this story presents the antitheses of the barrenness of isolation and the bounty of acceptance. Behind the irony of the title's double pun and the narrator interpolations lies an antinomian faith that views the end of the world as the token of a positive promise. A walk that initially seems futile or of infinite duration is used as the framework for man's search for the meaning of existence. This fairy-tale homecoming is at the same time a visionary resolution of metaphysical homelessness. The story is characteristic of the Biel period in its use of the most positive metaphor in Walser's poetic vocabulary, that of motion. In linking this metaphor with the fairy tale, Walser revives the motifs of play and transformation from his earliest fairy tales in a work whose peculiar locale for an extraterrestial paradise is an unmistakably bourgeois terra firma.

Homo ludens

Walser's move to Bern marks the beginning of the final phase of a literary career whose biographical and artistic consequences set him in a literary topography that was beyond the pale. The prose production of these years—which exceeds by well over two hundred works what had been known from prose collected by Carl Seelig in *Unveröffentlichte Prosadichtungen, Große kleine Welt*, and *Stille Freuden*—is more varied in quality and in style than Greven's chapter on the Bern period indicates (*Greven*, 136–175). Whether, as the contemporary Swiss author Paul Nizon has suggested, Walser had to continue to write to control his own demons, or whether he continued to write from his conviction of the value of a player-artist as a medium for resistance against monisms that limit individual consciousness, will depend on how the "amateurism" of this late work is read and received. Late in his career Walser described his prose pieces as "nothing other than parts of a long, plotless, realistic story." "For me," he continued, "the sketches I produce now and then are shorter or longer chapters of a novel."[29] Walser remained undeterred by the "disgrace" of his career. A late self-depiction in which he accepts the company of other "disgraced" authors begins: "Who reads me and how one reads me doesn't concern me" ("Etwas von der Schande" ["A Bit of Disgrace"], *Prager Presse,* March 28, 1936).

Walser himself viewed the move to Bern as the onset of a new period in his work. Contrasting it with Biel he said to Seelig: "Under the influence of the powerful, vital city I now began to write less shepherd-boy-like than I had in Biel—where I had used an affected style—more masculine and more internationally directed. It was a question of looking for new motifs and ideas . . ." (*Wdgg,* 21). The rarity of positive critical response at this time[30] and the lack of encouragement or financial assistance from publishers made these efforts to re-establish his reputation all the more difficult.[31] In his best work of these years Walser achieved a singular fusion of themes and style from his earlier writing. With the exception of an unusual number of topical references[32] and a notable increase in the frequency of dialogs, few elements of his style are new; the expansion the style undergoes comes from Walser himself. Transforming the wanderer-artist to player-artist, Walser further develops forms and a level of narrator discourse outside the path of normative literature. The characteristic form of the period is the monologist "essay" found in *Die Rose, Unveröffentlichte Prosadichtungen,* and work published in the *Prager Presse.* In its most extreme form, this "essay" unifies, only through the consciousness of the narrator, often unrelated subjects in segments of various length presented in random sequence. From center stage the monologist recites the diurnal occurrences of a solitary life and the insights and reflections that emerge from them. An intriguing forthrightness of masked self-identification is conveyed, yet the words spoken by one of the many author personae, "Das Kind," are extremely apt: "No one is justified in conducting himself towards me as if he knew me" (*FKR,* 202).

More insistently than before, Walser's writing depicts the inquiry into the meaning of existence uniting his earlier work (the motif of isolation from society, the homelessness of the novel heroes, interior life versus "the world," the fairy-tale-like resolutions or suspensions of this dichotomy, the motif of wandering) as investigations and practical experiments on the nature of art and the contrasts he associates with creativity in man. He mixes letters, addresses, reminiscences, plot résumés, fantasies, associations, dreams, dialogs, and "interior walks" in what he referred to in a letter as "a kind of combination" (Jochen Greven, "Rekonstruktion eines Werkes," *Neue Zürcher Zeitung,* October 23, 1965). The commitment to art in this work is as radical as Kafka's although his earlier antipathy to high art is now seen in a more drastic irony whose positive purpose is to concede to playfulness something of the weight Nietzsche had envisaged for it in a literature that would once again become the handmaiden of life (see Chapter Seven, Note 39). Since the problematic character of this work is most intimately related to the depiction of the creative personality and the symbolism in the narrator's depictions of self, the remainder of this section will be restricted to selections from the several hundred works from 'his period that illustrate these points.

A clear instance from the beginning of the Bern period of the artist as parodistic player may be found in the episodes that were published in 1923 from Walser's lost comic novel "Theodor." Of the three published novels, "Theodor" is most reminiscent of *Jakob von Gunten,* yet the differences are instructive. In place of a narrator-subject's private journal, Theodor records his experiences in an "almanac."[33] It is no longer the submerged inquiry of *Jakob von Gunten* into the justification of writing. Walser here approaches the irony of Gide's *The Counterfeiters*[34] when Theodor justifies to Frau Steiner his plan to fall in love with her in order to collect material for the novel he is writing. Although Frau Steiner is sympathetic and is willing to let him become *ami de la maison,* her scholar husband is uneasy. Her plea on Theodor's behalf reads in part:

> Theodor was on the wrong track, he had lost nearly all of his good humor. He had been looking for a fitting figure for his most recent novel book and he believes he has discovered the figure here. He had let himself be influenced by moods which—praise the Lord— are now a thing of the past. He came to me to recover. Humaneness alone would have obliged me to be indulgent . . .*

Theodor's explicit role as a writer becomes evident in the first episode, when he describes how he was hired as a secretary to the owner of an art gallery after he successfully managed to hide his "poetic character." The picaresque tone is still more pronounced in the final scene, a masquerade ball.[35] Before the ball the scholar visits Theodor in his rooms. Despite reciprocal courtesies which prevent them from discussing what is uppermost in both their minds—Theodor's relation to Frau Steiner—both men admit to having brought a pistol with them. The scene ends with Steiner—whom Theodor thinks of as "the poor devil"—

---

* Theodor war auf einem Abweg, er hatte fast alle gute Laune verloren. Er suchte eine passende Gestalt für sein neuestes Romanwerk und glaubt sie hier entdeckt zu haben. Beeinflussen ließ er sich von Stimmungen, die ihm nun gottlob fern liegen. Er kam zu mir, um sich zu erholen. Die Menschlichkeit allein mußte mich zur Nachsicht verpflichten . . .

angrily shouting: "The devil take you." These words play on Steiner's actions at the ball, where he appears dressed as "the poor devil." Steiner, wanting Theodor "to strike out on his own," forces him to leave the ball, and escorts him to the train station. Theodor escapes Steiner's carefully devised snare and spends the rest of the night with his brother, one "out in the midst of life," proudly recounting how he has made his own decisions in his most recent adventures.

Portrayed in a realistically sketched metropolitan milieu without the safeguard or asylum of an equivalent to the Institute Benjamenta, this artist-hero encounters the world as a literarily "helpless" comedian. This tells us something about how Walser sought to enlarge the scope of his work in Bern within the framework of the dichotomy between art and life. Although Walser continued to concede as little moment to the trivial "events" that figure as story in Bern as he did in Biel, Theodor's urbanity is symptomatic of a change in plot situations. The alternation between reveries and the enthusiasms elicited by minimal events in the Biel writing expressed a highly personal attempt to justify art while only indirectly revealing its problematic condition. Theodor transforms fantasy into intentional, public play. By depicting Theodor in an urban setting Walser abandons the Biel motif of the artist who "passes" as a burgher, acknowledges and accepts the artist as the embodiment of the opposite, and heightens through irony Jakob von Gunten's knowledge that in whatever guise, his commitment will always be to man.

"Theodor" is thus symptomatic of the shift in the depiction of Walser's view of art and the artist as the principal medium for an investigation, reminiscent of Jakob's, of the definition of individual freedom in contemporary society. Art is no longer the primeval, consuming vision that isolates the struggling germinal poet Oskar in the early dramolet "Dichter" (*KGS*, 20–31), nor is it the illusionary or compensatory dream it is for Fritz Kocher and the clerk of "Der Commis"; it is not the unacknowledged symbol of interior totality that is suppressed so as not to compromise the novel heroes in the world, nor is it, finally, the highly-conscious artistry masked as dream and solitary wandering in the Biel writing. In the extreme contrasts in theme, motif, and style of this period Walser's work carries further his demonstration of art as the actualization of opposites. In Greven's excellent analyses of the relationship between art and society in the Bern work (*Greven*, 141–156), he characterizes the view of the artist's attitude in this period as a "freies Sich-verhalten-zum-Sein" (*Greven*, 155). The antecedent for the admittedly more reflective expression of this view in Bern is implicit in Jakob's personality as it is expressed in his journal, in the narrative irony achieved by shifts of perspective in *Der Gehülfe,* and in the achievement within what has been referred to as immediacy of narration seen in *Fritz Kochers Aufsätze* through to and including the pieces discussed from the Biel period. The dominance of the narrator in the Bern work and his sententious reflections are not new, but their heightening does contribute to the transformation of the play of opposites into a symbol for the irreconcilability of art and existence and their eternal and necessary dialectic.

The dialectic of freedom and suppression is the theme of "Herren und Angestellte" ("Masters and Employees," *UP,* 24–28), where the narrator discusses a "problem" "that cuts deeply" "into contemporary conditions, which seem to veritably teem with existences who are employees, and who sometimes disregard this particular circumstance." What has been overlooked, the narrator suggests, is a unity inhering in contrasts by virtue of "the possibility" in each of them that it includes the other. "The employee waits, the master lets people wait." But the master, who is "something like an Overman," "nevertheless remains man and fellow man" and his superiority to his underling may become oppressive: " 'Blast it all,' he calls . . . , 'hasn't he had enough waiting, this man who is martyring me with his patience?' " (*UP,* 27). The "complementariness" of freedom and oppression is again brought out in an associative self-depiction entitled "Saubub" ("Brat," *Prager Presse,* April 10, 1932): "Perhaps the Swiss owe their freedom not only to Wilhelm Tell, the hero of the liberation, but to the freedom-disdaining Governor Gessler as well, who provided the former with the occasion to get moving" (cf. "Wilhelm Tell," *UP,* 208–210).

A Bern variant of the fairy-tale moralities that enlarge on the trap of emotional and intellectual inflexibility is the wise and capricious study of two emotionally different lovers who see only the shortcomings of the other ("Die nie fertig werden," *UP,* 244–251). In an earnest epilog that denominates humans as "actors and at the same time viewers" whose struggle to love one another gives present-day comedies a tragic touch and vice versa, Walser expands the motif of light and dark in *Jakob von Gunten* as he asks us to apply the "reason" of the benighted to human relations: "Why can't there be a light in the light instead of just in the darkness? Is it sometimes too bright in us?" (*UP,* 251).[36] The inevitability of antitheses even in "the absolute image of freedom," about which the narrator in "Freiheitsaufsatz" (*UP,* 210–214) says "in my opinion one cannot conceive, sense, reflect on, and esteem [it] multifariously enough," undergoes a transmutation into the antithesis of unreflective existence and intellectual activity in "Minotauros" (*GKW,* 168–171). Beginning with the proposition that being "awake as an author" means "I am a sleeping human being," the narrator produces a verbal and intellectual "maze" to demonstrate the absolute otherness of the abstract "problem" of "the future of nations." He unsuccessfully tries to think this through in comparison to the "absolute clarity" of the proposition "that a certain sort of sleep is useful, if only for the reason that it has its own specific life." By a series of digressions beginning with "the question, whether Langobards, etc. possessed anything like cultivation or not" this maze-runner understands that he is closest to the nation's meaning as being if he approaches it from the historically useless comparison with the thanes that arises from "the regularly breathing plot of the Lay of the Nibelungs." The reader emerges like "Theseus" from the labyrinth that came into being "out of knowledge and unconsciousness."

An analysis of "the uncanny quality of our age" is undertaken in "Der verlorene Sohn" (*UP*, 112–117). The "parable" specifies in word and in thought the glorification of the given of existence that Walser aims to embody in his capricious art. In an imaginatively tight-spun web of wordplays, cross-references between three separate narrative segments, and motif contrasts such as strength and weakness, intimidation and security, development and stagnation, marriage and bachelorhood, the grace secured by the return of the ragged prodigal son in the Bible is compared to the " 'incomparably uncanny man' " the narrator has recently seen once more. The mediocrity and facelessness of this master of "conventional cultivation"—who "is less dangerous than he suspects"—shares with "our epoch" its "homey uncanniness" (*heimelige Unheimlichkeit*). A narratively contrapuntal insert in this study depicts the relationship between Saul and David as an interdependent, vital, but antipodal relationship between art and life. A climactic, specific comparison is then made between the prodigal son's repentance and an age in which weaknesses are taboo, where, as the narrator suggests, "no one wants to repent anymore," since "we are too weak to disclose weaknesses." The final sentences expand the frame of this "letter on the prodigal son" to implicitly include the narrator, who, in the introduction, counted it "among the pleasantries of life to perceive the present as the eye of God," and who insists on the compatibility of "the man of the world and the pious man." Walser thus successfully transforms a biblical motif into the esthetically coherent knowledge that in "our epoch" the unsuccessful seeker of happiness still experiences punishment, but no understanding or atonement. The indeterminate perspective of the final sentence embraces both the infinite repentance of the prodigal son and the artful "amateurism" of the narrator: "Being happy overcomes, far outdoes all weakness and strength. Happiness is conjointly the most tremulous and the most stable thing" (*UP*, 116).

"Der verlorene Sohn" intimates the difficulty of maintaining art's salutary dissension in a culture whose proud comprehension, acceptance, and enthusiasm for what Walser might call the somnolence where art is created, forces the artist to new means of expression or to ironic disguise. In a fictitious reply to a request for "suspenseful novellas" ("Brief an einen Besteller von Novellen," *GKW*, 189–193), Walser makes a nearly programmatic statement on a related difficulty in contemporary literature. After reminding the "editor" in ebullient and convoluted language that the reality of present-day "civilization-centralization" precludes the development of story-telling talents such as Chekhov's or de Maupassant's, he places himself with the modern authors who "deal preferably with the problematic," which, while not gripping, "so to speak takes hold of the humane." Walser then analyses the refinement, the experimentation, and the reflection in contemporary writing as the result of the increasing difficulty of "not sending one's gaze out too far in what is relatively still too spacious a sphere."[37]

The most frequent device in the Bern period for the disguise of the artist is the use of a very great number of ironic, metaphoric masks. They parallel the development of the narrator's role in the novel because the more dominant is the masked figure in the foreground, the greater is the likelihood of his figurativeness. The generally transparent masks appear in prose pieces and dialogs as figures with names such as Ignaz, Kasimir, Lohengrin, Erich, Titus, "Das Kind," Parzifal, "Das seltsame Mädchen," Kurt, Fridolin, Wladimir, Manuel, Theodorli. If an explanation is given for the names, it is ironic.[38] Faced with the question "should one speak or be silent" posed at the end of a fictive "address" devoted to a family ensnared in "simulated considerations" and individual *idées fixes* ("Eine Art Ansprache," *Prager Presse*, August 22, 1925), Walser sets the caprice seen at Theodor's masquerade ball into his own work in an attempt to communicate "the pleasure in the mask, the good conscience of everything that is masked."[39] He underscores the metaphoric subjectivity of these naively immediate figures as a stimulant for our thinking: "in an I-book the I may possibly be modestly figurative and not authorative" (*FKR*, 203).[40] The game of art in the masks and the "figurative" ego provide the style and the motifs for the basic ontological tension of the Bern work, and as such, for the ultimate consequence of Walser's obsession with the insignificant and the diurnal—the polarity of freedom and the self-imposed limitation of belief, the exemplary character of which he acted upon as the artist's mandate. The masks are transparent as biography (the "life parallelism" Walser spoke of in "Brief an einen Besteller von Novellen"), but cryptic in their figurativeness. Their first-name appelations remind us of the anonymity of fairy-tale heroes. Thus these figures reflect the melding of what is confessional and what is disguise—the structural basis for the Bern work that Walser refined from Marti's double vision of the heart and the eye.

Still stressing the improvisational and the occasional, comic irony and moral earnestness become more tightly knotted as Walser seeks to fuse conscious and "lyric" levels of insight into an alogical, emotional entity with a skeletal or dismembered plot (cf. "Fragment," *Prager Presse*, December 25, 1929), a double plot (cf. "Mondscheingeschichte," *Prager Presse*, February 9, 1928), or a plot whose dramatic tension and insight into motivation depends on the figures' illusion that their discussion proceeds on an identical cognitive level (cf. "Zwei Männer reden," *Prager Presse*, July 26, 1931). An intellectually more rigorous sophistication of the circular discursiveness of *Jakob von Gunten* "hardens" the style through the greater use of ellipsis and hiatus,[41] but leaves more unfilled narrator space that the reader must occupy. The equipoise of autonomous parts and the related shifts of perspective and tense (cf. "Verkrüppelter Shakespeare, *UP*, 268–270) in prose pieces that often lack either a proper beginning or end correlate the interrelatedness of all phenomena to the unity inherent in the interdependence of opposites, the only unity which Walser concedes.

The principal axes around which these late transformations of self revolve—a "spätes Ich" as reliant on art as Gottfried Benn's, but standing for art's antipodal corroboration with what is ineffable in art—are the poles of art and love.

At the beginning of the Bern period, in "Der Künstler" (*Kunst und Künstler*, XIX. Jg., Nr. 11 [September, 1921]; now *GW* VII, 107–109), Walser reports his decision, made one evening when "the street was filled with people," not to lose heart when it was a matter "of revitalizing something significant." During the rest of his career Walser frequently saw himself characterized as a Primitive or as a wasted talent.[42] Referring to himself as a "person employed at home," a "technician," or "a newspaper writer," he produced practical illustrations of the everyday *terra incognita*—"the fresh, unmowed world" of "Der Commis"—which Walser continued to believe to be the province and the mandate of his art.[43] Along with prose pieces ridiculing the self-importance of writers ("Bildnis eines Dichters," *Prager Presse*, January 17, 1926) or their tragicomic introversion ("Literatursituation," *Prager Presse*, September 16, 1928), he points to the insignificance of success in art when compared with the reality of the suffering in the war ("Abhandlung," *Prager Presse*, November 27, 1925). A typically ironic-serious defense of his own writing is the piece "Die Glosse" (*Prager Presse*, April 1, 1928). Aware that from the point of view of "literary morality" the gloss "represents a depravity," it nevertheless "works in every direction." When the transparently masked figures comment on the work itself they frequently parody the presumptive primacy of plot. One piece begins: " 'Doesn't it sound megalomaniac to let pass my lips,' Titus was narrating, 'that my mother was a princess, and that bandits kidnapped me, to make me one of their ilk. But I only say that for embellishment, so that I won't be boring from the very outset' " (*FKR*, 167).[44] Even in the absence of masks, parabolic pieces are ironically recommended for their "sparse content" (*UP*, 12), or an "excerpt from a notebook" begins "This piece of prose might resemble a joke" (*UP*, 214), while one of the "interior walks" begins: "Without wanting to, I smile when I realize what I intend to tell you here. Naturally they are going to be inoffensive things" ("Eine Stadt," *op. cit.*).

In "Menschenfreunde?" (*UP*, 203–207) Walser justifies his own "inartistic" writing by varying a view anticipated in the Berlin piece "Lüge auf die Bühne" ("Put the Lie on the Stage," *GW*, VI, 30–34), in which he had protested against "realistic" theater by insisting that art is intrinsically different from real life. Here an "incongruity" has arisen from the excessive "cultivatedness" of the arts. "Life has remained too coarse; art, on the other hand, has become relatively too branchy, too boughy, too delicate and too refined. To my mind we would all be better off if art were more forceful, but life good and refined" (*UP*, 204).[45]

The player-artist demonstrates the irreconcilability between the demands of life and art, and their interdependence in Walser's art, in the frequent appearance of female figures, "beloveds" whose configurations vary but who most often appear either as "Edith," the muse that inspires but from whom the narrator needs to be independent in order to create, or as a girl—sometimes called "Alice," sometimes "maid"—who represents the autistic subjectivity in which creativity takes place, but who is selfishly exploited when the creation is committed to paper, self-pitying when the "healthy" narrator abandons her, and ultimately in need of being "rescued." "Das Kind" reports on a figure that was once a man, who "previously . . . wrote thick books" (*UP*, 199), but who "lost gruesomely much time with interior readiness to serve and with love" (*UP*, 200). The "falling asleep" that resembles "this perpetual not-being-able-to-disregard-women [*Frauennichtaußerbetrachtlassen*] in "Minotauros" (*GKW*, 168) causes the "literarily wakeful" narrator to balk at the "problem of nations" and approach it only by way of the sleeping Langobards and the "quietly breathing content" of the Lay of the Nibelungen. This "love" is defensible as participation in existence ("Did his 'love' signify a standstill?" [*UP*, 201]) but destructive to the writer ("Women had ruined the shrimp" ["Der Knirps," *Prager Presse*, September 4, 1932]). The late work contains "letters" to a beloved that elevate this variant of a "report" to the prerational medium in which creativity occurs and to the act of creativity in one. Characteristic for many of them and one of the sources of their intriguing mixture of lyricism, occasionally florid but wakeful verbal agility, and ironic essayistic detachment, is this double image of woman that represents a late variant of the double portrayal as muse and earth-bound creature of the principal female roles in the novels. The tone thereby introduced into these communications is a consciously more parabolic variant of the fairy-tale tone that is mirrored and heightened by a frequently-used situation in which the narrator is writing to one woman about one or more other women who are her "rival." The situation is typified in the conclusion of "Titus," who says of himself "I went over to writing, only to gradually give it up" (*FKR*, 168).[46] Although it is possible that a model for this relationship can be found in a maid in the home of the Swiss painter Ernst Morgenthaler with whom Walser was briefly acquainted in the early twenties,[47] only the literary projection of such a relationship—whether real or fancied—is crucial as the catalyst and inspiration for an addition to the repertoire of the creative imagination in the theme of the separation from and courting of a muse. On the one hand her disappearance is given ambiguous approval in return for the guarantee of the freedom to fulfill the human demands of participation in the world; on the other the muse in fact provides the inspiration for works in which she is cryptically inserted to bear witness to the transformation art has had to undergo.[48]

The depiction of these women is itself fluid. It depends not only on the complex stylistic devices brought to it but more on the phase of the cyclical life process that is being depicted. "Tagebuchblatt" ("Diary-leaf," *FKR*, 211–213) speaks of a woman who has never given the narrator more than "an adverse sign," but who "possesses" him, and yet "obliges me to look to myself." A section of "Etwas von der Schande" (*Prager Presse, op. cit.*) tells of the silent visits of "my beloved" to the narrator during his illness, when her visage and "her gentle bearing" said "I can't possibly be true to you and I beg you not to be offended." Now that the narrator is "revoltingly healthy" again he regrets the "generous" words he used to calm her then: " 'I'm not so fussy about that.' "

A more constructivist sublimation of a woman's attractions is shown in "Olympia" (*UP*, 88–96). This piece illustrates the degree to which Walser's combining of symbolic-abstract images has contributed to the development of the canon of modern narrative prose. The theme of "Olympia" is the difficulty of writing poetic prose; the success of the piece springs from its parabolic use of shifting perspectives. The ingratiating letter to a lady in a neighboring dwelling, with which the piece begins, is revealed in the remainder of the work to be a parody of Walser's literary "essays." The letter writer is interrupted by Olympia, who has been lying on the writer's sofa in splendid nakedness.[49] She asks him to continue in his "profession" and tell her "stories." After assuming the attitude of a writer before a mirror, he obeys this command from his "mistress" (*Gebieterin*). He tells three stories, but they leave Olympia unmoved—"in divinity-like imperturbability." He thus fails—on the plot level—to prove himself before the muse. Yet he does succeed esthetically by representing "an unusual way to spend one's life" in the third story. This story deals with the anonymity of the soldier's life. It too shows narrative irony but the irony here comes not from the narrator, but from two "distinguished" figures that appear, unintroduced, within the last story and designate it as not worthy of attention.

The surprise effect of the work derives from the apparent failure of the narrator to react to Olympia's charms. In fact, she unites a goddess sitting in judgment and Manet's *demi-mondaine* into a palpable symbol embodying the sensuousness and beauty that will go into the work as language. Finally, Olympia is also the watchword for the locale of the "contests" that take place in the writer's room.

Communications to a beloved are among the works published in the *Prager Presse*. In "Der Zapfenstreich" (March 29, 1927) and "Ich schrieb der Tränentrinkerin" (May 25, 1930) neither "muse" nor "maid" are present any longer, although both works have the search for them as theme and plot. The theme of "Der Zapfenstreich" is what the narrator himself demonstrates as the inability to create under the "high" inspiration of a muse. Yet the work successfully integrates a comic tone in the parallels in the "plot" to the punned-on meanings of the title [*Zapfenstreich* means "military taps;" Walser also uses it to mean "a cork's prank," basing this imaginary compound on the separate meanings of *Zapfen* (= cork) and *Streich* (= prank). He also uses *Zapfen* in its Swiss slang meaning (= money).] through the lyricism of the plea for the return of the beloved—despite the narrator's "directnesses"—to replace a pitiless muse:

> There are mothers—oh thou, my lovely vanished one, so strange and so rich in adversities—who elect a favorite from their host of children whom they perhaps stone in kissing, whose existence they undermine with the incontinence of their caressing preferment—*

* Es gibt Mütter, o, du meine schöne, so seltsame und so prüfungsreiche Entschwundene, die sich aus der Schar ihrer Kinder einen Liebling auswählen, den sie vielleicht küssend steinigen, dessen Existenz sie mit ihrer zärtlichen Bevorzugung, mit der Unenthaltsamkeit ihrer Liebe untergraben—

"Ein Flaubert-Prosastück" (*GKW*, 43–54) unites two otherwise disparate women of his imaginative life in a cryptic fantasy on a man's return to a woman whom he had no need to long for, "because she had always, always gone with him." As Christopher Middleton has suggested, the piece is likely based on Flaubert's return from Egypt, and represents the encounter with Flaubert's projection of himself into the figure of Emma Bovary. The parallels to Walser's own artistic existence are, however, so pronounced that the piece is also a covertly sensual depiction of Walser's own ambiguous relation to women. While the title and the style parody the psychological sensibility of Flaubert's narrative technique, the piece as a whole actualizes Flaubert's own stylistic ideal of being as omnipresent and invisible in a literary work as is God. It thus offers proof of the possibility of an individual, vital literary idiom within the imitation implied by parody.

Walser appears to have continued to write prose works until his removal to Herisau in 1933. The variety of motifs, tones, and styles, and the existence of genuinely superficial work along with the tightly written aggregates that resist dissection are greater in the Bern work than it has been possible to indicate here. The reappearance of themes from earlier work or from within this same period makes it difficult to posit developmental lines. The paradox of the work of this period is the retention of a unifying lyric tone—whether in the varied portrayals of the artist's imaginative self-sufficiency or the "healthy" acceptance of the "real" world in which creativity is obstructed. The paradox derives from the ability to infuse each realm with its opposite. "Der Einsame" ["The Lonely Man"], for example, the penultimate piece in *Die Rose*, depicts the artistic rejuvenation possible in human isolation while it demonstrates the metaphysical dignity of this autistically subjective mode of existence.[50] However, the subtitle of the piece reads: "It is uncertain whether he is sitting or standing" (*FKR*, 228). (The last piece in the book, "Die Geliebte" ["The Beloved"], is a monolog in which the muse admits that, although moving into a castle has made it impossible for him to reach her, he still "possesses" her.) Many of Walser's most blatant shortcomings as a writer are found in "Der Herbst" (*Prager Presse*, October 8, 1933). Nevertheless, in the last analysis, the piece is moving and effective as the progressively decelerating tempi of the fragmented narrative reveal the work to be a monolog admission of artistic failure spoken into the night. In his review of *Jakob von Gunten* (*Die Neue Rundschau*, 22 [1911]), Efraim Frisch admitted his uncertainity as to whether Jakob's departure into the desert was a movement towards us or away from us. The unidentified landscape from which these world-lonely and world-adoring reports were written was left intentionally ambiguous and open towards the past and the future. The late prose piece "Einer schrieb" reconstructs the insistently existential dualism of Jakob's love in more concentrated form. The piece, ostensibly a letter to a recently reencountered former love, tabulates the pleasurable temptations that continually kept the narrator from her. The run-on descriptions of other women encountered, however, form a subtle recapitulation of a writing career whose double allegiance to art and existence results in making "Einer schrieb" a communication to the muse as a demonstration of "plotless" art. In the second half of the final sentence, after a shift from a self-irony that characterizes the nature of Walser's art, we are told as forthrightly as we ever are in Walser about this love that will always sacrifice its artistically secured freedom to reappear in an infinite present: ". . . and now I am here, and love you, and I would be capable of mediatingly answering any questions you might put to me. In any case, I care for you very much" (*UP,* 56).

Notes

1. In an essay on a love scene in Stendhal's *The Red and The Black* ("Über eine Art von Duell," *Die literarische ˙Welt,* I [1925], Nr. 1, 4) Walser says: ". . . I had already read the book in Berlin, where I wrote six novels, three of which I found it necessary to tear up . . ."

2. See the quotation from the prose piece "Meine Bemühungen" on page 27. In 1944 Walser said to Seelig apropos of the novel: ". . . I realized that I had taken a fancy to a form that was too extensive for my talent" (*Wdgg,* 72).

3. See especially "Der neue Roman" (*P,* 127–130) and "Sonntagsspaziergang" (*FKR,* 126–130), written in Biel and Bern respectively. A letter from the publishing firm of Kurt Wolff, with whom Walser was corresponding in 1918 concerning the publication of a collection of prose pieces he intended to call "Kammermusik," encourages him in this direction. After the correspondent describes the prospects for "Kammermusik," he adds: "But then you really ought now to finish up this "small change" and think about writing a novel again. I am firmly convinced that in a short time you would then have it 'made.'"

4. Otto Zinniker first represented such a view in his short appreciation *Robert Walser als Poet* (Zurich, 1947). Bänziger's critically much more valuable study concludes by "explaining" Walser's artistic decline as the result of his psychological estrangement from his homeland. A more extreme interpretation that faults Walser for not having integrated himself into Swiss life is Paul Müller's essay "Aufbruch, Einfahrt, Zerfall. Bemerkungen zu Robert Walsers Prosa," (*Neue Zürcher Zeitung,* Nr. 2406, June 17, 1962). More recently Werner Günther's useful article on Walser's early fairy-tale comedies "Schneewittchen" and "Aschenbrödel" (*Neue Zürcher Zeitung,* November 22, 1964) speaks of the "precipitous" decline in Walser's work after his return to Switzerland in 1913. Gerhard Piniel's article "Robert Walsers späte Prosa" (*Schweizer Monatshefte,* November, 1966, 762–768), which appeared together with eight of Walser's

uncollected pieces on literary motifs, is another example of an uninformed literary bias. The essay, mistakenly positing "a great linguistic disorderliness and constriction of artistic will" in the late work, shows little critical insight into Walser.

5. "Rosa. Eine Novelle" (*Die Rheinlande* [1915], now *GW* VI, 180–188) and "Olga. Eine Novelle" (*Pro Helvetia* [1921], now *GW* VII, 116–121) are rare instances when Walser uses the genre name. In fact these two are no more novelistic than "Frau Wilke" (*P*); "Der Handelsmann" (*Der Bildermann* [1916], now *GW* VI, 234–238); "Frau Scheer" (*Die Rheinlande* [1915], now *GW* VI, 295–312); "Das Ehepaar" (*Die Rheinlande* [1915], now *GW* VI, 177–180); or the lyric, yet sociologically perceptive study "Zwei Männer" (*Die Rheinlande* [1918], now *GW* VI, 248–257). In Bern the term is used in the title of works intentionally not novellas: "Eine Art Novelle" (*Individualität*, III [1928], Bk. 1/2, 224–228); "Eine stilvolle Novelle" (*Simplicissimus* [1925], now *GW* VII, 194–196). Late in his career Walser himself wrote: "up until now I have perhaps yet to carry off as much as a single novella" ("Meine Bemühungen," *GKW*, 194).

6. An example of the after-effect achieved by a concluding remark by the narrator combining both commentary and lyricism is found at the end of "Zückerchen," a piece of the sort in *Die Rose* that Bänziger regards as indicative of the disintegration of Walser's style. The short piece consists of a series of unrelated lyrical remarks and statements of biographical facts. The title refers to a piece of sugar, ironically foreshadowed in the piece, which disappears after the narrator throws it into the air. The final sentence reads: "May we never be lost to sacred things" (*FKR*, 204). In his essay on Walser, Martin Walser associates this sentence with Hölderlin's poetic vision. In the context of Walser's work, the sentence is more accurately described as one of the experiments from the Bern period to preserve the sacred through play.

7. Attempting to correct the "rumors" attached to Walser, Martin Walser conjectures they have found currency, "because [they] don't really dare enter his clerical offices, where [Walser] lets destiny rule, as if his bookkeepers were named Hamlet or Richard III" (Walser, *op. cit.*).

8. Bänziger reads the story as a resigned reflection of Walser's "second self" (*Bänziger*, 66). In refuting this view Greven has pointed to the differentiated characterizations of other figures in the studies of clerical life as well as to the presence in them of a figure named Simon. Bänziger speaks of similarities in diction between Helbling and the novel heroes. The following quotation indeed shares with Jakob's diction a spatially limited subject lyricism that is part of the "fairy-tale tone" in "Helblings Geschichte," but it is difficult to associate his thoughts with any of the heroes:

> When the dream-like vanishes, however, I want to throw myself on the floor in my whole length and breadth, want to topple, hurt myself on the edge of a desk, so that I might sense the diverting enjoyment of pain (*AKD*, 269).

9. The earliest is a verse dialog entitled "Tobold" (*FKR*, 287–298; originally in *Arkadia. Ein Jahrbuch für Dichtkunst,* ed. Max Brod [Kurt Wolff Verlag, 1913]). Here an overly didactic presentation of the moral force of the novel heroes in a juxtaposition of poverty, weakness, and soul against material wealth, might, and art is enlivened by verbal and situational irony. In "Spazieren"

(*AKD*, 289; originally in *Die Neue Rundschau* [1914]) Tobold is a carefree wanderer. In "Der fremde Geselle" the narrator regrets having neglected an opportunity to become better acquainted with a figure that seems "poor and lonely" and "as if he knew much and was capable of telling much that was worth hearing" (*AKD*, 191). The imaginary name that the narrator gives Tobold "between sleeping and waking" suggests German *Kobold*, a hobgoblin or impish house spirit. The figure is possibly a transformation of the "homeless" *Teufelsjungen* of Simon's Paris dream. A final variation, "Aus Tobolds Leben" (*P*, 113–123) is a tepid reworking of the *Kleine Prosa* version.

10. The original idea for the work goes back to Walser's early plan to write a drama based on the battle (*KGS*, 6).

11. In his review of *Aufsätze* in *Die Neue Rundschau* (1913, Bd. 2, 1043–45) Max Brod designates Walser's fictive letters, the résumés of scenes from dramas, and above all the literary portraits (this volume included "Brentano," "Büchners Flucht," and "Lenz") as new literary forms.

    Heinz Politzer's perceptive review of *Große kleine Welt* (*Maß und Wert*, 1 [1938], Hft., 3, 467–469), speaks of Walser's ability to resuscitate used-up clichés of speech and thereby give his literary portraits the quality of being untouched by previous thought.

12. Unfortunately the integration of theme and style cannot be demonstrated within the limitations of this chapter. The conclusion merits quotation, however, as a historical example of the possibility in modern narrative prose of using irony to convey emotional involvement. The quotation below marks the end point of the narrator's disengagement during the concluding section of the story and it reestablishes his autonomy and authority; the last section begins with the description of an infernal coach ride from Thun, where the perspective is divided between a speechless Kleist, the sister who came to fetch him, and the narrator. If this conclusion—which is bolder than any of Jakob's diversionary conclusions—be compared with the sentimentally aposiopistic endings of the individual sections of Rilke's early prose poem *The Lay of the Love and Death of Cornet Christoph Rilke* (1904), a historical change in the actualization of emotion can be noted. "But finally one has to let it roll on, the mail coach . . . Thun is situated at the entrance to the Bernese Oberland and is visited annually by many thousands of foreigners. Thun had an industrial exhibition, I'm not sure, I think four years ago" (*KGS*, 208–209).

    The durability of Walser's fascination for Kleist is attested to by passing references in several prose works, a late poem ("Kleist," *UG*, 47), and the following prose pieces: "Was braucht es zu einem Kleist-Darsteller?" (*Die Schaubühne*, 3. Jg., Nr. 11 [March 14, 1907]; now *GW*, VI, 19–21), "Auf Knien," an ironic gloss on a scene in *Die Hermannsschlacht* (*AKD*, 57–58); "Porträtskizze," a study of Homburg and the actor who plays him (*AKD*, 59–61); "Heinrich von Kleist" (*UP*, 332–354); "Weiteres zu Kleist," (*Prager Presse*, September 10, 1936); and "Kleist-Essay" (*Prager Presse*, December 2, 1936).

13. Together with the walks published only in magazines and magazine versions that were later revised for book publication, Walser wrote over fifty such walks. They are frequent in Walser's first collection of prose after his return to Switzerland, *Kleine Dichtungen*, make up an important part of the volume *Poetenleben*, and, in the four unusually long descriptions of walks in *Seeland*, are determinative for the tone of this final volume published during this period.

14. Werner Weber, "In Sachen Robert Walser," *Neue Zürcher Zeitung* (June 24, 1962).

15. The interior walks range from the dry description of a walk from Bern to Geneva ("Genf," *FKR*), the self-portrait in "Schaufenster" (*FKR*), through the description of a city-wide masquerade using parallelism and contrast to the narrator's introversion ("Maskerade," *Prager Presse*, March 24, 1927), to the etherealized, physically passive, imaginatively kinetic city walk in "Eine Stadt" (*Prager Presse*, November 7, 1926), and the interior, ambulatory inventory of the reasons for and against writing in "Ich soll arbeiten" (*Prager Presse*, June 30, 1926) where, as in "Eine Stadt," nature and scenery are primarily figurations of Walser's experiment with his "essay" form.

16. A section of the prose medley entitled "Eine Ohrfeige und Sonstiges" expresses trepidation of the popular success equated with seeing one's name on a poster. "What a disagreeable fate! To come to flower on a poster, only to disappear . . . Am I too going to have my poster one day? Will it overpower me?" (*FKR*, 181). The letters to Resy Breitbach make clear that Walser's contradictory remarks on his personal fame have little relation with the thematically motivated dialectic of contrasts in the works, but are Walser's own admission of his secretly courted imago of fame.

17. This is how the narrator perorates his way toward the conclusion of this speech, after having stressed the artist's sense of duty and having recapitulated the walk up until then in acrobatic locutions:

> Den Spaziergänger begleitet stets etwas Merkwürdiges, Gedankenvolles und Phantastisches, und er wäre dumm, wenn er dieses Geistige nicht beachten oder gar von sich fortstoßen würde; aber das tut er nicht; er heißt vielmehr alle sonderbaren, eigentümlichen Erscheinungen willkommen, befreundet und verbrüdert sich mit ihnen, weil sie ihn entzücken, macht sie zu gestalthaften, wesenvollen Körpern, gibt ihnen Bildung und Seele, wie sie ihrerseits ihn beseelen und bilden. Ich verdiene mit einem Wort mein tägliches Brot durch Denken, Grübeln, Bohren, Graben, Sinnen, Dichten, Untersuchen, Forschen und Spazieren so sauer wie irgend einer. Indem ich vielleicht die allervergnügteste Miene schneide, bin ich höchst ernsthaft und gewissenhaft; und wo ich weiter nichts als zärtlich und schwärmerisch zu sein scheine, bin ich ein solider Fachmann! (*KGS*, 315–316).

18. At the conclusion of this essay Benjamin suggests a relationship between the fairy tale and Walser's figures:

> Diesen kindlichen Adel teilen die Menschen Walsers mit den Märchenfiguren, die ja auch der Nacht und dem Wahnsinn, dem des Mythos nämlich, enttauchen. Man meint gewöhnlich, es habe sich dies Erwachen in den positiven Religionen vollzogen. Wenn das der Fall ist, dann jedenfalls in keiner sehr einfachen und eindeutigen Form. Die hat man in der großen profanen Auseinandersetzung mit dem Mythos zu suchen, die das Märchen darstellt. Natürlich haben seine Figuren nicht einfach Ähnlichkeit mit den Walserschen. Sie kämpfen noch, sich von dem Leiden zu befreien. Walser setzt ein, wo die Märchen aufhören. "Und wenn sie nicht gestorben sind, dann leben sie heute noch." Walser zeigt, wie sie leben.

19. Werner Günther (*op. cit.*). His interpretation of those two works emphasizes the element of play and metamorphosis in them as preludes of the novel motifs. Biographically he sees them as a liberating memorial to Walser's mother. Since he disregards the nihilistic strain in Büchner's comedy, his identification of a literary model for the play element could as well have been made with the Brentano comedy Büchner himself used. His criticism of Greven's analysis (*Greven*, 34–40, 41, 43, 45–46) as overly intellectualized seems immoderate in view of the broad applicability of Greven's interpretation for Walser's work, as well as his inclusion of Günther's own basic approach (cf. *Greven*, 35, and 39: "[Snow White's] new life is beyond good and evil, is a free game regarding which no one can specify whether it is crime or innocence.").

20. A letter to the Insel Verlag dated February 16, 1903 shows that Walser's first literary portrait of Brentano (*AKD*, originally in *Die Neue Rundschau* [1910]) was already written at that time. The study "Doktor Franz Blei" indicates a knowledge of Brentano's poetry in 1899 or 1900 at the latest (cf. *KP*, 144). Walser's interest in Brentano was strong enough to occasion a second study, identically titled, probably written in Bern ("Brentano," *UP*, 323–327), portraying the artist as disillusionist.

21. The essay "Der gestiefelte Kater" (*Prager Presse*, September 15, 1929) refers not to Tieck's comedy of this title but to Tieck himself. Walser praises the humane, beneficial effect Tieck's work had on "the so-to-speak hospitalized cultivated humanity" of his day. Walser acknowledges his debt to Tieck and identifies with him, as these quotations from the piece show:

> . . . Ich selbst ließ mich von dem sozusagen in Vollgewichtigkeit, will sagen, in Stiefeln Einherschreitenden zeitweise inspirieren. Er gab sich gern plaudernd; ich nahm mir dies zum Vorbild . . . Dichtete dieser gestiefelte Dichter nicht ein Buch in der ausgesprochensten, durchdachtesten Dummkopfsprache? . . .
>
> Auch ich war einer dieser diesen einzigartigen Sprachgewandten Verehrenden, dem es zu irgendwelcher Zwecke willen vorteilhaft zu sein schien, läppisch, närrisch, komisch aufzutreten, was er vielleicht tat, damit sich die ihn geistig Aufnehmenden seelisch wegen seiner Sonderbarkeiten zu sorgen hätten. Etwas an ihm war im selben Atemzug kühn und zugleich vorsichtig; tiefsinnig und gedankenlos. . . . Schrieb ich nicht selbst mit Zuhilfenahme der Vortrefflichkeit seines Beispiels flott drauflos . . . ?

22. "Perhaps along with what is upright and good he also loved evil; along with the beautiful what was not beautiful. Good and evil, the beautiful and the ugly seemed inseparable to him" ("Der Arbeiter," *P*, 156); "The most varied encounters gave life something panoramic. He perceived anew and more vividly than ever, that good and bad are equally propulsive, one grows out of the other, mutually determines the other" ("Etwas über Goethe," *Pro Helvetia*, Jg. 3 [1921]; now *GW*, VII, 121–124).

23. Examples are "Zwei sonderbare Geschichten" (*AKD*), "Schwendimann" (*PS*), "Einer, der nichts merkte" (in "Lampe, Papier und Handschuh," *KP*), "Die Schneiderin" (*FKR*), and "Mori" (In "Vier Bilder," *Die Weißen Blätter*, 3 [1916], II; now *GW*, VI, 162–164).

24. "Fräulein Knuchel" (*KP*), "Die böse Frau" (*PS*), "Die Dame" (*UP*), "Kienast" (*KP*), "So! Dich hab ich" (*KP*).

25. Greven cites the "overdone" verbal irony of pieces such as "Gar nichts" (*KP*), "Basta" (*KP*), "Niemand" (*KP*), "Die Wurst" (*PS*), and "Na also" (*KP*) as examples of maneristic irony whose purpose is "the preservation and actualization of an absolutely free negative subjectivity" (*Greven*, 128).

26. Paralleling his excision of miraculous elements from both "Aschenbrödel" and "Schneewittchen," his first treatment of another folk fairy tale "Dornröschen" (*P*, 19–22) concentrates on recapturing the magic the love story in the fairy tale had for the narrator as youth in consciously ironic language. The happy ending is still a motif in a later verse dialog based on the same fairy tale and published at the end of Walser's Biel period ("Dornröschen," *Pro Helvetia*, 2. Jg., Nr. 12 [December 1920], 450–454). But this "fairy tale" is in fact a humorous epilog in which it is the purpose of the very workaday prince (here simply called "The Stranger") to persuade the assembled royal family, members of court, and palace employees that he had any right to awaken them from their slumber, or as the king says "to properly accreditize" himself. The miraculous elements in two very early works ("Zwei Geschichten," originally in *Die Insel*, 3 [1901–1902], Bd. 4) are likewise parabolic. In "Genie" a starving, freezing genius who is bored and lonely after having destroyed an unappreciative world, fills his own recreation of the world with a more amenable race of humans, but still remains out of sorts and disconsolate. The second story, "Welt," is an apocalypse, in ironic terms, of God's extinction of a perverse, chaotic, and purposeless world. The miraculous is also found in two fairy-tale moralities developed from cliché conceptions of death ("Zwei sonderbare Geschichten vom Sterben," *AKD*).

27. Cf. Max Lüthi, *Märchen* (Stuttgart: Metzler, 1964), p. 28.

28. Fort und fort lief das Kind, es dachte sich das Ende der Welt zuerst als eine hohe Mauer, dann als einen See, dann als ein Tuch mit Tüpfelchen, dann als einen dicken breiten Brei, dann als bloße reine Luft, dann als eine weiße saubere Ebene, dann als Wonnemeer, worin es immerfort schaukeln könne, dann als einen bräunlichen Weg, dann als gar nichts oder als was es leider Gottes selber nicht recht wußte (*GKW*, 9).

29. Cf. C. Seelig, "Robert Walsers Lebensbild," *Die Welt von Robert Walser* (Zurich, 1961), pp. 5–13.

30. An extremely laudatory review of *Die Rose* by Walther Petry (*Individualität*, I [1926], Bk. 3, 125–126) claims it can only be compared with Kafka's work, but is closer to life than Kafka. A review of the same volume by Ludwig Fürst (*Die Literatur*, 27. Jg. des "Literarischen Echo," Hft. 10 [July 1925], 622) praises "the penetrating observation and the classy, polished language" in an author who lacks Kafka's "complete maturity." A short general appreciation of Walser by H. W. Keller ("Robert Walser," *Individualität*, II [1927], Bk. 4, 116–117) counts Walser among the few poets alive in Europe. The levitation of his style is defended as a flight back into reality.

31. "In Bern I had to struggle hard, for years. At my age it's no trifling matter to take a new position by assault without financial support . . . I made enormous efforts to get back to the top again and to finally get hold of attractive ideas" (*Wdgg*, 71–72).

32. But for several indirect references to World War I in the Biel work, topical references before Bern are rare or are present by implication, such as the reference in "Abschied" (*Die Neue Rundschau*, 20 [1909]; now *GW*, VI, 79–82)

to the widely discussed disintegration of the Ottoman Empire. Topical references in Bern mirror Walser's concern for the future of European civilization, e.g.: the West's arrogance toward the East ("Exposé," *Prager Presse*, December 21, 1928); whether Europe's "soul" will recover ("Die weiße Dame," *Prager Presse*, November 21, 1926); the nature of the peace "guaranteed" at Locarno ("Abhandlung," *Prager Presse*, November 27, 1925); the wish that Germany recover ("Ophelia," *op. cit.*); whether Switzerland's culture is in a state of crisis ("Plauderei," *Prager Presse*, November 2, 1926); the justification for Swiss armament expenditures ("Menschenfreunde?" *UP*, 203); salutary effects of "the class struggle" ("Klassenkampf und Frühlingstraum," *Prager Presse*, February 18, 1926); reflections on people "all full of a contained condition of indignation at this age" ("Ich wanderte in ein Städtchen," *Prager Presse*, January 5, 1937); and Lindbergh's flight ("Das Drama," *Prager Presse*, July 12, 1931).

33. The word *Almanach* in German has broader connotations than its English counterpart. Its primary literary referent is the annual collections of belletristic writing which, in the last third of the eighteenth and in the first third of the nineteenth century, became the most popular form for publishing poetry. The first noteworthy literary almanac in Germany was the *Göttinger Musenalmanach* (1770–1804), the most important one was Schiller's *Musenalmanach* (1796–1800).

In using the term, however, it is likely that Walser also had in mind the so-called almanacs that German publishers began to put out annually in the second decade of this century. Along with the obligatory calendar and the small format taken over from the earlier almanacs, the modestly priced publisher's almanacs contained selections from recent and forthcoming books together with a list of the publisher's titles in print. Walser's "Lustspielabend" (*KGS*) had appeared in the almanac of the Kurt Wolff Verlag for 1914, *Das bunte Buch*.

Beyond the parody and self-irony implied by the reference to these two types of almanacs, calling Theodor's novel an almanac suggests not only that it was a short work, but that it was "fragmentary" in character, in analogy to the collection of short works or selections by diverse hands in genuine almanacs. Finally, the extant episodes indicate that Walser also meant *Almanach* in the popular sense it had acquired in the second half of the nineteenth century, as a collection of entertaining writings.

34. The published episodes do not indicate whether, in the rest of the novel, the ironic motif of the author gathering material for a novel extends as far as it does in Gide's *The Counterfeiters*, where, in chapters in Part II of the novel, Edouard discusses his theory of the novel and the author discusses his characters. Gide was interested in as varied a point of view as possible from fictionally distinct perspectives; Walser sought a plural perspective through the medium of a perspective-shifting single narrator.

35. Walser's "naive" art repeatedly sought a communal festivity as the frame for his work. One of the essays in *Fritz Kochers Aufsätze* is entitled "Jahrmarket"; one in "Der Commis," "Karneval." The figure of Hanswurst in "Maskenball" (*PS*, 13–19) is a clear anticipation of the Bern player-artist from the Biel period, decidedly free of stylistic mannerisms. A later, complex variant of the motif can be found in "Maskerade" (*Prager Presse, March* 24, 1927) (cf. Note 40).

36. Among other thematically related variants in which the fairy-tale tone is more pronounced are "Liebesgeschichte," (*Basler Nachrichten*, August 14, 1927); "Die Dame am Fenster," (*UP*, 45–50).

37. Da sich das Leben, wie ich gesehen zu haben und fernerhin sehen zu können meine, gleichsam in etwas Versuchhaftes, vorsichtig Tastendes verwandelt hat, so geschah dieses im Verlaufe der letzten Jahre mehr und mehr auch mit der Schriftstellerei, die ein Lebensparallelismus war und bleiben wird. Verfeinert sich das Leben, so wird auch die Kunst bedächtiger oder verantwortungsvoller, und die ruhige Erwiderung auf Ihre Anfrage, ob ich packend zu sein imstand sei, fällt dem darin Angesprochenen entsprechend aus, was ich Sie freundlich bitte, festellen zu wollen (*GKW*, 192).

38. "We are naming him Wladimir because that's an unusual name and he was indeed something rare" (*FKR*, 123); "Kurt was a boor, at least he was felt to be such" (*FKR*, 143); "We want to call him Erich because that's such a blond name, expressing innocence and idealism" (*FKR*, 165); "I called myself Lohengrin because I saw swans on my travels and when I poeticized now and then, I couldn't pardon myself, because it affected me as being something sissy" (*Prager Presse*, October 14, 1928).

39. Friederich Nietzsche, *Die fröhliche Wissenschaft*, Aphorism 77 (quoted in *Allemann*, 110). The quotation is from an aphorism on Bizet's *Carmen*, that reflects on the popular nature of the mask. In the particular context Allemann quotes Nietzsche's formulations for a naive-ironic art that deals with the possibility that "perhaps as parodists of universal history and [as] God's buffoons" the game of a naive-ironic art may in the future overcome "historical man."

40. The considerable fraction of Walser's entire production devoted to the theater attests to a life-long fascination for the simultaneity of reality and appearance on both sides of the stage, beginning with the "reality" of theater illusion within Snow White's fairy-tale world. Walser's frequent contributions to *Die Schaubühne* in the years 1905 to 1913 treated various aspects of theater life. Among Walser's works published so far, character sketches of actors, sardonic verbal exercises mocking Walser's own acting ambitions, highly personalized résumés of famous scenes from the classical repertory, wide-ranging variants illustrating the cathartic effect of the unreal in the theater, and many pieces in which the action on the stage plays against the events in the public are the most frequent types. In the thematically related descriptions of cabarets and honky-tonks the contrasts are crasser and more likely filled with ironized pathos. A late dialog entitled "Kabarettbild" (in "Drei Studien," *Die Neue Rundschau*, 38 [1927], II, 423–430) uses a variety of figures to enact situation contrasts. In one of them, an author mask, "The Bobby-Soxer," delivers a speech on the nature of reality amidst warnings from the Impressario that "you are ruining your own career."

41. "Following my own experience, that is, my own taste, it might always be highly desirable to be as inexact as possible with regard to place, time, geography . . ." ("Eine Art Novelle," *Individualität*, III [1928], Bk. 1/2, 224–228); the beginning of "Emil und Natalie" (*Prager Presse*, January 11, 1930) reads: "Once great flakes fell in a castle courtyard. I hardly need emphasize where it was. It's enough that it happened." Cf. "Die Berühmtheit" (*UP*, 20).

42. Cf. "Plauderei" (*Prager Presse*, February 11, 1926); "I wonder whether one can really only identify oneself as cultivated with printed manuscript in ones

pocket!" (*FKR*, 200); "Why did Walser once experience so much? . . . Why does Walser's fame leave him colder than it does others?" ("Walser über Walser," *Prager Presse*, July 27, 1925; now *GW*, VII, 217–219); "Der erste Schritt" (*Prager Presse*, June 24, 1928) speaks of the "marvelous problem" of colleagues who adore the "wonderful shepherd-youthfulness" of the narrator's first works but find that he now deserves a "juicy, spontaneous wallop" for his present "nicely rounded-off philistinism." In "Eine Erzählung von Voltaire" ("Zwei kleine Dichtungen," *Die literarische Welt*, 2 [1926], Nr. 14, 3) a visiting publisher says: "Why, your talent is simply lying fallow. Pardon my frankness."

43. Walser very precisely described the ambition of his own writing in an essay on the painter Cezanne, whom Walser thinks of as an "Asiatic" with "school-boyishnesses," who never traveled but to circle the limits of objects.

> Stundentagelang zielte er darauf hin, Selbstverständliches unverständlich, für Leichtbegreiflichkeiten eine Grundlage des Unerklärlichen zu finden. Er erhielt mit der Zeit lauernde Augen vom vielen exakten Herumschweifen rund um Umrisse, die für ihn zu Grenzen von etwas Mysteriösem wurden. Sein ganzes stilles Leben lang kämpfte er den lautlosen, und, wie man versucht sein könnte zu sagen, sehr vornehmen Kampf um die Gebirgig-machung . . . des Rahmens. . . .
>
> Alles, was er erfaßte, vermählte sich, und wenn wir von Musikalität bei ihm sprechen zu dürfen glauben, so entstand sie aus dem Reichtum seines Beobachtens, und dadurch, daß er jedes Gegenstandes Einwilligung zu erhalten, zu gewinnen suchte, sich ihm wesenhaft zu offenbaren, dadurch überhaupt erst recht, daß er Großes und Kleines in denselben 'Tempel' stellte ("Cezannegedanken," *Prager Presse*, March 3, 1929).

44. Walser's persuasion that "gripping" plots evade the problematic "politeness" of our age (*GKW*, 191) caused him to use their irreality for comic purposes in mock protestations of the inexorability of plot (*UP*, 101) and in the résumés of third-rate novels, to which Walser seems to have been addicted (cf. *UP*, 72). Two of the best of them, drawn from "kiosk sources" are included in an ambitious self-portrait of his artistic personality in *Die Rose*, the "series of meditations" entitled "Eine Ohrfeige und Sonstiges" (cf. *FKR*, 185f.). In "Fragment" (*Prager Presse*, op. cit.) two plots, both incomplete, are used to represent an unsuccessful attempt of a narrator-author to extricate himself from his "love" (see below).

45. The penchant for associative reflection sparked by trivialities that Jakob records as childish and Marti castigates in "Schlechte Gewohnheit" is now transposed into poetical observation: In "Was eine Frau sagte" (*Prager Presse*, September 18, 1932) the first-person narrator puns on German *Mache* (boastful pretentions) to insist on the conscious artificiality of all art: "for example in art everything has to be 'made.' "

46. Meine Hohe ist so schön, und ich beandächtige sie mit so heiligem Respekt, daß ich mich an eine andere hängen und damit Gelegenheit erhaschen muß, mich von der Anstrengung durchwachter Nächte zu erholen, der Nachfolgerin zu erzählen, wie lieb die Vergangene war, ihr zu sagen: "Dich hab ich ebenso lieb" (*FKR*, 170).

47. Cf. Ernst Morgenthaler, "Wie ich den Dichter Robert Walser kennenlernte," *Ein Maler erzählt* (Zurich: Diogenes Verlag, 1957), pp. 73–78.

48. The artistic actualization of the disappearance or reassessment of beauty in these works cannot be undertaken here. Greven has indicated a starting point for such a study by analyzing the two women in the final tableau of "Die Ruine" (*UP*, 223–244), the "singing woman" and the "domestic, frugal" woman as "the contrast of inner existence that leaves the subject free and presents it with the totality of life in the beautiful illusion of art and external existence where [the totality] must be lost" (*Greven*, 142). "Die Ruine" itself is an impressive example of the depersonalization of first-person narrative in the interior walks. Despite the dualities in the disassociative presentation in it of guilt, superficialities, surrealistic humor, "childishness" toward women, incontrovertible wisdom, and a real and figurative referent for the ruin of the title, the work has the cohesiveness only Walser can achieve when he simultaneously sings two varying melodies.

49. The descent of a muse from the lofty "heavens" recurs through Walser's work, nowhere as complexly ironical as in "Olympia." In Simon's dream of Paris, an appropriately unaccompanied cloud settles into the street in the utopistic city Simon equates with creativity (*T*, 219). "Die Göttin" (*AKD*, 217–218), a naked divinity the narrator associates with Greece, also arrives on a cloud. Her visit is an edifying one, but her departure in no way diminishes the beauty present in the scene before her arrival. In the less easily classifiable piece "Festzug" (*Pro Helvetia*, 3. Jg., Nr. 11 (November 1921); now *GW*, VII, 56–58), which is most likely a self-ironic but conceptually clearer interrelation between movement in street scenes and creativity than occurred in the novels, "a goddess, who at other times only put up on Olympus, descended into man's amusements on a snow-white, downy-soft cloud and looked about in awe; but no one saw her."

50. Es muß auch einen geben, der nachlässig ist und fröhlich glaubt, daß das nicht schadet. Nie endende Verjüngungen ummurmeln ihn. Er hört das Singen des Urstromes durch die stillen Stunden. Zu sich zurückstrebend erweiterte er sich. Vor den Menschen flieht er nicht. Wie gern säh' ich mich sympathisch, wie wünschte ich mich ihrem Kreis einverleibt. Doch glaub' ich getan zu haben, was ich vermochte, mich zu sparen. Ich blieb willig (*FKR*, 229–230).

8

WALSER IN PERSPECTIVE

The growing interest in German-speaking countries in Walser's writing along with the translations of individual works into English, French, Italian, and Serbo-Croatian are gradually helping to overcome the neglect shown his work in the past. Jochen Greven's new edition of Walser and the biography by Robert Mächler will make it possible for the first time to read Walser in his entirety and to establish his place in his literary generation. It is our purpose in this concluding chapter to facilitate the literary localization of Walser's work by comparing and contrasting it with a small selection of representative prose works written between 1902 and 1924. These works are interpreted in discussions centering around forms, themes, and motifs comparable to those found in Walser. In order to integrate the material in this chapter with earlier chapters it was necessary to either omit stylistic considerations or to summarize them with minimal documentation. Since our attention in this chapter is directed to elements in the works discussed that are comparable to Walser's work, we have not stressed the sometimes fundamental dissimilarities that exist between these authors and works in question. The comparison with Kafka must differ from the rest of the material because of the necessity to summarize the evidence of Kafka's knowledge of Walser, and the assumption of a more extensive knowledge of Kafka's works must be made because of the recurrence of themes comparable to Walser's. In this section, as in the entire chapter, the aim of the interpretive comment is to provide a basis for a better understanding of Walser's writing rather than to draw qualitative distinctions.

Rainer Maria Rilke's single, exactingly composed novel, *The Notebooks of Malte Laurids Brigge,* was published in March, 1910 after having been started in Rome in the winter of 1903–04. The novel poses the question of the possibility of a meaningful life for man as the actualization of his potential, in an urban society whose relation to reality is defective. Malte Laurids Brigge's search for identity as pure relation is depicted through a journal that reflects an acutely sensitive and initially solipsistic consciousness. The novel offers the student of Rilke a richly poetic, illuminating parallel to the author's development during the years of its creation—from the estheticism and mystic vitalism of *Das Stundenbuch* (1899–1903), through the *Dinggedichte* in the *Neue Gedichte* (1907–08), to the poetic maturity that enabled Rilke to write the first of the Duino elegies shortly after the completion of the novel. The work stands as a landmark in modern German fiction for the extremity of the human and artistic crisis it presents in the struggles of the writer-hero to reduce to essences and to re-evaluate unexamined generalizations. The concluding section of the book, a retelling of the parable of the Prodigal Son that was inspired by the appearance in German of Gide's reworking of the biblical story in 1907, is a prayer for a language able to express the existential experience of a contemporary world. As extreme as is the contrast between Walser's and Rilke's artistic temperaments, the emphasis in Malte's "eccentric orbit"[1] on the difficulty of writing, on masks, dispossessed nobility, and the appearance in the journal novel of Rilke's theory of *besitzlose Liebe* (love that foreswears possession) provide a basis for contrasts and comparisons to *Geschwister Tanner* and *Jakob von Gunten.*

Malte's contacts with urban life in Paris, where he is living in self-imposed exile and isolation, are for him an experience of moribundity, specifically corroborating the extinction of the line of Danish nobility whose last scion he is. Malte's father had symbolically sealed the death of this family with the irrevocable disavowal implicit in his arrangement to have his heart perforated after death. This ambiguous patent of liberty requires of Malte that he "begin from the beginning" (*MLB*, 140). Deprived of the rural basis for comparison from which Simon writes of the dehumanizing aspects of urban life (*T*, 138ff.), Malte's images bespeak a double dispossession. His memories of a fugitive domicile in the past are themselves fragmented (". . . it is no complete building; it is all broken up inside me . . . " [*MLB*, 30]), and the landed estate-house of his remembrance is spectral (cf. *MLB*, 124, 128). In the city he perceives a community of homelessness in a society in which "families can no longer approach God" (*MLB*, 118), as the deadly silence preceding the "frightful blow" of a wall's collapse at the height of a conflagration (*MLB*, 14), or as a row of homes in imminent "danger of falling down, since everything alongside had been taken away" (*MLB*, 46).

The first of the novel's two books stands under contrasting signs of death: the cheap, impersonal death in the cities and the "individual" deaths his forebears died. The writer, Malte, makes it his task and the offering of his loneliness to transmute the life-death symbiosis of his ancestors into his own "blood," thereby suspending its historicity and redeeming it as a life force. This process starts at an earlier stage of development than in any of Walser's novels: at the interior reflection of what Malte is "learning to see" on the Paris streets, showing him an "inner self of which I was ignorant" (*MLB*, 14–15). Malte's street life is invested with the unreal, sometimes theatrical quality found in Simon's dream of Paris and in Jakob's stirring experiences, but for Malte the masquerade is limited only to a dance of death with its images of disease and putrification. He flees a Mardi Gras street celebration "like a mad-man," trying to break loose from the crowds that were "gently swaying back and forth, as if they copulated standing" (*MLB*, 49). The community of existential fear Malte shares with man is enlarged upon in his identification with the man on the street suffering from Parkinson's disease and the moribund man in the *crémerie*—of whom he conjectures: "per-haps a great abscess had risen in his brain like a sun that was changing the world for him" (*MLB*, 50). These scenes, however, show Malte as the victim of his human encounters and not as the beneficiary of the humane solidarity that Walser's novel heroes share through all the modulations of their real and imagined street encounters. "I expend all the strength I have for the day," Malte says of his housekeeping chores in a room with "greasy-gray" evidences of former occupants, "and then when I get among people they naturally have it easy" (*MLB*, 50). Malte's experience is less solipsistic in the second half of "The Notebooks"; he still does not "even know how it is possible for school-children to get up in bedrooms filled with grey-smelling cold," he has "no conception of the amount of succor that is constantly being used up" (*MLB*, 180). Only in Malte's transformation of the parable of the Prodi-gal Son into a hypothesis of future existence is Simon Tanner's interior invulnerability during an exterior descent similar to Malte's isolation and impoverishment approached: "That was the time which began with his feeling of being general, anonymous, like a slowly recovering con-valescent" (*MLB*, 213). In the figure of the Prodigal Son, Malte finally exchanges his nobility for a more symbolic form of an earlier experience as an "outcast" (*MLB*, 42). But the only rescindment of Malte's words: "I have fallen and cannot pick myself up again because I am broken" (*MLB*, 52) occurs in the striving of his *besitzlose Liebe* to prove his existence by experiencing God. There is no intermediary for Malte, noth-ing to replace his fear, such as Simon's love of "the dangerous, the abysmal, the hovering and the uncontrollable" (*T*, 244), and no promise such as Simon's to keep picking himself up again as long as his strength endures.

Malte's acceptance of the disfranchisement of "nobility" is more difficult for him than for Jakob von Gunten, who actively renounced his, because the orientation of Malte's vision is taken from a past that he "achieves" only to find that it offers no comfort. Realizing that there is no longer a common denominator among people who do not use their God, that "despite discoveries and progress, despite culture, religion and world wisdom one has remained on the surface of life" (*MLB*, 28), Malte undertakes to combat his fear by writing (*MLB*, 23). He begins less out of the conviction of his artistry than as "the first comer" who "must begin to do some of the things that have been neglected" (*MLB*, 30). Malte's concept of his task is courageous; he equates it with Baudelaire's task in "Une Charogne": ". . . to see in this terrible thing, seeming to be only repulsive, that existence which is valid among all that exists. Choice or refusal there is none" (*MLB*, 67). Yet he does make a choice, since his attempted reintegration of life is based on "the infinite reality of my childhood" (*MLB*, 171). "The Notebooks" are the chrysalis of his development as a writer, from which he, like Jakob, is unable to write letters, since they would now be from a stranger (*MLB*, 15). His "process" is longer than Jakob's since he clings to the vision of a happy writer, sitting "in the quiet room of an ancestral house, among many calm, sedentary things" (*MLB*, 44). Paralleling the "corrections" and disillusionments that Walser's novel heroes experience in reality, Malte repeatedly faces the difficulty of writing after having sacrificed "everything I expected for reality" (*MLB*, 68, cf. 72f.). The nearly impossible task of reintegration Malte seeks to achieve through narrative. Yet by relating a tale coherently and with the causal cohesion whose single "real" correlation exists in the reconstructed integrality of Malte's heritage from his childhood, he secures only his own identity. Although the aperspectivism of this journal is not as extreme, not as "modern" as Jakob's, the external disorientation that does not submit to Malte's more traditional form of narrative limits the success of his transmutation and justifies the "notebooks" that Rilke referred to as "artistically . . . a poor unity, but humanly possible" (letter quoted in "Translator's Foreword," *MLB*, 8). Thus the link between Walser's and Rilke's journal novels is the esthetic realization, mediated by the narrator's imagination, of an existential fear whose symbolism transcends the hazard of personal extinction.

When Malte, as a "story teller," extends the "infinite reality" of his childhood to include the reality he sees around him, he does so by making his childhood the symbol for the eternal isolation of the artist. The second book of Rilke's novel develops the image of the selfless lover independent of the beloved into a circumlocution for art as religion. Thus, Malte's often unforgettable variations on the theme of loneliness in both books are climaxed by the Prodigal Son's wanderer existence, the successful transformation of Malte's loneliness into salvation and consolation. The "wilderness" the Prodigal Son enters, however, resembles Jakob's only in its provisional quality. The primarily esthetic justification for loneliness becomes clear in Malte's story of the solitary man who was distracted from his true self by the snare of fame and his counter image of the false Pretender Demetrius in the entry following. Malte's transformation of the fragmentary memory of a story read as a child on the final moments in the life of the Pretender Grishka Otrepioff into the fable of a man who attained complete realization of his true being behind "the mask which already he had almost renounced" (*MLB*, 164) is one of several undeniable proofs of Malte's artistry.

Early in the book Malte accurately predicts that "only for a little while yet" will he be able to "narrate" inner existence. What Jakob expresses as the disavowal of intellect in the recreation of being (and what bears a curious resemblance to Walser's metaphor in his remarks about the refusal of his "hand" to execute the "epic continuity" needed for the novel [cf. Chapter One, p. 11]), Malte communicates in the image of a disembodied hand which appeared to him in a childhood spiritistic episode. A later reminiscence by him of this incomprehensible episode from his youth (cf. *MLB*, 82–85) reveals the image of the hand to be the existence of a second, unknown, but spiritually more comprehensive self: "But there will come a day when my hand will be far from me and when I bid it write, it will write words I do not mean. The time of that other interpretation will dawn, when not one word will remain upon another, and all meaning will dissolve like clouds and fall down like rain" (*MLB*, 52).

"That other interpretation," in which no single meaning remains, is already intimated by Malte's childhood preoccupation with masks and metamorphoses, when "the more varied my transformations, the more convinced did I become of myself" (*MLB*, 92); in the second book it occupies a symbolically greater role in Malte's vain hopes for "a literal, unambiguous tale" (*MLB*, 148), in his progressive bewilderment as a "narrator" under the burden of his learning, and in the refinement of his human isolation into his retelling of the biblical parable.

"It will be difficult to persuade me," Malte begins this concluding section of the book, "that the story of the Prodigal Son is not the legend of him who did not want to be loved" (*MLB*, 210). Malte's parable transforms an earlier image of a God-seeking, medieval saint as "the solitary one" who resists "seduction," the one "who will perhaps hold out" (*MLB*, 158–159) into a metaphor for the artist, thereby apotheosizing an existence like his own. Although Malte's Prodigal Son often breaks his promise "never to love" out of "unspeakable fear for the liberty of the other" and "in order not to put anyone in the terrible position of being loved" (*MLB*, 212), his compulsion to preserve this liberty by penetrating "the loved object with the rays of his feeling, instead of consuming it in them" cause him to abandon hope "of experiencing the lover who should pierce him" (*MLB*, 213). His purpose "to learn to master what constituted his inner life," brings him back to the place of his "unachieved" childhood, certain that "his love was in all this and growing." At his return home the estranged man is recognized and forgiven in love. But he does not repent; preoccupied, he doesn't even reflect that there could still be love. The Prodigal Son throws himself at his family's feet in "the incredible gesture that had never before been seen—the gesture of supplication," "avowing to them that they had not loved."[2] The parable ends with the Prodigal Son's smiling self-assurance that their love could not "have him in mind" and his feeling that only God—Who "is not yet willing"—could now love him.

Malte's final transformation of the self here differs from Jakob's masks in that Malte seeks to eliminate human obstacles to the artist's transcendence (cf. Malte's description of humans interposing between him and the angel [*MLB*, 73]). A description earlier in the book of a blind newspaper vendor whom Malte perceives as proof of the existence of God, offers a parallel to Jakob's perception of Kraus as "a real God-creation, a nothing, a servant" (*JvG*, 409). Whereas Jakob's experience underlies his disavowal of fame and Kraus remains an allotropic image within the ironist who leaves the Institute Benjamanta with illusions revived by tolerance born of his own self-abandonment, Malte is only able to identify with this blind man—whose "misery [was] restricted by no precaution or disguise" (*MLB*, 179)—as an illustration of the imperfection of his art. Jakob's suppression of an artistic persona distinguishes him from Malte. Both share the hubris of an unrelenting ambition that they express in the various masks that project the apostasy of their prodigal youth. In his isolation Jakob seeks help and clarification through the human encounters he describes only to then experience the self-judgment imposed by the Institute Benjamenta. Malte's perception, late in "The Notebooks," of Venice, the impressionistic city par excellence, as the embodiment of artistic will, shows how Malte's loneliness has become a mask as impregnable as Grishka Otrepioff's, of whom

Malte conjectured that "the strength of his transformation lay in his no longer being anybody's son" (*MLB*, 162).

Rilke's own remarks on "The Notebooks" illuminate the disintegration between experience and expression that mark the words following the parable, "End of the Notebooks," as the finish of Malte's career as a writer.[3] "The Notebooks" and *Jakob von Gunten* are journals for different reasons. The lack of a specifiable time in what Malte writes strengthens the mythic quality of the stop-time past of his youth as a safeguard against self-sacrifice. And despite the similarity of theme, motifs, and narrated space in the two journals, Malte's entries are necessarily longer than Jakob's. Were Malte to equivocate as does Jakob, the esthetic credibility and coherence of his entries would be undermined. Malte most often describes exterior reality that has been internalized by the intensity of his response to it. By contrast, Jakob addresses himself to and describes the surface of symbols—indeed, he equates the symbol with its surface. Jakob can suggest the fear and the promise of existence from the outset—although his only partially cohesive narratives are usually limited to visions, dreams, and fantasies—by treating the impetus for a particular entry and its underlying theme in emotional abbreviations that are simultaneously relentless self-exposures and externalized interior description. When Malte sees the life-stained interior wall of a tenement that has been bared by the demolition of the adjoining building it is excruciating for him. The tenement wall "is at home in me" (*MLB*, 48), he says. Jakob's experience of the "wall of sorrows" in the passageways of poverty (*JvG*, 428), which he approaches with the perception of suffering endured through the centuries, but before which he then plays "comedy," is only apparently less excruciating for Jakob; he substitutes an ironic "objectivity" for Malte's internalized exterior description to more accurately represent the danger to "things" both authors aim to redeem through their journal heroes' distance from them. The continuing fear of the loss of things leaves Malte's Prodigal Son seeking the language for his work (cf. *MLB*, 213) but Jakob creates an idiom whose gradations between imagination, emotion, and analysis encompass a broader spectrum of human experience than does Malte's. Both of the journal novels exhibit a unity of style and subject, but the more radical postulation of the evanescence of a single meaning in *Jakob von Gunten* is in large measure due to Jakob's refusal to regard his masks and projections of himself as the redeeming burden of artistry. Jakob, too, is no longer anyone's son, but without Rilke's artistic premises about poverty, Walser makes Jakob's sense of human solidarity more credible. Malte's single adumbration of human community is his estheticized perception of the folk's mythologization of the hero in Malte's story of the death of Karl the Bold (*MLB*, 166).

James Joyce's apprenticeship novel, *A Portrait of the Artist as a Young Man*, dating from 1904 and published in 1914, is the lyric portrayal of the estrangement and liberation of the artist Stephen Dedalus. It fashions the first step towards the disappearance of "the personality of the artist," the personality that, as Stephen says, "finally refines itself out of existence, impersonalizes itself so to speak" (*PA*, 219). The novel handily attests to the recurrence of related problems of social, esthetic, and individual cognition throughout Europe at the turn of the century. Thematic and stylistic correspondences to Walser's novels can be found in Stephen's movement away from the family (Stephen's counterpart to the mythological Dedalus' escape from the labyrinth is echoed in his "cave" images); in the amalgam of styles used as much to portray varying internal rhythm as to recreate external reality; in the proximity of the symbol of poetic imagination ("the enchantment of the heart" [*PA*, 217]) to somnolent states of consciousness; and in Joyce's associations of kinesis with imagination.

A wanderer "among the snares of the world" (*PA*, 165), Stephen obeys "a wayward instinct" (*PA*, 169) to follow "his destiny . . . to be elusive of social or religious orders" (*PA*, 165). His fear of the uncertainty of the future is not as crippling as it is for Malte Laurids Brigge because Stephen's fear is countered, as is Jakob's, by a return from the "brief pride of silence," "glad to find himself still in the midst of common lives, passing on his way . . . fearlessly and with a light heart" (*PA*, 180). In contrast to Malte's response to the death of his childhood in the unpossessive love of objects that turns them back upon themselves, Stephen survives this death with von Gunten fortitude and resilience that is implicit in Stephen's acceptance of a world in which the proximity of lyricism and lice (cf. *PA*, 238) is projected into the juxtapositions of style. Admittedly "The Portrait" shows Stephen's life before a Malte-like self-imposed exile in an unrelievedly existential world, deprived of any community but that of fear; what distinguishes the isolation of both Stephen and Malte is their corresponding "search for the essence of beauty" (*PA*, 180) and Malte's unpromising search for a cohesive narrative link between infinite experience and expression. As the concluding sections of "The Notebooks," "The Portrait," and *Jakob von Gunten* make clear, all three protagonists set out on what Malte calls the "long love to God, that silent, aimless labor" (*MLB*, 214). Although Joyce's novel lacks both the sustained existential power of "The Notebooks" and *Jakob von Gunten's* unabatingly ironic perception of human pre-

cariousness, his work stands closer to Walser's journal-novel. Rilke's aus-
tere, sometimes sentimental hero has nothing to fall back on but an
extinct nobility and reflects Rilke's response to the social and linguistic
isolation of the German-speaking people of Prague in a private myth
of socially and culturally distinguished forebears. On the other hand,
Stephen's transmutation of the family when "He felt that he was hardly
of one blood with [his mother and siblings] but stood to them rather
in the mystical kinship of fosterage, fosterchild and fosterbrother" (*PA*,
101) corresponds to the enlargement and liberation of the family in
Walser's work. The simultaneity in Stephen of interior unrest and "quiet
obedience" (*PA*, 86, 159) relates him both to Joseph Marti at the Toblers', and to Jakob at the Institute Benjamenta in their common readiness
to forsake what they love. Stephen's thought of himself as "a heretic
franciscan, willing and willing not to serve" (*PA*, 224) is also reminiscent
of the quest of Walser's novel heroes to secure freedom through service.
Stephen thereby anticipates his final prayerful pledge of devotion to
life in the terms of the lore of his homeland, that he, like Walser's
heroes, takes with him into exile: "Welcome, O life! I go to encounter
for the millionth time the reality of experience and to forge in the smithy
of my soul the uncreated conscience of my race" (*PA*, 257).

Joyce's portrayal of the development of his artist-hero provides a mirror of the search for art through the depiction of alternating internal
rhythms in the hero and through the conscious leit-motifs of recurrent
images (especially water, evening, and flight). Stephen's sensibility and
imagination as a child is sanctioned and nurtured by the doctrinal teaching of his Church (*i.a. PA*, 106–108). The first chapter shows how the
Church instills imagination while setting limits on it (cf. *PA*, 20).
Stephen loses his innocence when his search for liberty leads him
through the purgatory of sensuality (*PA*, Chapter Three). This experience which he obediently tries to extirpate by "chastizing" the senses
(e.g., *PA*, 143), he later recognizes as the birth of the soul (*PA*, 207).
As his esthetic sensibility awakens, sensuality is transmuted into the
warrant of Stephen's calling (*PA*, Chapter Four), then transmuted further into a sensuality of language later equated with the life-giving
force of water, the "liquid life"—"like waters circumfluent in space"—in
which "the liquid letters of speech, symbols of the element of mystery,
flowed forth over his brain" (*PA*, 227ff.). Joyce's kinetic water images
in the novel span and reconcile the conflicts in Stephen's soul that are
depicted, in the indirect interior monolog as the book opens as both
separate and hostile.[4] During the epiphany on the beach the water image
becomes the greeted "advent of life" (*PA*, 176).[5]

Walser and Joyce resemble one another most in their lyric use of the "epiphanies" of real, imagined, and dreamed human encounters. Jakob's descent to the lower passageways, his divination of Kraus, the mixture of megalomania and disillusion in his dreams and fantasies, and his reaction to Johann's world come to mind when Stephen declares his only arms for the future to be "silence, cunning, and exile" (*PA*, 251). Similarly Marti's Sunday walk, his dream in the military prison, his fantasy on the lake, as well as Simon's evening on the lake shore, his discovery of Sebastian, his Paris dream, and his snow-child fantasy are signs that support the secret, outwardly unrealized inner life of Walser's superficial heroes and reassure them as Stephen's epiphanies support him in "an undivined and squalid way of life" (*PA*, 80).

Instructive comparisons can be drawn between the two authors in their use of style and in the role they see for the artist.[6] The problem of language for Walser and Joyce, no less than for Rilke and Kafka, was complicated because of the anomalous role each of these languages held in the homeland from which each wrote. With the exception of Kafka, who early developed a lean, uncluttered language of unusual esthetic economy, each of the others overcompensated to secure his language as a creative tool. It developed in Walser's and Rilke's case in the direction of *Jugendstil* and in Joyce's case from the *fin-de-siècle* heritage of the Celtic Twilight. The lure of these contemporary styles for them was in each case the same: they mistakenly hoped the emotiveness of the style could be an esthetically adequate vehicle for the representation of modern consciousness. To the extent that "The Notebooks," "The Portrait," and all three of Walser's novels illustrate the creation of personal literary idioms, they also represent their authors' reaction to the pathos of contemporary styles. Joyce's hero cannot speak the words "*home, Christ, ale, master*," "without unrest of spirit"; his "voice holds them at bay," his "soul frets in the shadow" of this language (*PA*, 194). Joyce creates a language closer to the range of tones and registers in Walser's novels than to Rilke's rarely relieved soulfulness that portrays Malte's difficult discipleship to art. The language in "The Portrait" ranges from the child's inchoate utterances and rimes to the intellectual and emotional shorthand of the journal with which the novel ends. Seeking a "fluid and lambent narrative" (*PA*, 219), Joyce's language takes pleasure in ecclesiastical costume and pomp, in the rarefied latinisms of doctrinal theology (*PA*, 193), in the florid imagery of moral tracts (*PA*, 109), and in the rhetorical hyperbole of Father Arnall's hell-fire depiction, from which the narrator often borrows images of feculence. The rhythm of the novel's language is modelled after "the vital sea"; it inspires sentences like "But the tide was near the turn and already the day was on the wane" (*PA*, 176), or that seen in the peace and reprieve of the image that cools the hell fires, when "the tide was flowing in fast to the land with a low whisper of her waves, islanding a few last figures in distant pools" (*PA,* 177), or a phrase like "the spell of arms and voices" (*PA,* 257). Too frequently, however, the effect of this poetry is outweighed by a strained pursuit of "the cloistral silver-veined prose of Newman" (*PA,* 257). At worst, a Dublin variety of literary dandyism results, a verbal form of Stephen's "elaborate adoration" (*PA,* 170) that gives too great a precedence to the emotional weight of words (cf. *PA,* 168, 170f., 196), causing a literary imbalance comparable to that of *Fritz Kochers Aufsätze.* The unfolding of Stephen's consciousness brings with it a supererogation of similes, metaphors, and adjectivally overladen images, where, within single paragraphs, estheticized perception, verbal play, and puns alternate with successful verbal "epiphanies," lyric leit-motifs, and associative repeats. The linguistic catholicity in *Jakob von Gunten* could be said to resemble that in "The Portrait," although there is none of the intellection based on Stephen's reading and the Newman-inspired estheticism. The narrative style of *Jakob von Gunten* telescopes states and levels of consciousness which in "The Portrait" are distributed developmentally, in rough approximation to Stephen's chronological age. The same easy crossing from states of wakefulness to reverie and imagination in Joyce's novel is of course frequent in Walser's two earliest novels, but it is Jakob who splices with insight the childishness of remarks such as those made by Stephen as a child: "that was called charcoal . . ."; "Suck was a queer word"; "There was every kind of news in the paper . . ." (*PA,* 42, 11, 24). Indeed, Walser, in Jakob's journal, progresses even further along the uncharted linguistic road Joyce entered upon in the final pages of the novel. He shows the same personal fearlessness that Stephen enunciates to Cranly.[7]

With the development of a journal form within his novel, Joyce, more than Rilke in "The Notebooks," explores the possibilities of human expression in the novel. Joyce, however, outdoes Rilke in the deification of the artist when he makes the word incarnate "in the virgin womb of imagination" (*PA,* 221), or writes of the sacramental image of the transmutation of "the daily bread of experience into the radiant body of everliving life" (*PA,* 225). Malte's monkhood strives for an absolute called God that resembles more a purified, fear-shorn image of himself as an artist, or a supreme, accessible esthetic arbiter to replace a *deus absconditus.* Stephen's certainty of his future fall (*PA,* 165) is, like Jakob's somber apprehension that such a fall be permanent (*JvG,* 156), a salvation in terms of human limitations. The crowning of Stephen as the "cunning worker" of his surname takes place as the form changes from lyric biography to journal. Joyce begins with a style of narrative Naturalism disguised as childlike perception and moves through the post-symbolistic prose poetry that alternates with the easy flow of narrative and dialog traditional in the English novel (cf. *PA,* 88f., 94) until, in the final pages of the book, he has made Stephen an impersonalized artist who mixes themes and motifs from the novel as chronicler, player on internalized emotion, first- and third-person narrator, and free artificer. In finding the language that Rilke, through Malte, still seeks in his parable of the Prodigal Son, Joyce makes of his novel not only an evocation of the past, but an artistic exorcism that clears the way for the experiment of *Ulysses.*

Nietzsche's attack on the stultification of German education in his second essay in *Unzeitgemäße Betrachtungen,* "Vom Nutzen und Nachteil der Historie für das Leben" (1874), provided the immediate impetus for the school novels that are characteristic of German letters at the turn of the century and which remained a part of the literary scene as late as 1930 with the popular success of Friedrich Torberg's *Der Schüler Gerber.* Around 1900 the school motif provided a convenient vehicle among intellectuals for expressing their reform spirit as well as the youthful personality with its newly-won literary respectability. Frank Wedekind used this motif as early as 1891 for grossly satirical scenes in his lyrical drama *Frühlings Erwachen.* Heinrich Mann's school novel *Professor Unrat* (1905) follows Wedekind in using the motif as the medium for a caricature of Wilhelmenian Germany. In Mann's overdrawn parody, however, the school is no more than the background for the sordid failure of a *Gymnasium* teacher to purge himself of middle-class mentality even after "breaking out" of his narrow school world.

Jakob von Gunten, because it elevates the school motif into a permanently fluid tension symbolizing the individual responsibility of freedom versus the transitoriness of all institutions, deserves a place of honor in this otherwise ephemeral and rarely distinguished sub-category of literary history. Robert Musil's first novel, *Die Verwirrungen des Zöglings Törleß* (1906), can be compared with *Jakob von Gunten* in his theme of the relation between intellectual and imaginative cognition. However, Musil's novel is too often forced to bear stylistic comparison with *Jakob von Gunten,*[8] while the school motif is nothing more than the mechanism for sparking a study of youth that is rich in psychological-philosophical insights.

Before discussing points of similarity between these two school novels, we want to refer briefly to two novels, one by Emil Strauss and one by Hermann Hesse, that are more typical in their use of the school motif. Heiner Lindner, the hero of Strauss' *Freund Hein* (1902), is the mortal victim of a conflict between the demands of his uncompromising, instinctive personality—represented in his unusual musical gift—and the demands of an equally insistent, but impersonally abstract world, represented by the *Gymnasium*. The specific theme of this "life history" is the price exacted by life for securing ties in this world. Karl Notwang, Heiner's brilliant, rebellious school comrade, is the only figure in the novel with the sensitivity, love, and spiritual independence from abstract formulas to sense that the pressures exerted on Heiner to finish school mean his ruin. "The devil take you all," he cries to Heiner's baffled parents when he is certain that his friend has taken his life, "with your 'To the best of my knowledge and conscience,' if you don't have a spark of feeling for the inviolability of pure nature." Heiner is incapable of protecting himself by assuming a masking mimicry such as Notwang urges upon him in order to save himself and his talent. By naming his hero with a colloquial variant of the folk euphemism for death seen in the title, the author wants the freedom that Heiner achieves in suicide to be understood as a negative renunciation based on a failed spiritual parturition.

Hermann Hesse's *Unterm Rad* (1906) has, as does Strauss' story, autobiographical sources and deals again with the problem of talent. Hans Giebenrath, the soulful student, no longer finds purpose in his calling after he gradually realizes that his ambition had been encouraged only by the selfishness of those who made his career as a theological student possible. He is accompanied by a second, more resilient author-projection—comparable to Karl Notwang—in the person of Giebenrath's blood friend Hermann Heilner. Heilner refuses the lifetime security the state school offers in return for conformity, he castigates—as does Notwang— the spirit-deadening hypocrisy of piety towards the classics, and he finally escapes the teachers' pedantry and fear of talent by running away from the school. Hans Giebenrath, on the other hand, suffers an unclarified death by drowning after an unsuccessful and so-called "unnatural" attempt—during a recuperation from nervous collapse—to make good the childhood his mentors had robbed him of. The symbolism of Giebenrath's loss of Heilner is latent in Giebenrath's inability to extirpate the elder-inspired revulsion and shame at his failure in school, but is left undeveloped in the novel. Whereas Strauss is able to redeem his work from the conventionality and inherent sentimentality of some of his motifs by alternating narrative realism in one part of the novel with conscious, objectivized irreality in all that deals with the development of Heiner's inner life, Hesse undercuts his gifts for the lyric evocation of small town life by the mediocrity of his conception and by an esthetically untempered irony.[9]

Musil's school novel, *Young Törless* (*Die Verwirrungen des Zöglings Törleß*), concentrates on the spiritual development of an adolescent during his stay at a select boarding school in an eastern province of the old Austro-Hungarian empire. Conventional narrative fillers on curriculum and the narrow-mindedness of teachers are missing. Musil develops the school motif into the symbol of a commencement that is definitive as personal destiny and thus elevates the question of the meaning of school to an inquiry into the authority of reality, as does Walser in *Jakob von Gunten.* Hindsight tells us, but it would have been difficult to predict that the author of "Törless" would be the author who, in *Der Mann ohne Eigenschaften,* went on to create a massive, breathtakingly intellectual torso of a non-novel. In a novel whose "story" consists of not telling the story it is supposed to (*MOE,* 1640), essaysim is substituted as the basis for the "constructive irony" of a utopia perceived in the here and now.[10] Precisely the motifs that bear comparison with *Jakob von Gunten,* rather than Musil's narrative style and language,[11] are the motifs that presage the later author.

The novel depicts Törless' struggle and ultimate failure to rationally comprehend, although he eventually welcomes them as positive and natural, the unfolding of forces within him that are induced in the seemingly anomalous circumstances of brutality, school-boy sexual perversions, reverie, and dream. That the source of Törless' confusions relates to the ineffability of intense emotions in the language of reason is clear from the Maeterlinck quotation Musil uses as a motto for his novel; that the novel's latent theme is the search for an artistic language to render Törless' cognition of reality when he leaves the school is not as evident, but can be surmised from the narrator's suggestion of Törless' "great future" (*YT,* 28), the somewhat ingenuous prediction of Törless' later developed into a "young man of very fine and sensitive spirit"—one of "those esthetically inclined intellectuals" (*YT,* 169)—from the visionary experience of the garden wall (*YT,* 86–93) foreshadowing visions of poetic inspiration, from the narrator's equation of Törless' remembrance of autonomous imagination with artistic intuition (*YT,* 137f.), and, finally, from the duality of perspective that Törless retains after the overly tidy resolution of his confusions. The implication that, at the end of the novel, Törless has found the language able to render his maturer cognition of the fluidity of reality—"this mental perspective that he had experienced which alternated according to whether he was considering what was distant or what was near by" (*YT,* 216)—is rendered ambiguous by the social conservatism with which Musil chooses to depict Törless' acceptance of the reality of both worlds. It is true that the language with which Törless answers questions before a school board inquiring into the brutal mistreatment of Basini by his fellow pupils, where Törless himself feels he will speak "clearly, coherently, and triumphantly" (*YT*, 209), can only be so judged by the measure of art and not rational reason.

If we compare Jakob von Gunten with Törless we note that both experience what Musil's narrator refers to as "that manifold amazement and bewilderment in the encounter with life" (*YT*, 202). Yet Jakob's childish-wise actions in the ironic experiment of his life and his writing show that he advances the education of the soul through humiliations found in "The Portrait" and "The Notebooks" as well as in "Törless" further toward the fusion in Törless' final knowledge of the dynamism of the "easily effaced boundary-lines" that "had sunk deep into him, sending out its wan and shadowy beams" (*YT*, 216).[12] Törless shares with Jakob the "different, more internalized certainty" that carries beyond the "gap in the causality of our thinking" (*YT*, 216). Musil's hero attains the knowledge that we can't manage with thinking alone through mortifications such as his associative confusion of the prostitute Bozena with his mother (*YT*, 40f.), that is as disturbing to him as the dream in which Jakob strikes his mother is to Jakob (*JvG*, 362). Like Jakob's forced sacrifice of the illusion regarding the Benjamentas, Törless has to acknowledge the distasteful reality of the personalities of his classmates Beinberg and Reiting and of his own short-lived passion for Basini.

To help convey the vitality of Törless' inner life, the narrator tells us that the hero's images are "unstable, varying and accompanied by an awareness of their random nature" (*YT*, 135) or that the thought emerging from a great insight signifies neither the depth of the perception nor the aid it needed from the "dark loam of our innermost being" (*YT*, 211). Yet the complementary cohesiveness of thought and emotion, fused into the humane spirit that perceives the "easily effaced boundary-lines" around human beings, remains too much an intellectual construct in the novel. Clarity and dream alternate for Törless for much the same purpose they do for Jakob; their aim is "to try to see lucidly" (*JvG*, 352). In the maturing of Törless' spirit, the images of narrow doors, walls, confining borders, trap doors, and dark guards give way to the knowledge that no matter how unsettling an image or thought is from the distance, from a nearer perspective it will somehow be accommodated to a human measure. In *Jakob von Gunten* Walser fuses intellectual and imaginative volatility into a single symbolic figure; the only hint in "Törless" of the contrapuntal dynamism Musil later achieves within the stasis of narrative essayism is a static narrator whose intellectualism leaves very little esthetic space for Törless himself to emerge as more than an exercise in cognition. Consequently, although Törless is comparable to Jakob in his acceptance of reality when he says: " 'Now I'm not perplexed by riddles. It all happens: that's the sum total of wisdom . . .' " (*YT*, 191), the failure to inspire the context of such an insight with either the emotion of discovery or the esthetic objectification of its paradox, relegates the statement to the realm of precocious resignation. Similarly, that the "fissure" between thinking and emotion still exists for Törless when he faces the authorities questioning him on Basini, even though Törless has overcome his fear ("'I know, things are just things, and they will probably always be so . . .' " [*YT*, 212].), indicates not only that Walser's and Musil's school novels were related in their theme of cognition, but also that we find in Musil's novel little of the simultaneity of utopian hope and renunciation developed in Jakob's perception of the same "fissure." Because the intellectual perception of the double image of reality (cf. *YT*, 84–86; 89f.; 212) is so much more decisive in the work than its linguistic re-creation, "Törless" today seems like a novel inspired by an empathetic reading of Hugo von Hofmannsthal's "Lord Chandos Letter," but compromised artistically by a knowledge of Bergson and Freud.

Klaus Wagenbach's biography of the young Kafka[13] mentions Walser and Heinrich von Kleist as the most enduring literary influences on Kafka. Wagenbach does not specify the nature of "the strong influence of Robert Walser" (*Wagenbach*, 116) other than to claim that *Jakob von Gunten* played a role in the conception of *The Castle* (*Das Schloß*) (*Wagenbach*, 158). Taking Kafka's praise of *Jakob von Gunten* in the draft of a letter from the year 1909 as the earliest evidence of Kafka's knowledge of Walser, Wagenbach says it is "questionable" whether Walser could have influenced Kafka's first book, *Betrachtung*, published in 1913 and consisting of prose pieces written between 1904 and 1910. The possibility of a literary relation between the two authors goes back to Robert Musil's review in *Die Neue Rundschau* in 1914[14] and Walter Benjamin's essay on Walser. Reviewing Walser's *Geschichten*, Kafka's *Betrachtung*, and the separately published first chapter of *Amerika, Der Heizer*, Musil had suggested that Kafka erred in trying, in *Betrachtung*, to imitate Walser's prose. Max Brod's description in his autobiography of Kafka's enthusiastic reading of some of the prose pieces that Walser wrote in Berlin[15] gave new impetus to the intimations of an inter-relationship between Kafka and Walser. This notion is understandably attractive in view of Kafka's generally severe or noncommital judgment of contemporary authors as well as of the difficulty of identifying immediate stylistic or thematic influences in his work. Yet the most authoritative recent scholarly studies of Kafka have either ignored Walser altogether (Sokel) or made only peripheral reference to Kafka's knowledge of Walser (Emrich, Politzer). Typical is Beda Allemann's insistence at the end of his study of *The Trial* (*Der Prozeß*) that the theme of justification that emerged with the "breakthrough" in Kafka's story "Das Urteil" (written 1912) effectively excluded "all of Walser's perambulations and slight oddity for Kafka from then on."[16]

Without a detailed stylistic comparison of Kafka and Walser it is difficult to establish a direct influence on Kafka that is specifically distinguishable from the acknowledged influences of Hebel, Flaubert, and Kleist.[17] It is, however, possible to show that Kafka's first reading of Walser took place at an earlier date than critics have heretofore surmised and to explore the range of Walser's work in which thematic and formal parallels exist in the work of the two.

Five of Walser's prose pieces appeared in the last three monthly issues of *Die Neue Rundschau* for 1907; the series thus made up, together with prose pieces in the January and March issues of the next year, are no doubt the "many monthly issues" of the magazine Brod refers to in establishing the time of Kafka's discovery of the Walser (*Brod*, 393). Kafka's first written reference to Walser follows shortly thereafter, in a letter describing to Brod his difficulty in selecting a birthday gift for him. If Brod's report of the degree of Kafka's initial enthusiasm for Walser can be credited, the familiarity implied in Kafka's reference in the letter to "the book by Walser" would suggest he himself had read it, although this is not clear from the context of the letter.[18] In 1909 Kafka drafted a letter to Director Eisner, an office superior in the *Assicurazioni Generali,* who had evidently suggested a resemblance between Kafka and the figures in Walser's novels. "Walser knows me?" Kafka writes in this incompleted draft, "I don't know him, *Jakob von Gunten* I do know; a good book" (*Briefe*, 75). Even though he goes on to say that he had not read any other books by Walser, the rest of the letter draft defends Simon Tanner[19] as representative of the struggle to move spiritually out of the nineteenth century. He explains the unaccustomed view of reality in the novel as the consequence of the difficulty of ever regaining a normal view of life once one is out of step with it. Simon's is "a very poor career," Kafka writes, "but only a poor career gives the world the light that a still imperfect, but already good writer wants to create, but unfortunately, at any price" (*Briefe*, 76).[20] Kafka's third and last reference to Walser in his correspondence is in a letter to Brod from Switzerland in 1911, which suggests that by this time Kafka may have read *Der Gehülfe:* "To put it briefly for now, in forming an opinion of Switzerland I would stick to [Conrad Ferdinand] Meyer rather than Keller or Walser" (*Briefe,* 91). The single other written reference to Walser[21] is at the end of a journal entry from 1917. Kafka had described his indebtedness to Dickens in his first novel while specifying some of Dickens' narrative artifices: "Walser's connection with [Dickens] in his blurring [*verschwimmenden*] employment of abstract metaphors" (*Tgbch,* 536). There is no evidence to indicate that Kafka's formulation of a salient element in the ambivalence of Walser's style was occasioned by a reading of Walser's *Kleine Prosa,* the collection of prose pieces published in 1917, where this element of style is particularly marked.[22]

To these conjectures based on ascertainable facts, it remains only to add that Kafka's active interest in Walser must have lasted beyond the "breakthrough" in 1912. There is strong circumstantial evidence that Kafka was acquainted with *Aufsätze,* published in 1913. One of Kafka's favorites, "Gebirgshallen," first appeared under this title here; Brod has written of "Lenz" (*AKD,* 144–150), an imaginary dialog in the same collection: "this dramatic scene, too, [was] a favorite piece in the readings Kafka gave among his friends."[23] There are no known written references by Walser to Kafka who claims to have hardly known Kafka's work. When Seelig mentioned Kafka's interest in his work to him Walser answered drily that there were more exciting things to read in Prague than "Walserades" (*Wdgg,* 107).

Parallels and contrasts between Kafka's and Walser's work do exist beyond the ultimately questionable verifications provided by real or supposed literary influences. These parallels and contrasts offer some insight into two artistically and humanly elusive personalities who lived total existences as artists (cf. *Tgbch,* 420) but harbored indomitable middle-class longings and ideals. Both Kafka and Walser devoted their outwardly uneventful lives to writing what they regarded as private expressions of their private isolation and weakness.[24] Participating in contemporary literary life only marginally except for their reading, instinctively distrustful of the pathos of the artist's role, these two constitutional bachelors[25] made their "weakness" the instrument of what Kafka called a "higher variety of observation," "fact-observation" (*Tgbch,* 564). In the distorted reality of what both Kafka and Walser were persuaded was a re-creation of everyday life, they both regarded the inalienable reality of fact as the stuff of a literature that demonstrates not so much "the absurdity of fact" (*Middleton,* 414) as fact as the anchor in the free flow of existence (cf. the parallel "swimmer" images implying freedom and subjection to the universal law in both *Jakob von Gunten*

[*JvG*, 430f.] and a prose fragment by Kafka ["Hochzeitsvorbereitungen," p. 287]).

In their art, both writers sought the creation of an autonomous realm which they consciously disavowed as inconsistent with the laws governing human life.[26] Walser's work no less than Kafka's has as its theme the justification of man that both of them expressed in their own existences and with insights gained at their own expense—Walser with a gaiety that is too insistent to dismiss as superficial, Kafka with the sadness whose hopeless love is expressed only in the humor and irony found even in his most somber works. The literature of accreditation for man they both wrote shows a broad contemporary sensibility working within formal and thematic limitations. Kafka's intuition expressed in the draft to Director Eisner that Walser created the illumination in his novel "unfortunately at any price" is similar to his own intention to overcome his "incapability of writing" by directing "at least one line against himself each day" (*Tgbch*, 12) or his later statement that he had access to the archimedean point at the price of his exclusion from life ("Hochzeitsvorbereitungen," p. 418). It was this sacrifice of individuation in order to discover and secure what Kafka later spoke of as "the indestructible" that very possibly made compelling even the undeniably mannerized pieces he first read by Walser. If indeed, as Brod reports, "Kafka was an enthusiastic troubador for Walser's art, especially for the novel *Jakob von Gunten*" (*Die Zeit*, April 7, 1955), then his enthusiasm must have been related to the self-preserving sacrifice of individuation found in Jakob. The "breakthrough" story, "Das Urteil," hints that, for Kafka, the double father image, from which Jakob escapes only to be reunited with Benjamenta, the more threateningly tyrannical one of the two, must have exerted a profound attraction.[27]

Kafka's depiction of the interior life in "Das Urteil," "Die Verwandlung," and *Amerika* illustrates parallels in the work of the two writers, although Kafka is from the outset more rigorous, and more skeptical of the "free existence" it promises. Georg Bendemann's death verdict is the symbolic outcome of the disavowal of the "friend" in St. Petersburg who represents the free existence of childhood, the sacrifice of individuation in imagination needed to realize the father's love, and simultaneously the weakness of such a personality in the everyday world. Gregor Samsa's "metamorphosis" into a giant bug follows from his inability to acknowledge the reality of his interior life and from his family's refusal to accept their inner beings as representing a separate and yet common truth that relates them. Karl Rossmann, the hero of Kafka's first novel, portrays an attempt, less successful than Jakob von Gunten's, to become part of a larger human family in the freedom imposed on him by the separation from his own family. Kafka claimed that the resolution of the novel in the incomplete final chapter, which Brod titled "Das Naturtheater von Oklahoma," was to lead to a happy ending and a reconciliation with Karl's family (Brod's Afterword to *Amerika*). Something of the sort is intimated when Karl finds Giacomo, the elevator boy with whom he had worked in the hotel, whose name is the Italian form of Karl Rossmann's rich uncle's and his own son's. But the "horse man" (Rossmann) Karl has no better control of the two realms of nature and theater than does the imaginary horseman mentioned in Kafka's letter on Walser over his steed, or Kafka's country doctor over his wagon team. This final chapter in *Amerika* also represents Kafka's most comprehensive, at that time, although hidden inquiry into the possibility of artistic existence. Kafka sublimates the artist—as does Walser—into the figure of an intelligent, consciously naive and wakeful observer.[28] Karl Rossmann projects Kafka's own ambiguous artistic ideal of what might be called a dream vision of clarity in the two poles of his longings—to become an engineer and to give expression to his interior being in music. Karl is provisionally taken on in the troupe of players under a false name and a false (or masking) title that indicates Kafka's own uncertainty about his art: "Negro, technical worker" (*Amerika*, 213). His departure into the wilderness to join a troupe of players is as equivocal as Jakob's final departure, however as a stylistically ironized departure into artistic isolation it lacks the utopian human hope that encourages Jakob in his.

In the course of his work, Kafka's association of the metaphor of motion with the freedom of interior being underwent a progressive reduction of mobility and space to end in *The Castle* (*Das Schloss*) with the "standing march" that was supposed to lead to K.'s death by exhaustion, and in "Der Bau" (1923) with the maze-running burrowing animal in Kafka's final depiction of the artist in autonomous isolation. The flowing river, the symbol of integrated existence in "Das Urteil," is already inaccessible for the hero of Kafka's earliest work, the posthumously published "Beschreibung eines Kampfes." Kafka's later representation of autistic artistic existence in the spool-shaped, patchily clothed, homeless figure of Odradek in "Die Sorge des Hausvaters" that may "one day . . . bounce down the steps before my children's and their children's feet with trailing threads of twine" (*Erzlgg*, 172) is curiously similar to Walser's depiction in "Märchen" (*UP*, 117–118) of a more forthright projection of the artist transformed by "some unknown power" into a ball which "rolled and bounced around instead of walking."[29]

The novels of the two writers point to their recognition of a valid absolute in the self to which man is responsible. A discrepancy between Kafka's articulation of this absolute in his journal, letters, and conversations with Janouch and Brod and its fictional representation in *The Trial* and *The Castle* is explained by depiction in these novels of human existence in a world whose order blocks or distorts man's entrance into what Kafka called the law. Jakob's relation to the laws of the Institute Benjamenta and the acceptance of insignificance that makes possible his discovery of the subterranean sanctum of the laws within himself offer some thematic parallels to these two Kafka novels. Joseph K. never realizes that the court that has arrested him wants nothing of him but that he realize his own life "process," or that he can only become the prey of the court if he seeks it out. He never realizes that his justification of himself in the résumé of his life that he is asked to write must necessarily be the proof of a lie. Only in the moments before his death does he pose the questions that contradict logic, and if asked sooner, might have extended the possibility of redeeming self-sacrifice rather than the demeaning death whose shame he fears will outlive him. Jakob by contrast gains entrance to an understanding of the laws through its guardians and victims, the Benjamentas, who are Jakob's superiors before the law but his servants in his freedom. Whereas Joseph K. defends himself by attack, Jakob can—in his vision—apprehend the source of the laws at the Insitute Benjamenta during his descent to the lower passageways because he accepts and experiences both his transitoriness and his death as equal possibilities in his destiny. Joseph K. is never participant as is Jakob in preservation of the laws through the symbol of exterior self-sacrifice through insignificance or their rescue from estranged anonymity through play and mask—except, perhaps, in the stricken chapter "Das Haus." Jakob's knowledge is closest to that of Titorelli's in *The Trial*, who tries in vain to have Joseph K. exchange the courage of his absolute concept of freedom for the courage to accept Titorelli's knowledge that such freedom as exists encompasses servitude. In fact the heroes of Walser's novels occupy a position as close to the laws as Titorelli's; they too subject themselves to an absolute law whose tangible manifestations they recognize as compromised. The danger absolute freedom implies to the common order of life, the knowledge implicit in Walser's Bern work and his walk-episodes that such freedom is accomplished at the price of the human loss of the things we love (cf. Jakob's Kafkan vision of freedom as cold, beautiful and not permanently endurable in the lower passageways [*JvG*, 429]), Kafka portrayed most implacably in "Ein Hungerkünstler" (1921/22) and "Der Bau" (1923). K., the hero of Kafka's final novel, *The Castle*, resembles his predecessor Joseph K. in his absolutist aims. The motif of the "inner chambers" in *Jakob von Gunten,* which Kafka transposed into the inaccessible castle in this modern variant of the German *Bildungsroman,*[30] would seem to be less important to the conception of the novel than the theme of self-justification embodied in Jakob's risking the entire individual to encounter existence as completely as possible. Jakob does this through his infractions against the laws he reveres. He thus experiences the synthesis between personal freedom and the universal application of the law that exists as a possibility for K. in the Bürgel scene in *The Castle.* But in contrast to K., who believes the castle officials would not accept the self-accreditation he himself would write because it would be too amateurish (*Das Schloss,* 377), Jakob does write an exact counterpart of such a testimonial in his *curriculum vitae* and thereby expresses as language the combination of consciousness of intention and unconscious reality of being which Emrich has specified as K.'s unrealized possibility.[31] Jakob's subversion of the school's regulations is motivated by his insistence on communicating with Benjamenta as a human being and not as the official of the law he represents. In so doing he undermines the institution of the law and frees its victim, whereas K. frustrates Bürgel's secret human hope to be liberated from the machinery of the law.

The vain attempt by K.'s two "assistants," the playful childish creatures assigned him by the castle to alleviate and humanize the rigidity of K.'s attempts to gain access to the castle, and K.'s own misguided attempt to personalize and objectify the mythic, emblematically conceived force of Klamm, suggest that the most pervasive influence from Kafka's reading of *Jakob von Gunten* may be this devious acknowledgment that the exhausting exertions of so many of his central figures to mediate between freedom and the limitations governing life in the world had to remain useless without a break in the logic of their own will.

The source of Kafka's attraction to Walser can be adduced from the coincidence in their works of a constitutive, unresolved dialectic as movement in repose. In Walser's novels this movement underlies Simon's reflection on nature to the male nurse, the narrator's description of the four seasons in *Der Gehülfe,* and the dream quality of street encounters. The parallel in Kafka is the "functional space"[32] that isolates Kafka's three novel heroes and makes impossible a resolution based on genuine encounter. The reduced development in Kafka's and Walser's novel heroes becomes progressively more pronounced in a common pattern of reduced time phases. The effective suspension of time underlines thematic iteration in chronologically interchangable sections, which, linked in an additive series, reinforce the fairy-tale atmosphere of narrative hermeticity through the omission of elucidating exposition. In Kafka's work the structure of movement in repose not only comprehends the rhythm of individual narrative segments where the emotional and verbal kinesis is emitted by the unattainable object of the central figure's longing (cf. the father's "resurrection" in "Das Urteil"; Gregor Samsa's expulsion from the living room in "Die Verwandlung"; the gallery visitor's breathless descent to the circus ring at the end of the first paragraph in "Auf der Galerie" and his disheartened acceptance of exclusion from the charmed circle of art in the second, after realizing the dichotomy between the intrinsically misleading but empirically real allure of the exhibition of artistic skill; Joseph K.'s illness during his visit to the chancellery in *The Trial;* K.'s frustrated attempt to encounter Klamm in *The Castle*), but also pervades his imagery and even his sentence structure. Whether the sentences in Kafka that reproduce movement in repose by suspending or absolutely qualifying the statement in them are modelled on Walser or whether such sentences represent an independent, parallel development that began as the attempt to describe simultaneity of perception in *Beschreibung eines Kampfes,* Kafka's use of these, as well as Walser's use of disillusionistic "corrections"—which serve in *Jakob von Gunten* to suspend intellectual and linguistic presuppositions—demonstrates how similar was the narrative device of a double optic which both authors used to actualize the process of cognition. While Kafka substituted the dialectic of contradictory detail for Walser's fluidity of narrative point of view in *Der Gehülfe,* Kafka's mastery in conveying his central figures' point of view and that of their adversaries from a single narrative position suggests that the attraction of Walser's short prose (particularly "Gebirgshallen" and "Lenz") must have lain in its combination of a negative and positive view within a narrative space that is consciously restricted to what is directly perceptible. (Cf. the mixture of irony and sympathy we have described in *Der Gehülfe, Jakob von Gunten,* "Kleist in Thun," and in "Die Schlacht bei Sempach.")

As self-incriminating surveyors of reality, both Kafka and Walser amassed detail of seemingly minimal importance to the esthetic statement of their work in order to give shape to the invisible and ineffable. Their reliance on detail is of course directed toward different narrative objectives: Kafka concentrated his efforts increasingly on the seamless, logically inseparable detail of absolute "stories" while Walser, by apparently random detail, fragmentized the sparse traces of story for absolute narration. Yet, for both, the copiousness of detail is the evidence of the activity of parabolic description and surveillance that more and more dominates their late work. The motion within the static space surrounding Kafka's central figures, that functions as a demonstration of their beings, can also be found in *Jakob von Gunten* and in the prose pieces in Walser's *Aufsätze*. The accelerated dialectic of paradox that provides the stylistic counterweight for the reduced mass of this space in Kafka's late work (cf. *Das Schloss*, "Josephine, Die Sängerin," "Der Bau," and "Forschungen eines Hundes") has a counterpart in the reduction implicit in the internalization and abstraction of Walser's late "walks," in which Walser's verbal and intellectual montages illustrate the difficulty he noted in "Brief an einen Besteller von Novellen" of "not sending one's gaze out too far in what is relatively still too spacious a sphere" (*GKW*, 191). For both writers, detail objectifies a compulsion for justification that is inseparable from the themes, forms, and style of their work. Although the desire for the seeming completeness of detail can be documented in the early work of both writers,[33] the greatest detail— whether logical and cohesive, like Kafka's, or indirect and discursive, like Walser's—only documents the incompleteness of a partial view.

Kafka's work is incomparably more astringent than Walser's, intellectually more rigorous, and psychologically more consistent. Walser wore his self-indulgent gaiety on his sleeve, but only in a letter to Brod in 1922, when Kafka summed up his own career, did he speak of his writing as "only a construction of the addiction to pleasure" (*Briefe*, 385). Kafka never lost his "hand" as Walser later described his situation following the completion of his novels in Berlin; one reason, however, that Kafka failed to complete and publish his novels was that he felt a disparity in the continuity in them as compared with some of his short work. At a time before the writing of *The Trial*, Kafka judged the level of his novel writing to be "in the disgraceful low country of writing" (*Tgbch*, 294). What he agreed to publish was only what had been created "in the fire of contiguous hours" (*Briefe an Felice*, p. 153). Walser in his dissipated writing was always willing to risk more, although he too expressed a similar standard for his work in a letter to Morgenstern from early in the Berlin period. There Walser justified his reservation about an author continually writing novels by describing novel writing as "an exacting craft that requires a continually flourishing fire" (quoted in *Mächler*, 114). The uncertainty of his role as an artist, that Kafka only articulated clearly in his final stories although it is latent from the earliest work on, Walser risked admitting in order to secure a distinction between art and life and thus to avoid the maze both had created as a symbol of the desire for their correlation ("Der Bau" and "Minotauros").

While it was not the aim of this section to illustrate Walser's and Kafka's use of language, it should be noted that the critical distance both retained to a language that was learned outside the home (cf. Kafka's journal entry October 24, 1911 [*Tgbch*, 115–116] and *Wdgg*,

109) is mirrored in their seemingly instinctive ability to use puns as commentary on the thought and emotional patterns of language. Walser's garrulousness plyed the richness of connotation in German into verbal thickets that represent his criticism of the certainty in intellectual monism; Kafka moved more towards a brittle, transluscent language whose logic bared the bones of emotion in language. Both writers could view silence as a tenable alternative to art because they shared a knowledge of the imperfection of art as a presumptively prime medium for expressing the truth of human existence.

Historically Walser belongs to the generation of writers whose earliest works reflect the crisis in art, language, and cognition that distinguishes artistic endeavour at the turn of the century. From the outset Walser's work incorporates the basic transformation in techniques and forms that characterize modern literature. Correspondences in Walser's work to modernist trends have been obscured by his connotative and eidetic intelligence, by his unorthodox cultivation of the short prose form, and by the consequences of Walser's ambivalence toward art, as it is expressed throughout his career in the use of art to suspend itself. The themes of his work, however, show the necessity of re-evaluating his contribution to German literature in the first third of the century. In the progressively more restricted format of his work he depicted his perception of a contemporary age through the symbol of writing himself. The walker and the wanderer-artist are Walser's formulation of the pervasive modern theme of a directionless life journey. As symbols for the recurrent knowledge in modern literature that art is at present not created by members of a community but by the isolated, they effectively reflect modern man's experience of human isolation and his difficulty and resistance to communication. The ambivalence toward art, which in Walser is formulated in the duality of his central figures, has, since Walser, become a sometimes-arbitrary tenet of modern writing. But the same ambivalence has been the base from which artists have sought to elicit a response appropriate to an increasingly problematic world. As in Walser, this ambivalence represents a legitimate attempt to reconstitute the necessary dialog between art and its audience. Although the themes in Walser of the proximity of freedom and confinement, the absence of identifiable truth, and the unalterable reality of death give his work the artistic and human tension we identify as modern, it is the ambiguousness of his style that embodies the irrational hope strong enough to counterbalance, if not suspend, the unanswerable question of the meaning of existence. The novels are the earliest artistic statement of an individual, paradoxical vision that celebrates and vindicates man while it witnesses his inadequacy and failures. This vision is refined, fragmented, and reworked, but never abandoned through the rest of his career.

Despite the literary unpretentiousness of Walser's novels, they successfully convey a direct experience of the complexity of a new era. This experience is given literary form in the discrepancy between their restricted, uneventful plots and Walser's instinctive reaction to the unusual cultural demands made on this literary genre in our century—in the form of a double plot in *Geschwister Tanner,* a myopia deriving from Marti's vision of the heart, and Jakob's irony of hope. Walser's more conscious response to his own personal experience of a crisis in the novel was to substitute the short prose he called the chapters of a single plotless novel as a vicarious novel form. The abstraction and experiments in the later prose permitted Walser thematic and formal investigations; the unique blend of the rustic and the baroque in his language was the medium for linguistic queries. Thus the minimalism in Walser— which is born of chastened "poetic" illusions—symbolized for him the incommensurability of modern existence in the only terms he could accept as articulable—that is, as the reassurance in language that every human phenomenon is a complex web of spiritual, natural, and therefore significant relations.

Through the novel heroes' socially amoral experience of life before the portals of society's institutions, the novels represent Walser's basic expression of man's absolute justification in the absence of a binding law for mankind in society. By their very suppression of the theme of art, the novels contribute to Walser's transformation of the *fin-de-siècle* illusion of art into the wittingly unsuccessful game of art he plays in the Bern period. This "game" is the self-victimizing symbol of Walser's hope that the irresoluble antithesis between freedom and limitation is in fact an unpredictable interdependence, the specific elements of which are determined by man's realization of himself as perpetually in transition. This symbolic relativism underlies both the didacticism and the irony of the transparent masks of the Bern work as well as Walser's pleasurable experiments to find an "unknown vitality" in language (*GKW*, 198). A late prose work communicates something of this experience through a "letter," purportedly in answer to a query from an intellectual who has "not penetrated into the light" ("Brief an ein Mitglied der Gesellschaft," *Neue Schweizer Rundschau,* 20. Jg. [1927], 886–888). In his search for happiness the addressee wants to believe in and model himself on the narrator, but he is cautioned against this. Since the "colossally unmolested" personality of the "member of society" hasn't yet realized that life—"if this great life really pretends to be life"—ultimately "accumulates into a bit of faith," the narrator recommends the "self-surveillance" to "look into every day life with the greatest possible attentiveness." In this late variant of the restricted present in which Walser was able to intimate the recurrent creativity of encountered existence, the narrator points out: "I am not your path, I am rather one who has to risk reminding you that you are not only one path for yourself, but numerous paths."

Notes

1. The term is borrowed from Eudo C. Mason's *Exzentrische Bahnen. Studien zum Dichterbewußtsein der Neuzeit* (Göttingen: Vandenhoek und Ruprecht, 1963).

2. M. D. Herter Norton translates the words ". . . sie beschwörend, dass sie nicht liebten" as "imploring them not to love" (*MLB*, 216). This translation, I feel, contradicts the parabolic sense of the story.

3. "These journals," Rilke wrote in 1912, "in applying a measure to very far-developed sufferings, indicate to what height the bliss could mount that would be achievable with the fullness of these same powers" (*MLB*, 8). Another letter from the same year cautions against giving way "to the temptation" to go "parallel with this book"; "in its essence, it will be pleasureable only to those who undertake to read it, *against the current*, as it were" (*Selected Letters of Rainer Maria Rilke. 1902–1926*, Tr. R. F. C. Hull [London, 1947], p. 209).

4. Specifically the "cold, slimy water" of the square ditch; the sea that "was cold day and night: but . . . was colder at night" (*PA*, 17); the homesick reverie of holidays at home that is based on warmth (*PA*, 20–21); the expression of insecurity in the longing for sleep and in Stephen's death reverie; and the terror and disillusion in the experienced reality of dissension in his home (*PA*, 27–41).

5. The fabled Daedalian thread that Joyce obliquely refers to in the simile "like threads of silken light unwound from whirring spools" (*PA*, 229) is of course too intricately wound not to anticipate water as fulfillment even in Chapter One, in the soft dark simile concluding the chapter ("like drops of water in a fountain falling softly in the brimming bowl" [*PA*, 60]), which reproduces in image and sound Stephen's self-fulfillment in his victory in the Father Nolan episode. The hopeful sea reverie in the infirmary (*PA*, 27) is truncated by the death of Parnell.

6. Walser's work lacks completely the unmistakable political overtones in Joyce's novel that are even present in Stephen's answering the call of his "kinsmen" in order "to discover the mode of life or of art whereby [his] spirit could express itself in unfettered freedom" (*PA*, 250).

7. "I do not fear to be alone or to be spurned for another or to leave whatever I have to leave. And I am not afraid to make a mistake, even a great mistake, a lifelong mistake, and perhaps as long as eternity too" (*PA*, 251).

8. Contemporary comparisons between Musil and Walser were made in reviews of "Törless" and *Geschwister Tanner*. Felix Poppenberg (*Die Neue Rundschau*, 18 [1907]) preferred Walser's novel, although he may have misread Musil. Franz Blei (*Die Opale*, I, 2[1907], 213f.) singled out the two—Walser for his poetic intuition, Musil for his intellectualism—as novelists whose work would endure from an otherwise unpromising literary epoch. More recently, "Törless" has been described as "almost conventional" compared with *Jakob von Gunten* ("A Miniaturist in Prose," *Times Literary Supplement*, July 21, 1961).

9. Theodore Ziolkowski's recent study of Hesse's major novels (*The Novels of Hermann Hesse: A Study in Theme and Structure* [Princeton, 1965]) discusses aspects of Hesse's novels from *Demian* on that would seem to warrant comparing themes and motifs in his work with Walser. Particularly suggestive in this regard are Ziolkowski's remarks on Hesse's exploitation and transformation of "structures that go back to historical Romanticism" (342); Hesse's use of a fairy-tale structure to achieve a double perspective which is based on the realism of everyday life (200–206); Joseph Knecht's "awakening" to a commitment to man as the cause of his defection from the "pedagogical province" Castalia in the highly etherealized school novel, *Das Glasperlenspiel* (1943); and, finally, the emergence of humor, from *Der Steppenwolf* on, to temper the despair of Hesse's tortured heroes.

Hesse had an intimate knowledge of Walser's work, at least through the publication of *Poetenleben* in 1917, which he reviewed in the *Neue Zürcher Zeitung*. He published Walser during his period as co-editor of *März*, and, following the publication of *Jakob von Gunten*, he wrote the first comprehensive essay on Walser ("Robert Walser," *Sonntagsblatt der Basler Nachrichten* [September 5, 1909]).

Without overburdening a comparison, it should be noted that the earnest lightness Leo, the servant, porter, and "Oberste Ober des Bundes" in *Die Morgenlandfahrt* (1932) tries to teach H. H. and Leo's certainty that humility will preserve him into old age remind us of two aspects of Jakob's person at the Institute Benjamenta. Similarly Jakob's descent to the lower passageways to "see" himself in contradictory aspects of life under the guidance of an idealized woman he later abandons resembles Harry Haller's descent into "Hell" in *Der Steppenwolf*, his experience of the possibilities of personality in the "magic theater," and his "murder" of Hermine. Jakob's playfulness and his acceptance of good and evil as a unity resemble the "immortality" implicit in the lowly, but exemplary figure of Pablo in the same novel. Whether Hesse learned from Walser or not, by the time he wrote the review of the second edition of *Der Gehülfe* (*Neue Zürcher Zeitung*, August 9, 1936), the vexed admiration for Walser's effectiveness despite his "mistakes" and "playfulness" in the 1909 essay had given way to a view of estheticism more like the one he was then struggling to realize for his own final novel: "Now and again behind the appearance of playfulness genuine estheticism—one that is no longer playful—becomes visible: that attitude that says Yes to the entirety of life, because it is magnificent and beautiful as a spectacle, from the moment one can regard it dispassionately."

10. Two useful studies of Musil's novel are: Beda Allemann, *Ironie und Dichtung* (1956), pp. 177–220, and Albrecht Schöne, "Zum Gebrauch des Konjunktivs bei Robert Musil," *Euphorion*, 55, 2 (1961), 196ff.

11. Wilhelm Braun's systematic presentation of the development and portrayal of intense emotions in Törless ("The Confusions of Törless," *GR*, XL, Nr. 2 [March 1965], 116–131) has been of considerable use for this section. The treatment of "Törless" in Gerhart Baumann's book on Musil (*Robert Musil. Zur Erkenntnis der Dichtung* [Bern and Munich: Francke Verlag, 1965], pp. 119–130) is nearly exclusively concerned with intimations in "Törless" of the coincidence of opposites Baumann sees as the structural basis of Musil's work.

12. The hero of Walser's journal novel is closer to the creative spirit Musil describes early in *Der Mann ohne Eigenschaften:* ". . . It doesn't acknowledge what is permissible and what is not permissible, for everything can have a quality by means of which it is one day part of a great, new relation. Secretly it hates like death everything that acts as if it were fixed once and for all . . . It regards no single thing as firm, no I, no regulation; because our knowledge can change daily, it doesn't believe in any tie, and everything possesses the value it has only until the next creative act . . ." (*MOE*, 158).

13. Klaus Wagenbach, *Franz Kafka. Eine Biographie seiner Jugend. 1883–1912* (Bern: Francke, 1958), p. 159.

14. Now in Robert Musil, *Gesammelte Werke in Einzelausgaben,* ed. Adolf Frisé, II, *Tagebücher, Aphorismen, Essays und Reden* (Hamburg: Rowohlt, 1955), 686–688.

15. According to Brod, Kafka first called Brod's attention to Walser when *Die Neue Rundschau* published Walser's prose pieces in "many" consecutive issues. "When the issue arrived," he continues, "the first thing Kafka did was to rush to open the back pages of the text. He read many of Walser's pieces out loud to me. Some many times." Brod then describes the gusto with which Kafka read Walser's "Gebirgshallen" (*AKD*, 54–56). When he was no longer able to repress his laughter at a climactic moment in the text, "Kafka broke up, and, for a while, couldn't be quieted" (*Brod*, 393–394).

16. Beda Allemann, "Der Prozess," *Der deutsche Roman,* ed. Benno von Wiese (Düsseldorf: Bagel, 1963), II, 289.

17. In his Kafka biography Brod repeatedly stresses Kleist's stylistic influence on Kafka. Closer examination of this widely held view may reveal the influence to be predominantly thematic. A comparative textual study of themes, style, forms, and imagery in Kafka and Walser would, I believe, not only reveal a significant area of correspondence in their work but would place Kafka's achievement in more intimate relation to the themes prevalent in the first decade of the century than has so far been the case in studies of his work.

18. "What are books in comparison! [The birthday letter accompanied the gift of a stone and two books.] A book begins to bore you and never stops, or your child tears the book up, or, like the book by Walser, it is already falling apart when you get it" (*Briefe*, 57). The book in question could have been "falling apart" after frequent use or been a defectively bound paper-cover edition.

19. Kafka's acquaintance with Simon Tanner may be based on reviews of *Geschwister Tanner* in 1907 in two magazines to which he subscribed, *Die Neue Rundschau* (XVIII, Bd. I, 376–377) and *Die Opale* (1. Halbband, 2. Teil, 213–214).

20. The letter indicates a close identification with Walser and expresses the certainty that Walser's myopic world is indeed the human world. The letter is of further interest for the facility in its second half of a change of perspective—that could indeed be an imitation of Walser to assert the inevitability of the reality of the world—and the use of an image from his later work, a recalcitrant horse, as the symbol for the impossibility of fruitfully incorporating sensuality into modern man's life (cf. "Ein Landarzt").

> Natürlich laufen auch solche Leute, von außen angesehen überall herum, ich könnte Ihnen, mich ganz richtig eingeschlossen, einige aufzählen, aber sie sind nicht durch das Geringste ausgezeichnet als durch jene Lichtwirkung in ziemlich guten Romanen. Man kann sagen, es sind Leute, die ein bißchen langsamer aus der vorigen Generation herausgekommen sind, man kann nicht verlangen, daß alle mit gleichregelmäßigen Sprüngen den regelmäßigen Sprüngen der Zeit folgen. Bleibt man aber einmal in einem Marsch zurück, so holt man den allgemeinen Marsch niemals mehr ein, selbstverständlich, doch auch der verlassene Schritt bekommt ein Aussehen, daß man wetten möchte, es sei kein menschlicher Schritt, aber man würde verlieren. Denken Sie doch, der Blick vom rennenden Pferde in der Bahn, wenn man seine Augen behalten kann, der Blick von einem über die Hürde springenden Pferde zeigt einem sicher allein das äußerste, gegenwärtige, ganz wahrhaftige Wesen des Rennbetriebs. Die Einheit der umliegenden Gegend in der bestimmten Jahreszeit usw., auch den letzten Walzer des Orchesters und wie man ihn heute zu spielen liebt. Wendet sich aber mein Pferd zurück und will es nicht springen und umgeht die Hürde oder bricht aus und begeistert sich im Innenraum oder wirft mich gar ab, natürlich hat der Gesamtblick scheinbar sehr gewonnen. Im Publikum sind Lücken, die einen fliegen, die anderen fallen, die Hände wehen hin und her wie bei jedem möglichen Wind, ein Regen flüchtiger Relationen fällt auf mich, und sehr leicht möglich, daß einige Zuschauer ihn fühlen und mir zustimmen, während ich auf dem Grase liege wie ein Wurm. Sollte das etwas beweisen? (*Briefe*, 76).

21. *Der Gehülfe* is mentioned in the published section of "Richard und Samuel," the fragmentary novel co-authored by Brod and Kafka ("This arrangement, of conducting business enterprizes in villas, reminds me very much of R. Walser's novel 'Der Gehülfe'" [*Erzlgg*, 307]), but Middleton correctly notes that the work "betrays at this point the stamp of Brod's style, not that of Kafka's" (*Middleton*, 427).

22. A less likely possibility is that Kafka is referring to the style of Walser's prose piece "Dickens" (originally in *Pan*, I, 10 [March 16, 1911], where Brod published his "Kommentar zu Robert Walser" in the same year [October 15, 1911], although Walser's hyperbolic praise conceivably stimulated the reading of Dickens in the summer and fall of 1911 that preceded the writing of the first chapter of *Amerika* in the fall of 1912 (cf. *Tgbch*, 60, 77).

23. Max Brod, "Erinnerung an einen Dichter," *Die Zeit*, April 7, 1955.

24. Cf. Walser's "Aus meiner Jugend" (*UP*, 254–257), Kafka's remarks to Gustav Janouch describing his "scribblings" as "attestations of loneliness, private notes or playfulness" that were "proofs of weakness" (*Janouch*, 23), and Kafka's journal entry criticizing his life and his writing as unreal play (*Tgbch*, 561–562).

25. Kafka's list of reasons for and against marriage in his journal entry in July 1913 (*Tgbch,* 310–312) concludes with the irreconcilability of marriage and writing. Walser's much later dialog "Zwei Männer reden" (*Prager Presse,* July 26, 1931) ironically demonstrates that the artist Almador must marry.

26. Compare two "terminal" statements by Kafka and Walser, each of them a renunciation of their artistry: the "heightened redemption" as the artist heroine of Kafka's last story "Josephine" disappears in the anonymity of her race and Walser's remark to Seelig: "I want to live with the folk and disappear in it. That's the most appropriate thing for me" (*Wdgg,* 87).

27. Jakob escapes first from his industrialist father, whose very competence and success was a tyranny; Jakob feared "being suffocated by his excellence" (*JvG,* 340). Compare Kafka's unsuccessful sorties into an "active life" which his father prescribed must be modeled after his own success. Kafka must likewise have recognized in the awesome giant Benjamenta a Draco such as the figure he described in "Brief an den Vater," both of them alternating between peremptory severity and human evasion.

28. Kafka had already intimated the free existence of youth as a symbol for the artist in the departure of the children in "Kinder auf der Landstrasse" for a land of night where "fools" never sleep. The danger and the isolation of this "childhood" Kafka had depicted in the final story in the *Betrachtung* collection, "Unglücklichsein" (1910) and in Georg Bendemann's alter ego in "Das Urteil."

29. The image of encirclement in one of Kafka's first journal entries is still positive; it is the unbroken ring securing the continuity of our lives in the "river of time." If we somehow leave this circle we become "one-time swimmers, current walkers" (*Tgbch,* 22). In one of the "definitive" entries from winter 1921–22 the circle image is one of impassable enclosure: ". . . I have continually made a running start toward the radius, but again and again had to interrupt it" (*Tgbch,* 560).

30. Cf. Walter H. Sokel, *Franz Kafka – Tragik und Ironie. Zur Struktur seiner Kunst* (Munich and Vienna, 1964), pp. 488–489.

31. Wilhelm Emrich, *Franz Kafka,* p. 389.

32. Martin Walser, *Beschreibung einer Form,* Literatur als Kunst. Eine Schriftenreihe, ed. Kurt May and Walter Höllerer, Nr. 2 (Munich: Hanser, 1961), p. 125.

33. Cf. Simon's explanation for the detail of his chronicle to the manageress (*T,* 322), the insistence of the one walker in Kafka's earliest prose work to the other that he won't listen to stories told "piecemeal." "Tell me everything from beginning to end. Anything less I won't listen to . . ." (*Beschreibung eines Kampfes,* p. 22), and Kafka's 1911 journal entry, where the possibility of transcribing a self-insight is related to the possibility of the "greatest completeness, down to every immaterial consequence . . ." (*Tgbch,* 37).

Index

DATE DUE